COSTA RICA

A Natural Destination

COSTA RICA

A Natural Destination

THIRD EDITION

Ree Strange Sheck

John Muir Publications
Santa Fe, New Mexico

John Muir Publications, P.O. Box 613, Santa Fe, NM 87504

Third edition. First printing September 1994

Library of Congress Cataloging-in-Publication Data
Sheck, Ree.
  Costa Rica : a natural destination / Ree Strange Sheck.—3rd ed.
  p. cm.
  Includes bibliographical references and index.
  ISBN 1-56261-144-5 : $17.95
  1. Costa Rica—Guidebooks. 2. Natural parks and reserves—Costa Rica—
Guidebooks. 3. Outdoor recreation—Costa Rica—Guidebooks.
  I. Title.
F1543.5.S52 1994   94-19011
917.28604'5—dc20   CIP

Distributed to the book trade by
W. W. Norton & Company, Inc.
New York, New York

Typeface: Garamond Book
Typography: Jill Epstein
Cover Art and Book Design: Susan Surprise
Map Art: Michael Taylor
Printer: Publishers Press

Contents

Río Celeste near Magil Forest Lodge (Photo by Ree Strange Sheck)

Acknowledgments

I first came to Costa Rica in 1968. I came as a visitor to this country that has been my home now since 1990, when I finished the first edition of this book. I express my deep appreciation to Yehudi Monestel, a longtime friend and fellow journalist, who walked the trails with me in 1968. Thanks to his parents, *don* Bolívar and *doña* Elena, who have opened their hearts and their home to me since that time.

In October, as a member of the press, I was invited to attend Expotur, an international meeting of tourism wholesalers and retailers in San José. That experience helped get the first edition of the book off the ground. I would like to thank the Costa Rican Tourism Institute (ICT) and the staff of Expotur for their assistance then and since. Special thanks go to those who work in the ICT information offices at the Plaza de la Cultura and the airport: Grettel Agüero, Miguel Aguilar, Guido Carbajal, and Nelson Villalobos. Their courtesy and sincere desire to help are remarkable, especially in light of the fact that they hear the same questions day after day.

To the naturalist guides I have been privileged to travel with and to learn from, to tour operators, to the owners of private nature reserves and hotels visited, thanks for gracious attention.

Travels in national parks, reserves, and refuges have given me profound respect for park rangers, who often live and work under difficult circumstances. Thanks to each one who has taken time to talk or walk with me.

On the home front, thanks to my co-workers at the Monteverde Conservation League for their support during revisions for this third edition and to the Eston Rockwell and Omar Coto families in Monteverde for seeing me through any number of emergencies as I struggled to meet deadlines.

My sister Ruth Hamilton traveled with me during part of the research for this edition—her presence and her spirit helped me remember to savor the adventure.

For unfailing support during the research and writing of the book, from the first edition to the third, thanks go to Ronald Sheck and to my daughter, Claren Boehler-Sheck. Continuing love and gratitude go to my son, Curt, whose death in 1984 was the beginning of a new journey for me, a journey that led me back to Costa Rica and to this book.

Finally, I express my appreciation to the people of Costa Rica for their generosity of spirit, those I know and those whose names I will never know—for smiles, for helping me get on the right bus or the right road, for walking with me to the corner to point to the street I needed, for reminding me that neighborliness transcends international boundaries. And I am forever grateful to those who have worked to preserve the extraordinary richness of Costa Rica's tropical ecosystems.

1
Why Costa Rica?

Costa Rica touches the heart and mind, not through elegant boulevards, towering cathedrals, or an imposing place in history but through its incredible natural beauty and a gracious people disposed to peace, kindness, and a generosity of spirit. No one feels a stranger here for long.

It is one of the most biologically diverse countries in the world—a treasure house of flora and fauna unequaled in so small an area. Casual tourist and dedicated nature traveler alike come under the spell of a natural wonderland studded with tropical forests, rushing rivers, exotic animals, uncrowded beaches, high mountains, and awesome volcanoes.

Struggling to explain why increasing numbers of people are making their way to this small Central American country, one observer finally said simply, "The greatest tourist attraction in Costa Rica *is* Costa Rica."

With more than 100 years of democracy under its belt in a region with a history of political strife, Costa Rica boasts "teachers, not soldiers." The country has had no army since 1948. It lays claim to one of the highest literacy rates in the world and a national health care system that covers all its citizens. The people's inclination toward modesty, simplicity, and friendliness, along with the country's commitment to peace, create a climate of trust for travelers.

And what a place to travel! Visitors can walk among rain forest giants, see green turtles nesting, get a ringside view of one of the

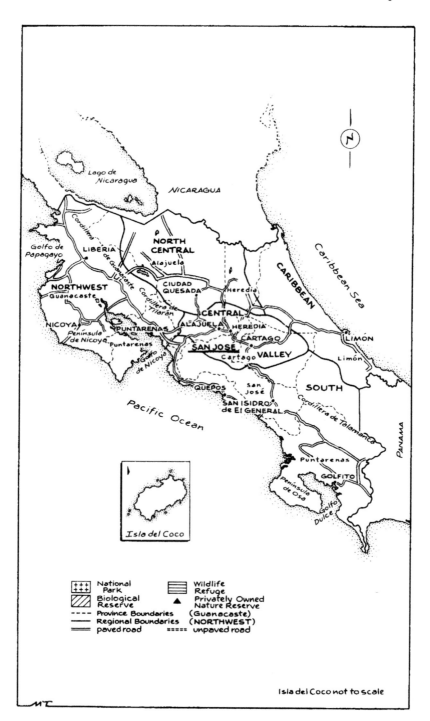

National Park
Biological Reserve
---- Province Boundaries
— Regional Boundaries
══ paved road

Wildlife Refuge
▲ Privately Owned Nature Reserve
(Guanacaste)
(NORTHWEST)
═════ unpaved road

Isla del Coco not to scale

most active volcanoes in the world, ogle at the keel-billed toucan, and hear the howler monkey. Pristine beaches beckon on the Caribbean and Pacific. Trees alive with their own miniforests of bromeliads, lichens, and mosses assume mysterious forms in the high cloud forests; orchids grow wild amid lush vegetation that tumbles down along road cuts. Miles of coffee *fincas* (farms), sugarcane fields, and pineapple and banana plantations bear witness to a rural heritage and the influence of agriculture on the life of the country today.

Travelers can enjoy world-class white-water rafting, sunning on deserted beaches, bicycle touring, surfing, swimming, fishing, bird-watching, hiking, or shopping, or simply sit on the Plaza de la Cultura in the heart of San José and people-watch.

A small country, a little smaller than West Virginia or Nova Scotia, Costa Rica abounds with plant and animal species: North American, South American, and those native to the area.

It is possible to drive from Puntarenas on the Pacific to Port of Limón on the Atlantic in less than six hours, even allowing time to maneuver through the traffic of the capital city of San José en route.

Elevations go from sea level to 12,529 feet (3,819 m). In general, temperatures are moderate, varying more with altitude than time of year. San José's average high is 77°F (24.9°C), its low, 61°F (16.3°C). Lowland zones range from the 70s to the 90s (21° to 37°C). Most people are surprised to learn that frost and ice can occur on some of the loftier peaks.

Costa Rica is known around the world for its national park system, now protecting about 12 percent of the land. With the aid of other reserves and parks, almost 28 percent of its territory is protected, an enviable record for any country—remarkable for a developing one. That commitment to conservation makes it possible for resident and tourist alike to encounter the natural world in a special way. An agouti and I once surprised each other on a park trail; a paca (called in Costa Rica by the marvelous name of *tepezcuintle)* amazed me by rushing from bushes to plunge into a pool at the base of a waterfall where I had just been swimming. Giant blue morpho butterflies can turn any ordinary day into a mystical experience. There is the chance that one will come face-to-face with a white-faced monkey or catch a glimpse of a scarlet macaw. Tropical trees towering to 150 feet and delicate, tiny flowers blooming in a high Andean-like climate open us to not only the magnificence of the universe but also the interrelationship of all living things.

This guide is offered as a companion for your journey in Costa Rica, to help you touch and be touched by the land and people on paths most comfortable to you. It includes information about the national parks and privately owned nature reserves, beaches, volcanoes, and towns. It also tells what you will find at the end of the trail: a private room and bath with hot water or a bunk in a dormitory atmosphere with a shared bath and cold water. It lets you know whether you can fly in or drive in, or whether access is by foot, boat, or horseback.

There is a nutshell version of the country's history, focusing on what makes Costa Rica stand out from its neighbors, tips on what to bring along and how to call home, and a few highlighted odds and ends such as where and when you might see a quetzal, which beaches turtles lay their eggs on, water safety, and coffee from bean to harvest.

The book is intended to help you find your own adventure, to sense the heartbeat of this special place, from the quiet rhythm of its rural landscape to busy San José. Your experience will be your own. Just bring an open heart to contain it.

2
Marching to a Different Drummer

There's something different about Costa Rica. It is a country without an army in a world that counts tanks, missiles and nuclear warheads as the measure of a nation's strength. The national hero is not a general but a young, barefoot *campesino* (farmer). Schoolchildren, not soldiers, parade on Independence Day. While other countries debate the issue, Costa Rica abolished the death penalty more than one hundred years ago.

Located in a region where violence has too often been the order of the day, Costa Rica lives in peace. It has a literacy rate of 93 percent and a Social Security system that offers health care to all its people. Costa Ricans like to say they have gained through evolution what other countries try to attain through revolution.

Travelers often ask what has led this country on a path that sets it apart from its Central American neighbors. A brief look at Costa Rica's history, economy, and political and social systems will answer some of the questions visitors ask most.

Historical Highlights

When Christopher Columbus dropped anchor off Costa Rica in 1502, near present day Port of Limón, he still thought he had found a new route to the East and believed he was on the southeast coast of Asia, near Siam. Even today, some people confuse Costa Rica with another Caribbean locale: Puerto Rico.

Stories about great wealth to be found here began at that time. The Indians offered Columbus gifts of gold, and Spanish explorers began to refer to the area as *costa rica*, or "rich coast." Later expeditions touched along the Caribbean and then the Pacific coasts, but it was not until the 1560s that the first permanent European settlement took root. Cartago in the Central Valley became the capital of what would become a province under the Captaincy General of Guatemala.

The first Spanish inhabitants of this new land found neither mineral wealth nor a large indigenous population that could be used as forced labor. The Indians they did find were not keen on servitude. Resistance ranged from warfare to retreat into the forested back country. Colonizers were effectively reduced to small landholdings that they and their families could work themselves. Communication was hampered by rugged terrain and lack of roads, made more difficult by seasonally heavy rains. Efforts went into survival rather than commerce, with the agrarian society based on subsistence farming and ranching.

Throughout the colonial period, Costa Rica was a poor, neglected outpost of the Spanish empire. The poverty and isolation gave rise to a simple life, individualism, hospitality, and a spirit of equality that cut across social class lines, creating the beginnings of rural democracy.

Even the name Costa Ricans call themselves, *ticos*, is said by some to come from a colonial saying: "We are all *hermaniticos* [little brothers]." Diminutive endings of *-ito* and *-ico* are characteristic of everyday speech. For example, you may hear *pequeñito* for "small" rather than *pequeño*.

The Latin American wars for independence from Spain were far removed from this peaceful enclave. When victory came in 1821, Costa Rica received word about a month later. A popular story is that a messenger on a mule delivered the official letter. Costa Rica joined the Central American Federation for a time but declared itself an independent republic in 1848.

The war that did have an impact on the country came in 1856, when William Walker, a U.S. adventurer who had gained control of the armed forces of Nicaragua and dreamed of controlling all of Central America, invaded Costa Rica. The strong national identity forged during the colonial period of isolation brought volunteers from around the country to defend the nation. In a battle that lasted only a few minutes, the well-armed invading force was routed at Hacienda Santa Rosa in Guanacaste. (The site of the confrontation is now protected in Santa Rosa National Park. When you visit there, remember how remote it was at the time; the ragtag citizen army of 9,000 marched twelve days from San José to get there.) The army pursued Walker's forces into Nicaragua, where a second battle occurred. In the fighting at Rivas, a brave young *campesino* from Alajuela named Juan Santamariá volunteered to set fire to the Walker stronghold, losing his life in the act. He became the national hero for his part in this crucial battle. Walker's dream ended in 1860 before a firing squad in Honduras.

The first true popular elections came in 1889, which is why Costa Rica claims more than 100 years of democracy. The president at the time tried to cancel the promised vote to name his own successor, but the elections were held when peasants invaded San José and demanded their say. By this time, the exportation of coffee was ending Costa Rica's isolation. Soon, bananas thrust it further into international commerce. Population grew, frontiers expanded, and transportation routes carried produce out and the world in.

Costa Rica's own brief "revolution" came in 1948, when Congress annulled the presidential election to keep the opposition candidate from taking over. It was a short but savage civil war in which more than 2,000 people died. The leader of the revolt was José ("Pepe") Figueres, who took control of an interim government for eighteen months before the elected opposition candidate assumed office. Figueres abolished the army; military facilities were converted into schools, a prison, and the National Museum. The Constitution of 1949 set up a government full of checks and balances.

Succeeding governments have spent money on roads, schools, hospitals, electricity, and running water instead of arms. Com-

Monument in Alajuela honoring Costa Rica's national hero, Juan Santamaría
(Photo by Ree Strange Sheck)

promise and negotiation are the key words in resolution of conflict. Citizens do, however, take to the streets to protest or pressure the government for action.

Today, large landholdings exist alongside small farms; wealth exists alongside poverty. But there is still a genuine faith in peace as a force, in democracy, and in fundamental human dignity. Social, economic, and political mobility are possible. The national character is still tied to the land. Even in urban centers, Costa Ricans tell you their strength is in the hard-working, loyal campesino and the land. How this idealization of the past will hold up as more and more campesinos become *peónes* (day laborers) and the pressures on the land increase will be interesting. You can be sure of one thing: it will be a Costa Rican solution.

Political System

Governmental power is divided among executive, legislative, and judicial branches, with a Supreme Election Tribunal in charge of elections. The decentralized form of government reflects Costa Ricans' aversion to concentration of power.

A president is elected every four years by secret ballot and cannot be reelected. Two vice-presidents are elected at the same time. Numerous checks and balances were written into the 1949 constitution, under which the country is governed, to prevent abuse of power, especially by a strong president. The unicameral Legislative Assembly is considered to have more power than the president. Its fifty-seven deputies are also elected every four years and may not serve consecutive terms. Seats are allocated according to population in each of the country's seven provinces.

Magistrates of the Supreme Court of Justice are named by the legislature for staggered eight-year terms. These magistrates name justices at the provincial level.

To safeguard against electoral fraud, a kind of fourth branch of government is set up as an autonomous body. This Supreme Election Tribunal oversees everything from voter registration to the actual counting of votes. It also oversees registration of politi-

cal parties and keeps an eye on political campaigns for miscon-
duct. As a further check, six months before the election, command
of the Civil and Rural Guard, essentially police forces, passes from
the president to the tribunal.

Campaigning can get dirty, but election day itself is a party. Even
children turn out to help get people to the polls, wave party flags,
and shout slogans. Organized travel tours come just to observe the
process and join in the civic fiesta.

Do not, however, mistake fanfare for frivolity. Ticos take their
voting seriously; turnouts are high. Women have the vote, as do
eighteen-year-olds. Even those who cannot read and write are enti-
tled to cast a ballot. Women have been elected to high office—
both in the legislature and as vice-president.

Municipal elections take place at the same time as national elections. These are the two important levels of government.

Political parties come and go, the two principal ones today being
the National Liberation party and the Social Christian Unity party.
Factions split off and coalitions form. The Communist party is recognized but does not have much weight at the polls.

Costa Rica has a large bureaucracy. The government produces
electricity, runs the telephone service and a national banking system, builds houses, and distills liquor, along with all the other
things one expects a government to do. More than 16 percent of
the country's workers on fixed salaries are employed in the public
sector.

Social Welfare and Education

The Social Security system, referred to by ticos as the *Caja* and
identified by the initials CCSS, was instituted in 1941 by the same
president who helped enact a labor code that set minimum wages
and guaranteed workers the right to organize. Though complaints
about inefficiency and the level of care are common, no one
denies the vital role Social Security has played in improving health
care. Infant mortality rates are among the lowest in Latin America.
Life expectancy at birth in the early part of the century was 40

years; today it is 75 years. When the system started, coverage was limited, but now practically all citizens have access to care, whether they have paid into the system or not.

Rural health care programs geared to both prevention and treatment touch the lives of the poor even in remote corners of the country. Scenarios may include a paramedic-staffed center supplemented with regular visits by doctors and nurses. I was once visiting a rural highland school when the doctor came for his scheduled community visit, using one room of the two-room school for consultations. In a coastal Caribbean village, a young mother told me the doctor came by boat once a month. Poor urban neighborhoods are also targeted.

As you travel around the country, you will see clinics in small towns and a growing number of regional hospitals. The Red Cross, or *Cruz Roja* as it is called in Spanish, is a strong, highly respected organization in Costa Rica with dedicated staff members and volunteers in many communities. It works closely with health care agencies and provides ambulance service.

Costa Rica and schools are practically synonymous. The country was one of the first in the world to mandate free, compulsory, tax-supported education. This 1869 constitutional provision preceded passage of such laws in the United States. About 21 percent of the national budget goes to education.

In a rural place, the schoolhouse may be one room, with six grades divided between morning and afternoon classes. Continuing on to secondary school can mean real commitment for students, for while primary schools are abundant, secondary schools are centered in areas with larger populations. Two young people who stopped to rest near me on a mountain road explained that they were on their way to the nearest bus stop for a thirty-minute ride to school in Turrialba. The daily walk to and from the bus stop was an hour and a half each way, with the return trip after dark.

Costa Rica has four state universities in the Central Valley, with branches in outlying areas. University education is not free, but tuition is generally low and scholarships are available. Technical and vocational schools are also located outside the San José metropolitan area to put higher education within reach of more students as well as promote other regions in the hope of stemming the flow of people into the heavily populated Central Valley. There are a number of private institutions of higher learning.

Most visitors ask about the rationale behind school uniforms for primary and secondary students. This, too, harks back to egalitarian roots. The idea is to minimize differences between social classes. Private schools also have uniforms. Secondary schools may petition to have a uniform that differs from the traditional blue shirt and navy pants or skirt.

Debates on the quality of education, and even what constitutes an education, rage here as elsewhere. Resources are stretched thin, and urban areas have an advantage because of backup facilities such as libraries and easier access to educational support. It is sometimes difficult to retain teachers in small, isolated areas. The overall picture, however, looks positive. Schools are frequently the nucleus around which a sense of community forms. Dedicated teachers do exist, often working with few of the materials teachers in the United States or Canada take for granted. Innovative projects include radio programs aimed at primary schoolchildren in rural areas, one of which focuses on environmental education. Bilingual materials in the six surviving Indian languages (Maleku, Cabecar, Térraba, Boruca, Guaymí, and Bribrí) are incorporated into the curriculum on Indian reserves, including history and legends that have passed down through oral tradition.

Housing is another focus of social programs, and it has been particularly emphasized in the last few years. Both urban and rural public projects have been implemented in an attempt to meet a serious housing shortage.

Economy

Starting from a base of subsistence agriculture in colonial times, Costa Rica moved into the world economy only in the latter half of the nineteenth century with the exportation of coffee to Europe. Exportation of bananas followed soon afterward. A Costa Rican

The coffee bean brought Costa Rica into the world market (Photo by Ree Strange Sheck)

journalist, lamenting his country's dependence on agricultural exports, once said to me, "What makes it worse is that the country produces *postres* [desserts]—coffee, bananas, sugar, and chocolate. When importing countries are in an economic bind, demand for these things drops first."

If you hear Costa Ricans refer to the "crisis," they are talking about the years from 1979 to 1982, when the country went through probably the worst economic crunch in its history. World prices for its traditional crops collapsed at the same time that petroleum costs soared. Since Costa Rica imports all its oil, the dynamics were devastating. The country had borrowed heavily from eager banks with the money used largely, as one Costa Rican put it, "to maintain our accustomed standard of living." It has been difficult to cut social programs citizens take as their due. National spending still outstrips income earned from exports and taxation, while juggling foreign debt payments demands enormous energy. (Average per capita income, by the way, is $2,013.)

However, there is light on the horizon. Investment in nontraditional products to increase exports and cut dependence on the postres is starting to pay off. In 1988, for the first time, nontraditional exports edged past traditional ones in dollar value. Textiles, fresh flowers, ornamental plants, pineapples, frozen fish, macadamia nuts, and melons are among the items filling out the menu. Check the label of the next shirt or pair of pants you buy. It could very well say, "Assembled in Costa Rica." The country has become one of the largest brassiere manufacturers in the world.

The nation's stability, a large and educated middle class which provides a high quality work force, lower labor costs, and national and international incentives are drawing foreign firms into joint ventures with Costa Ricans. The U.S. Caribbean Basin Initiative, which provides preferential customs treatment to many products from the region, has been a stimulus; the United States is the country's biggest business partner, but multinational companies from Europe and the Far East are also setting up shop. Tourism has edged out coffee and bananas to become the country's number one foreign exchange earner. This is a result of both increasing numbers of visitors and decreasing income from those traditional crops because of falling prices, competition, and restrictive trade agreements.

Someone once observed that Costa Rica has a way of turning fatal flaws into saving graces. Perhaps the national debt is a case in point. "Debt-for-nature" swaps have been used to reduce the debt while providing money for in-country conservation projects. The plan works like this: Conservationists raise funds to buy a piece of the debt on the secondary market—usually in dollars—from a foreign bank or institution willing to sell for less than the face value. It is usually the Central Bank of Costa Rica that buys the debt from the conservation group through interest-bearing government bonds, in local currency. The conservation group must use the money to finance environmental projects. The foreign bank gets what it considers a bad debt off its books, Costa Rica lightens its burden, and money flows into the preservation of natural resources.

SOME CONSERVATION ORGANIZATIONS

Many small, nonprofit groups around Costa Rica are hard at work to protect the environment of this biologically rich country. All can use a helping hand. A few are listed here:

APREFLOFAS is a volunteer force that helps patrol protected zones to combat illegal hunting and lumbering, and works to increase conservation awareness through environmental education. Apartado 1192-1007, San José, telephone 240-6087.

APROCA, the Costa Rican Aquatic Conservation Association, promotes conservation and rational and sustainable management of marine, river, and lake resources. Apartado 1604-1000, San José, telephone 224-0399, fax 224-9169.

Friends of Lomas Barbudal (AMILOBA) is dedicated to the conservation of tropical dry forest, focusing on the Lomas Barbudal Biological Reserve in Guanacaste. An initial and continuing concern has been wildfires, one of the greatest dangers facing the reserve. Some are set by hunters to flush out game, some are the result of carelessness, some start accidentally from neighboring fields being cleared. Through the conservation group's efforts, fire prevention and control strategies are now in place. It also offers environmental educa-tion programs at the group's center in Bagaces, and operates a visitor center at the northern entrance to the reserve. Volunteers, preferably Spanish speakers, are needed for special projects. In the United States, write to Gordon and Jutta Franke, 691 Colusa Avenue, Berkeley, CA 94707-1517, fax (510) 528-0346. In Costa Rica, telephone or fax 671-1029 or 671-1203.

ARBOFILIA has reforestation projects, organic farming, and wildlife conservation programs principally in rural communities around Carara Biological Reserve. A small center in El Sur de Turrubares is open to visitors, who can swim in clean rivers and explore the zone on horseback. The organization was founded by small farmers with a goal of economic and environmental restoration. Write to ARBOFILIA, El Sur de Turrubares-6009. Telephone 240-7145, fax 240-8832.

The Monteverde Conservation League owns and manages the first international children's rain forest and has programs with neighboring communities in environmental education, information, reforestation, and some small-scale sustainable development projects. Some volunteer opportunities exist. Apartado 10581-1000, San José, telephone 645-5003, fax 645-5104.

Natural Resources

Historically, Costa Rica's Indian population was low and dispersed, causing little human impact on the land. Spanish colonial settlement was also limited, both in size and location, being focused in the centers of San José, Cartago, Alajuela, and Heredia. As the limits of the frontier began to widen after independence from Spain, first around the Central Valley and then fanning out from transportation routes to the coasts and eventually to the north and south, occasional legislation began to appear to protect natural resources. Initial concerns seemed to be with wildlife and hunting or with prohibiting private ownership of certain tracts of land or a volcano crater. Precedents were set, though early enforcement was not terrific.

As time went on, foreign naturalists, who first began to arrive in the mid-nineteenth century, came in increasing numbers, drawn by the biological richness of the area. By the middle of this century, natives and foreigners alike began pressing for preservation: Unprotected, forests were obviously not going to last forever. Costa Rica began building a national park system that today protects nearly as many bird species as is found in all of North America and almost half its number of plant species. There are more butterflies in this tiny country than in the entire United States.

While preservation was the necessary initial step, the goal and challenge of protected areas today is not only conservation of biodiversity but also putting people into the conservation equation. Population pressures are increasing at a time when public land available for new settlement is practically gone.

Neighbors who receive some benefit from those protected lands will be more inclined to preserve them. New concepts are going beyond promotion of the areas for scientific research, nature tourism, and environmental education, all of which, when carefully carried out, can benefit local people. In some of the parks, for example, local residents are being incorporated into park operations as rangers, teachers, caretakers, and even researchers. Their livelihoods will come from the parks.

Throughout the country, the challenge is to teach people that they can make a living from natural resources without destroying them. This is a crucial concept since practically all forest reserves are in private hands, and about 12 percent of the parks are still privately owned. Sustainable development is the watchword. Managed harvesting of trees, plants, or seeds can bring more money than clearing the forest, and the resource survives. Carefully planned, responsible tourism can bring benefits to those who live around protected areas.

Government and private reforestation efforts are a long way from replacing what is cut every year, but they are growing. Research and plantings with native trees are under way. A project that encourages natural regeneration of a tropical dry forest could have implications for projects around the world.

Costa Rica has come a long way from its beginning, poor and forgotten by the world. Its accomplishments in health and literacy put it in the ranks of highly developed nations. In conservation and commitment to peace, it seems like a giant.

3
Lay of the Land

Rising up between the Atlantic and the Pacific as part of the land bridge between North and South America, Costa Rica lies in a region unique in the world. The land is home to plants and animals from both North and South America as well as to species native to Costa Rica. The cultural mix is as rich as the biological one. Indigenous peoples, though small in number compared with their neighbors to the north and south, were influenced by the advanced civilizations of both Mesoamerica and South America.

The rugged terrain of this small Central American country, wedged between Nicaragua on the north and Panama on the south, springs surprises on those who come expecting the tropical temperatures to always be balmy. At some times of the year, ice forms at the highest elevations.

Topography

From sea to shining sea in Costa Rica can be as short a distance as 74 miles (119 km). However, where the country is narrowest, near Panama, it is also the most rugged and hardest to cross. The chain of mountains that forms a backbone down the length of the land becomes higher and wider as it curves from northwest to southeast.

In the north, near Nicaragua, the chain is known as the Guanacaste Cordillera (*cordillera* is the Spanish term for mountain range), giving way as it progresses southeast to the Tilarán Cordillera and Central Cordillera, all of which were formed as a result of volcanic activity. The Cordillera of Talamanca in the south is an uplifted mountain range which contains the country's highest peak: Chirripó, reaching 12,529 feet (3,819 m) above sea level.

You won't be in Costa Rica long before you hear people talking about the Meseta Central, or Central Valley. Since colonial times, this region has been the center of population. But it is not just the area around San José, as many visitors assume. In addition to the lower and larger valley of San José, where the capital is located, along with towns such as Heredia, Alajuela, Grecia, Naranjo, Atenas, and San Ramón, there is the higher, eastern valley of Cartago, which contains the colonial capital of Cartago as well as Paraíso and Turrialba.

VOLCANOES

Volcanoes are a hot topic. Some 112 craters, including the two on Coco Island, mark the landscape of Costa Rica. They range from extinct to dormant to active and from a mere remnant rising 328 feet (100 m) from the Tortuguero Plains to majestic peaks more than 11,000 feet high (3,350 m) that still fuss and fume along the country's spine.

If you have never heard a volcano breathe, consider a visit to 5,358-foot Arenal (1,633-m), one of the most active in the world. Hearing the huff of its breath one unforgettable morning made me one with primitive peoples; the mountain became a living being. When it hurled fiery blocks high in the air, not a doubt remained: Arenal was angry. It has been angry enough to kill people since it
began its current phase of activity in 1968, including a tourist who climbed up its slopes. Be prudent when you visit: keep a respectful distance.

Activity at 8,884-foot (2,708-m) Poás Volcano has caused Poás National Park to close at times since 1989. The Volcanological and Seismological Observatory of Costa Rica at the National University in Heredia (telephone 237-4570) monitors Poás and other active sites. It has published a map that pinpoints the craters and gives the elevation and type of volcano.

Other volcanoes with some level of activity include Irazú at 11,260 feet (3,432 m), Rincón de la Vieja at 5,925 feet (1,806 m), Miravalles at 6,653 feet (2,028 m), and Turrialba at 10,925 feet (3,330 m).

Elevations in the Central Valley range from almost 2,000 to 5,000 feet (600 to 1,500 m). Separating the two depressions is the Continental Divide, which runs through the mountains known as La Carpintera at 5,085 feet above sea level (1,550 m). The San José Valley drains toward the Pacific via the Virilla and Grande rivers, tributaries of the Tarcoles River. The Cartago Valley is drained by the headwaters of the Reventazón River, which flows to the Caribbean.

The third major intermountain basin, the General-Coto Brus Valley, is between the high Talamanca Range and the coastal mountains in the southwest. Elevations here are lower than in the Central Valley, ranging from about 330 to 3,200 feet (100 to 1,000 m). Significant population has spilled over into this rich region only in the last half of this century, with San Isidro de El General serving as a center for shopping and transportation in a largely rural landscape of dispersed settlements. Two tributaries of the great Térraba River—the General and Coto Brus—drain the basin toward the Pacific.

The spine of mountains that winds its way down the country separates two coastal regions that have noticeable differences. A number of hilly peninsulas jut out from the Pacific coastline (Santa Elena, Nicoya, Herradura, Osa, and Burica); there are two large gulfs (Nicoya and Dulce) and many small coves and bays, creating natural ports. The two major commercial ports are Puntarenas and Puerto Caldera. For the most part, mountains come close to the sea on the Pacific side. The greatest expanse of flatlands in the Pacific lowlands is inland, centering around the Tempisque River drainage at the north end of the Gulf of Nicoya and narrowing northward to Nicaragua.

The Pacific coastline is almost 780 miles (1,254 km) long, but the Caribbean coast, by contrast, is only 132 miles long (212 km) and has a natural harbor only in the Moín-Limón area. The largest area of lowland plains in the country stretches back from the eastern coast: the Plains of Guatuso, San Carlos, Tortuguero, and Santa Clara form a wedge-shaped lowland reaching from the San Juan River, the border with Nicaragua, nearly to Limón. These *llanuras* make up about one-fifth of Costa Rica and generally have an eleva-

Loading cane at Drake Bay, Osa Peninsula (Photo by Ree Strange Sheck)

tion of less than 330 feet (100 m). There are small volcanoes even here, but the tallest rises less than 1,000 feet (300 m) above surrounding lands. This region contains the only rivers navigable for any distance inland. You will not see large ships, but the San Carlos and Sarapiquí rivers allow smaller-boat travel for about 30 miles (50 km) from where they flow into the San Juan River. These rivers were important early transportation routes.

Climate Patterns

Costa Rica lies in the tropics between eight and eleven degrees north of the equator, about the same latitude as the southern tip of India. Because it is a small country without much latitude variation, one might expect the climate to be relatively uniform. Wrong. Climate can vary over short distances because of the rugged mountain chains that affect such factors as wind, rain, and temperature. The result is a series of microclimates where altitude is the key to change.

Microclimates make countrywide generalizations about rainfall and temperature misleading. What is helpful to the traveler are some rules of thumb for various regions, backed up with specifics for a few locations. We are going to hit the high spots; my apologies to climatologists for ignoring the intricacies.

Temperatures

Remember that temperature goes down as elevation goes up: it is cooler in the mountains than at sea level. Temperatures are generally higher on the Pacific side than on the Caribbean at the same elevation. (There are more clouds on the Caribbean watershed year-round than on the Pacific.) At sea level on either side, the annual average is always going to be above 75°F (24°C).

Some of the highest peaks in the Central Mountain Range and Talamanca Mountains average 54°F (12°C), though temperatures can fall below freezing. The lowest temperature yet recorded was in the Talamancas: 16°F (-9°C) at Chirripó, the highest mountain in the country.

Variation in temperature is much greater from night to day than from season to season. Differences between the hottest month and the coldest at a particular location average only 4° to 5°F (2° to 3°C), while the daily fluctuation averages 14° to 18°F (8° to 10°C). The greatest daily fluctuation occurs during the dry season, when cloudless skies permit lots of sunshine in the daytime and lots of heat radiation at night back out into the clear sky. Add some wind, and it can be downright chilly.

Following are some average annual highs and lows at particular locations to illustrate the differences, along with median averages derived from the two (totals are rounded off). Elevations given are of the measurement sites.

From November to January, cold air from the north can funnel down through the mountains of North America, and though much weakened by the time they get to Costa Rica, the breezes bring a bite to the air. This is one of the few places in the world where polar air gets this close to the equator, so the coolest month anywhere in the country is probably going to be November, December, or January; the warmest March, April, or May.

Place/Elevation	Average High °F (C)	Average Low °F (C)	Average Median °F (C)
San José 3,845 ft. (1,172 m)	77 (25)	61 (16)	70 (20)
Limón 10 ft. (3 m)	87 (30)	71 (21)	78 (25)
Puntarenas 10 ft. (3 m)	92 (33)	73 (23)	81 (27)
Liberia 279 ft. (85 m)	92 (33)	72 (22)	81 (27)
San Isidro de El General 2,306 ft. (703 m)	88 (31)	64 (18)	76 (25)
Golfito 49 ft. (15 m)	91 (33)	72 (22)	82 (28)

Rainfall and Seasons

While spring and fall have little meaning here, summer and winter are tied to rainfall. Ticos call the dry season summer, which can stretch from December through April in some parts of the country. The winter designation is reserved for rainy months, generally from May through November. It reverses the standard Northern Hemisphere understanding of which months are summer and which are winter, but it makes sense to ticos.

There are some rainfall rules of thumb, always keeping in mind microclimatic differences. On the Pacific side, particularly from the central to the northern area, the rainy season usually begins at the end of May and ends in November. The wettest months are September and October. However, the length of the wet season increases the farther south you go. January to March are the only dry months in some places, and by the time you reach the Golfo Dulce area, there may be practically no dry season. Rainfall amounts vary from less than 59 inches (1,500 mm) in the northwest and central part of the country to 197 inches (5,000 mm) in the south.

Cataloging Costa Rica's species at the National Biodiversity Institute (Photo by Ree Strange Sheck)

On the Atlantic side, the rainy season can begin in late April and end in January. The wettest months are usually November, December, and January, while some areas also have higher amounts in July as well. Annual rainfall averages are higher on the Caribbean than on the Pacific side. The heaviest rainfall is inland, not along the coast; in some places on the eastern—windward— face of the northern mountains, it exceeds 355 inches (9,000 mm) per year. In the rest of the Caribbean lowlands, annual rainfall usu- ally averages from 118 to 200 inches (3,000 to 5,000 mm).

Throughout Costa Rica, less rain falls on valley bottoms, so places like San José and San Isidro de El General are drier than the surrounding slopes. The country's most prevalent rainfall pattern is in the range of 79 to 158 inches (2,000 to 4,000 mm). Here are some specific locations and their average annual rainfall.

Place	Inches (mm)
San José	74 (1,881)
Limón	138 (3,499)
Puntarenas	63 (1,598)
Liberia	63 (1,600)
San Isidro de El General	117 (2,974)
Golfito	196 (4,976)
Tortuguero	214 (5,437)

Precipitation can come in the form of a tropical downpour—a gully-washer complete with impressive lightning and thunder—or a steady rain. The downpour is called an *aguacero*; a continuous rain for several days is a *temporal*.

Other weather terms you may hear are *veranillo* (little summer), which refers to a brief dry period in July in the Pacific zone; *papagayos*, strong winds blowing inland from the Pacific; and *nortes*, the winds coming down inland from the north toward the Pacific. Both of these winds are very strong in Guanacaste from January through March. *Alisios* are the northeast trade winds, felt during the dry season over the Pacific slope, except in the south.

Do not imagine that rain is constant throughout the wet season. Sunshine can dominate several days in a row. When the rains come, they usually begin in early afternoon in the Central Valley and other highland areas and later in the afternoon in the Pacific lowlands. Rain can drum steadily at night in the Atlantic lowlands and valley bottoms.

Each season has its beauty and its particular cares. In wetter times, plant life is profuse, with a vibrant greenness that seeps into the soul. In the dry season, a subtler background is a perfect canvas for orchids, bougainvillea, and *reina de la noche* (queen of the night), with its large white or pink trumpet-shaped flowers, as well as for deciduous trees that flower only at that time.

Biological Diversity

Costa Rica is species rich. This small country, which covers less than three ten-thousandths of the Earth's surface, is home to 5 percent of all the plant and animal species known to exist. As a matter of fact, species are still being discovered in the country's rich mix of tropical habitats. The National Biodiversity Institute (INBio) has begun a multiyear project to discover and catalog all plant and animal species found in the country. Here are some numbers from INBio to give you an idea of what is known to exist: birds, 850 species; arthropods (insects, spiders, crabs with segmented bodies and jointed limbs), 366,000; plants, 13,021; mammals, 209; reptiles, 220; amphibians, 163; freshwater fish, 130. Some scientists believe that as many as a half-million species exist in Costa Rica, with a number of them—5 species of mammals, 6 of birds, 41 amphibians, 24 reptiles, and 16 species of freshwater fish—not found anywhere else in the world.

As a land bridge between the continents, a bridge that dates back about 3 million years, Costa Rica became a corridor for the movement of plant and animal species north and south. This interchange was slowed by the gradual growth of humid tropical forests which became widespread in the last 2 million years. Today Costa Rica has flora and fauna from both North and South America as well as some endemic species. They live in a variety of habitats: tropical dry and seasonally deciduous forests, rain forests, cloud forests, mangrove swamps, coral reefs, rivers, and *páramos* (high, cold, humid landscapes). Costa Rica is the northern limit for Andean páramo vegetation. You will find it above the tree line at Cerro de la Muerte and on Chirripó and other of the Talamancas' highest peaks.

Descriptions of Costa Rica often mention its twelve life zones. Defined by L. R. Holdridge, they classify vegetation based on temperature, rainfall, and their seasonal variation and distribution. Basically, the zones are tropical dry, moist, wet, and rain forests, with their premontane and lower montane versions, plus the tropical subalpine rain páramo.

Gigantic *sombrilla del pobre* plants in Braulio Carrillo National Park (Photo by Ronald Sheck)

The Tropical Science Center, a private nonprofit Costa Rican association that focuses on natural resources in the tropics, has a striking map of the country showing these zones in color. It is a vivid picture of variation over small distances—the microclimates mentioned earlier. The map is for sale at the center's office in San Pedro, outside San José, along with other interesting publications for the serious nature traveler (telephone 225-2649). The Tropical Science Center also operates the Monteverde Cloud Forest Preserve.

Forest was the natural cover of this tropical land since about 2 million years ago, and until this century, the forests continued to dominate. However, with commercial logging and the clearing of land for agriculture and settlement, less than one-third of the country remains forested, a substantial amount of it in protected lands. Though trees are still being cut, private and government efforts and national and international attention are focused on integrating conservation and sustainable development to preserve what remains. But private and public reforestation projects under way do not keep up with the number of trees cut every year.

Reforestation is tricky. Complex relationships between flora and fauna are not fully understood. What *is* understood points dramatically to the intricacies of nature. For instance, there are 65 species of fig trees in Costa Rica, adapted to a variety of habitats. Each of these species is pollinated by a different species of wasp. After the female wasp pollinates the fig, she lays her eggs inside the fruit. The wasp depends on the fig, and the fig depends on the wasp. Remove either and the cycle of survival is broken.

Animals are more important to seed dispersal of plants in tropical forests than in temperate ones, where wind is the primary factor. Maintaining the rich animal mix is crucial to maintaining the diverse plant species in a tropical forest.

Around the world, species are being lost before they have even been identified, much less studied for their importance to humanity. Plants are gone before their medicinal values is known. Disappearance of a species of fauna can cut a link in a food chain that affects several other species.

We are beginning to appreciate the necessity of maintaining natural forests. Replacing a primary forest of mixed species with one or two types of trees will not maintain the diversity: the fig wasp is not going to make it in a eucalyptus grove. While reforestation projects on already-cleared lands are essential—erosion control and watershed protection alone merit the effort—they are not going to replace what has been lost.

Costa Rica's creation of national parks, reserves, and refuges is a step toward preserving a biological diversity that is important far beyond its national boundaries. Maintaining them in the face of increasing economic and population pressures may have to be a shared responsibility.

Population Patterns

The Central Valley, home to most of the country's 3.2 million people, has been the center of population since colonial times. As was the pattern in other Central American countries, settlement centered in the highlands. Early Spanish colonists in Costa Rica shunned the hotter, rainier coastlands to settle in this mountain valley with rich volcanic soil. It was an enclave in the New World that continued in relative isolation until the nineteenth century. As late as 1700, Cartago, with a population of 2,535, was the country's only permanent urban center. In 1821, when Costa Rica gained independence from Spain, 60,000 people lived there, with 90 percent in the Central Valley. About 5 percent had ventured out toward Esparza and Bagaces to raise cattle, and another 5 percent were indigenous peoples living in dispersed settlements on their traditional lands in the north and south.

A small bean introduced into Costa Rica around the beginning of the nineteenth century ended up transforming the life of this agrarian society, pushing the frontier farther and farther away from the Central Valley. Coffee was its name. The export of coffee led to the opening of a road to Puntarenas, since the first loads went to Panama, then Chile, and finally to Europe via the Strait of Magellan. To transport the beans to the Port of Limón for more direct access to the European market, a railroad was built, which indirectly brought about the beginning of large banana plantations on the

Caribbean. Blacks brought to work on the railroad and plantations, mainly from Jamaica, added another ethnic group and an English-speaking component. The Afro-American population today is about 2 percent. The estimated Indian population is less than 1 percent.

As land values went up in the Central Valley, small farmers sought new territory. Satellite towns took shape around colonial centers, but Costa Rica still had an abundance of unoccupied land at the beginning of the twentieth century.

In 1938, banana activity moved to the southern Pacific coastal region from the Atlantic; roads followed, and so did settlement. With the opening of the Pan American Highway south of the Central Valley to San Isidro de El General in 1946, the trickle of pioneers who had braved Cerro de la Muerte on foot or horseback became a flood of immigrants looking for new land, following the transportation route as it made its way to Panama in the sixties. (The Pan American Highway is called the Inter-American Highway in Costa Rica, as it is throughout Central America.)

Immigrants added to Costa Rica's population. Italians, for example, developed San Vito, and Quakers from the United States settled Monteverde. New transportation routes helped drain some of the population pressure in the central region. In 1956, Costa Rica

POPULATION

Costa Rica	*3,166,962*
Provinces	
San José	*1,152,817*
Alajuela	*564,209*
Cartago	*356,198*
Heredia	*254,136*
Guanacaste	*252,386*
Puntarenas	*353,558*
Limón	*233,628*

Source: Dirección General de Estádistica y Censos, January 1, 1993 census figures

had 1 million inhabitants; by 1976, 2 million. The limits of settlement extended to the Plains of San Carlos and Sarapiquí, to Guanacaste and Tilarán, to the Nicoya Peninsula, and to the San Isidro de El General and Coto Brus regions.

Today, for the first time in its history, Costa Rica is facing the pressures of a growing population with little remaining public land. Most of what exists is in Indian reserves, forest reserves, national parks, and wildlife refuges. Since one of the frontier legacies is a belief that every campesino has a right to a piece of land to work, pressure on this protected land is going to be enormous.

As you travel on the road to San Isidro de El General, remember that most settlement along here dates from the middle of this century. As you drive over the new road to Limón through Guapiles, look at what has developed in this decade. If you sense a frontier spirit as you get to know outlying areas, you will understand why.

4
Ticket to Enjoyment: Planning the Journey

Entry Requirements

For citizens of the United States and Canada, entry requirements are simple: No visas are necessary. With a valid passport, you are on your way. In lieu of a passport, you can use a birth certificate or voter registration document along with photo identification, such as a driver's license, to buy a $2 tourist card when you check in at the ticket counter of the airline flying you to Costa Rica. You do not need a tourist card if you have a passport. Citizens of other countries can check with the nearest Costa Rican consulate or the Costa Rican Institute of Tourism for entry requirements.

From the date of entry, U.S. and Canadian citizens with passports can stay for ninety days; however, those who have no passport but enter with a tourist card are limited to thirty days. The law requires travelers to carry a passport or tourist card at all times while in the country.

Allow me a plug for passports: Routinely accepted at banks when you change money and at hotels when you register, a passport simply makes travel easier. If you don't have a passport, consider applying for one.

Immunizations

No immunizations are required. But even when staying at home, it is wise to have inoculations up-to-date. Is your tetanus booster current?

Incidence of malaria has increased in some parts of Costa Rica with the influx of refugees from neighboring countries. Mosquito eradication programs are used to control its spread. Most cases have been in the northern border area and around Limón. Dengue, also carried by mosquitoes, has reappeared. Signs everywhere are evidence of a countrywide campaign to avoid the spread of cholera—which so far has been minimal. Check with your physician or contact your local health office for advisory information.

Exit Requirements

All tourists must pay a departure tax, currently less than $7. You may pay it at the airport in either dollars or *colones*. That is all that is required if you leave before your original permission runs out. Whether you can legally extend your stay depends on your entry documents. Tourist cards good for thirty days cannot be renewed. If you are traveling with a passport, you can apply for an exit visa, good for thirty days from the date it is issued, which automatically extends your stay. However, the airport departure tax then jumps to what Costa Ricans pay, about $45. To remain legal, apply for an exit visa just before your original permit expires. Each month or part of a month that you stay beyond the original permission in your passport costs an additional $3.

The painless way to get an exit visa is to let a San José travel agency do it for you. The charge is about $4, and you spare yourself the frustration of standing in lines at government offices. The travel agency will need your passport for a couple of working days, so copy the first pages with your name, photo, and passport number as well as the page showing your date of entry. Copy machines abound downtown; just look for a sign advertising *Copias*.

Airlines

Time, distance, and political considerations lead most tourists from the United States and Canada to opt for air travel to Costa Rica, which means landing at Juan Santamaría International Airport,

twenty minutes from San José. Don't be startled if you hear the
pilot say the plane will touch down at Cocos International Airport;
Cocos was the previous name. You are in the right country.

By the time you come, the Tomás Guardia airport near Liberia
may have become Costa Rica's second international airport. Liberia
is a gateway to Guanacaste Province and its beautiful Pacific
beaches, folklore towns, and a number of the country's spectacular
national parks.

Various airlines fly into Costa Rica from the north, some direct,
others with stops at Mexico City, San Salvador, Tegucigalpa, San
Pedro Sula, or other places. Intermediate stops change on some airlines with the day of the week; be sure to inquire if you want to
minimize your ups and downs.

Commercial carriers include American, Continental, and United
(U.S. carriers), Aero Costa Rica and LACSA (Costa Rica), Mexicana
(Mexico), SAHSA (Honduras), and TACA (El Salvador). Phone numbers for these airlines are listed in Practical Extras at the back of
the book. Some of their departure points are:

Dallas: American

Houston: SAHSA, TACA, Continental

Los Angeles: LACSA, Mexicana, TACA, United

Miami: American, LACSA, Mexicana, SAHSA, TACA, United

New Orleans: LACSA, SAHSA, TACA

New York: LACSA, Mexicana, TACA, United

Orlando: Aero Costa Rica, LACSA

San Antonio: Mexicana

San Francisco: LACSA, Mexicana, TACA

Tampa: Aero Costa Rica, LACSA

Washington, D.C.: TACA

If possible, have your ticket written up as if issued by the airline
with an office in San José. For example, if you fly from Atlanta to
Miami on Delta and Miami to San José on American, be sure the
ticket is written up on American stock. If you have to make a
change for the return trip, American will help you if the ticket is
on its stock; otherwise, you have to try to deal with Delta, which
has no office in San José. I learned that the hard way.

From Canada, several companies have scheduled direct charter
flights: Air Transat (514-987-1616) out of Montreal, Fiesta Holidays

(416-498-5566) out of Toronto, Mirabelle (514-632-0510, fax 514-632-5598) out of Quebec and Montreal, and Fiesta West (604-689-5664) out of Vancouver, Calgary, and Edmonton. Their airfare/transportation packages are sometimes less expensive than airfare alone from the U.S. KLM and Iberia fly in from Europe.

Whichever airline you choose, it is best to reconfirm your return flight at least twenty-four hours before departure. Addresses and phone numbers of the airline offices in San José are listed in Practical Extras.

You will be told to be at the airport two hours early. It is good advice; check-in lines can be long, and you need time to pay the departure tax and change your remaining colónes into dollars. The airport bank is open from 8:00 a.m. to 4:00 p.m. Monday through Friday.

Here's a tip to save possible embarrassment at the airport. Porters who carry your luggage from curbside will leave it as close as possible to the check-in counter. Many an unsuspecting tourist has followed his or her luggage, only to receive disapproving looks from fellow passengers for not going with it to the end of the line. Waiting your turn is a surviving piece of the "everyone is equal" mentality born in colonial times. No one is exempt. In fact, the more important a person is, the more essential it is that this tenet be respected. I observed this for myself one lunchtime when I noticed the Costa Rican president entering a downtown McDonald's. It was almost as if a ritual—understood by all the players—was being performed as he took his place in line and looked for an empty table. That president was Oscar Arias, winner of the Nobel Peace Prize.

The same decorum is expected when waiting for a bus or to be helped at a department store counter. (The sign that says *Haga Fila* means "get in line.")

What to Bring

Having read the weather section in chapter 3, you know that you can encounter everything from frost in the early morning on the high mountains to a hot midday sun on the coast. Even in San José, the nights can be chilly, so bring a sweater or sweatshirt and jacket. Light clothes that can be layered will serve you well.

Costa Ricans dress on the conservative side. Women do wear pants or jeans even in downtown San José, but shorts are seen more on tourists than local men and women except in coastal areas or for sports. In a nice restaurant in the evening, men may have on coat and tie or at least a dress shirt; women, a dress or skirt and blouse.

Cotton and polyester long pants are good. It takes forever and a day for jeans to dry in the rainy season, but they are good for horseback riding or hikes in chilly climes. A long-sleeve shirt or two is wise for protection from the sun—remember, its rays are direct at ten degrees from the equator—and from insects and scratches on narrow forest trails. Shorts are not recommended for hiking in rain forests. Bring your bathing suit; nudity on public beaches is not acceptable in this culture.

Many researchers and naturalist guides prefer tennis shoes to hiking boots for forays into the tropical world. Whichever you choose, just be sure the footwear is comfortable and can get wet; even in the dry season, some trails lead through small streams. In rainy times, rubber boots are a joy, and they are available in Costa Rica for less than $8. (Some lodging places have a few pair for their guests.) You can buy the boots, which are standard footwear for campesinos, in central markets and many shoe stores throughout the country. If you don't want the extra weight going home, make a gift of the boots to the last nature reserve you visit. If you have large feet, consider bringing a pair from home.

There is a lively debate on rain ponchos versus umbrellas for experiencing the rain in a tropical forest. Just remember, sweltering under a poncho can leave you just as wet from sweat as from the rain. I pack an umbrella and a lightweight, hooded poncho that opens up on both sides so I can drape it over my shoulders and let more air circulate. The poncho gives better protection to backpacks or fanny packs, binoculars, and cameras, and it is handy for boat rides or trips on horseback. The umbrella is great for town time and for when you are not carrying thirteen other things on the trail. Bring an inexpensive one so that if you would rather stick an extra poster or gift in your bag when you leave, you can present

Rubber boots *(botas de hule)*, standard gear for tropical trails (Photo by Ree Strange Sheck)

the umbrella to the maid or bellboy, who will probably be your friend by now. Reasonably priced umbrellas are available in San José.

If you will be staying at hotels or nature reserves that have shared baths, consider a lightweight sweatsuit for trips to the shower. It can double as sleeping attire if the night is chillier than expected or as something comfortable to change into after a day of sightseeing or travel.

Here is a checklist of other items:

Wide-brimmed hat—for rain or sun
Flashlight—for nighttime hikes, to get from your cabin to the dining room in the middle of the forest, and in case the power

goes off in town or the generator is shut off before you are ready
for bed at one of the remote reserves.

Sunscreen

Insect repellent

Pocket calculator—simplifies currency calculations.

Moist towelettes

Pocketknife

Small mirror—some rustic facilities lack a bedroom mirror.

Anti-itch ointment—an antihistamine cream for insect bites or
even an antihistamine to take orally to reduce discomfort. If you
do find yourself with bites and no ointment, juice from the stem
of the impatiens (*china*) plant, abundant in many parts of Costa
Rica, is an excellent natural remedy.

Antidiarrhea medicine—better to have the kind you are comfortable with, just in case.

Washcloth—most Costa Rican hotels do not supply them.

Reclosable plastic bags—small ones are ideal for keeping a
passport or other important papers dry; a larger one is handy for
packing a wet bathing suit, or even for your camera or extra lens.

Plastic water bottle or canteen—for some independence in
what and where you drink.

Binoculars—to see the expression on the face of the sloth high
in the tree.

Antifogging agent for eyeglasses—especially during the rainy
season, when putting binoculars or camera to your glasses can
result in one big blur. (If you are in the forest with Amos Bien of
Rara Avis, he can show you a plant leaf that will do the trick, but
otherwise, you had better bring your own stuff.)

Old tennies or sandals—for climbing over rocks at the beach
to explore tide pools.

Tissues or toilet paper—public rest rooms may not have any.

Coin purse—to accommodate an ever-growing supply of
change. (Unfortunately, only the small denominations seem to
self-generate: coins of 50 céntimos or one or two colones.)

If you stay in the rustic facilities at some parks, you need to bring
soap, towel, and sleeping bag or sheets.

Leave expensive jewelry at home. Much to Costa Ricans' dismay, thievery is on the upswing, especially in San José. I had a chain snatched from my neck on a downtown street at midday.

The electric current is 110 volts, the same as in the United States and Canada. Plugs and outlets are standard. Be aware, however, when packing electric razors, hair dryers and such that travel in the boonies may put you in a room without an electric outlet. Some outlets do not accommodate the larger grounding plugs on new appliances, so you may need an adapter without the larger prong.

When packing your bags, remember that travel to remote spot by small plane, boat, or jeep may limit what you can take. Some domestic airlines limit luggage to 26 pounds per person. You will generally be able to store your larger bags at the hotel until you return, so include a small bag with enough room to carry a change of clothes, swimsuit, toilet articles, another pair of shoes, umbrella or poncho, camera, and so on. A day pack also comes in handy, even for city sightseeing. You can stick in a jacket, camera, umbrella, guidebook. Be sure it closes securely. To further foil the light-fingered in heavy street traffic or on crowded buses, put your fanny pack in front or move your day pack to your shoulder where you can control access to it. A water-resistant pack helps.

As for film, you can get Fuji, Kodak, Agfa, and other brands in San José and some outlying towns, but it is best to bring a few rolls just in case. Slide film is sometimes hard to find outside San José. You will not find the variety of ASA ratings and types of film you may be accustomed to. Don't forget spare camera batteries.

Imported goods are expensive, so if you run out of toilet items, consider local brands. Keep any medicines you require with you, not packed in luggage to be checked.

One item you should not bring along is impatience. Leave it at home. Who knows, after a time in Costa Rica without it, you may find you do not need to lug it around anywhere anymore.

Reservations

Reservations are highly recommended for visits from December to April and are increasingly advisable in the low season, now marketed as the Green Season. They are essential for Christmas time and Easter week. Think about reservations not only for hotels but also for lodging at the privately operated nature reserves, where the number of rooms is limited. Even hotels, with the exception of some in San José and a few beach resorts, tend to be small. I emphasize smaller hotels, many of them owner-operated, because I believe they give the traveler a better opportunity to taste the flavor of the country. Some hotels offer substantial discounts during off-season months, especially in beach areas. Phone numbers and faxes for hotels, private reserves, and tour companies are included in this book, but there are no mailing addresses because service is slow and unreliable. Call once you are in the country to reconfirm reservations you made from home, and bring copies of your confirmation to the hotel. Prices listed for hotels are valid for January 1994. However, rates may be adjusted every six months, based on ICT evaluations.

Tourist attractions also feel the impact of Costa Rican vacationers during school vacation from December through February and again during the midyear break for two weeks in July. Beaches and parks are prime destinations.

Thoughts on Itineraries

The first-time visitor to Costa Rica can feel overwhelmed by the banquet of choices: tropical forests to explore, steaming volcanoes to photograph, beaches to comb, mountains to climb, rivers to raft, flowers to smell along the way. Hire a guide? Take a tour? Travel independently?

Here are some suggestions to help you get started. If it is your first trip, do not slight San José. It is big city, crazy traffic, and crowded downtown sidewalks, but it also is worthwhile museums, peopled parks, and the center of culture and government. Go on a day trip with a professional naturalist guide to a park or reserve in the first day or two. (See chapter 9 on tours for possibilities.) With a good introduction to the tropical world, your travels afterward will be richer.

On the guided day trip, you will generally get Costa Rica's history in a nutshell, learn something about current economic realities, and have a chance to ask questions about what you are seeing or want to see. A naturalist guide knows where the crocodiles hang out, what time the scarlet macaws fly over the trail, what tree the hummingbird nest is in, and which orchids are in bloom. You will get an early taste of what is out there waiting for you while you leave the driving to someone else. If you want to see a monkey, there is no reason to go home without having seen one.

But you don't want to limit your stay to San José. Costa Rica's essence is tied to its rural roots. Its people and its natural resources are the biggest part of what it has to offer. Several smaller towns now have adequate hotels, restaurants, and transportation to serve as bases for travel to nearby areas of interest. Traditional destinations are Limón, Puntarenas, and coastal resorts, but think about staying in such places as Turrialba, San Isidro, or Liberia. See chapter 6 for some possibilities. Chapter 8 is a rundown of several privately operated nature reserves that cater to ecotourists; one will have the level of comfort and adventure just right for you. Chapter 7 guides you to the national parks. In chapter 5, there are suggestions on ways to move around the country.

All prices given are in U.S. dollars. Hotel rates were given to me as valid for the 1994 high tourist season, but prices go up in Costa Rica as everywhere else. I have included the taxes in hotel rates. Bus and plane schedules change, so check once here at one of the places listed under Tourist Information in chapter 5.

By definition, vacations have to do with moving beyond one's ordinary activities. Let some of your dreams come true in Costa Rica: sail in a yacht, raft down a river, sit on a beach, walk in a cloud forest, hike in a jungle miles from nowhere, visit a banana plantation, see birds and animals you know only from National Geographic specials, bathe under a waterfall. Meet a warm and gracious people. Walk softly, with an awareness of your own impact on the culture and environment.

5
Bienvenidos: Welcome to Costa Rica

Bienvenidos means "welcome." This chapter is intended to help you feel more comfortable as you move about city and *campo* (countryside). Here are details about money, calling home, where to find out what is going on, and how to get to where you want to go. You'll find health and safety tips, with a special focus on nature travel, a list of holidays to plan around, and typical foods and drinks to try.

Language

Spanish is the official language of Costa Rica. However, major hotels have bilingual receptionists, and some restaurants have menus in English and Spanish. (The English translations can be delightful.) English is taught in some public schools, so you will come across ticos who want to speak English with you or will try to help out if you do not speak Spanish. Do not, though, expect to find people who speak English wherever you go. Your taxi driver may not speak English, and no one at the bus station may understand a word you say. However, Costa Ricans are genuinely nice people on the whole, and they will try hard to help as long as you are polite.

Ticos are delighted when you try out whatever Spanish you know, so learn a few words and phrases—at least *por favor* (pronounced por fah-VOR) and *gracias* (GRAH-see-ahs), "please" and "thank you." You will soon be saying *buenos días* (boo-EN-nos DEE-ahs), "good morning," with the best of them.

At the Airport

One of the first welcomes you may receive after you make your way past *migracíon* (immigration) and *aduana* (customs) is from Nelson Villalobos, chief of the Costa Rica Tourism Institute's airport information office (ICT), or one of his staff. Look for the ICT counter after clearing customs. It is open from 8:00 a.m. to 9:00 p.m. every day of the year except Thursday and Friday of Holy Week, December 25, and January 1. For sixteen years, Nelson has been helping people at the airport, and he or his people will have answers to your questions. They can help you make hotel reservations and give you a road map of Costa Rica, and a free poster (if they have any in stock). You can pick up brochures put out by ICT as well as by hotels and tour companies. If there is no time to stop at the airport tourist booth, you can get information at the ICT office in San José.

COSTA RICA ODDS AND ENDS

Population: 3.17 million

Area: 19,730 square miles (51,100 sq km)

Capital: San José
population 305,278 in municipal limits; greater metropolitan area contains half of total population elevation 3,809 feet (1,161 m)

Official language: Spanish

Official religion: Roman Catholic; 80 percent of the people are Catholic

Government: Constitutional, democratic republic; elections every four years

Currency: Colón

Time: Central standard, no daylight savings time

Electric current: 110 volts

Telephone country code: 506

Highest point: Mount Chirripó, 12,529 feet (3,819 m)

Seasons: rainy—May to November; dry—December to April

The bank at the airport is open from 8:00 a.m. to 4:00 p.m. Monday through Friday. It is across from the ticket counters on the ground floor. There is also a money exchange booth in the immigration area of the airport (before you go through customs), but it will not be open if you arrive on a late flight.

A taxi ride for the 11 miles (18 km) into San José is about $10 in U.S. money. Fare on the frequent public buses is less than 50 cents, but there are no luggage racks, so if you have big bags, forget that option. You would also still have to get to your hotel from the bus terminal at Avenida 2, Calles 12/14.

Outside the front door of the terminal are the offices of several rental car agencies, but be sure to read the section on transportation in this chapter before you rush out and rent a car.

On the way into town, if you arrive during coffee harvest, you may get a whiff of something pungent as you cross a bridge—not exactly the sweet tropical fragrance you had expected. It is not the person next to you but *broza*, pulp washed from coffee beans during processing, which ends up in the river. Welcome to Costa Rica.

Money Matters

The monetary unit is the *colón* (co-LONE). Its symbol is ¢. Take time to look at the coins—some are *colones* (co-LONE-ess) and some are *céntimos* (SEN-tea-mos). Each is clearly marked, but it pays to recognize that the coin marked "20" is 20 colones, not 20 céntimos. Bills come in denominations of 5, 10, 50, 100, 500, 1,000, and 5,000. Coins are 10, 25, and 50 céntimos, and 1, 2, 5, 10, and 20 colones. (Few coins of 10 and 25 or bills of 5 and 10 are in circulation now. The 5-colon bill, however, is a beauty. It has the *guaria morada* on one side and a copy of the mural in the National Theater on the other.) Rumor has it that a 50-colón coin will be issued.

The colón floats in relation to the U.S. dollar; as of May 1994, the exchange rate was 155 to the dollar. Continuing mini-devaluations will change this rate.

From my experience, you can expect to pay a premium for colones in a departure airport, so change a minimum or wait until you get to Costa Rica. You may change money legally at banks there or at your hotel. It is certainly more convenient at the hotel, but sometimes the cash drawer is low, so do not wait until the last minute to ask. You will find accommodating people who offer to change dollars as you walk around San José, especially on Avenida Central near the Central Bank. This is illegal; both buyer and seller can be prosecuted. The difference in the legal and black-market rate is only a few colones, and you risk receiving counterfeit money or being otherwise shortchanged.

Hotels and banks usually charge a small amount for changing traveler's checks or give a lower exchange rate. Ask. Some have a minimum service charge whether you change $50 or $500 worth of checks. Do not assume that all hotels will accept credit cards, especially outside San José. Be sure to inquire when you make your reservation.

Do not take off for the countryside with only 5,000-colón notes, because small restaurants or shops may not have change; keep some smaller bills with you wherever you are.

Banks

Hours vary, but except on holidays and weekends, banks are open at least from 9:00 a.m. to 3:00 p.m. One with longer hours is Banco Nacional de Costa Rica, which is just south of the Metropolitan Cathedral at Avenida 4, Calle Central/2. (This means it is on Avenida 4 in the block between Calle Central and Calle 2. See the San José section of chapter 6 for more on addresses.) It is open from 7:00 a.m. to 6:30 p.m. weekdays. Another is the Morazán branch of Banco Nacional de Costa Rica, which is on the corner of Avenida 1, Calle 7. It is open from 8:00 a.m. to 6:00 p.m. weekdays. Banco Metropolitano (Avenida 2, Calle Central/1) is open from 8:15 a.m. to 12:30 p.m. and 1:30 to 4:30 p.m.—the charge for changing traveler's checks there is only one colón for every dollar changed. Just tell the guard at the door of any bank that you want to change dollars (that much English everybody understands), and he will point you in the right direction.

Before you take a place in any bank line, ask again to be sure you are in the right one. You sometimes must hand over your identification documents (passport, tourist card) at one window and complete the transaction at another. It can be a happy five-minute experience, or it can take half an hour or more, depending on the lines. That is why it may be easier to change money at your hotel if you have the option. Many hotels stick to the official rate, posted for all to see.

Remember that banks are closed on holidays. (See the list in this section.)

Credit Cards

The number of establishments accepting credit cards is increasing, but check before you spend if you are depending on plastic.

With an American Express card, you can write a personal check to buy traveler's checks in dollars. The American Express office, open 8 a.m. to 4 p.m. Monday through Friday, is in Banco de San José across from the Hotel Europa, Calle Central, Avenidas 3/5. Telephone 221-9911.

With Visa or MasterCard, you can get cash advances in colones but not in dollars. A handful of hotels provide this service for their guests. Ask at yours. Otherwise, Credomatic accepts both Visa and MasterCard. One of its offices is also in Banco de San José, open from 8 a.m. to 5:30 p.m. Monday through Friday. Another is in Centro Comercial Omni, Avenida 1, Calles 1/3 (third floor), open from 8 a.m. to 7 p.m. Monday through Friday. The main Credomatic office is at Avenida Central, Calles 29/33 (second floor). It is open from 8:00 a.m. to 7:00 p.m. weekdays and from 9:00 a.m. to 1 p.m. Saturdays, telephone 253-2155. If that seems too far to walk, use this as an opportunity to try the city bus system. Take a bus marked San Pedro, which starts east of the National Theater on Avenida 2, and watch the street signs. Get off at the bus stop (*parada*) near Kentucky Fried Chicken; Credomatic is half a block east of the colonel. By the way, there is a good restaurant called Paprika in the same building.

For Visa, I have also used the Banco Crédito Agrícola de Cartago, Avenida 4, Calle 2, near the Metropolitan Cathedral, open from 9 a.m. to 3 p.m. Decals on bank windows indicate which credit cards can be used there. You will need to show your passport or tourist card for any transaction.

Some establishments add a surcharge for use of a credit card. You may want to ask when you make your hotel reservation.

Tourist Information

In addition to the office at the airport mentioned earlier, ICT has an office in the heart of downtown San José, underneath the Plaza de la Cultura. Go down the stairs facing Calle 5, between Avenida Central and Avenida 2, and you will find some very kind people who can answer questions in English as well as Spanish about attractions, services, and transportation. You can get a free ICT road map and a list of guides who have completed a training program. Hours are 9:00 a.m. to 5:00 p.m. weekdays and 9:00 a.m. to 1:00 p.m. Saturday. You may call there for information: 222-1090. If you need help when that office is closed, call the airport office at 442-1820. There also are ICT offices at the northern and southern borders for those who enter by land, and at Puerto Caldera.

INFOtur is a new computerized service that offers information on lodging, restaurants, bus schedules, embassies, museums, souvenir shops, and travel and car rental agencies. The bus list is a marvel, with departure times, addresses, and telephone numbers. Offices are at the ICT Plaza de la Cultura and airport information offices and at Calle 5, Avenida 2 (INFOtur's main office). Hours at the main office are 8:30 a.m. to 6:00 p.m. Monday through Friday, 8:30 a.m. to 1 p.m. Saturdays. Personnel there speak English, Spanish, German, and Italian. Telephone 223-4481 or 223-4482, fax 223-4476. INFOtur will make reservations for you. The airport office is open from 8:30 a.m. to 9:00 p.m. A regional office is in Liberia.

If you have a modem, the information is also available via computer for just the cost of the telephone call. Dial 257-2000 or 253-2000, adding Costa Rica's country code (506) if you are outside the country. If you are a net user, the code is 0712211201000. Press H (capital) and "Enter," then enter Ninfrac-211201000 and press "Enter." You can talk to the system via menus, entering the two first letters of the option. Internal selections are made by number codes.

Communications

Mail

Some hotels sell postage stamps and will mail cards and letters for guests. However, it is fairly painless to do it yourself at the local post office; Spanish usually is not necessary. Just hand the card to the person at the window, who will sell you beautifully colored stamps to stick on; insert the card or letter in the slot marked *Exterior* (foreign). There may be a slot specifically for the United States and Canada. The line moves quickly at the Central Post Office in San José, Calle 2, Avenidas 1/3. Hours of window service are 7:00 a.m. to 9:00 p.m. weekdays, 8:00 a.m. to noon on Saturday.

The first automated stamp machines were introduced in 1993 at several locations in San José: the Central Post Office, Gran Hotel Costa Rica (Avenida 2, Calle 3), Soda Palace (Avenida 2, Calle Central), and Hotel Alameda (Avenida Central, Calle 12). Instructions are in English and Spanish.

Telephones

International calls are too easy. From a private phone, you can dial direct, using the appropriate country code (001 for the United States and Canada), followed by the area code and the number. You can call person-to-person collect, or charge a call to your credit card by dialing 09, the country code (1 for the U.S. and Canada), area code, and phone number. An operator will come on the line for billing and person-to-person specifics. You can also dial 116 for the international operator, but service is quicker and cheaper using the 09 service. At most hotels, you must go through the switchboard, and there may be a fee. Ask.

Radiográfica Costarricense in downtown San José, Avenida 5, Calles 1/3 is open from 8:00 a.m. to 10:00 p.m. weekdays and 8:00

a.m. to 8:00 p.m. weekends, and Comunicaciones Internacionales on Avenida 2 just around the corner from the Gran Hotel Costa Rica and Plaza de la Cultura is open daily from 7:00 a.m. to 10:00 p.m. Both have phones where you can call the United States and Canada and pay on the spot. You can also call collect or use a telephone credit card. Comunicaciones Internacionales also has an office in Puntarenas.

From any phone in the country, you can contact an operator in Canada or the United States to place collect or credit card calls. For the United States, dial 114 for AT&T, 162 for MCI, and 163 for Sprint. You can contact an operator in Canada by dialing 161.

To make a local call from a public telephone, have a supply of 5-colón, 10-colón, and 20-colón coins. Place the coin in the slot; if the phone is working properly, it will drop only when your call goes through. Sometimes a series of beeps at the beginning makes conversation impossible, but persevere. If the phone starts beeping after you have talked awhile, feed it another coin or you will be cut off. When calling a friend, give the person the number you are calling from (posted near the phone) so she or he can call you back and avoid the problem.

Some hotels, groceries, and department stores have public phones that are quieter than those on the street. Public phones do not have phone books. Calls from your hotel can be expensive.

Notice the many public telephone signs as you travel around the country. Often they are in the local grocery or sometimes even in a private home. To call from one of these, give the person in charge of the phone the number to be dialed. Time is metered, and you pay when you finish. To call within the country, just dial the number; there is no long-distance code. Even on in-town calls, charges are based on time used, which is one reason most businesses do not let the public use their private phones. It costs them.

NOTE: As of April 1, 1994, it is a whole new ball game with telephone numbers in Costa Rica. Every number in the country went from six digits to seven. Numbers in this book, which went to press before the changeover, are the new ones assigned by the Costa Rican Electricity Institute. I have my fingers crossed that havoc ensuing from the change will be brief. Be patient.

Telex and Fax
If your hotel does not offer this service, go to Radiográfica or Comunicaciones Internacionales in San José, where you can both send and receive by telex and fax. Most post offices have telegraph services.

Taxes and Tipping

Be aware that a 10 percent service charge is automatically added to restaurant bills (along with a 10 percent tax). Tipping beyond that for extra-good service is at your discretion. Tips for hotel bellboys and porters are about 50 cents per bag. Taxi drivers appreciate but do not expect tips; let it depend on courteous service as well. Do not forget the housekeeping staff.

Tour guides expect tips, and do not overlook the naturalist guide at the private reserve; his or her tip is not included in the package. Consider a minimum of $1 per person per day. If your tour has been by bus, give something to the driver as well. Some people prefer to tip individually, but another option is to combine tips from everyone in the group and present it on the last day. Perhaps you also want to leave a monetary thank you for the cook at the private reserve who turned out those good meals, or the young girl who shyly served you every day.

Taxes, however, have nothing to do with courtesy. Hotels are going to charge you a 10 percent sales tax and a 3 percent tourism tax, which is similar to a lodger's tax.

Business Hours

We have already covered banking hours, which are at least 9:00 a.m. to 3:00 p.m. Government and professional offices are usually open from 8:00 a.m. to 5:00 p.m., though some government offices close at 4:00 p.m. Shops are generally open from 9:00 a.m. to 7:00 p.m., though some still observe the long lunch hour—

closing from noon to 2:00 p.m. Downtown San José used to close up at midday Saturday and reopen on Monday. These days, more stores observe weekday hours on Saturday, and a few are open on Sunday. Some restaurants close on Sunday, some on Monday; check before you charge off in a cab.

A note on daylight hours. Since Costa Rica is near the equator, it does not have the seasonal variations in daylight hours we to the north have. If you get up with the sun, you will be getting up between 5:00 and 5:30 a.m. Darkness falls between 5:30 and 6:30 p.m. year-round.

Transportation

You have options for getting around that you may not have considered. In San José, taxis and buses abound. To get out into the countryside, taxis, buses, planes, boats, bicycles, and rental cars are available.

The miles of paved roads grow yearly; Costa Ricans tell you the increase is always greatest the year before a presidential election. But highway construction and maintenance are expensive in this

Ferry across the Tempisque River, approaching the Nicoya Peninsula (Photo by Ree Strange Sheck)

mountainous, rainy nation, to say nothing of the havoc wreaked by hurricanes and earth tremors. I traveled over the newly paved road between San Isidro de El General and Dominical in southern Costa Rica in 1987, just after it was finished, marveling at what an easy, quick trip it was through a spectacular landscape. Six months and Hurricane Joan later, the landscape was still spectacular, but some of it had shifted onto the roadbed, and potholes required full driver attention. You can encounter superb highways, potholes, unpaved gutbusters, and charming country roads, and even the most recent road map cannot keep up with all the changes.

Taxis

Taxis are supposed to use meters, called *marías*, for distances of up to 7.5 miles (12 km). Do not be embarrassed to ask the driver before you get in if his maría works, or look below the front dash to see if it is on. If the meter is not working, agree on a fare before you get in, as you should do with longer trips. If you are taking a taxi from the hotel, ask the receptionists or doorman what the fare might be. Rates are reasonable by U.S. standards.

A taxi driver who does not use his maría can be fined if the passenger files a complaint at the Ministry of Public Works and Transport. If you want to do this, be sure to get the taxi's number and driver registration number, and note the time.

If you phone for a taxi, the driver can turn on his meter where he got the call, and can legally charge up to 20 percent more for service between 10 p.m. and 5 a.m.

Taxis will slow down beside you when you do not need one, but they are, of course, impossible to catch when you are running late at rush hour on a rainy afternoon. Drivers are generally courteous, though some will refuse to take you if they consider the distance too short or the traffic too fierce. Do not be surprised if this happens to you at the taxi stand on Avenida 2 in front of Gran Hotel Costa Rica. It gets my vote for the greatest percentage of surly drivers.

Drivers can be incredibly kind as well. One picked me up as I ran down a dark suburban street, carrying a backpack, to meet a 5:00 a.m. downtown departure for Tortuguero. Though he could not take me all the way because he was going off duty, he dropped me at the nearest bus stop without charging me a single colón and admonished me for being out alone: "Es peligroso, señora." (It is dangerous).

You can hire a taxi to go practically anywhere there is some kind of road. In outlying areas, taxis are often four-wheel-drive jeep types. Drivers have remarkable skill. If you do not fancy going on an organized tour to a particular location or do not want to take a bus or drive, you could hire a taxi. The fare will be based on distance and time. You should figure on a minimum of $5 per hour, but it will be considerably more if the trip is over bad roads. If you do not want to arrange it yourself, ask your hotel to call and get the fare and reserve the taxi. The advantage is that the driver will stop wherever you want to take a picture or have an extra moment to soak up the scenery; the disadvantage is that he may not speak English. (Airport drivers usually speak some English, but their rates are higher.) There are a number of taxi companies. (See Practical Extras for a few numbers.)

Buses

Bus service in Costa Rica is reliable and inexpensive. It offers a good opportunity to mix with the people, perhaps in closer quarters than we of automobile-prone societies are accustomed to. You may actually have to rub shoulders with someone, but you will sense the nature of those people by the time the trip is over. And they might have a glimpse of yours.

My bus travels have revealed a genuinely courteous people— helpful, friendly, good-humored, dignified. No pigs and chickens in these buses. The vehicles are usually clean (unfortunately, some carry a sign advising passengers to throw trash out the window rather than litter the bus!), and so are the Costa Ricans who use them. I have encountered some foreign tourists in Costa Rica who must have thought that "back to nature" in the tropics meant going without a bath. Not so for Costa Ricans: for them, cleanliness is truly next to godliness.

Let's talk first about intercity bus travel, leaving San José and the greater metropolitan area for last. You can take a bus from the capital to any destination in the country that has bus service for less than $10 one way. For that reason, I do not include exact fares with bus information in later chapters. I know some of us have to count pennies when we travel, but just allow $10 per ride and you will come out below budget. (Departure points in San José for various towns are listed in Practical Extras.)

Sometimes seats can be reserved with advance ticket purchase. If not, go to the bus stop at least an hour early. If the bus line has an office there, buy your ticket and get in line. If there is no office, you will buy your ticket from the driver or his assistant. Get in line, but be sure to ask if you are in the right one. Verify that it's the right bus when you get on. Some buses carry only the number of passengers there are seats for; on others, if you can get on or hang on, you can go. Check to see if your ticket gives you an assigned seat.

Some buses have compartments underneath for luggage; some have overhead luggage racks that usually are too small for anything but a sack or tote bag. Some have nothing but a small space toward the front where bags can be piled. Do not take any more luggage than you would be prepared to hold on your lap or put under your feet during the trip, and you will be OK. Some of the newer long-distance buses have adequate legroom, while some of the old ones bring back memories of riding on a school bus: The seats are the same, but you are bigger.

I include length of trip with bus information for specific destinations, so you can judge whether it appeals to you. Remember that the country is small. By the Inter-American Highway, it takes only six hours to get to Nicaragua from San José, eight to get to Panama.

On longer trips, there is a short rest stop. I usually carry juice or fruit; your plastic water bottle or canteen will come in handy. Do not expect a rest room on board.

Tell the driver where your destination is, and he will generally let you off as close as possible. Taxis usually wait where buses stop in towns.

Watch your belongings and, if you end up standing in a crowded bus, your pockets. Even with those courteous, helpful, friendly, dignified people around you, a bad apple may be on board (probably a foreigner). Be especially careful with checked luggage. Get off the bus quickly to claim it at your destination. I usually try to watch at intermediate stops to see that no one else claims my bag. If you put a bag on an overhead rack, keep your eye on it as well.

I look forward to bus trips off the major highways. They are so human. The driver may stop to chat a minute with the driver in the bus you meet or be flagged down by a housewife asking him to pick up something in town and drop it off on the return trip. These buses are a lifeline in rural areas. Once while I was on a trip from Monteverde, the bus stopped so the driver's assistant could move a piece of milled lumber to the side of the road. A few bumps later, another piece and another stop. Then another. Soon everyone on the bus was craning to see the next piece, laughing about the truck ahead that would arrive without its cargo, telling the driver to keep the pieces and add a room to his house. Even non-Spanish-speakers were caught up in the fun of it.

Some ability in Spanish makes bus travel easier, but with politeness, persistence, and imagination, someone who does not speak the language can manage. Carry a map and point to destinations, or write the destination down and show it when asking for guidance. *Bus* is spelled the same in Spanish but is pronounced "boos."

Thousands of people ride buses in San José every day. You can, too. City fares and even fares to other towns in the greater metropolitan area are minimal. You can take a bus to the airport or Alajuela for less than 50 cents, or to some of San Pedro's good restaurants or the art museum at La Sabana Park for less than 15 cents. You do not need correct change. Hotel staff members or the ICT office can tell you where stops are. Wait your turn in line and pay as you enter; the fare may be posted on the front window.

If there is no vacant seat, hang on. Men and women passengers relinquish their seats to pregnant women, parents with a small child or two in tow, the handicapped, and frail, elderly persons. It is not uncommon for men to surrender seats to females in any form, but that is strictly by choice. I have sometimes felt I was given a seat because I was a foreigner—a nice feeling after traveling in some other parts of the world. Microbuses cost more but are quicker, and you are guaranteed a seat.

Again, watch your money and passports. I had a coin purse lifted so skillfully on a Sabana-Estadio bus that I have yet to figure out how it was done. But I have ridden the bus hundreds of times in Costa Rica and have had that happen only once. Buses are great for people-watching, for eavesdropping, and to get glimpses of people's everyday lives.

When it is time to get off, push a button, pull a cord, or yell "*parada*," and the driver will stop at the next scheduled place.

Planes

SANSA is the national domestic airline, with scheduled service from San José to several locations. It flies to Quepos, Palmar Sur, Puerto Jiménez, Golfito, Coto 47, Barra del Colorado, Tortuguero, Tamarindo, Nosara, Sámara, and Tambor. One-way rates range from $42 to $53. Tickets are available at the SANSA office, north of the corner of Calle 24 and Paseo Colón, and some hotels and tourist agencies. Flights leave from Juan Santamaría Airport, but SANSA offers van service between its main office and the airport. Telephone 233-0397 or 233-3258, fax 255-2176.

Travelair has daily scheduled flights to Barra del Colorado, Tortuguero, Golfito, Puerto Jiménez, Nosara, Carrillo, Tambor, Palmar Sur, Quepos, and Tamarindo. One-way fares range from $37 to $70. San José departures are from Tobias Bolaños Airport in Pavas. Telephone 220-3054 or 232-7883, fax 220-0413.

Schedules for both of these airlines are in Practical Extras at the end of the book. Baggage is limited to 26 pounds (12 kilos) on each. Store your extra luggage at your hotel. Flights are generally less than one hour. Because planes are small, it is advisable to reserve as far in advance as possible, especially in high season.

Several charter companies provide air service. Three are Aeronaves de Costa Rica (232-1413), VEASA (232-1010), and Aero Costa Sol (441-1444). Look in the phone book for other possibilities.

Do not schedule yourself too tightly, and be aware that flights can be canceled because of bad weather, more of a threat in the rainy season. Once on a charter flight from Marenco, humidity and temperature led the pilot to ferry two passengers and luggage to Palmar Sur, returning for the other three of us. From Palmar Sur we flew to San José together. Standing on the short grass runway at Marenco with ocean on one side and rain forest on the other, not one of us questioned the pilot's decision.

Trains

The famous Jungle Train from San José to Limón is no more. It came to an end in 1991 when passenger service between the Central Valley and the Caribbean shut down. The Puntarenas service was also discontinued that year. But rail buffs need not despair. Swiss Travel Service runs the Banana Train on narrow-gauge tracks through banana country on the Caribbean slope, daily except Sundays, at $70 per person for the round-trip bus/train package. The train portion, which begins at Guapiles, is two to three hours, ending at a banana plantation for a tour of the operations. Swiss Travel's telephone number is 231-4055, fax 231-3030. TAM has a Green Train tour that offers a ride in a restored 1930s train. The guided tour begins by bus from San José to Guapiles through Braulio Carrillo National Park and switches to rail from Guapiles to Siquirres, with a return by bus. Passengers have lunch on board, and the train stops along a river to allow a trek or a swim. A guided tour of a banana operation is included. The Green Train has scheduled runs on Tuesdays and Saturdays, other days with a minimum of fourteen people; the cost is $70 each. TAM's telephone number is 222-2732, fax 221-6465.

You can also board interurban commuter trains between San José, San Pedro, and Heredia (departure in San José from the Atlantic station, Avenida 3, Calles 19/21), San José and Pavas (departure in San José from the Pacific Station, Avenida 20, Calle 2), and between San José and Cartago (from the Atlantic station). Ask at ICT about the Intertrén schedules.

Ferries

On the Pacific side, car/passenger ferries cross the Gulf of Nicoya from the mainland to the Nicoya Peninsula. The Puntarenas-Playa Naranjo ferry operates from 3:30 a.m. to 9 p.m. (See Practical Extras for departure times from each port.) The charge for a standard car is less than $10; passengers pay less than $1.50 each. The company has a new fleet of boats that can carry 30 to 40 cars each and make the trip in about an hour. Telephone 661-1069 or 661-3834.

The ferry across the Tempisque River operates hourly between Puerto Níspero and Puerto Moreno from 5 a.m. to 7 p.m., starting from the mainland side. The rate for a standard car with driver is less than $3; passengers pay a pittance for the half-hour trip. Telephone 685-5295.

A passenger launch makes the trip from Puntarenas to Paquera on the southern end of the Nicoya Peninsula for those heading from there to Montezuma. It leaves behind the Municipal Market in Puntarenas three times a day. (See Practical Extras for the schedule.) The cost is less than $2 for the hour-and-a-half trip. Telephone 661-2830.

A passenger launch also operates between Golfito and Puerto Jiménez, crossing the Golfo Dulce for a sea link between the mainland and the Osa Peninsula. It runs once a day, leaving Golfito at noon and Puerto Jiménez at 6 a.m., for a voyage of about an hour and a half.

Car Rental

To rent a car, you need a valid driver's license, passport, and credit card. The minimum age is usually from 21 to 25 depending on the company. All major car rental agencies have offices in Costa Rica, and there are several local companies as well. Offices are at Juan Santamariá International Airport and in San José either at major hotels or concentrated in the Paseo Colón area. Several beach hotels now offer car rentals, and there are agencies in Limón, Liberia, and Golfito.

Sample costs range from $21 a day plus 21 cents a kilometer, or $38 a day with unlimited mileage, for a small standard car to $31 a day plus 31 cents a kilometer, or $54 a day with unlimited mileage, for a four-wheel-drive vehicle. You can rent a nine-passenger van for $34 a day plus mileage. Shop around. Some companies require purchase of insurance; others do not. Deductibles can be high. Weekly rates are discounted, and travelers in the low season from May to November may pay as much as 20 percent less. You may get better rates by reserving your car before you come, through international reservations.

Some agencies also rent coolers, surfboards (Toyota), beach chairs, and tents. You can even rent a driver for your rental car if you like. Ask for a handout sheet on basic Costa Rican traffic regulations.

Gasoline is sold by the liter. Regular and diesel fuels are available, and some stations have lead-free fuel, called "Super." All petroleum is imported and refined in Costa Rica by RECOPE, the national refinery. In rural areas, watch the gas gauge. You will not find a service station at every intersection. While round-the-clock service is available in San José, service stations in other areas may open at 6:00 a.m. and close at 6:00 p.m.

The maximum speed limit is 50 miles (80 km) per hour on toll roads and primary highways unless posted otherwise. It has been raised to 56 miles per hour (90 km) on some stretches. You will see plenty of 40- and 60-kilometer-per-hour signs. Remember that the speedometer indicates kilometers, not miles. Speeders are subject to heavy fines, as are people in the front seat who do not buckle up.

Be sure to check the car over for dents, scratches, or other damage before you accept it, and have those noted in writing by the agent. It could save you some problems. Also be sure to check the spare and jack and such details as brake fluid, oil, water, and lights.

Before you rent a car, please read the section in this book on traffic hazards. Just know what you are in for. If you do rent, do not leave belongings visible even in a locked car, and do not leave luggage in the trunk at night or even unattended during the day. In fact, do not leave anything of value in an unattended car.

Because of road conditions, driving times are usually longer than expected. (See the Intercity Buses section of Practical Extras for some idea of driving times.)

Bicycles

Bicycle tourism is beginning here. If you are going to do it on your own, remember that bike lanes do not exist. If it is your first trip to Costa Rica, you might consult one of the tour companies before you set off; there are roads you should avoid.

Hitchhiking

Hitchhiking on major roads is practically nil since bus fare is so cheap. However, local people wait by the road for a ride in rural areas where bus service is nonexistent or infrequent. Tourists do not generally hitchhike in Costa Rica except in an emergency. For example, when my return flight from Golfito fell through and I had to be in San José the next day for an appointment—and all the buses were sold out—I hitchhiked for the first time in my life. At the end of the seven-hour trip, the charming young man who had rescued me said, "Ree, you should not do this any more. Not everyone is good." He delivered me right to my door.

Traffic Hazards

For a tourist, there are easier ways to get around San José than by rental car. Parking space is limited, and traffic is fierce. I would suggest you walk or take a taxi or bus.

In the countryside, roads are for cars, buses, trucks, cows, dogs, chickens, people, and landslides. Be careful out there.

Some specific driving habits to look out for are passing on curves, use of climbing lanes by cars going downhill, and driving on whichever side of the road has the best pavement or fewer rocks or ruts. Tailgating is a national pastime.

Watch out for two-lane roads that feed suddenly into one-lane bridges, for lethal *huecos* (oo-AY-cos), or holes in the pavement that can knock passengers and vehicle for a loop, and for tree branches laid across the road that warn of trouble ahead. Geography and climate team up to create landslides big and small.

Fog is a permanent possibility on the highest section of the Inter-American Highway south of San José toward San Isidro de El General—the range known as Cerro de la Muerte. The earlier you get through that section, the better. The scenery is magnificent. The same advice goes for the new road to Limón through Braulio Carrillo National Park, though at least the road is wider there. It is prone to landslides as well.

On the miles of the San José-Puntarenas highway that have yet to be widened, you may find yourself in a string of cars and buses and trucks belching diesel fumes on a narrow, winding road. Adrenaline flows as vehicles jockey for position without a clue as to what may be approaching just around the curve. I would avoid that road on weekends and after dark. In fact, for safety's sake, I would avoid driving at night in general.

Even with road map in hand, you will need to ask directions when traveling off main roads. Additional signs are going up along main tourism routes, but choices to be made outnumber signs, especially on dirt roads. In the rainy season, always ask about the condition of the roads you plan to take before setting out each day.

Rental cars, marked by their license plates, are targets for some transit police. If you are stopped and cited, fines must be paid to a bank, or the rental agency will handle it for you. You should not pay the officer—if he says you should, take down his number and report him.

Safety

Theft is a worldwide phenomenon. Use common sense: do not wear expensive-looking jewelry, do not flash lots of cash, watch your belongings. Do not leave cameras or binoculars lying unattended on the beach. Watch your pockets and purse on crowded buses and streets. Use a sensible purse, one that closes securely; choose a bag that can be carried with a strap over the shoulder, held tightly between arm and body. Travel stores now carry all kinds of hidden pockets and pouches to wear on practically any part of the body; investigate which serves your purposes. Keep your passport separate from your money. Carry only the credit cards you need.

Be alert on the street if approached by an overly friendly person who claims to have met you somewhere. There are expert pickpockets around. I lost a watch while trying to explain to a man that I did not believe I knew him. I would know him now.

One of the most dangerous things facing a traveler in Costa Rica is crossing a downtown San José street. Your job as a pedestrian is to keep out of a driver's way, whatever he or she may decide to do. The tico's gentle nature seems to give way to rampant individualism once behind the wheel. Cars turning right do not yield to pedestrians even though the new traffic law requires it. Expect no mercy if the light change finds you in the middle of the street. To meet the challenge, I get beside a Costa Rican woman who is hanging onto at least two small children. When she goes, I go. By watching the natives, I have also learned that if I do not see the light turn green at a wide street like Avenida 2, the safest thing to do is wait a full cycle and be ready to sprint across when it next turns green. You do not want to be in front of four lanes, or more, of cars gunning their engines when they get the signal to go.

One other word of caution: back up on corners where buses make turns on narrow streets; you could actually be hit by the bus while standing on the sidewalk.

The pedestrian walkway along Avenida Central between the Central Bank and the Plaza de la Cultura is a delight; there is limited vehicle access, but generally you can walk right down the middle of the street. Lots of people crowd the narrow sidewalks; a study revealed that at one corner of the Central Market, an average of sixty-five thousand people a day pass by.

Staying Healthy

Costa Rica feels like a healthy place to travel, but some precautions make travel anywhere healthier. Give your body a break: keep to a diet it can recognize at first, adding a few new things each day. Get plenty of rest. If you would not eat in a "greasy spoon" or buy food from a street vendor at home, why risk it elsewhere in the world?

Food and Drink

I used to say it was OK to drink the tap water in San José and most other cities in the Central Valley. Then in 1991, a study revealed that only 50 percent of the country has water not contaminated by fecal material. Costa Ricans have demanded action by government officials to remedy the situation, so it is improving. I tend to exercise more caution in coastal areas and try to follow the saying, "When in doubt, don't." When you stay at a hotel or reserve in a rural area, you have every right to ask what the source of water is. Bottled water—*agua mineral*—is available almost everywhere, as are bottled carbonated drinks, beer, and packaged fruit juices. Contaminated ice continues to be a problem, mainly from the poor hygiene of those who handle it.

A good substitute for water on a hot day on the coast is the liquid from a *pipa*, a green coconut. And remember, if you don't trust that the water is safe to drink, do not brush your teeth with it either.

You can get *té de manzanilla* (chamomile tea) practically anywhere, with water that most likely has been boiled. Several companies offer a variety of delicious, packaged herbal teas. Buy a box to carry with you in case the restaurant does not offer herbal tea. Some of the private reserves at low and medium altitudes have lemongrass (*zacate de limón*) in the garden. If you ask, the kitchen staff is usually delighted to brew a tea from it. It is not only delicious but also used as a remedy for gastrointestinal problems and colds. You can always get fine coffee.

The two largest dairy product companies are Dos Pinos and Borden; both are reliable and offer pasteurized products. Even laser-treated milk that does not have to be refrigerated until opened is available.

Raw fruits and vegetables that can be peeled are safer. (That is one reason you carry a pocketknife.) Be sure to try the *mamón chino* (an exotic-looking red, spiny fruit with a succulent white flesh inside that you suck off a large seed), several varieties of mangoes, pineapples, bananas with the taste of the sun still in them, and *cas* (wonderful in juice or ice cream). Be careful with the colorful cashew fruit (*marañón*)—it causes an allergic reaction in some people.

If you hike, raft, or engage in a lot of physical exertion, remember that the salt content of sweat goes up with rising temperatures. Drink plenty of fluids and add salt to your food if you are sweating heavily.

Nature Travel Tips

Insects and snakes come with the tropics. Try to observe them on your terms. Plants can offer some surprises, so look before you grab hold of a tree along a steep or slick trail. It could have a protective coat of spines. If you choose to experience the jungle at night, take along a good light and go with a guide.

Remember that rivers can rise substantially with rain upstream; the river you waded across in the sunshine can look quite forbidding under a leaden sky. When you plan to hike along the beach, inquire about tides. Some beaches disappear at high tide, which also can make the mouth of a river dangerous to cross.

Remember, too, that the sun's rays are more vertical than you may be used to, so you can sunburn more easily. Be especially careful of the midday sun. Wear a hat with a brim large enough to protect your face and lips, and use sunscreen. If tanning is a goal, limit yourself to brief exposures in the early morning or late afternoon, increasing the time gradually.

Long sleeves and long pants protect you from sun, insects, and scratches whether you are in open grassland or forest. Leave the shorts for leisure time at the beach. Loose-fitting clothes are cooler, and baggy pant legs can get the first full dose of venom in the unlikely case of a snakebite.

Insects

I am well acquainted with two insects in particular: chiggers (*colora-dillas*—co-lo-rah-DEE-lyahs) and ticks (*garrapatas*—gahr-rah-PAH-tahs). Chiggers are actually mite larvae and live in grassy, bushy areas waiting to climb up the legs of passersby. Their bites itch like crazy, and the red bumps get worse if you scratch them. To discourage chiggers, dust sulfur powder on socks, feet, ankles, and lower calves before you walk in the grass. Put some on your pant legs. Mosquito repellents are not effective. For bites, Caladryl or Eurax cream helps; some people take an antihistamine for severe itching. The effect of the bites can last for weeks.

Ticks hang out especially where horses and cattle are found. You may notice some itching, but you also may feel nothing and then discover their reddish black bodies under your skin when you undress. Be careful not to leave the biting end embedded (a tick doesn't really have a head) because it can fester and cause infection. Apply alcohol, gasoline, or kerosene to the bite or hold a

The spiny pochote tree (Photo by Ree Strange Sheck)

lighted match or cigarette close to the tick to get it to let go and come out. Squeeze gently to help it along. Ticks can carry disease, so if you get a fever after being bitten, see a doctor.

In an area where mosquitoes are bothersome, use repellent and wear protective clothing. Some places provide mosquito netting for beds; if not, inexpensive mosquito coils, or "spirals" as they are known in Costa Rica, keep the population down. Buy them in groceries. The smoke from the end of the lighted spiral does the trick, but you also breathe that smoke. I would not recommend putting it next to your bed.

Ants in a wonderful assortment of sizes and colors will bite or sting if you are where they do not want you to be. Try not to stand still without first checking out the area. Sounds easy, but the advice is hard to remember when you have just spotted a great green macaw or a coati and you freeze so it won't go away. Be alert in innocent-looking grass. A group of us waiting for a plane on a grass airfield were bitten by ferocious little black ants, and when we landed back in San José, we had to do battle again with the swarms that had infiltrated our luggage. For hikes and trail rides, hats and long-sleeve shirts give some protection against ants that live in trees you may brush against.

If you are bitten by no-see-ums, the gnats known as *purrujas* in Costa Rica, use an antibiotic salve. You will not only be in more agony if you scratch the bites but also risk infection. They live near the coast, but you can visit the coast many times and never encounter them; they prefer areas near salt marshes. Repellents are not effective; protective clothing works best.

African (killer) bees arrived in Costa Rica in 1982, and you would do well to assume that all bee colonies are now Africanized. Keep your distance from hives or swarms. The stings of Africanized bees are no more venomous than those of your garden variety bee, but these insects are aggressive and attack with less provocation. The cumulative effect of many bee stings is dangerous. If attacked, move in a zig-zag motion; you can probably outrun them. Head for water if any is nearby, and cover your head. If someone with you is attacked and cannot move, cover both of you with something light in color and get the person to safety. Remove stingers with a knife or fingernails, being careful not to squeeze more of the stinger's venom into the bite. Apply ice or cold water, and, if badly bitten, see a doctor.

I routinely shake out boots or shoes before I put them on, and shake and inspect my clothes. Having been bitten once by a scorpion when I did not, I rarely forget.

Snakes

Running on a path to catch a bus, I once came face-to-face with a snake racing to catch a gigantic frog. I had turned my head to glance at the frog as it leaped by and looked forward again to see a spectacular black snake with a luminous bright green stripe the length of its long body about four feet in front of me. The top half of that body was reared in the air, the head at about the level of my thighs. Startled, we stopped in our tracks and stared at each other for a timeless moment. Then in one graceful move, it melted to the ground and slid off into the leaves at the side of the trail. The lesson: if a giant frog passes you with incredible leaps and bounds, consider the possibility that something is in hot pursuit, headed your way.

Although seeing a snake in the tropical forest can be thrilling, be respectful and keep your distance. Minimize unpleasant surprises. First, running is not a good idea. Take time to look around. Never sit on or step over a log or rock without checking out the other side. Some snakes live in trees, with protective coloration, so watch where you put your hands and your head. Most bites, however, occur below the knees, so consider high boots.

Two pairs of eyes are better than one, so walk with a friend. At night, carry a strong light. If you want to familiarize yourself with which snakes are poisonous and which are not, visit the Serpentarium in San José, Avenida 1, Calles 9/11, open daily from 9:00 a.m. to 6:00 p.m., or visit the Clodomiro Picado Institute in Dulce Nombre de Coronado, about thirty minutes from downtown San José, open to visitors only on Fridays at 2:00 p.m. Ask for directions at the ICT information office. Fewer than five hundred snakebites—mostly of farmworkers—are reported each year, with fewer than fifteen fatalities. The fer-de-lance, or *terciopelo*, accounts for almost half the bites.

Most naturalist guides carry antivenin kits. Ask. All Social Security hospitals, Red Cross stations, and National Guard posts have antivenin available. Bite marks of venomous and nonvenomous snakes differ, so if someone is bitten, look to see whether there are fang marks. There also may be small marks made by teeth. The bite of a nonpoisonous snake shows two rows of teeth marks but no fang marks. If the bite was by a poisonous snake, keep the victim still (especially the affected part), and squeeze out as much venom as possible with your mouth or hands within the first ten minutes after the bite. (Tourniquets and incisions are not recommended for amateurs.) Get medical attention as quickly as possible. A description of the snake is helpful. There is an anticoral serum and a polivalent serum for use against all other venomous Central American snakes.

Swimming

Fungus infections, especially in the ears, from swimming in pools or rivers is not uncommon. To prevent infection, clean out your ears with rubbing alcohol and a cotton swab after swimming. If you are swimming in a river, check the water for visible pollutants before getting in, and bathe with soap and water afterward. Read the information on water safety in this chapter before you swim in the ocean.

Medical Care

Costa Rica has good doctors and modern medical facilities, in both private clinics and its public health care system. (Tourists have access to treatment in the Social Security hospitals and clinics in case of accident or sudden illness.) One of the largest private hospitals is Clínica Bíblica: telephone 223-6422. Most hotels will contact a doctor for you, or the ICT information office in San José can help. (U.S. and Canadian Embassy addresses and phone numbers are listed in Practical Extras.) There is a private air ambulance service with a 24-hour emergency number: Ambulancia Aérea, 225-2500. Pharmacists often diagnose ailments and prescribe remedies. In addition to patent medicines, some medicines requiring prescriptions in the U.S. may be sold over the counter in Costa Rica.

Typical Fare

Gallo pinto is the staple of the Costa Rican diet: black beans and rice. Try to eat it somewhere other than a first-class hotel. A *gallo* is something with a tortilla wrapped around it, such as beef, cheese, beans, chicken, or pork. When faced with an unfamiliar menu in the countryside, you usually cannot go wrong ordering

WATER SAFETY

The beaches in Costa Rica are no more dangerous than those in southern California, according to Donald Melton of Quepos, who has pushed lifesaving efforts in coastal areas for many years.

Basic rules apply whenever you swim in coastal waters: Do not swim alone, on a full stomach, or while intoxicated. Do not swim at the mouth of a river, where currents can be treacherous. For the same reason, be careful around rocky points. Look before you leap. How deep is the water? Are people standing? Is the slope gradual or is there a steep drop-off?

According to Donald, about 80 percent of the two hundred people who drown each year in Costa Rica are victims of riptides. Some rips are called permanent because they are always in the same place. Ask local people how safe the water is. In other areas, rips can come and go. Some telltale signs are discoloration of the water—brown spots where turbulence is kicking up sand—and areas where breakers do not return directly to the surf but run parallel to the beach for a bit. Take a few minutes to watch the action of the sea before you go in.

If you are caught in a rip, remember that it will only take you out, not drag you under. Panic is a factor in drownings. Do not fight the current. See if you can use the energy of a big wave to push you toward the beach. Motion to shore for help, but while it is coming, swim parallel to the beach, and then as the current weakens, swim at a forty-five-degree angle toward shore. Never try to swim directly toward the beach. If you cannot swim, float; keep your legs and body close to the surface. If you can walk when you feel yourself being pulled out, also go parallel to the shore as fast as you can to try to get out of it.

Some dangerous beaches are Playa Bonita near Limón; near the entrance to Cahuita National Park; Doña Ana and Playa Barranca near Puntarenas; Jacó; and south Espadilla Beach at Manuel Antonio.

---

one of the rice dishes such as *arroz con pollo* (chicken and rice) or a *casado*, which often comes with beef, chicken, or pork and vegetables such as *yuca* (cassava, a tuber similar to a potato), plantain, or squash with the ever-present rice and black beans. A vegetarian casado may also be available. *Olla de carne* is a soup of beef and vegetables—chunks of yuca, squash, potato, corn on the cob, plantain, or whatever is the house recipe for olla de carne.

Tico tamales, traditional at Christmas, are wrapped in banana leaves rather than corn husks, with a filling of pork most common, though it can be chicken. Try a *tortilla de queso*, a substantial tortilla with cheese mixed in the cornmeal. *Pupusas* are, I believe, of Salvadoran origin, but they have found their way into typical restaurant menus in Costa Rica. Basically they are two tortillas fried with cheese inside—tasty and greasy.

Sea bass (*corvina*), prawns (*langostinos*), and lobster (*langosto*) are among the fresh seafood available. An appetizer of *ceviche*, certain types of raw seafood "cooked" in lime or lemon juice and mixed with onion and coriander leaves, can serve as a good light lunch. Ceviche is, however, being served less now because of the threat of cholera.

The big bunches of bright red or orange fruit you see for sale along roadsides are *pejibayes*, a palm fruit that has been harvested for food since Indian times. When boiled, it is often served as an hors d'oeuvre with a dollop of mayonnaise on top. Try it. You may not like it. The flesh is quite dense and on the dry side. Most ticos love them. Another product of the pejibaye palm is *palmito*, or heart of palm, served cooked or fresh. Some palm species do not resprout when cut for the "heart." The pejibaye does, and commercial plantations now supply the market. So you do not have to worry that your heart of palm salad cost a forest tree its life. Natives also make a fermented drink from the sap when a tree is cut. Have a guide point out the tree, a stately palm with hairy spines on the trunk.

Refrescos, or natural fruit drinks, may come mixed with milk, in which case they will be listed as *en leche*, or with water (*en agua*). Let your surroundings guide you as to which is safest, or stick to bottled drinks. I often order *agua dulce* in the campo, a hot drink made of boiling water and brown sugar. You can also have it mixed with milk, *con leche*. It is especially good in the mountains when there is a chill in the air. Cane-based guaro is the national liquor.

For sweets, try a dessert (*postre*, POS-tray) of flan, a sweet custard, or *tresleches*, a moist cake. *Cajeta* is a fudge.

Current Happenings

The *Tico Times* is an English-language newspaper published every Friday. It is an excellent source of information on what is going on in Costa Rica. Several downtown San José newsstands sell it, or look for it in gift shops, hotels, or in the Candy Shop in the row of stores off the Plaza de la Cultura, Calle 3, Avenida Central/2.

Costa Rica Today comes out every Thursday. It is distributed free at many hotels and other tourist-related businesses throughout the country. It has a restaurant section and articles on health, language, hotels, and tours, plus a calendar of events and delightful natural history pieces.

Holidays

Gaily decorated trucks carrying costumed children brightened the dusty road. We discovered it was the day of San Isidro, patron saint of the farmer, celebrated in the area we were passing through with a local fair and blessing of animals and carts and other vehicles. Many such religious or civic festivals occur throughout the year. Ask at the ICT Information Office where festivals will occur during your visit.

On official national holidays, most businesses, including banks, close. Holidays are listed here so you can plan around them.

January 1—New Year's Day
March 19—St. Joseph's Day, patron saint of the capital, San José
Holy Week—Maundy Thursday and Good Friday rival Easter in importance. Banks and businesses close, some of them all week.
April 11—Day of Juan Santamariá, national boy hero from the battle against William Walker and his filibusterers in 1856
May 1—Labor Day
June 29—Day of St. Peter and St. Paul
July 25—Annexation of the Province of Guanacaste, formerly part of Nicaragua

August 2—Day of the Virgin de Los Angeles (Our Lady of the Angels), patron saint of Costa Rica

August 15—Mother's Day

September 15—Independence Day (independence from Spain)

October 12—Discovery of America, Columbus Day, celebrated here as Día de la Raza

December 8—Immaculate Conception

December 25—Christmas (many businesses close from Christmas to New Year's Day)

6
What to See and Do

If you have not guessed by now, I should tell you straight out that I love Costa Rica. My only reason for writing this book is to help other travelers discover the beauty it has to offer. This section presents an overview of what awaits you in different parts of the country: the towns, parks and wildlife refuges, privately owned nature reserves, hotels, beaches, rivers, and good places to try typical food. You also will find out about some of the country's important agricultural crops.

Not so long ago, most visitors used San José as a base for one-day trips into the countryside. Other towns now offer adequate hotels and services, opening up the option of staying in an area to explore it rather than returning to the capital every night. Places such Turrialba, Liberia, Golfito, and San Isidro de El General are not crowded with tourists; to experience the day-to-day rhythm of life in these areas puts you more in touch with the rural roots of Costa Rica than dodging traffic on San José's Central Avenue. Many small hotels and lodges in outlying areas offer tours for their guests, so you can visit a forest or a beach from a base in the countryside. Consider spending a few nights on nature reserves, either public or privately operated, to hear the birds as they greet the day, to have time on a forest trail, and to sit quietly after supper and visit with the owner, the guide, the cook, or the ranger.

As for accommodations, I emphasize smaller lodges and hotels when possible because I believe they are generally more con-

ducive to giving the traveler a sense of place and are more in keeping with the wonderful smallness and variety of the country itself.
The connection, both with people and nature, is easier to make. I
have tried to cover a range of price possibilities. Information on
tour options from lodges and hotels is mentioned.

There are some excellent nature-oriented package tours to
places mentioned in each region. Some companies feature naturalist guides and offer day trips customized to fit the wishes of as few
as two people. Details on what some companies offer and price
information are in chapter 9. How to get to the national parks and
reserves on your own is included in chapter 7 with a discussion of
what each has to offer the tourist. The privately owned nature
reserves described in detail in chapter 8 are mentioned here; some
of them offer one-day as well as multiday visits. We already talked
in chapter 5 about the options of travel by public transportation,
renting a car, and hiring a taxi or van with a driver.

Costa Rica is a country of the unexpected. You may spot a sloth
in a tree as you pass along a busy highway, round a bend to discover a herd of cows meandering along the road, watch monkeys
swing from tree to tree on shore as you swim in warm ocean
waters, or spot a flock of parrots in downtown San José. It is a
place to try things you have never done before: go rafting or kayaking, be pampered on a cruise, tramp along trails in a tropical forest, ford rivers with water to the hood of the car, stay up all night
trying to photograph a volcanic eruption, or take off on horseback
to explore the countryside. The following pages guide you to the
level of adventure you choose.

San José

Like most cities, San José (founded in 1737) has its good and bad
sides. It is the center of government, theater, and art, as well as of
air pollution and congestion. It has beautiful parks and museums,
along with a few beggars on the streets. It is big and often noisy,
but even from its crowded downtown streets, one can manage a
view of surrounding mountains, green against the sky. I find it a

Artwork on Plaza de la Cultura, next to the National Theater (Photo by Ree Strange Sheck)

friendly, interesting city. Increased theft, however, is a reality. Be alert, and be careful.

With all the traffic, it is hard to realize that the era of the automobile began here only in the fifties. It is not uncommon to see carts scattered among the cars even now, though they are generally pulled by a person rather than oxen or a horse, as you may still encounter in the countryside. Walk along Avenida 1 to the area around the Central Market, Calles 6/8, or Borbón Market, Avenida 3, Calles 8/10, in the early morning to see carts being loaded and unloaded.

Avenida? Calle? These are words to add to your vocabulary. *Avenida* (pronounced ah-vay-NEE-dah) means "avenue." Avenidas run east and west in the city. Calle (CAHL-lyay) means "street," and calles—you got it—run north and south. It helps if you can get your bearings early, because when you stop to ask for directions, the answer probably will be in terms of so many meters to the north, east, south, or west. A city block is about a hundred meters long, so a helpful person will tell you to go "200 *metros al norte*," two blocks north. *Metros* is pronounced "MAY-tros."

About the hardest thing you will do in San José, other than get safely across its busy streets, is keep the street numbering systems straight. Calle numbers originate from Calle Central, with odd-numbered streets running parallel to the east of it, even-numbered streets west. Avenida numbers originate from Avenida Central; odd numbers are north of it and even numbers south. For example, if you go north from Avenida Central, you cross in succession Avenida 1, Avenida 3, Avenida 5. Walking west from Calle Central, you encounter Calle 2, Calle 4, Calle 6. Few buildings have numbers, so a typical address is Calle 1, Avenidas 2/4. This means the place is on Calle 1 in the block between Avenida 2 and Avenida 4. Look at the map of central San José to fix the system in your mind.

Street and avenue numbers are posted on buildings at some intersections. Keep looking as you walk, and you will eventually find one. The Costa Rica Tourism Institute (ICT) map of the country has a city map on the back. Get one and carry it with you.

The Plaza de la Cultura, above the downtown ICT office, is a good place to people-watch. A mime, juggler, marimba band, magician, or storyteller may be performing for whatever is collected when the hat is passed. Civic functions, book fairs, or a visiting music group from the Andes draw clusters of onlookers. Artisan booths have become common, creating an arts and crafts fair atmosphere. The adjacent open-air terrace of the Gran Hotel Costa Rica is a popular place to have refreshments or a meal while watching the activity or listening to the music.

On the Avenida 2 side of the plaza is a source of pride for ticos, the National Theater. Inaugurated in 1897, the building was paid for by coffee growers through a voluntary tax on every bag of coffee exported. The reason? A famous European opera star appearing in Guatemala had refused to perform in Costa Rica for lack of an adequate theater. National honor in this case resulted in a work of art. Perhaps you can attend a performance there. The theater is open for tours weekdays from 9:00 a.m. to 5:00 p.m., with an admission fee of $2.50.

Museums and Such

San José museums can be a good way to get a feel for the country before you take to the road. Most have reduced or free admission for students with an identification card.

National Museum (Avenida Central/2, Calles 15/17). An exhibit on modern history joins pre-Columbian art, natural history, and religious art in this nineteenth-century building which was converted from a military fortress after the army was abolished. The Plaza de la Democracia next door, dedicated in 1989, commemorates one hundred years of democracy in Costa Rica. The museum is open from 8:30 a.m. to 5:00 p.m., except Mondays. The admission charge is less than $1. The museum has a good gift shop, with copies of Indian artifacts and ceramics.

Museum of Costa Rican Art (Calle 42, where Paseo Colón comes to La Sabana Park). La Sabana Park used to be the international airport (Charles Lindbergh landed here), and the museum is in the old terminal building. After looking over the art exhibits downstairs, climb to the second floor to see the Golden Room, whose embossed walls depict the country's history. It is open 10:00 a.m. to 5:00 p.m., except Mondays. Admission is less than $1. The Sabana-Cementerio bus will get you from Calle 7, Avenida Central to the museum.

Jade Museum (Avenida 7, Calle 9). The museum is on the eleventh floor of the Instituto Nacional de Seguros (National

Insurance Institute) building. In addition to the marvelous collection of jade objects, there are pre-Columbian ceramic and stone works as well as displays with archaeological and ethnographic information. You also get some good views of the city from this height, and the rest rooms are clean. (Public rest rooms are in short supply.) The museum is open from 9:00 a.m. to 3:00 p.m. weekdays, except holidays. Admission is free.

Gold Museum (Calle 5, Avenidas Central/2). Located underneath the Plaza de la Cultura, this spectacular collection of indigenous gold art belongs to the Central Bank of Costa Rica. It is open Fridays from 1:00 to 5:00 p.m., and weekends from 10:00 a.m. to 5:00 p.m. Admission is free.

National Railway Museum (Avenida 3, Calles 19/21). Housed in the old Atlantic Railroad station, the museum contains a few his-

San José statuary, near Central Bank: Presentes (Photo by Ree Strange Sheck)

toric pieces of rolling stock, photos, train bells, telegraph equipment, period furniture, rail memorabilia such as tickets, and historical documents. It is open from 9 a.m. to 4 p.m. weekdays, 9 a.m. to 2 p.m. weekends. Admission is less than $1.

Museum of Natural Sciences (Colegio La Salle) across from the southwest corner of La Sabana Park. Though some of the specimens appear a bit moth-eaten, exhibits show many of the mammals and birds to be found in Costa Rica. It may be your only chance to see the harpy eagle, an endangered species, even if it is stuffed. Some signs are in English and Spanish; some are only in Spanish, with Latin names. (See Practical Extras for a list of some of the more common animals in Costa Rica, with their English and Spanish names.) Do not overlook the butterfly collection above the shells. A few crocodiles and caimans live on a small island on the patio. Take the Sabana-Estadio bus from near the Cathedral on Avenida 2 and ask the driver to let you off at Colegio La Salle for the Museo de Ciencias Naturales. The museum is down a tree-lined drive, near the Ministry of Agriculture. It is open from 7:00 a.m. to 3:00 p.m. weekdays, 7:00 a.m. to noon Saturdays. Admission is less than $1.

Insect Museum (University of Costa Rica campus in San Pedro). This small museum in the basement of the Music Arts Building (Facultad de Artes Musicales) has a dazzling display of butterflies. There are also bee specimens, exotic-looking beetles and walking sticks, poisonous spiders, the large *bala* ant found in the Atlantic zone, and a 162-pound wasp nest from near San Isidro de El General. Another display shows how animals protect themselves by mimicry and coloration.

The entrance, at the bottom of the stairs, may be locked. Ring the bell. Hours are from 1:00 to 4:45 p.m. weekdays; admission is less than $1. The easiest way to find it is to go by taxi. Buses to San Pedro, leaving across from the National Theater on Avenida 2, will get you to within a ten- to fifteen-minute walk. Get off at the church in San Pedro and follow the street in front of it as it curves around to the north side of the campus. Watch for the Facultad de Artes Musicales and Museo de Insectos signs. It is a pretty campus, and students are extremely helpful when you ask directions.

Serpentarium (Avenida 1, Calles 9/11). You may not encounter a single snake during your forays into the natural world, so here is a good chance to see some of what lies hidden there: the boa constrictor, coral snake, brightly colored tree viper, and fer-de-lance. More than 45 species of reptiles and amphibians (including the tiny poison dart frogs) are here, and there is also a nice photographic exhibit of Costa Rican wildlife. Most signs are in English and Spanish. Take time to look at the illustrations showing how to distinguish between venomous and nonvenomous snakes. You can also buy posters, T-shirts, postcards, nature books, and slides. A bilingual biologist is on hand. The Serpentarium is open from 9:00 a.m. to 6:00 p.m. year-round; admission is $2. There is a sign at the entrance on the street, but the Serpentarium is upstairs. Telephone 255-4210.

Clodomiro Picado Institute (Dulce Nombre de Coronado). Snakes are "milked" at this snake "farm" for the production of serum to be used against Central American snakes, including most coral species. The low fatality rate from snakebites in Costa Rica is attributed to the widespread availability of antivenins, which the lab also exports. The institute is about thirty minutes from San José. It is open to visitors Fridays at 2:00 p.m. Admission is free. Take a taxi or the bus to Moravia (from Avenida 3, Calle 3).

Parque Bolívar—the zoo (Calle 9, Avenida 11). The zoo tends to be jammed with local folks on weekends. Most of its wildlife is from Costa Rica, but an African lion, Bengal tiger, and assorted other foreign species round out the picture. The facilities themselves are on the shabby side, but the setting is beautiful, and improvements are under way. Bolívar once again has a tapir, and a new herpetological aquarium displays all five of Costa Rica's colorful poison dart frogs. The zoo is open daily from 9:00 a.m. to 4:30 p.m. Admission is less than $1.

Zoo Ave (La Garita de Alajuela). More than 700 birds and a few species of mammals (including all four species of Costa Rica's monkeys) await the visitor on the spacious grounds of this former coffee plantation. You can see the king vulture, toucans, parrots, scarlet macaws, green macaws, and many other species that are so elusive in the rain forest. Signs give English and Spanish names. The animals are well cared for by owners Dennis and Susan Janik.

Hours are 9:00 a.m. to 5:00 p.m. daily. Admission is less than $6 for adults and $2.50 for children. From Alajuela, you can take a La Garita or Atenas bus, which passes in front, or go by taxi for about $4. Telephone 433-9140.

Walk in a world of butterflies—I recommend it. In the San José area, several possibilities exist.

The Butterfly Farm in La Guácima de Alajuela has a garden of native plants that are home to thirty-six species with about a thousand breeding butterflies. Visitors can see all stages of the butterfly life cycle. Joris and María Brinkerhoff have created a beautiful opportunity to observe and to learn and to photograph butterflies and tropical flowers. The two-hour guided tour touches on butterfly defense mechanisms, predators, host plants, and reproduction, along with a film and a visit to the breeding facilities. In addition to butterflies, you can learn about bees in an hour-and-a-half tour that offers a peek inside a hive to see the queen depositing her eggs, plus fascinating details about such things as the importance of these busy insects in nature and medicinal uses of honey. It ends with a treat: honey tasting. Either tour includes a ride in a painted *carreta* (oxcart). Admission for the butterfly tour is $9 for adults, $4 for children; for the bee tour, adults are $8, children are $4; or you can combine the two at $16 for adults and $7 for children. The Butterfly Farm is open daily from 9 a.m. to 5:00 p.m., with the last tour beginning at 3 p.m. The restaurant is open from 7 a.m. to 5 p.m. A Butterfly Farm bus runs three times a day from San José hotels: the round trip costs $9. Call 438-0115 for reservations, bus information, or instructions on driving there.

Butterfly Paradise in San Joaquín de Flores, 7 miles (14 km) from San José, features more than 3,000 butterflies, representing seventy-five species, in a tropical garden with some fifty species of host plants, plus a botanical exhibit. Visitors can spend the day if they like. The fee of about $7 for adults and $3.50 for children includes a film and a walk through the laboratory (cocoons are exported), gardens, and a small museum. Butterfly Paradise is open from 9 a.m. to 4 p.m. Call 224-1095 for information.

Located near El Pueblo Shopping Center not far from the heart of San José is Spirogyra, a smaller garden that nevertheless showcases about 300 butterflies of some twenty-five species. Visitors learn about the whole process from egg to metamorphosis to feeding habits and defense systems. The garden is open daily except Tuesdays from 9 a.m. to 4 p.m. Admission is $4 for adults and $1 for children. Spirogyra is in the Guadalupe district, about 100 yards east and 150 yards south of El Pueblo. Telephone 222-2937.

Souvenir Shops

You can buy a wide variety of quality products in San José: jewelry, wooden items, furniture, T-shirts, leather goods, and artwork. Many of the shops also sell park posters, postcards, and slides; most accept credit cards.

La Casona (Calle Central, Avenidas Central/1). Two floors of shops, open from 9:30 a.m. to 6:00 p.m. except Sundays.

CANAPI (Avenida 1, Calle 11). Open from 9:00 a.m. to 6:00 p.m. except Sundays.

Mercado Nacional de Artesanía (Calle 11, Avenidas 4/6). This is behind La Soledad Church, which offers a quiet place for reflection in this busy city and impressive stations of the cross. The artisan center is open weekdays from 9:00 a.m. to 12:30 p.m. and 1:30 to 6:00 p.m., Saturdays from 9:00 a.m. to 12:30 p.m. and 1:30 to 5:00 p.m.

Travelers' Store, Costa Rica Expeditions (Calle Central, Avenida 3). Attention bird-watchers: You can get a locational checklist of birds of Costa Rica here. It is open from 10:00 a.m. to 7:00 p.m. daily.

Annemarie's Boutique, Hotel Don Carlos (Calle 9, Avenidas 7/9). There is lots of artwork along with one of the most complete selections of handcrafts around—something for every budget and taste. Shopping here gives those not lucky enough to stay in this hotel an excuse to see it. The shop is open from 9:00 a.m. to 6:00 p.m. every day.

Suraska Gallery (Avenida 3, Calle 5) and La Galería (Calle 1, Avenidas Central/1) show off their handcrafts and elegant jewelry like the works of art that they are. Do not fail to go upstairs in each. They are open weekdays from 8:30 a.m. to 12:30 p.m. and 1:30 to 6:00 p.m., Saturdays from 8:30 a.m. to 12:30 p.m.

Quiet breakfast at Hotel Grano de Oro (Photo by Ree Strange Sheck)

Central Market (Avenidas Central/1, Calles 6/8). Handcrafts are sold here along with rubber boots, fish, flour, herbal remedies, shirts, and pots and pans. Be ready for crowds, and watch your belongings.

Do not miss Atmósfera on Calle 5 between Avenidas 1 and 3. Art and handcrafts are beautifully displayed on three floors in a lovely old building that is itself worth the visit. Atmósfera is open Monday through Saturday from 8:30 a.m. to 6:30 p.m.

Galería Doble A is a twenty-two-store mall on Calle Central, Avenidas 5/7, near the Hotel Europa. It has a beauty shop, travel agency, textiles, jewelry, wooden items, and a small art gallery. It is open from 8:00 a.m. to 7:00 p.m. daily.

The nearby town of Moravia, which is famous for its leather goods, also has shops offering a variety of other gifts. It is an easy bus trip to do on your own or about ten minutes by taxi from downtown San José. In addition to the many small shops, an artisan mall has thirty shops—ask for Mercado de Artesanía Las Garzas. You can find everything from jewelry and clothing to Costa Rican coffee. The mall is open from 8:30 a.m. to 6:00 p.m. Monday through Saturday, 9:00 a.m. to 4:00 p.m. Sunday.

General Shopping

Head west from the Plaza de la Cultura on Avenida Central to find Librería Lehmann (Calles 1/3) for books and magazines, Librería Universal (Calles Central/1) for books, posters, maps, film and developing, and department store items, and La Gloria department store (Calles 4/6).

Next to the Avenida 1 "back door" of Librería Universal is a photo shop (look for the Fuji sign), where you can get film and same-day print developing. Credit cards are accepted. An IFSA photo shop is at Avenida Central, Calle 5.

The Bookshop, one block east (Avenida 1, Calles 1/3), has English-language books, newspapers, and magazines.

The supermarket closest to the Plaza de la Cultura is La Gran Via, just west of the plaza; other large ones downtown are Mas por Menos (Avenida Central, Calle 13), and Automercado (Avenida 3, Calle 3). Pharmacies (*farmacias*) abound, but there is a very complete drugstore/pharmacy about seven blocks from the Plaza de la Cultura on Calle Central, Avenidas 8/10. Look for the Botica Mario Jiménez sign. Another is in Fischel at Avenida 2 and Calle 3. Remember, some stores require that you check packages when you enter, and you sometimes pay for a purchase at one counter or window (*caja*) and receive it at another (*empaque*).

Restaurants

San José and surrounding towns have many fine restaurants serving typical fare as well as French, Italian, Chinese, German, and Japanese cuisine. Look in the English-language weekly newspapers, *Tico Times* and *Costa Rica Today.* American food chains are here: Pizza Hut, Mr. Pizza, Kentucky Fried Chicken, McDonald's, Burger King, Hardee's. A 10 percent tax is included in your restaurant bill.

If you want a light meal, look for a *soda.* San José also has good ice cream shops, such as Pops, two of which are near the plaza, and Monpik. Churrería Manolo (Avenida Central, Calles 9/11) has a typical Costa Rican breakfast for less than $3. *Churros* are those long, thin donutlike pastries for sale at the front. A larger Manolo's is at Avenida 1, Calles Central/2.

Three hotels with excellent international cuisine are Amstel Morazán (Avenida 1, Calle 7), Fleur de Lys (Calle 13, Avenidas 2/6), and Villa Tournón (Barrio Tournón). Try the breakfast buffet at the Hotel del Rey (Avenida 1, Calle 9) and the unusual fare at the Hotel Grano de Oro (Calle 30, Avenidas 2/4). At El Pueblo Commercial Center, you can have typical food at La Cocina de Leña or seafood, with good service, at Rías Bajas. For a typical Costa Rican mid-day meal, try the third-floor restaurant at the Hotel La Gran Vía (Avenida Central, Calles 1/3)—it is inexpensive and tasty. San Remo (Calle 2, Avenidas 3/5) also has good inexpensive *platos del día* (daily specials) and pastas. Other eateries worth returning to are Ambrosia (with vegetarian dishes and good crepes) in San Pedro; Tomy's Ribs (Avenida 6, Calles 9/11); El Balcón de Europa, excellent (Calle 9, Avenidas Central/1); Peperoni La Corte, Italian of course (Avenida 8, Calles 15/17); and La Galeria in San Pedro, German food with classical music.

A favorite of mine is La Hacienda—nice atmosphere, good food, and friendly staff. Nils and the other waiters will do their best to make sure you enjoy your meal (Calle 7, Avenidas Central/2). The *flan de coco* is yummy for dessert. The second floor is now a pizza and pasta place with the same ownership. The Cafe Ruiseñor in the National Theater on the Plaza de la Cultura is a delight—memorable pastries and capuccino and the best *limonada* in the country—as is the Ruiseñor in Los Yoses on the way to San Pedro. Across the street in Los Yoses is Azafrán, with excellent sandwiches, crepes, salads, and heavenly desserts.

Las Orquídeas, about 7 miles (12 km) north of San José on the road to Braulio Carrillo National Park, has a nice atmosphere, good food, and good service. Few people can resist the ambiance of the outdoor terrace at the Gran Hotel Costa Rica next to the National Theater and Plaza de la Cultura. At happy hour time, music from inside mingles with the sounds of a city getting ready to go home.

When I cannot stand the thought of one more meal in a restaurant, I drop by Spoon at Avenida Central, Calles 5/7, and choose among wonderful pastries, sandwiches, and desserts for a carryout lunch; you can get natural fruit juice drinks to go, too. Morazán and España parks are a few blocks away on Avenida 3, a place to join ticos eating their sack lunches, and watch playing schoolchildren and the park's birds—blue-gray tanagers, a few parrots, a woodpecker or two. The metallic school building you see nearby was built in the 1890s, the plates designed by Alexandre Gustave Eiffel of Eiffel Tower fame and shipped from Belgium by boat to be assembled here. The National Park, farther down Avenida 3 at Calle 15, is another good place to escape the crowds.

Hotels

This is not a comprehensive list of hotels, but it represents a range of prices, with more of an emphasis on smaller places. I do not list any that I would not stay in myself, depending on my pocketbook at the time. The approved rates should be posted in the rooms.

Prices listed here include tax. If you arrive without a reservation, the ICT airport office will help you, but reservations are recommended. When calling from outside Costa Rica, use the country code, 506, before the number. Because mail service can be slow and unreliable, it is better to phone or fax for reservations.

I use the term "shower-head hot water" throughout the book to indicate that hot water is from a thermo-electric device on the shower head—in which case you will probably not have hot water from the bathroom sink faucet.

Costa Rica has a youth hostel association, with offices at Avenida Central, Calles 29/31. The Costa Rican Network of Youth Hostels offers its members lodging at Toruma, its own facility in San José, and reduced rates at a growing number of other sites, including Rara Avis and Islas del Río in Sarapiquí, Santa Clara Lodge in Guanacaste, Rincón de la Vieja Mountain Lodge, Burio Inn in La

KEEP IN MIND

Hotel rates quoted are those given to me for the 1994 high season, generally from late December to April. The Costa Rican Tourism Institute reevaluates lodging facilities about every six months and can change what establishments are allowed to charge. Rates for the Green Season, or rainy months, may be considerably lower, especially in beach area

Fortuna, and Hotel Marparaiso en Jacó. For information, telephone or fax 224-4085.

The Costa Rican Bed and Breakfast Group is an association of more than 160 B&Bs in practically every part of the country. Pat Bliss at 228-9200 (telephone or fax) or Debbi McMurray at 223-4168 (telephone) can give you information and will make reservations for you.

TURCASA is an association that offers stays in more than 400 rooms in Costa Rican homes where travelers have an opportunity for close contact with the people and the culture. There are homes in San José, Tres Rios, Heredía, Alajuela, Manuel Antonio, Cariari, Tortuguero, Cartago, Turrialba, Talamanca, Puerto Viejo de Limón, Monteverde, Limón, Liberia, and Santa Cruz. Some offer private baths, in others, they are shared, all with hot water and breakfast included. For more information, contact the central office. Telephone 234-9905, fax 225-1239.

The following hotels are in the San José greater metropolitan area. Some listed in the Central Valley section are close enough for easy access to San José and the airport, and may be even closer to the airport than those listed here.

If your tastes run to larger hotels, here are a few you can contact, all with the amenities you would expect from a full-service hotel: air conditioning, restaurants, shops, cable TV, casino, etc.

Sheraton Herradura Hotel & Spa. The least-expensive single is $132, double $143. It is five minutes from the airport, 20 minutes from San José. Telephone 239-0033, or in the U.S., (800) 245-8420; fax 239-2292.

Aurola Holiday Inn. Rooms start at $128 for a single, $139 for a double. Avenida 5, Calle 5. Telephone 233-7233, or in the U.S., (800) HOLIDAY; fax 255-1036.

San José Palacio. Rooms start at $125 for a single, $132 for a double. On the highway in from the airport, ten minutes from downtown. Telephone 220-2034, fax 220-2036 or 231-1990.

Corobicí Hotel and Spa. The least-expensive single is $122, double $134. Near La Sabana Park close to Paseo Colón. Telephone 232-8122 or 231-6512, or in the U.S., (800) 227-4274; fax 231-5834.

Hotel Irazú. Rooms start at $88 for a single, $101 for a double. It is fifteen minutes from downtown and has a daily bus to its sister hotel at Jacó Beach. Telephone 232-4811; in the U.S., (800) 272-6654; in Ontario, (800) 387-8842; in Vancouver, (800) 668-8355; fax 231-6485.

The hotels and inns that follow are smaller, arranged according to price. Many are in what were once lovely old homes in residential areas whose use has changed as the city grew. It is a nice trend.

Hotel L'Ambiance was one of the first to take the charm of a historic building and turn it into a hotel that feels like an elegant home. Six rooms plus a suite open onto an interior courtyard and the large entry hall, or *zaguán*, typical of Spanish colonial construction. Antiques collected by owner William Parker are throughout. Polished wooden floors in rooms contrast with original tile in the hallways and courtyard. Sounds of water in the fountain mix with soft classical music in an intimate dining room, also open to the public, which specializes in fine French cuisine.

Rooms are air-conditioned and have cable TV. The concierge can arrange a private car with a driver. A single is $80, a double $105. Credit cards are not accepted. Calle 13, Avenidas 9/11 in Barrio Amón. Telephone 222-6702, fax 223-0481.

Hotel Le Bergerac in pretty Los Yoses is roses on the table, balconies and gardens, a sun terrace, fountains, Monet prints on the walls, spacious rooms, and personalized service. The French Canadian owners pay attention to detail. The two-story house with the flavor of a fine French inn has eighteen airy rooms. Framed, padded headboards match the soft tones of the bed coverings, and each room has ceiling fans, cable TV (including the French and German channels), hardwood floors and baths with dark forest-green fixtures. The standard room for one or two people is $89, ($101 with a garden or balcony), including a continental breakfast. The restaurant next to the central garden, for guests only, also serves drinks and *bocas* in the afternoon and evenings, and dinner. Telephone 234-7850, fax 225-9103. Le Bergerac is half a block south of Avenida Central on Calle 35.

The Hotel Amstel Amón is a newcomer in the historic Barrio Amón section. The four-story, ninety-room hotel has souvenir shops, a restaurant, bar, beauty shop, spa, gym, travel agency, conference center, and underground parking. Rooms for single or double occupancy are $86, junior suites $105. Credit cards are accepted. Telephone 222-4622, fax 233-3329. Avenida 11, Calle 5.

The Britannia Hotel is at Avenida 11 and Calle 3 in a 1910 mansion I have long admired. Great care has been taken in its restoration and conversion into a twenty-four-room hotel. The entrance is grand, giving one the feeling of having arrived somewhere special. Even the standard rooms are large: $84 for a single, $97 for a double. Deluxe rooms are $96 for a single, $110 for a double; suites are $124 for two. Included is a breakfast buffet served in a former patio. Rooms have hardwood or carpeted floors, tiled baths with tubs and showers (hair dryers in suites), cable TV, writing desks, pretty comforters with matching window treatment, and wallpaper wainscoting; some have king-size beds. There is a gift shop, parking, restaurant, conference room, and bar. Telephone 223-6667, fax 223-6411.

Hotel Rosa de Paseo is in a restored century-old residence on Paseo Colón, the boulevard that brings you into San José from the airport. The twenty-room hotel has some beautiful antique pieces—chests, benches, wardrobes—painted stenciled friezes at ceiling level in some rooms, charming alcoves and bay windows on the front, some beautiful painted tile floors, and stained glass. Rooms have high ceilings (how long since you stayed in a room with a transom?), matching drapes and bedspreads, a wardrobe, desk, and large baths with bathtubs. A lovely two-story addition in keeping with the older house shares a pretty garden. Nice sitting areas have attractive wicker furniture. A single is $80, a double $92, a suite (with Jacuzzi) $149; a tropical breakfast is included. Credit cards are accepted. The gift shop has fine jewelry, paintings, and other artwork. The restaurant serves light meals. Telephone 257-3213 or 257-3225, fax 223-2776.

Hotel Milvia is past San Pedro on the way to Tres Ríos, only fifteen to twenty minutes by bus from downtown San José. The wooden residence, built more than fifty years ago, has been renovated as a five-room hotel surrounded by a lovely garden. Rooms are large, with antique furniture, cable TV, telephone, mini-bar, hair dryers, and private baths with hand-painted tiles. There is a boutique with hand-painted ceramics by Milvia, the namesake and gracious proprietor along with her husband, Mauricio. There is a library, terrace, and parking. A single is $80, a double $92. Credit cards are accepted. Telephone or fax 225-4543.

Hotel Grano de Oro is a personal favorite—I am partial to bath-tubs, and these are spotless and large in charming blue and white bathrooms with brass and porcelain fixtures. Cushions in white wicker chairs match comforters on the beds in restful rooms. Each has a writing desk, TV, and wardrobe closet, No-smoking rooms are available. Starting out in a gracious turn-of-the century mansion, the hotel has expanded next door—with thirty-six rooms in all. Inner patios and courtyards with fountains connect the old and new. By day, one can see volcanoes from the rooftop terrace where there is a Jacuzzi and bar—at night, city lights sparkle. If you can-not stay here, come try the creative bocas—the restaurant is open to the public—as well as delicacies such as chicken and mushroom lasagna, enchilada pie, beautiful salads, or stuffed palm heart pie. There is a gift shop and parking. Standard doubles are $79, supe-rior $88, deluxe $97, and suites $132—depending on room size and type of beds. Singles are $5 less. Credit cards are accepted, but there is a service charge. Hotel Grano de Oro is on Calle 30, Avenidas 2/4, just a block and a half south of Paseo Colón. Tele-phone 255-3322, fax 221-2782.

La Casa Verde is another of the lovely Barrio Amón mansions that has been renovated as an exclusive small hotel. The green Victorian house at Avenida 9 and Calle 7, La Casa Verde has five rooms and two suites, with king- or queen-size beds, cable TV, ceil-ing fans, and private baths (I saw one with a claw-foot tub). The loving restoration was supervised by owner Carl Stanley. The upstairs Victorian lounge, with its 110-year-old German-made baby grand piano, wicker furniture, and polished wooden floors, is stun-ning. You could get lost in one of the enormous suites. Artwork for sale on the walls gives the hotel the air of a gallery. A breakfast buf-fet is served on a garden patio. The coffee shop is for guests only. A single is $74, deluxe rooms $83, suites $99. Credit cards are accepted. Telephone 257-1054, telephone or fax 223-0969.

The Fleur de Lys Hotel is about a block from the Plaza de la Democracia at Calle 13, Avenidas 2/6. The renovated three-story house, built more than sixty years ago, has twenty unique rooms, each named for a flower and all tastefully furnished. They offer cable TV and private baths. Some of the original tile and hardwood floors remain; rooms are carpeted. Fresh flowers brighten comfortable sitting alcoves. Skylights bring the sunshine in. Singles are $75, doubles $80; suites start at $92. There is a tour agency (the hotel belongs to the same company as Aventuras Naturales, which specializes in rafting, mountain biking, and nature tourism) and a fine restaurant specializing in Swiss-Italian cuisine. Dishes are a visual as well as gastronomic delight. A superb executive lunch served from noon to 2 p.m. changes daily; it's about $5 from soup or salad to dessert. Service is superb, and the setting is intimate. If you cannot stay at the Fleur de Lys, try to eat there. You won't find a menu like it elsewhere in Costa Rica. Telephone 222-4391 or 257-2621, fax 257-3637. Credit cards are accepted.

Hotel Presidente has grown to 110 rooms. Some are carpeted, some have rich tones of parquet; carved doors set a nice tone. Standardized new rooms are nice, but the older ones, in various shapes and sizes, also have appeal. Amenities include satellite TV, Jacuzzi, sauna, small gymnasium, solarium, air conditioning, and concierge. There is a piano bar, restaurants, and parking. New rooms have a special glass to shut out street noise. A single is $69, double $80. Credit cards are accepted. Avenida Central, Calle 7. Telephone 222-3022, or in the U.S. and part of Canada, (800) 972-0515; fax 221-1205. There is free pickup at the airport for guests who reserve via the 800 number.

Gran Hotel Costa Rica, in the very heart of San José next to the Plaza de la Cultura and the National Theater, has been a meeting place since it opened in 1930. The terrace cafe is open twenty-four hours a day; daytime diners are treated to marimba music. The 108 pleasant, carpeted rooms have satellite TV and writing desks. The single rate is $59, double $68; a suite is $138 for two. Credit cards are accepted. There is also a casino and parking. Avenida 2, Calle 3. Telephone 221-0796, fax 221-3501.

Hotel del Rey is an appealing and comfortable hotel of 104 rooms right downtown at Avenida 1, Calle 9. The large gracious lobby with tropical plants and cushioned wicker furniture groupings says welcome. The six-floor neoclassical structure has a sky-light-covered central atrium that washes the building with light. Rooms are carpeted and have soft-colored quilted bedspreads, cable TV, direct-dial telephones, private baths with tubs, and wash-cloths! The hand-carved wooden doors to each room depict quet-zals, butterflies, iguanas, a coffee picker, and other Costa Rican motifs—real works of art. The hotel has a travel agency, gift shop, attractive streetside bar, casino, car rental, parking, and restaurants. Standard singles start at $63, standard doubles $78; deluxe rooms are $86, single or double. Master suites, which can include as many as three bedrooms, begin at $143 for two people. Credit cards are accepted. Telephone 221-7272 or 255-3232, fax 221-0096.

Mansión Blanca Inn is an eleven-room, second-story hotel six blocks from the Plaza de la Cultura. Rooms have gleaming hard-wood floors, high ceilings, and tasteful furnishings. Owner-oper-ated, it offers guests personalized tour arrangements. A single is $62, double $76, continental breakfast included. Credit cards are accepted. Telephone or fax 222-0423.

Las Orquídeas Inn outside Alajuela is a charming eighteen-room inn in a lovely garden setting, like a country estate. Ample rooms have arched windows that let in lots of light, colorful bedspreads, fresh flowers (orchids, of course), and private baths. Note the glass-topped tables on old Singer sewing machine bases. Owners Fred and Darlys McCloud serve up Buffalo-style chicken wings in the Marilyn Monroe Bar as complimentary *bocas*—you can get your popcorn fix here. Guitarist, composer, singer Rolando and daughter Leidy give a great evening performance most weekends. There is a gift shop, a pretty swimming pool, and paths to walk on and admire the tropical plants on this 5-acre (2-ha) estate. Keep your eyes open for the sloths that drop by. Las Orquídeas can fix you up with a van and driver for custom tours (Poás and waterfall, $60 for two people for half a day; Sarchí $40), and the McClouds offer a mystery trip to a destination off the beaten path. The inn is on the road to Sarchí and Poás Volcano, just ten minutes from the international airport and twenty minutes from San José. Singles are $57, doubles $69 with fans, $10 more for air conditioning. Visa and MasterCard are accepted. Two large suites are also available. No children under thirteen are permitted. Telephone 433-9346, fax 433-9740.

Hotel Vesuvio is a twenty-room, owner-operated hotel on Avenida 11, Calle 13/15 in a residential setting. The carpeted rooms are decorated in soft colors (the print in the comforter matches the curtains), each with ceiling fan, desk, and TV. There is a bar and a restaurant featuring Italian specialties. Parking is available. Singles are $57, doubles $69, junior suites $97, continental breakfast included. Credit cards are accepted. Telephone 221-7586, telephone or fax 221-8325.

Hotel Santo Tomás, with twenty rooms, is in a renovated mansion that dates back to the turn of the century. Each room is different, but all have high ceilings and reproduction French provincial furniture. Persian rugs decorate hardwood floors. Corridors and some other areas have handmade tile floors. Some bathrooms have tubs. There is cable TV in the comfortable parlor area, along with reading material. Staff members help arrange tailored tours. Parking is nearby at a discount. Standard rooms are $57 for singles, $63 for doubles; superior rooms are $69 for singles, $75 for doubles. Continental breakfast is included. Credit cards are not accepted. Avenida 7, Calles 3/5. Telephone 255-0448, fax 222-3950.

The Hotel Europa on Calle Central, Avenida 5 has seventy-two carpeted rooms and a pretty outdoor swimming pool surrounded by plants right in the heart of town. Good-sized carpeted rooms have cable TV, air conditioning, large closets, and a writing desk—and some rooms have a balcony. A few baths have tubs. Singles are $57, doubles $69, suites $114. Credit cards are accepted. There is a restaurant, a cozy downstairs bar, meeting rooms, an art gallery, and a gift shop. Telephone 222-1222, or in the U.S., (800) 223-6764; fax 221-3976. A second Hotel Europa will be opening on the road out of town toward Braulio Carrillo National Park.

Hotel La Gran Vía is on Avenida Central, Calles 1/3, just a half-block from the Plaza de la Cultura. The thirty-two carpeted rooms are nicely furnished in soft colors, lace curtains and drapes. The avenida is closed to through traffic in this block, so car noise is reduced. The upstairs restaurant serves simple, inexpensive, flavorful food. A single is $56, a double $71. Credit cards are accepted. Telephone 222-7737, fax 222-7205.

Hotel Amstel Morazán on Calle 7, Avenidas 1/3, has fifty-four air-conditioned, carpeted rooms and a fine restaurant that attracts travelers as well as local people. It has a travel agency in the lobby, a bar, a casino, and parking nearby. Singles start at $54, doubles $64. Credit cards are accepted. Telephone 222-4622, fax 233-3329. The Amstel group also has the twelve-unit Apartotel San José (with kitchenettes) on Avenida 2 across from the National Museum. Singles are $53, doubles $61. Telephone 222-0455. At the sixteen-room Amstel Escazú, a country inn with pool and gardens, a single is $63, double $69. (Telephone 228-1764).

Hotel Torremolinos, at Calle 40 and Avenida 5, two blocks from Centro Colón near La Sabana Park, has seventy-two rooms and suites, each carpeted and with cable TV and either air conditioning or ceiling fans. There is a pool in a garden area by the restaurant, a Jacuzzi, sauna, and parking. Rooms are $52 for a single, $63 for a double, $86 for a junior suite, and $97 for a suite. Telephone 222-9129, fax 255-3167.

Hotel Edelweiss is in a remodeled forty-five-year-old house on Avenida 9 between Calles 13 and 15. Each of the sixteen rooms has distinctive wallpaper, custom handmade furniture (the fold-out writing desk is a gem), a ceiling fan, and private bath with hot water. The bar is in a covered patio enhanced with many orchids and other tropical plants. The dining room specializes in cuisine from Austria and Germany (the birthplaces of two of the four owner-managers). Singles start at $52, doubles at $75. Credit cards are accepted. Telephone 221-9702, fax 222-1241.

Casa Morazán in Barrio Amón was the home of a former president; now it is a stylish eleven-room hotel. Rooms have restful green and rose carpeting, air conditioning, high ceilings, cable TV, telephones, and large private baths with tubs; some rooms have king-size beds. Lovely watercolors hung throughout are for sale. The dining room opens onto a patio and there is a comfortable sitting area. Guests can enjoy a quiet dinner, with selections such as lasagna, crepes, and stroganoff, for about $10. The Costa Rican owner-operators are happy to help arrange tours. Parking is available. Singles rooms are $46, doubles $75, and suites $105 and $114; continental breakfast is included. Credit cards are accepted. English and French also are spoken. Telephone 257-4187 or 257-

4175, fax 221-3826. Casa Morazán is at Calle 7 and Avenida 9, about two blocks from Morazán Park.

Hotel Dunn Inn is centered in a tastefully renovated 1924 home at Avenida 11, Calle 5 in Barrio Amón. The two-story house had an interior courtyard that owner Pat Dunn turned into a tropical garden restaurant. Lovely exposed brick walls are a perfect backdrop for original art. Each of the twenty-seven rooms—including a newer addition—carries a Bribrí name. Striking stained glass uncovered in the restoration is the focus of a small sitting area. Rooms are carpeted and well-lighted, with pretty comforters and reading chairs. There is also cable TV, ceiling fans, and arranged parking (with the hotel paying half). A single or double is $53, and a suite $102. Credit cards are accepted. Telephone 222-3232 or 222-3426, fax 221-4596.

Hotel Petit Victoria is a two-story Victorian house, more than seventy years old, near the Sala Garbo theater off Paseo Colón (Calle 28, Avenida 2a). It has elaborate tile floors in the reception area, wood floors in some of the high-ceilinged rooms, and a carpeted upstairs. Pretty quilted bedspreads brighten the rooms, some with king-size beds and cable TV. Singles are from $50 to $55, doubles from $65 to $85 in the fifteen rooms with private baths. Seven rooms with shared baths are $40 each for doubles. A complimentary continental breakfast is served on the patio. Telephone 233-1812 or 233-1813; fax 233-1938. Swedish and English also are spoken.

Hotel Royal Dutch is on Calle 4, Avenida Central/2. This twenty-six-room hotel has carpeted, air-conditioned rooms, but local TV only. There is a pleasant second-floor restaurant. Parking is available. Singles are $47, doubles $62; some suites have very large rooms. Credit cards are accepted. Telephone 222-1414, fax 233-3927.

Hotel Don Carlos in Barrio Amón has character: patios with fountains, lots of plants, walls covered with artwork, rooms stuck away here and there, and a two-story shop (Boutique Annemarie) loaded with gifts. The twenty-five comfortable rooms range from $46 to $57 for singles and $57 to $69 for doubles, including complimentary continental breakfast. Some rooms have patios; all have cable TV. The hotel has its own tour company that offers rafting and trips to Tortuguero and volcanoes with a bilingual naturalist guide, and it also books for Travelair and SANSA. Credit cards are accepted. The restaurant serves light meals, offering such things as ceviche, tamales, chicken and rice, or gallo pinto. Its staff is multilingual. Annemarie's is open from 9:00 a.m to 6:00 p.m. daily—it is great for one-stop shopping even if you are not staying at the Don Carlos. Telephone 221-6707, fax 255-0828. Credit cards are accepted. The Apartotel Don Carlos in Los Yoses, with a fully equipped kitchen, has weekly ($400) and monthly ($1,029) rates.

Hotel Hemingway is in a Spanish-style house built in 1930 by the family of one of the current owners. Each of the eighteen rooms is named for a twentieth-century author—you could be in the Steinbeck, Faulkner, or T. Williams room. Shoulder-high wooden wainscoting, hardwood floors, and high ceilings predominate. Rooms have private baths with shower-head hot water and cable TV. The complimentary continental breakfast is served in an interior courtyard. Singles are $46, doubles $57. Credit cards are accepted. Telephone or fax 221-1804. The architecturally distinctive two-story hotel is at Avenida 9, Calle 9 in Barrio Amón.

Diana's Inn is next to Morazán Park at Calle 5 and Avenida 3. The eleven rooms in the three-story wooden building (no elevator), which once was home to a former president of the country, are different shapes and sizes, each with telephone, TV, and private bath with hot water. The Costa Rican owners offer a family atmosphere, and the staff is helpful. Singles are $46, doubles $52 ($10 more for air conditioning); continental breakfast is included. Visa and MasterCard are accepted. There is no smoking in rooms. Telephone 223-6542, fax 233-0495.

Hotel Pico Blanco is located on 12 acres (5 ha) above San Antonio de Escazú, about twenty minutes from San José at an elevation of 5,000 feet (1,524 m). The twenty pleasant rooms have private balconies with breathtaking views of the Central Valley below. Most rooms have queen-size beds. A single is $46, a double $57. A fireplace in the restaurant area, which also has good views and is open to the public, is welcome—nights can be chilly. You can hike on nearby trails, rent horses, or swim in the pool. Owners John and Flor are gracious hosts and proud caretakers of a pair of free-flying macaws. Telephone 289-6197, fax 289-5189.

Tres Arcos Bed and Breakfast in the lovely Los Yoses area, a twenty-minute walk from downtown, has five homey rooms with private bath ($57 for a double) and two with a shared bath ($46). A complimentary light breakfast is served on the terrace. Each room is different, but all have big windows that look out on the pretty garden and a tall, tall tree decorated with gorgeous bromeliads. Owners Lee and Eric Warrington will help you arrange tours. Telephone 234-9073, telephone or fax 225-0271. Avenida 10, Calle 37.

Hotel Ave del Paraíso in San Pedro is a seventeen-room bed-and-breakfast in a quiet area near the University of Costa Rica. Owners Marek and Kattia Adamski are attentive hosts—they can also speak to guests in English, French, Polish, German, or Russian. It is a friendly place. There are sitting rooms, the upstairs one opening onto a balcony. Rooms are carpeted and have big windows, pretty oval mirrors with wooden frames, and TV (local stations only). Private tiled baths have shower-head hot water. There is an outdoor area for the full breakfast included in the price: $40 for singles, $52 for doubles. Credit cards are accepted. Telephone or fax 225-8515. Ave del Paraíso is 350 meters north of Hispanidad Fountain; watch for the sign.

Hotel Plaza is a six-story building right downtown on Avenida Central, Calles 2/4. The size of the forty simple rooms varies; some are quite small, but all have in-room phones, TV with local stations, ceiling fans, and private baths with central hot water. The pleasant street-level restaurant looks out on the pedestrian boulevard in front. Singles are $40, doubles $52. Credit cards are accepted. Telephone 257-1896 or 222-5533, fax 222-2641.

Hotel Rey Amón is in the pink building at Avenida 7 and Calle 9. The thirteen rooms are light, carpeted, with high ceilings, cable TV, and private baths with shower-head hot water. Notice the 100-year-old floor tile in the large lobby and reception area. A single is $40, a double $57, with continental breakfast included. There is also free parking and a tour desk. Telephone 233-3819, telephone or fax 233-1769.

The Garden Court Hotel is also a favorite of mine. Rooms are quiet, beds comfortable, and yes, the bath has a tub. There is an outdoor swimming pool next to the breezy open-air restaurant, a tour company, and free parking. Rooms are carpeted and air-conditioned. The only drawback is that the neighborhood is risky, but friendly staff members will call a taxi for you. Singles are $38, doubles $52, with a buffet breakfast included. Telephone 222-3674, or in the U.S., (800) CR-BOOK-H; fax 232-3159.

Hotel Joluva is an eight-room bed-and-breakfast on Calle 3B between Avenidas 9 and 11 in the Barrio Amón district. The single-story building with a row of pretty palo verde trees in front has high ceilings, some with gold motifs. Some rooms are carpeted; others have hardwood floors. Six have private baths, and the shared bath also has hot water. Room sizes vary. The complimentary continental breakfast is served on a former patio. Rooms with private baths are $35 for a single, $46 for a double; with shared bath they are $29 and $35. Credit cards are not accepted. Small group tours are offered. Telephone or fax 223-9901.

Hotel Diplomat, with twenty-nine rooms, is on Calle Central, Avenidas Central/2. Rooms are bright, clean, and generally small, though closets are large. The upstairs restaurant has a nice atmosphere. Singles cost $31, doubles $41, MasterCard and Visa are accepted. Telephone 221-8133, fax 233-7474.

Hotel Belmundo reminds me of New Orleans' French Quarter architecture. There is definitely Southern hospitality inside from India and David Norman, who own the place, and their three children. Each of the twenty-two rooms is different; some on the second floor have small porches that look out on city roofs and the mountains beyond. All rooms have a private bath with windows and hot water. Pretty comforters brighten the rooms. Singles are $29, doubles from $35 to $40. There are some dormitory-style rooms with four or five single beds and a private bath for $17 per person. Credit cards are accepted. Rates cover a hearty natural food breakfast. The outdoor dining room serves delightful home-cooked dinners every night, for guests only. There is a TV area, small gymnasium, and tour desk. Telephone or fax 222-9624. The Belmundo is at Calle 20 and Avenida 9, a short walk from Paseo Colón.

Hotel Galilea on Avenida Central, Calles 11/13, has twenty-three rooms, all on the second and third floors (no elevator). The captain and staff befriend guests—making it a home away from home. There is cable TV in the small lobby. Rooms are simply furnished and clean; private baths have central hot water. A single is $27, a double $33. Credit cards are not accepted. Telephone 233-6925, fax 223-1689.

Hotel La Amistad Inn is a German-owned and -operated bed-and-breakfast at Avenida 11 and Calle 15, a ten-minute walk to the Plaza de la Cultura. The twenty-one rooms have private tiled baths with hot water, cable TV, ceiling fans, and orthopedic mattresses. Singles range from $23 to $40, doubles from $35 to $57, with suites at $69; all include a German-style breakfast. Credit cards are accepted. Telephone 221-1597, fax 221-1409.

Pensión de la Cuesta, Avenida 1, Calles 11/15, has eight simple rooms and three baths. A sunny common room with big windows looks out on a small garden area. A single is $25, a double $35, with light breakfast included. Telephone 255-2896, telephone or fax 257-2272.

Petit Hotel is on Calle 24 between Paseo Colón and Avenida 2. It has fifteen basic rooms. Singles with private bath are $21, doubles $29; with shared baths, rooms begin at $19. There is a television in the lobby and a bright interior courtyard. Guests have kitchen privileges (there is no restaurant), and coffee is free. Telephone 233-0766, fax 233-1938.

Toruma Youth Hostel has been remodeled so that guests now have more security and privacy The twenty-one rooms have 107 beds. Nonmembers pay $10 per person, members $7 in shared rooms. Private rooms are $22 for two, with a shared bath. A small restaurant is open to the public and has very reasonable prices. There is a minimal charge to guests for the use of a washing machine and iron. Toruma stores luggage and has safety deposit boxes. Telephone or fax 224-4085. The hostel is at Avenida Central, Calles 29/31.

Pensión Americana is on Calle 2 between Avenidas Central and 2. The 100-year-old house contains thirty-five high-ceilinged rooms that put me in mind of old-style European pensions, the kind you find near train stations in Portugal and Spain. The furnishings are eclectic, and some of the original ceilings are quite ornate. The shared showers and toilets are basic; there is a deposit for towels. All the rooms, costing $5.50 per person, are on the second and third floors; there is no elevator. Telephone 221-4171 or 221-9799.

One-Day Package Tours from San José

Because of the country's small size and San José's central location, the traveler who wants to use the capital as a base can touch many parts of Costa Rica in one-day air excursions.

National parklands with easy access are Irazú and Poás volcanoes and Braulio Carrillo. Package tours by air bring Tortuguero and Barra de Colorado national parks into the picture. Guayabo National Monument, the only archaeological park, and the Tapantí National Wildlife Refuge are also good road trips. A cruise in the Gulf of Nicoya or a tour to Carara Biological Reserve takes you to the Pacific. Exploring the historical and biological treasures of the Central Valley is possible with tours to the Orosi Valley, Lankester Gardens (for orchids), the colonial capital of Cartago with its religious shrine, and the handcraft city of Sarchí. One-day tours take you rafting or kayaking on the country's waterways and hiking on Barva Volcano. (Specifics on all these are in chapter 9.)

If, after all this physical activity, you could use a relaxing massage when you return to San José, it's about $17 at Integree. Herbal wraps and a sauna are also available. An incredible three-hour "tune-up," for $80, is a treat you owe yourself. Manager Nazira Naranjo and her staff are qualified professionals, and the facilities are pleasing. Telephone 233-3839. Integree is on Avenida 14, Calles 1/3, and is open Monday through Friday from 9:00 a.m. to 6:00 p.m., Saturdays from 9:00 a.m. to noon.

Central Valley

The four colonial cities of Costa Rica were San José, Cartago, Alajuela, and Heredía. Each had its own character and strong sense of identity. That is still true today. When a man tells you he is from Alajuela, he has centuries of pride in his voice.

As you travel to or through these places, remember that this land was once covered with forest. Try to imagine what travel must have been like on foot or horseback up and down these mountains and across the rivers now spanned by bridges. Life here was hard; it forged the national character.

Escazú ox cart parade (Photo by Ree Strange Sheck)

Beauty, not hardship, is the sensation one experiences when traveling through this land today. Patches of protected forest remain, but the landscape is largely one of coffee fields, sugarcane, small farms, picturesque villages, and pastures for dairy cows. Each rural house has its flowers, a porch to sit on when the work is done, a few banana and coffee plants, some fruit trees, and perhaps some beans, squash, and corn—a link back to agrarian self-sufficiency.

Alajuela (population 46,070) was the home of Juan Santamaría, the country's national hero. He is honored here with a statue and the Juan Santamaría Cultural and Historical Museum, open every day except Monday from 10:00 a.m. to 6:00 p.m. The Central Park is a veritable orchard of mango trees. Blue-gray tanagers are among the birds that flock to eat the ripe fruit when it falls on the ground. In July, the Festival of Mangoes brings nine days of music, parades, farmers' markets, and an arts and crafts fair. Alajuela can be a stop on your way to Sarchí and Poás Volcano, or you can take a half-hour bus ride from San José (leaving from Avenida 2, Calles 12/14) to explore the town. This is the capital of the province of Alajuela.

Since Alajuela is five minutes from Juan Santamaría International Airport, some travelers choose to stay here or nearby. You can ask about possibilities at the ICT airport office. Here are a few:

Apartotel El Erizo in Alajuela has eight apartments with kitchenettes and four rooms. All have cable TV, ceiling fans or air conditioning, private baths with hot water, and telephones. Two-bedroom apartments are $89, one-bedrooms $78, rooms $70. Telephone or fax 441-2840.

Las Orquídeas Inn is a delightful Spanish hacienda in a country setting north of Alajuela on the road to Poás. See particulars in the hotel section for San José.

Sarchí is an artisan center where even the trash cans and bus stops are decorated with colorful paintings. The most famous product is the painted ox cart. Ox carts played a vital transportation role in earlier times, carrying coffee from the highlands down to the Pacific for export. Carts, painted and unpainted, still transport produce. Farmers are usually pleased to stop to let you photograph their carts and oxen when you encounter them on a rural road. At Sarchí, you find the genuine item as well as replicas turned into bars, napkin holders, and miniatures, complete with a few beans of coffee stuck on. There are salad bowls, wooden fruit, lamps, furniture, jewelry, and more. At the Joaquín Chaverri store and factory, watch artisans paint the delicate designs freehand.

Plaza de la Artesanía has thirty-four stores exhibiting arts and crafts of Costa Rica as well as other countries: pottery, sculpture, paintings, jewelry, leather goods, glassware, textiles, and wood and bamboo furniture. The shopping center offers parking, an ice cream shop, restaurants, and restrooms. For information, call 454-4755.

The bus to Sarchí leaves Alajuela every half-hour. Some tours to the magnificent Poás Volcano National Park stop here. (See chapter 7 for further information about Poás.)

Nearby is another natural destination: La Providencia Ecological Reserve, a private reserve on a farm that has 395 acres (160 ha) of primary forest. Denizens of this forest include the resplendent quetzal, ocelots, coyotes, armadillos, emerald toucanets, peccaries, hummingbirds, and tayras. Giant ferns abound; there is the huge-leafed *sombrilla del pobre* (poor man's umbrella) and magnificent oak forests, one of which is white because of acid rain from the volcano.

The panorama from La Providencia when the weather is clear is impressive: the Central Valley, the Pacific, lakes in Nicaragua, and Arenal Volcano. The elevation is 8,200 feet (2,500 m). Visitors are welcome for both day tours and overnight stays. The reserve has five rustic wooden cabins with private baths. (Electricity from a generator gives hot water.) A short distance away is a small restaurant where meals are cooked on a wood stove. Nighttime brings candlelight meals.

A three-hour horseback ride takes visitors on the slopes of the volcano through primary and secondary forest (including the "white" oaks) and to waterfalls, paramo, and view points, in the company of a biologist guide. The cost is $19 including breakfast, $22 with lunch. The rooms for two are $55, and meals are $5.50 for breakfast, $9.50 for lunch, and $10.50 for dinner. Bring warm clothes and rain gear. Telephone 232-2498, fax 231-2204 (marked "for Amalia").

The black shade cloths covering fields on the way to Poás Volcano are sheltering ornamental plants and flowers, a growing nontraditional export. Strawberries grow there as well, and you can often buy them at roadside stands.

Heredía (population 27,998) is the gateway to another volcano, Barva. It is also the home of the National University and a church built in 1796. The tower of an old fort remains in pretty gardens near the church. Buses for Heredía leave San José from Calle 1, Avenidas 7/9, every ten minutes. The twenty-five-minute trip has stops in Tibás and Santo Domingo. Microbuses to Heredía leave from Avenida 2, Calles 10/12 and from Avenida 2, Calle 4. You can also take the interurban train. Heredía is the capital of the province by that name.

Three lodging possibilities in the Heredía area are especially appealing for nature travelers. Bougainvillea Santo Domingo Hotel in Santo Domingo de Heredía is located on 10 acres (4 ha) of gardens. The forty-four nicely furnished, carpeted rooms are spacious, with a separate sitting area, cable TV, and private baths (tub and shower). Each opens onto a balcony. Sculpture and paintings by Costa Rican artists are scattered throughout the hotel. Facilities include tennis courts, a swimming pool, and a jogging trail. The fine restaurant is known for its cuisine and its service. There is hourly free shuttle service to San José, about fifteen minutes away. Singles cost $75, doubles $86. Credit cards are accepted. Telephone 240-8822, fax 240-8484.

Finca Rosa Blanca Country Inn is outside Santa Barbara de Heredía, a half-hour from San José. It is exquisite. The building seems to soar above surrounding coffee plantations, with great views of the Central Valley and Irazú Volcano through enormous windows. Inside, interesting architectural details abound. Beautiful tropical hardwoods gleam in floors and walls—the wood was salvaged from a road-widening project. Each of the eight rooms is unique; one has a mural by an artist from nearby Barva that flows from a large window and continues the landscape on the wall. Bathrooms are unique. There is a walking trail where butterflies await, 200 fruit trees on the grounds to attract birds, and a river. A swimming pool as unusual as the building is in the works. Rooms range from $132 to $229 for two people, $117 to $217 for singles, including a full breakfast. An organic garden supplies produce for the restaurant, which is for guests only. Tours that focus on Costa Rica's natural beauty are arranged for guests. Telephone 269-9392, fax 269-9555.

North of Heredía is Hotel Chalet Tirol, thirty to forty-five minutes from San José. Located at about 5,900 feet (1,800 m), the main lodge, chalets, and suites are in a rain forest setting. Paths through the forest allow guests to see trogons, motmots, hummingbirds, and trees and ferns typical of this altitude. You can play tennis or go trout fishing, horseback riding, or bicycling. Chalet Tirol offers a number of tours, including visits to Barva Volcano, coffee farms, a butterfly collection, and an ornamental plant operation, and a hike in the cloud forest. The hotel's fine French restaurant is well-known. Rooms and chalets are $92 for two; suites are from $114 to $172, including continental breakfast. Telephone 267-7371, fax 267-7050.

Barva Volcano is in Braulio Carrillo National Park. The resplendent quetzal and a variety of other birds can be seen here. Even veteran hikers have gotten lost, so consider going with a guide. To get to Barva Volcano, take the Paso Llano bus from the Central Market in Heredía. A walking trail then leads you about 4 miles (6 km) to the park entrance. The lagoon is about 2.5 miles (4 km) farther on. There are two or three buses a day. Check with ICT for the times.

On the road between Heredía and the jumping-off place for the volcano at Sacramento is the historic town of Barva, with its large church and tiled-roof adobe houses. Farther along, in the area of San José de la Montaña, are three hotels that offer a chance to hike, bird-watch, and spend the night in this chilly clime. Bring a coat, it is cold at night and brisk in the early morning, and I have wished for my long johns to sleep in.

Hotel Cypresal has a swimming pool, Jacuzzi, sauna, gift shop, conference rooms, restaurant, and a bar with a fireplace. Rooms have a private bath with hot water, color TV, and telephone. The larger unit has a separate bedroom and sitting room and a private terrace. The smaller rooms have a sitting area in front of the fireplace. A single costs $57, a double $63. The hotel is quadrupling its twenty-four rooms. You can rent horses, and airport pickup can be arranged. Telephone 223-1717 or 221-6455, fax 221-6244. Cypresal is about 13 miles (20 km) from San José.

Within walking distance up the road is the fourteen-room El Pórtico, which has a Jacuzzi, sauna, pool, and restaurant. El Pórtico also has a river trail. Rates are $43 for a single, $66 for a double. Telephone 237-6022, fax 260-6002.

Cartago (population 30,273) lies 13 miles (21 km) southeast of San José, on the other side of the Continental Divide. Once the colonial capital, it now is the capital of the province of Cartago.

If you like markets, stop by the one here, which has gorgeous vegetables. The ruins of a church surround a tranquil garden of trees, flowers, and fountains; the town gave up trying to finish it after a severe earthquake in 1910. In front is an example of a cobblestone street from the colonial era. The most famous church in Cartago—in the entire country, in fact—is the Basílica de Nuestra Señora de los Angeles, built in honor of La Negrita, Costa Rica's patron saint. An image of the dark-skinned Virgin first appeared in 1637. Holy water from a spring flows out behind the basilica, where people can fill bottles or jars. Many miracles are attributed to the saint. On August 2, thousands of pilgrims gather at the shrine; the road from San José to Cartago is jammed with them

COFFEE

Coffee was Costa Rica's number one export from the middle of the last century until this decade, when bananas edged it into second place. Today it is the third largest foreign exchange earner, after bananas and tourism. Its cultivation and export brought the country into the world market and initiated a cash economy in a land previously tied to subsistence agriculture. But the instability of world market prices for coffee brings good years and bad years, and even though Costa Rica is working hard to diversify its economy through nontraditional exports, a drop in the price of coffee still sends a shudder through the country.

Coffee, which originated in Ethiopia and Arabia, was brought to the New World by the French, Spanish, and Portuguese. Seeds were first planted in Costa Rica around the beginning of the nineteenth century, but coffee did not become a substantial export until 1840. Most of the crop today is sold to Germany, the United States, and Great Britain.

According to a coffee specialist at CATIE, the agricultural center at Turrialba, the best flavor comes from coffee grown above 4,000 feet (1,200 m) on land where temperatures average between 59° and 82°F (15° and 28°C). A definite dry season helps because plants then flower evenly once the rains start. That means the fruit will mature over a few months, creating a short harvest period. Coffee is picked by hand; only mature fruit is taken. Since all the berries, even on a sin-gle plant, do not ripen at the same time, much labor is involved. Reducing the duration of that labor-intensive period is economically important to the grower.

Coffee plants are grown in nurseries until they are about one year old, and then they are transplanted to the field. After two years, they begin to bear commercially. Some growers harvest from coffee trees for fifteen or twenty years and then prune them way back for twenty more years of production before replacing the plant. (Coffee wood is highly prized for cooking because it burns slowly and produces little smoke.) Other growers replace their trees more often.

In some fields, trees are planted to shade the coffee, reducing the need to add nutrients to the soil. Some trees used, such as the poró, *are legumes that add nitrogen to the soil as well as provide shade. Sometimes fields have banana or citrus trees for shade.*

Coffee is planted in May and June. Harvest time depends on the elevation: October to January in the Central Valley, June to October or November in Turrialba and Coto Brus. Pickers are paid by the cajuela, *the basket you see workers fill. A good picker can earn about $10 a day. All ages take to the fields for the harvest. Each berry, which turns from green to red when ripe, contains two seeds. These seeds are the coffee beans. The pulp of the fruit must be removed and the beans dried before they can be roasted or exported.*

beginning the preceding day. Some arrive from as far away as Nicoya, Guanacaste, Panama, and Nicaragua.

Cartago has felt the effects of activity from Irazú Volcano as well as several severe earthquakes. The drive to the volcano offers spectacular views of the valley. Farmers tend fields of potatoes, onions, and cabbages. Milk cows move along the road. When we stopped once to photograph a young man forking hay into an ancient-looking barn, he insisted on taking us inside to see his bull.

An adventurous way to see Irazú Volcano is by horseback with Magic Trails, a nature tour operation run by the Chavarría family. The three-hour horseback portion of the all-day tour leaves from Hacienda Retes, their farm on a mountain next door to Irazú, and goes through Prusia National Forest Reserve. The cost is $75, including transportation from San José, horse, naturalist guide, and lunch. If you are not up for that, for $50, Magic Trails will take you from San José to the volcano by car, followed by a visit to the hacienda for lunch and a walk on its nature trails with a guide or an optional horseback ride. (Rental is $5 per hour extra.) There is a three-person minimum for these prices.

An overnight stay at the rustic century-old main house, made of oak logs, can be combined with either the Irazú trip for $115 or a visit to the farm for $90, including transportation, meals, and guided tours. Bring your jacket to enjoy this almost 9,000-foot (2,700-m) elevation. Telephone 253-8146 (weekdays), fax 253-9937.

From Cartago it is a fifteen-minute drive to Lankester Gardens, operated by the University of Costa Rica. Begun by Charles Lankester to preserve local flora—especially orchids, bromelaids, and arum plants—as well as to regenerate a natural forest, the Jardines Lankester stands as a gift from one nature lover to thousands who have walked these paths. Most come to see the more than 1,000 species of orchids. Some are blooming at any time of year, but the peak months are February through April. Trails lead over brooks, under arbors, to greenhouses, through a breathtaking display of flowers and trees that attract at least 150 species of birds. The gardens are open daily from 8:30 a.m. to 3:30 p.m. Guided walks leave on the half-hour. Admission is about $3.50, children 20 cents. Tours come from San José; a bus from Cartago for Paraíso (Paradise) brings you close to the entrance. Ask the driver where to get off. A taxi from Cartago costs about $3. Telephone 551-9877.

From Paraíso, roads go east and south for magnificent views of the Orosí Valley, Reventazón River, and the lake formed by the Cachí Dam. The east road leads to ruins of the seventeenth-century church of Ujarrás. Archaeological digs show that the colonial town that once surrounded it lies over pre-Columbian roads. There is a restaurant at the view point (*mirador* in Spanish) overlooking Ujarrás. Ten minutes away by car is the Charrarra Recreation Park on the lake, with swimming pool, restaurant, picnic areas, tour boat, and trails. The distinctive call of the oropendola, a large dark bird with yellow tail feathers, resounds through the trees. Crowded on weekends, the park is peaceful on other days. The road continues on to the dam.

The road south of Paraíso goes to the town of Orosí and its eighteenth-century church. Beside the church is a small historical museum, closed on Mondays. A mirador before you reach Orosí offers glorious views. Just beyond the town is Hotel Río Palomo, on the Palomo River, with its popular restaurant. Cabins with a small living room and private bath (with hot water) are $22 for two people; those with kitchenettes and beds for up to six people are $32 for two. Tours are offered to Tapantí, Orosí, Ujarrás, and a coffee plantation. Horseback tours are also available, and there is a large swimming pool by the restaurant. Telephone 533-3128 or 533-3057.

The Tapantí National Park is about 6 miles (10 km) from Orosí. Tours combine some of these sites near Cartago in day trips from San José. Public buses from Cartago go to Orosí and Ujarrás (ask at ICT), with a taxi extension for Tapantí. Or you can get a taxi from Cartago or Paraíso, where they are more plentiful. If you are driving, you can make a loop from Ujarrás around the lake, but the unpaved section from the dam to Orosí is very bumpy (and dusty in the dry season).

The road from Cartago to Turrialba is spectacular as it winds up and over the mountains. This was the route to Limón before the shorter highway from San José to Guapiles opened. When you get

Coffee harvested by hand near Turrialba (Photo by Ree Strange Sheck)

to the town of Cervantes, watch on the left for the Posada de la Luna restaurant. I am unable to pass this place without stopping for a freshly made *tortilla de queso* (cheese tortilla) and a glass of hot *agua dulce con leche*. Some people swear that the best *gallo pinto* (beans and rice) in the country is served here; buy some *cajeta* (fudge) to take with you. Showcases hold bits of history from Indian artifacts to flatirons. La Luna is quite a place. It is open from 8:00 a.m. to 8:00 p.m., except Mondays.

The agricultural lands around Juan Viñas are among the most beautiful in Costa Rica. Fields of sugarcane wave across this top-of-the-world setting. Then comes the winding descent into the Turrialba Valley.

Only 40 miles (64 km) from San José, Turrialba, with 30,268 people, is the center of a rich agricultural region and is increasingly a destination for tourists. Kayakers and white-water rafters use the town as a base for forays on the mighty Reventazón and Pacuare rivers. Its location makes it ideal for travelers interested in archaeology, agriculture, and nature. From here you can visit Guayabo National Monument 11 miles (18 km) away, Turrialba Volcano, plantations of coffee, macadamia nuts, cardamom, sugarcane, and bananas, and tour CATIE, a tropical agricultural research and education center. Located a few miles from Turrialba, CATIE prefers that visitors come with an organized group. A tour can include a look at meat and dairy operations, forest management, orchids, coffee, cacao, macadamia nuts, plantains, and plant genetics, with a stop at the center's seed laboratory and seed bank. Individual visitors can go on the nature trail but will not have access to the facilities. For CATIE's tourist office, telephone 556-6431, extension 210, fax 556-1533.

Hotel Wagelia has two locations. The eighteen-room downtown building offers parking and a restaurant with good food and a pleasant atmosphere. The eleven-room annex is on a quiet street backed by coffee fields at the edge of town. It has a bar, restaurant, and swimming pool. Rates at either are $42 for singles, $62 for doubles; superior rooms with air conditioning, TV, and refrigerator are $60 for singles, $77 for doubles. Both types of room have private baths. Area tours include rafting trips and visits to Guayabo, Turrialba Volcano, and CATIE. Telephone 556-1566, fax 556-1596.

SUGARCANE

Sugarcane was brought to the New World by Columbus and was introduced into Costa Rica in 1530. Though it is grown in most of the country, the major cane-producing regions are the Central Valley around Atenas and Grecia; the Turrialba and Juan Viñas area of the Central Valley; Guanacaste; San Carlos; and Pérez Zeledón and Parrita to the south. Some 101,200 acres (42,000 ha) are in production.

At 3,280 feet (1,000 m) or less, cane takes twelve to eighteen months to reach harvest; above that elevation, it takes twenty-four months. Almost all the cane is cut by hand except in Guanacaste, where machines are used because there is insufficient labor. In Costa Rica, most cane is burned first to make the cutting easier: A worker can cut two to three tons of unburned cane per day compared with three to six tons of cane that has been burned. The harvest season is from January to May, though in higher regions around Juan Viñas, it can last until August. Large sugar mills are called inge-

nios, and companies often provide a school and housing for workers. Small trapiches, where juice is extracted by ox power, can still be found.

More than 4,500 people have cane operations, ranging from a few acres to 7,400 acres (3,000 ha). Some 60,000 workers and their families depend on cane production. In some places, especially in the Central Valley, the cane harvest alternates with the coffee harvest.

The United States is the biggest buyer of Costa Rican sugar, and has been since 1963 when it stopped buying from Cuba. Nicaragua and Trinidad also buy tico sugar. Some cane is used to produce alcohol for fuel, which is also exported to the United States, at distilleries in Cañas and Liberia.

The price of cane is fixed by the government, and the Sugarcane Agricultural and Industrial League (LAICA) regulates buying and selling and conducts research to improve production. Costa Rica is third in the world in production per hectare.

Do not plan to sleep late anywhere in town. Its peaceful air will be broken by three strong blasts of the town's fire alarm announcing 6:00 a.m.

You can get from San José to Turrialba by express bus. (See Practical Extras.) If you have a car, there is a back door to Turrialba that winds through San Isidro de Coronado and Rancho Redondo, dairy country, and oak forests often shrouded in mist.

The last time I was on this road was a Corpus Christi Sunday. Flowers strewn in the road marked the path of religious processions in village after village. In one, a milk cow stood in the middle of the road eating the flower petals while worshipers sang in the church. Past Llano Grande is the turnoff for Irazú Volcano. Continue on to Cot and Pacayas for Santa Cruz, watching for waterfalls on the skirts of Turrialba Volcano. At Santa Cruz, turn to Turrialba. This road is passable even in the rainy season. From Santa Cruz, a jolting road—which is supposed to be surfaced this year—goes on to Guayabo and the national monument.

A small mountain lodge called La Calzada on the road between Guayabo and the park has four doubles with a shared bath, but construction is under way on three rooms with private baths. The cost is $24 per room for one or two people. Visa is accepted. An Indian road (*calzada*) passes through the property, and a walk along the road through plantains, macadamia nuts, and coffee to the forest and river may reveal potsherds. José Miguel and Grettel García are great hosts. Food at the thatched, open-air restaurant is typical fare—delicious. Stop by on your way to the park even if you do not spend the night.

La Calzada is a ten-minute walk from the park. Call for reservations: 556-6091, 556-0465. The bus from Turrialba to Guayabo passes in front. Check the schedule: It runs only once a day, never on Sunday.

Two other small mountain lodges are located outside Turrialba on the road toward Limón. Turrialtico is about 4 miles (7 km) away. Twelve rooms with private baths with hot water are above the locally popular restaurant. Owner Hector Lezama will pick you up in Turrialba, or you can go by bus. He arranges tours to Guayabo and to macadamia nut and coffee plantations, rafting trips, and, with enough notice, a trip to Turrialba Volcano—part by car, part on horseback. Rooms are $23. Credit cards are not accepted. Telephone or fax 556-1111.

Pochotel is 7 miles (11 km) from Turrialba. From its mirador on a clear day, you can see not only the Reventazón Valley but also Cerro de la Muerte, Chirripó, Irazú Volcano, Turrialba Volcano, and the Caribbean coast. Eight bungalows with private baths and shower-head hot water are simply furnished but have charm; new units have a small fireplace. The rate is $35 for two people, $5 per person extra for more. The restaurant has a wood-burning stove (*cocina de leña*) in the dining room so guests can be a part of this traditional way of cooking. When I was last there, an organic garden was in the works—it may be reflected in the menu by the time you arrive. A taxi from Turrialba is about $5. Owner Oscar García will arrange tours for you to Turrialba Volcano, a fishing lake, a waterfall, or a *trapiche*, where you can see juice extracted from sugarcane in the old style. Visa is accepted. Telephone 556-0111, fax 556-6222.

On the banks of the Reventazón River off the road to La Suiza 15 minutes southeast of Turrialba is Casa Turire, a splendid country house on the Atirro Hacienda. Situated in a curve of the Reventazón River, Casa Turire reigns over nearby forest as well as fields of sugarcane, coffee, and macadamia nuts. The hacienda belongs to the Rojas family, who extended their enterprises to include tourism in 1991. The twelve-room, four-suite grand "plantation house" sits amid formal gardens, with a pool, Jacuzzi, tennis court, and six-hole golf course. Rooms are elegant and furnished in soft tones, with two full beds in each, satellite TV, shower with tub, ceiling fan, hair dryer, and direct dial telephone. Each room has a stunning view of the mountains from a private balcony. Floor-to-ceiling windows welcome light that shines on polished hardwood floors. Singles are $97, doubles $114, suites from $149. No children under twelve are permitted; building not equipped for handicapped.

Guests at Casa Turire can choose from mountain biking, rain forest tours, horseback riding, kayaking, and white-water rafting. There are tours to Guayabo National Monument and to see the sugar mill where cane is processed. Coffee and macadamia nuts are processed right on the hacienda. The restaurant is open to the public for lunch and dinner with reservations. Telephone 531-1111, fax 531-1075.

The privately owned nature reserve, Rancho Naturalista, a favorite with bird and butterfly enthusiasts, is near Turrialba, southeast through La Suiza. (See chapter 8).

North Central

Mountains, plains, volcanoes, lakes, rivers, forests, fruit farms, and cattle ranches form a colorful and diverse mosaic in this region of Costa Rica. Several routes take the traveler into the north-central area from San José. To get to the La Fortuna-Arenal-Tilarán areas from the Inter-American Highway west of San José, you can go north through either Naranjo, Zarcero, and Ciudad Quesada, or San Ramón and La Tigra.

Travelers can also go northwest out of San José through Varablanca and San Miguel and either head west for Lake Arenal or Caño Negro, or go east to the Puerto Viejo area. (There are several towns named Puerto Viejo in Costa Rica; this one is Puerto Viejo de Sarapiquí.) The road northeast out of San José through Braulio Carrillo National Park toward Limón is another gateway to Puerto Viejo, turning north before Guapiles and going through Las Horquetas.

If you are in Guanacaste in the northwest region, you can visit the north-central section by either heading northeast at Cañas for Tilarán and the Arenal area or taking the mostly unpaved road from La Cruz near Nicaragua to Upala. The western entrance to Caño Negro National Wildlife Refuge is accessible via an unpaved road from Upala. (Many visitors arrive on the eastern side via a paved road to Los Chiles, a stone's throw from Nicaragua.)

Buses run throughout this area. (Check the bus section in Practical Extras at the end of the book.) Direct buses from San José go to Ciudad Quesada, Puerto Viejo de Sarapiquí, Braulio Carrillo Park, and Tilarán, with connections to other destinations. For instance, there are two buses a day each way between Ciudad Quesada and Tilarán for access to Lake Arenal.

Let's begin with the route through San Ramón. If you are driving, watch for killer speed bumps near San Ramón—the signs say "*Reductor de velocidad.*" Part of the magnificent primary forest along this road is in the Alberto Manuel Brenes Biological Reserve, and some of it is Bosque Eterno de los Niños, the first international children's rain forest, owned by the Monteverde Conservation League. The children's rain forest sectors around La Tigra are not

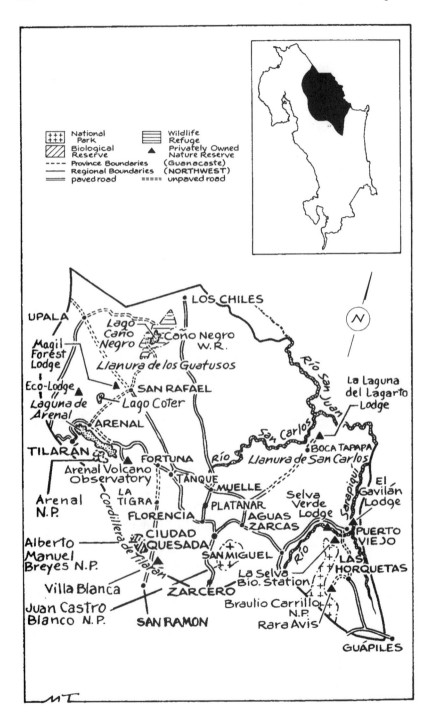

open for tourism, but you can see the magnificent forest-covered mountains as you drive between La Tigra and La Fortuna, forest protected by gifts from children and adults around the world.

About 12 miles (19 km) north of San Ramón is a private nature reserve called Villablanca. Guests stay in a replica of a colonial village nestled next to a cloud forest. (See chapter 8.)

A few miles north of the turnoff to Villablanca is Valle Escondido Lodge, where you can combine treks in fantastic forest with walks through acres of ornamental plants grown for export, while enjoying very nice quarters. The lodge itself has twenty rooms, each opening onto a covered gallery with a magical view of a valley and green, green mountains that appear and disappear according to the mists. Large frogs convene on the porch in the evenings. Rooms are large and bright, carpeted, with beautiful polished hardwood furniture, including an ample writing desk. Bathrooms have big lighted mirrors and come with bidets, not common in Costa Rica. Singles are $51, doubles $63. Credit cards are accepted.

The restaurant, a short walk downhill from the rooms, offers an international menu with Italian specialties: breakfast in the $4 to $5 range and main dishes for other meals generally from $5 to $10. Food is a feast for the eyes as well as the palate. Don't forget to take your binoculars to the dining room to enjoy the birds in the garden at the back while you eat. The restaurant is open to the public and is only a five-minute drive from the highway turnoff.

Owner Marco Hidalgo exports the more than twenty species of ornamental plants grown here to Italy, the Netherlands, and Belgium. Guests can also visit the greenhouses and packing sheds.

The farm includes about 150 acres (60 ha) of forest and an abundance of mountain streams. The understory of the tall forest is a natural tropical greenhouse with a variety of heliconias and fascinating tree roots. I watched as one masked tityra fed another. An aracari, a member of the toucan family, frustrated my attempts to photograph him but allowed wonderful glimpses. Near one trail is a huge tree with enormous buttresses where bats live. The wide forest trails begin and end at the plantation. The lodge offers a tour—either on foot, horseback, or mountain bike—to the San Lorenzo River, where you can swim in a natural pool. Or you can hike to a three-tiered waterfall. Horses cost $5 per hour, and mountain bikes $3.50. Boots are also for rent.

The elevation is about 2,000 feet (600 m), and the temperature ranges from 68° to 86°F (20° to 30°C). Valle Escondido Lodge is 21 miles (33 km) from San Ramón and 56 miles (90 km) from San José. English and Italian also are spoken here. Telephone 231-0906, fax 232-9591. Call about the availability of day visits that include a tour of the ornamental plant operation. The lodge can arrange transportation, or you can take the public bus to San Ramón and a taxi from there for less than $20 or continue by public bus to the turnoff.

The route through Naranjo takes you to Zarcero, a mountain town famous for its animals—that is, animals sculpted from plants, topiary art. The fantastic gardens in front of the church hold an evergreen elephant, bull, and rabbit, plus dozens of other forms. Roadside stands offer fruits, *cajeta*, delicious cheeses, and other specialties of this rural center of some 3,300 people. The food known as *palmito* is not made from heart of palm, as some visitors deduce from its name. It is a layered ball of white cheese.

Ciudad Quesada (population 29,000) is a center of this rich agricultural area. Located on the edge of the San Carlos Plains about 60 miles (95 km) from the capital, it is often referred to as San Carlos. The first view of the extensive plains from the mountains is always a little surprising for those who think of Costa Rica as all rugged terrain. Both of these towns can be reached via the Ciudad Quesada bus from San José. Some one-day tours to the Arenal area include a stop in Zarcero to see the church and pass through Ciudad Quesada.

In 1992, a national park named Juan Castro Blanco was created east of Ciudad Quesada, but it has no developed facilities for visitors.

Five miles (8 km) northeast of Ciudad Quesada on the road to Aguas Zarcas is the Hotel El Tucano Resort and Spa, a country inn set among the trees, complete with restaurant featuring Italian food, tennis courts, swimming pools, paths through a primary forest, a sauna whose steam comes from hot springs, and two Jacuzzis supplied by water from the hot springs. The waters are said to be effective for treatment of arthritis, skin and kidney disorders,

Arenal Volcano, one of the most active in the world (Photo by Ree Strange Sheck)

rheumatism, and sinus problems. Guests can also bathe at the base of a small waterfall in the cold river water and choose the temperature they like best by their distance from the hot springs along the shore. Fresh flowers grace the desks in the ninety spacious, carpeted rooms, which have both showers and bathtubs. Singles are $62, doubles $75; suites begin at $100. A tour office arranges trips nationally and to such local attractions as Arenal Volcano, Caño Negro National Wildlife Refuge, and Venado Caves. Hotel-provided transportation from San José is $60 one way for up to six people. Telephone 460-1822, fax 460-1692.

A public nature reserve and springs next to El Tucano is open to the public for less than 40 cents. Ask for directions to El Tucanito.

Just a piece farther down the road toward Aguas Zarcas is La Marina zoo, which has 40 species of birds and 60 of mammals and reptiles, including toucans, a crested eagle, jaguars, white-tailed deer, a tapir named Clarisa, and peccaries (including one albino). Alba María Alfaro, the owner, says most of the animals were brought to La Marina because they were sick or wounded or had been abandoned either by former owners or in the wild. The small zoo is open daily from 8:00 a.m. to 4:30 p.m.; admission is less than $1.50 for adults, 75 cents for children. Donations are gladly accepted.

North of Ciudad Quesada at Platanar is the attractive Hotel La Garza, built along the Platanar River with a view of Arenal Volcano. The twelve rooms are in bungalows with ample windows and French doors that open onto porches looking out to the river and landscaped grounds. There are in-room telephones, hardwood floors, a modern bath with shower-head hot water, and ceiling fans. The restaurant and bar of this new hotel is in what was the gracious main house of the Hacienda Platanar. Access to the restaurant is across a hanging foot bridge over the river. La Garza (*garza* means egret or heron and hints of the abundant bird life to be seen) has 740 acres (300 ha) of primary rain forest with trails open to guests, and it is also a dairy and cattle ranch. Perhaps the pool will be finished when you arrive. Tours can be arranged. A single is $74, a double $79, including breakfast. Credit cards are accepted. Telephone 475-5222, 475-5230 or 222-7355, fax 475-5015.

Fourteen miles (22 km) north of Ciudad Quesada at Muelle is the Tilajari Resort Hotel, located in a rural setting on the banks of the San Carlos River in sight of Arenal Volcano. Facilities include pools, three lighted tennis courts, racquetball courts, sauna, restaurant, and bar. Guests may rent horses and tennis equipment as well as canoes to use on the Peñas Blancas River.

Tours operated from the hotel include visits to the Caño Negro National Wildlife Refuge (a full day with drive to Los Chiles and boat trip on the Río Frío through the refuge is $48 each for a minimum of four people), Venado Caves, the waterfall in Fortuna, Arenal Volcano (a late afternoon/night tour that allows time at the Tabacón hot springs complex is $45, plus the fee at Tabacón), fishing, and nature walks in a tropical forest. Guides for the trips are trained for the job and are bilingual. I was fortunate to travel to Caño Negro with Miguel Benavides, who was not only knowledgeable about local history and geography but also excellent at spotting species along the road and from the boat.

Rates for the sixty rooms are $74 for singles, $85 for doubles; suites are also available. All have air conditioning, fans, and private baths with hot water. Credit cards are accepted. The rooms are quiet, located apart from the sports areas, restaurant, and pools, and are surrounded by manicured lawns and gardens. The large rooms open onto covered terraces where you can enjoy a variety of birds. Crocodiles amble along the river bank. In low trees near the restaurant are keel-billed and chestnut-mandibled toucans who were raised here and have decided to stay—their wings are not clipped. They seem to enjoy posing for photos. Owners Jaime Hamilton and Ricardo Araya hope that two scarlet macaws that have been added to the menagerie will do the same. I saw a young sloth curled up in one of the many fruit trees that supply produce for the restaurant. You may want to investigate travel packages that include round-trip transportation from San José for two people, the cost for two days and one night is $124.50 per person double occupancy; for three days and two nights, it is $166. For four people, costs drop to $96.50 and $138, respectively. The Tilajari is 73 miles (117 km) from San José. Telephone 469-9091, fax 469-9095.

West of Muelle, about 4 miles (6 km) from La Fortuna, is Hotel Rancho Corcovado. Arenal Volcano looms in the distance. The thirty-four rooms are in buildings facing a good-sized swimming pool, rather like a motel. Rooms are spacious, with telephones, central hot water, and a tiled porch that runs the length of each building. The restaurant and bar are in a large open-sided structure overlooking a small lake, where you may spot a crocodile or two. Birds abound. The hotel is a family-run operation. One son is the architect, another is a pilot who can bring guests from San José to a landing strip on the property, and daughter Agnes oversees operations. Tours can be arranged to Caño Negro and other area sites. A horseback tour shows crops such as yuca, ginger, plantains, tiquisque (a tuber), and corn. Guests can also walk through a 4-acre (1.4-ha) forest. A single is $34, a double $45. Credit cards are accepted. Telephone or fax 479-9090.

A couple of private nature reserves accessible from this area offer opportunities to experience the region's variety of natural beauty. (See chapter 8.) The rustic Magil Forest Lodge is west and north of Muelle, 12 miles (19 km) from San Rafael de Guatuso, on a line between Lake Arenal and Caño Negro on the map. It is on the skirts of Tenorio Volcano. La Laguna del Lagarto is east and north of Muelle, through Pital, an extremely pleasant town, and Boca Tapada. Yes, there are *lagartos* (caimans) there, and monkeys, and colorful frogs.

If you are going on to Lake Arenal from Ciudad Quesada or La Tigra, the road takes you to La Fortuna (population 6,000). Arenal Volcano is nearby, visible from town. You can stop by the Tourist Information Center, past the park and soccer field, and talk to Gabino about such area attractions as the 230-foot (70-m) waterfall, the hot springs at Tabacón, Caño Negro, and nearby walking trails. He has a microbus and offers night tours to the volcano as well as other tours. Another tour information center is across from the soccer field.

Hotel Las Colinas, a block off the main street, has seventeen spacious, plain, but clean rooms, each with private bath and shower-head hot water. Rates range from $12 to $34 per room, depending on the number of people. MasterCard and Visa are accepted. Telephone 479-9107.

Hotel San Bosco is two blocks north of the gasoline station. In the sixteen-room, two-story addition, singles are $32, doubles $40. The rooms have ceiling fans, and the private baths have shower-head hot water. The eleven older rooms are less expensive. Credit cards are not accepted. Most tours are arranged through the information center belonging to a family member, but San Bosco has its own waterfall tour, costing $14. Telephone 479-9050, fax 479-9109.

On the main street is the eight-room Burio Inn with private baths, shower-head hot water, and ceiling fans. The rooms at $20 per person, are a bit dark but clean, with high ceilings and cement floors. German also is spoken. Credit cards are not accepted. Tours include horseback riding to a waterfall, a $35 all-day visit to Caño Negro, a $10 night volcano tour, Venado Caves for $17, and sunset on Lake Arenal for $28.

West of Fortuna 2.5 miles (4 km) is Jungla y Senderos Los Lagos, which contains four forest trails and two lakes. Boats and horses may be rented.

Just a piece farther down the road is Tabacón Resort at the base of Arenal Volcano. The complex offers four pools with thermal waters and one with cold water. The beautiful landscaped grounds center on paths along the river and a waterfall of hot water that steams against the greenery. The water from the hot springs is more than 126°F (52°C).

The admission charge of $10 for adults and $4 for children covers use of the pools, which range from 80° to 102°F (27° to 39°C), the gardens, bar, a Jacuzzi, the river, and a half-mile (1 km) trail along the forest through volcanic rock to a small volcanic lake. Visitors may eat in the restaurant overlooking the gardens (Italian and Costa Rican food) without paying the admission fee; it is open from noon to 10:00 p.m. Telephone or fax 479-9033, telephone 222-1072, or fax 221-3075.

Across the road is another, less expensive, no frills opportunity to bathe in the hot springs' water.

Arenal is one of the world's most active volcanoes, thundering and blowing since 1968. A number of dirt roads take you near enough to watch from. Climbing to the crater can be hazardous to your health; in fact, it can be fatal. Arenal Observatory Lodge, discussed in chapter 8, is a privately owned nature reserve that offers a front row seat for nighttime viewing, and day tours as well.

Archaeological studies show that Indians had small settlements around Lake Arenal, near the volcano, as long ago as 2000 B.C. Today the lake has been greatly enlarged by a dam built to provide hydroelectric energy. Twenty-four miles (39 km) long, Lake Arenal is a favorite for fishing and water sports such as wind surfing and kayaking. The road around the northeast side takes you over the dam and on to the new town of Arenal, built by the Costa Rican Electrical Institute to replace house by house the old Arenal, which was flooded because of the dam.

If you are driving around the north side of the lake, be alert for one-lane bridges that seem to be mostly on curves. And be aware that the road is more potholes than pavement in some places, and the pavement ends altogether at Nuevo Arenal for about a 6-mile (9-km) stretch going east toward the dam—slow going. While paving seems imminent, I hesitate to predict it will be done by your arrival.

Just past the dam and up a mountain through a macadamia nut farm is the very pleasant Arenal Lodge. Rooms in the front have impressive views of the volcano, while those in back are around a covered courtyard graced with orchids. The twelve view rooms have bathtubs and showers with central hot water. A single is $79, a double $90. The six standard rooms, with showers only, are $57 for a single, $68 for a double. The master suite with a private balcony and king-size beds is $113. Breakfast is $6, dinner $12, plus tax. Credit cards are accepted. There is a Jacuzzi, a sauna, and a small library. Guests will probably see howler monkeys in the forested area at the edge of the lodge and may even spot a tayra or anteater. Hummingbird feeders and platforms for fruit bring a variety of birds to the gardens. The lodge offers lake fishing and tours to Caño Negro for $50 and also to Venado Caves, the hot springs, the base of the volcano, and the La Fortuna waterfall. English, German, French, and Flemish also are spoken. Telephone 228-2588, fax 228-2798.

For a taste of Switzerland, check out Los Héroes back on the main road around the north side of Lake Arenal. You can't miss the imposing chalet-style structure. Eleven carpeted rooms, some with balconies, have private baths with central hot water, some with bathtubs. Prices range from $76 for a double with no balcony to $108 with a balcony and a view of Lake Arenal, including continental breakfast. Credit cards are not accepted. There is a nice pool and Jacuzzi with a lake and volcano view. The restaurant, with decor right out of the Swiss Alps—big cowbells, lace curtains—is open to the public. If you are tired of rice and beans, you can choose from a menu that includes meat and cheese fondue, roesti (a delicious potato dish), spaghetti, and sausages. Entrées range from $5 to $12. Tours can be arranged to Arenal Volcano, Arenal Botanical Gardens, and other sites. Telephone 228-1472 or 441-4193, fax 233-1772.

About an hour from La Fortuna and 2 miles (6 km) before the town of Arenal is the sign for La Ceiba, a bed-and-breakfast with four bright and airy rooms that open off a tiled terrace with a panoramic view of Lake Arenal. Rooms are $20 per person with breakfast. Owners Ursula and Julio are artists; their paintings are displayed in the rooms. Private baths have central hot water. The house is on a working cattle and goat farm. Guests may see three kinds of toucans, howler monkeys, or sloths on paths in the forest.

The owners, who also speak German and English, will serve evening meals featuring produce from their organic garden. A sailboat tour for up to four people can includes a visit to islands in the lake, a close-up view of the volcano, or fishing. For those who do not come by car, the hosts arrange tours to the volcano or Venado Caves, costing $30 for two people. Fax 695-5387.

Heliconias, begonias, orchids, tree ferns, gingers, anthuriums, euphorbias—1,200 varieties of plants from around the world thrive in the Arenal Botanical Gardens, including many that are native to Costa Rica. Owner Michael LeMay, who has collected plants for 15 years, began to convert degraded pastureland into a breathtaking garden in 1991, and opened it to the public in 1993. Easy trails weave through dazzling displays that were laid out to look like a natural forest but with groupings that permit the visitor to stand in one area and see varieties in the same genera or family. There are 200 kinds of bromeliads, 200 varieties of orchids, and 100 of ferns. Visitors are led on guided walks where they hear where the plants originated, how they got their names, whether they have medicinal value, and what kinds of habitats they need. The entrance fee of about $4 covers a guided walk that generally lasts from one to two hours. In addition, there is a trail through a natural forest that can take up to an hour. Flowers attract butterflies and birds, including six species of hummingbirds. The gardens are open from 9:00 a.m. to 5:00 p.m. daily, but are closed in October.

Michael, who can tell you where he got each plant, set up the garden to preserve native species of plants, create a habitat for birds, insects, and other wildlife, and provide a living classroom for the study of plants. He is developing a computer-based information center. (He is also a whiz at opening a locked Toyota for a certain writer who locked her keys in the car. Thanks, Michael.) Arenal Botanical Gardens is 2.5 miles (4 km) east of the town of Nuevo Arenal.

Just down the road is Chalet Nicholas, a small bed-and-breakfast with a front-porch view of Arenal Volcano. A double room is $56. Credit cards are not accepted. Guests can hike in a nearby protected forest, and the Nicholases can arrange horseback riding and a canoe ride on the lake. Catherine has a small orchid garden and an aviary of 25 birds, including a laughing falcon, red-legged honeycreeper, and aracaris. Fax 695-5387.

Past the town of Arenal near Lake Coter is a private nature reserve called the Eco-Lodge. It has marvelous nature trails through its biologically rich forest. (See chapter 8.)

An inviting white portal on the main road around the lake marks the entrance to Albergue Club Alturas de Arenal, a small, two-story, twelve-room hotel with a pleasant dining area open to landscaped grounds that slope toward Lake Arenal. The carpeted rooms are small but pleasant, with a large mirror. A single costs $48, a double $55. Credit cards are accepted. The hot tub sits amid tropical flowers, and a pool is in the works. The hotel is on an 82-acre (44-ha) farm where coffee, macadamia nuts, ornamental plants, and fruit trees are cultivated. It includes 25 acres (20 ha) of forest; trails lead into a habitat where white-faced and howler monkeys live and where you may see birds such as a collared aracari, a chachalaca, or an oropendola. Night tours to Arenal Volcano from the lake side are $25 a person, and the hotel has a houseboat that can offer dinner tours on the lake or a two-day outing. Breakfasts are $5.50, lunch and dinner $6.50, plus tax. Telephone 222-6455, fax 222-8372.

Not far down the road, at kilometer 40, is Rock River Lodge, with rooms in cabins above and behind the main building which houses the bar, dining room and a small library. Most nights find a fire going in the fireplace at the far end of the open-air dining room. There are views of the lake and the volcano. The simple rooms are wood-paneled and a bit dark, but there is a brightly lit mirror in the bathroom, and shower-head hot water; windows open onto a balcony facing the lake. Single or double rooms are $40. Credit cards are not accepted. Breakfast is $5 and dinner $10, plus tax. Tours can be arranged to the Corobicí River, Palo Verde, or other sites, and there are horses for rent. Telephone 222-4547, fax 221-3011.

Mirador Los Lagos is on the slopes above the lake, and its eleven rooms and open-air restaurant have an unobstructed view of both lake and volcano. The rooms are plain but clean, and each has a porch with chairs to sit on and enjoy the panorama. Owners

Alejandro and María have an organic vegetable garden and raise their own chickens. Italian dishes are a specialty—it is a tradition to serve gnocchi on the 29th of every month. Lake tours are arranged, and there is hiking in a nearby forest. Baby-sitting can be provided. English, Italian and French are also spoken. A local bar down the mountain has live music on weekends—it is a favorite with locals, and María says guests often enjoy going there. But the music also drifts up the hill. Telephone 695-5169, fax 695-5387.

Near the northeastern edge of Lake Arenal is the Hotel Tilawa and its WindSurf Center. The imposing two-story building sits on the slope above the lake. Every room has large windows looking out on either the lake or attractive gardens, two queen-size beds with orthopedic mattresses, a writing desk, and bathrooms with both a tub and a shower. Colorful Guatemalan bedspreads brighten the rooms. There are twenty-four standard rooms (a single is $54, a double $71, breakfast included) and four junior suites with sitting area and furnished kitchenette for $112. Credit cards are accepted. There is a main restaurant and a poolside bar and restaurant.

Trails take off in the forest next to the swimming pool—howler monkeys were calling when I was there, and you have a good chance of seeing keel-billed toucans. Guided tours to the volcano are available by either boat or car, as are trips to the Corobicí River, Venado Caves, and the hot springs at Tabacón. There also is tennis, sailing, horseback riding, and rental of mountain bikes and cars. The strong suit at Tilawa, however, is windsurfing. Lake Arenal is gaining a reputation as one of the top areas for this sport, and the lakeside WindSurf Center offers equipment for rent and lessons for adults and children.

Hotel Tilawa offers airport pickup in San José, $130 one-way for up to four people. Packages for seven days and seven nights, double occupancy, are $589.50 for sailors (with unlimited use of equipment) and $248.50 for non-sailors, breakfast included. Telephone (800) 851-8929 in the U.S.; or 695-5050, fax 695-5766 in Costa Rica.

From the hotel property on clear days, you can see not only Arenal Volcano but also three others: Rincón de la Vieja, Miravalles, and Tenorio. These majestic peaks are also visible from the road between Tilarán and the lake.

Tilarán (population 8,423), about 2 miles (3 km) from Lake Arenal, is a pleasant town laid out around the traditional square.

Across the street from the south side of the cathedral is the Hotel Naralit. The seventeen rooms, small but pleasant, have ceiling fans, reading lamps, and private baths with shower-head hot water. The cost is $16 per person. Visa and Mastercard are accepted. The staff will arrange lake fishing and boat trips to the volcano. Telephone 695-5393.

If you are in Tilarán about mealtime, you may want to check out the Restaurante Catalá around the corner from the Hotel Naralit. The food is very tasty. If you have yet to try the typical *casado*, here is your chance to enjoy a good one, with the full meal and drink costing about $6. Hours are 6:30 a.m. to 10:00 p.m. There is also a pleasant bar open to a pretty garden, with access to the Hotel Naralit.

Just north of the park is Cabinas El Sueño, a second-floor, twelve-room hotel with most rooms around an open courtyard with a fountain in the middle. The carpeted rooms are pleasant and have ceiling fans; all have private baths with shower-head hot water. Singles are $15, doubles $25. Credit cards are accepted. Staff members will arrange full-day or night tours to the volcano and trips to Venado Caves, Tabacón, and La Fortuna waterfall ($45 with guide, meals, and transportation) as well as horseback riding with a guide or mountain biking. There is a supermarket below. Telephone 695-5347, fax 695-5387.

Cabinas Mary is on the south side of the park downtown. The hotel's sixteen rooms above a restaurant are simple but very clean, and the staff is attentive. Rooms with shared bath have no hot water, while private baths have shower-head hot water. No credit cards are accepted. A single is about $5.50, a double about $7. Telephone 695-5479.

The route from San José to the north-central region through Varablanca is spectacular, with Barva Volcano and Cacho Negro on one side and Poás Volcano and Cerro Congo on the other. Just before Varablanca is a turnoff to Poás Volcano. On a clear day from the heights, you can see the plains stretching to the coast. The winding descent passes gorgeous waterfalls—the most photographed being the Peace Waterfall. The river that feeds the waterfall rises in the forests of Poás.

At San Miguel, roads west and north take you to Aguas Zarcas and Ciudad Quesada, destinations already discussed. To continue to Puerto Viejo, head northeast. Several privately owned nature reserves offer opportunities to learn about tropical flora and fauna in this region. One of them is Selva Verde Lodge near Chilamate. (See chapter 8.) Selva Verde has a butterfly garden open to the public just down the road from the Chilamate school, across from the lodge. Watch for the large floral butterfly on the hillside. Admission is $5 per person for a guided walk on the 2.5 miles (4 km) of trails, open from 8:00 a.m. to 4:00 p.m. Peter Knudsen has added plantings to attract the butterflies (more than 700 species are found in the area) and provide host plants for larvae to feed on. Here, the butterflies are free, without enclosures, but it is not uncommon to see twenty-five to fifty species in a morning. Peter can show you the wallpaper vine that becomes a cut-leaf monstera. Lacking toxins to protect it from insects, the plant, early in its life, pastes itself to a tree. There is also a section for medicinal plants. Before or after the butterfly walk, you may want to drop by the Selva Verde gift shop managed by Betty Ann Knudsen to see the variety of interesting locally made handcrafts.

Islas del Río near Chilamate has thirty rooms. A double is $50 per person with shared bath, $57 with private bath and shower-head hot water, meals included. Credit cards are accepted. Guests have access to three small forested islands in the Sarapiquí River and a nature trail behind the lodge where river otters, armadillos, monkeys, anteaters, and sloths can be seen. Rooms are simply furnished, large, and airy, with fans. There is a pool and small conference center. The intent is to provide a family environment where guests have a chance to get to know the staff. Bilingual guides are available, with activities such as a night walk, at $12 per person, and a visit to La Selva, costing $25. Horse rental is $10 per hour. The guided island walk is $12.

Las Islas is starting an ecological center that will include an organic gardening project in which participants from local communities sell their produce to hotels along the Caribbean Telephone or fax 710-6898, telephone 233-0366.

Continuing on to the town of Puerto Viejo (population 6,060), you enter an area where large banana plantations have developed in recent years. Unfortunately, primary forest sometimes fell to make way for the bananas. In town is El Bambú, an eleven-room hotel with private baths, shower-head hot water, and ceiling fans. Rooms for up to two people are $51. Credit cards are accepted. Bamboo furniture decorates the pleasant rooms. A restaurant and bar are on the ground floor, open on one side to the greenery outside. The hotel offers trips on the San Juan River to Barro del Colorado as well as bird-watching trips and boat rides. Telephone 766-6005 or 225-8860, fax 766-6132 or 234-9387.

Mi Lindo Sarapiquí is a modest hotel next to the soccer field right downtown. Six simple, clean rooms above the restaurant have private baths with shower-head hot water. A single is $12, a double $19. Credit cards are accepted. Staff members will arrange tours in the area and to Tortuguero. Telephone 766-6281.

Just outside Puerto Viejo is the entrance to La Selva Biological Station, a private nature reserve operated by the Organization for Tropical Studies. (See chapter 8.)

Local naturalist guides trained by the Organization for Tropical Studies at La Selva will accompany individuals or groups in the Puerto Viejo area and to Braulio Carrillo Park and other areas in the Central Volcanic Range. The charge is less than $7 for a half-day, $14 for a full day. English-speaking guides cost more, but all the local guides have received some instruction in English. Hiring them will give you the interpretive skills of a naturalist and also support a community-based project that ties rural self-development to conservation. Call 710-6580 at La Selva.

Across the road from the entrance to La Selva is the road to El Gavilán Lodge, which lies between the Sucio and Sarapiquí rivers. It has four rooms in a building near the dining room, and ten more in two-room bungalows. All have private baths and ceiling fans, some with central and some with shower-head hot water. Orchids decorate the spacious grounds, along with other flowering tropical plants. There is an outdoor Jacuzzi, a thatched *rancho* with hammocks and chairs for reading or watching the birds that visit the gardens, and a small open-air conference center.

Green coconuts, called *pipas* in Spanish, are served as natural refreshment, along with drinks from other fruits that grow there:

star fruit, oranges, guayabas, passion fruit, mangos, and pineapples. Cas is a favorite of mine.

Guests can choose from a variety of activities: horseback riding to a private forest reserve for $15 per person, a guided hike in the reserve for $15, a trip to the San Juan River and hiking in the forest for $60, and a boat trip on the Sarapiquí for $20. On the Sarapiquí, I saw crocodiles, iguanas, parrots, a great blue heron, and howler monkeys. The plant life along the banks was exuberant: fragrant heliotrope, colorful heliconias, vines trailing into the water.

Rates for bed and breakfast are $40 for a single and $30 each for a double. Credit cards are accepted only if you pay in San José. Lunch and dinner are $8 each. Packages include transportation, lodging, meals, a bilingual guide, boat rides, horseback riding and hiking. A one-day trip is $78, including either the boat ride or horseback riding; two days and one night is $150 with the boat ride and horseback riding; three days and two nights is $200 with a chance to hike as well. Telephone 234-9507, fax 253-6556.

Adventure companies in San José offer trips on area rivers. Trips to view wildlife along the banks are popular, too. If your hotel or lodge does not offer one, look for local entrepreneurs with boats in Puerto Viejo. In the days before roads, when waterways were the area's main transportation routes, some of the forty-niners made their way from the East Coast of the U.S. to California by traveling on the San Juan River through Lake Nicaragua to the Pacific. Though the river, which forms the boundary between Nicaragua and Costa Rica, is actually Nicaraguan territory, Costa Rica has a perpetual treaty right to use it.

You may also enter the north-central region through Braulio Carrillo National Park. Where the highway crosses the Sucio River as you drop down toward the lowlands, still inside the park, pull off to look at the joining of the Hondura River with the Sucio, which is dirty-looking because of mineral content carried from its origins on Irazú. The interplay of the blue and brown waters as they flow together is fascinating. There is a wide place to park after you cross the bridge. Travel on the Río Frío-Puerto Viejo de Sarapiquí bus will also let you see the joining of the rivers and will take you to some of the sites described in the Varablanca-Puerto Viejo section, providing a nice loop.

Just 2 miles (3 km) after the bridge over the Hondura and Sucio rivers is the entrance to El Tapir, which its owners call an eco-touristic reserve. Five trails, ranging from easy to hard, take you through premontane tropical rain forest. The 247-acre (100-ha) reserve is adjacent to Braulio Carrillo, so mammals that need large areas to survive can be found here, including the tapir and the jaguar. Species you are more likely to see include deer, armadillos, monkeys, coatis, and peccaries. The crested guan lives here, as do manakins, trogons, owls, tanagers, and hummingbirds. Boots and raincoats can be rented.

You can check on the status of bamboo and cane cabins being built by calling 226-2570. The entrance fee is $5. A natural history bilingual tour guide costs $15 per person for the day or $8 for half a day. If you do not take the guide, a security officer, costing $2 for a full day and $1 for half a day, will accompany you.

Not far away is the Rain Forest Aerial Tram project, which will let visitors experience the species-rich canopy of the rain forest on six-person cars passing into and above the treetops along an almost-mile-long route. Donald Perry, who is developing the project, describes it as a "school in the treetops." Walking trails will allow visitors a ground-level look into a lowland gallery forest. The target date for opening is May or June 1994. According to Perry, the restaurant, gift shop, tram, and at least one of the walking trails should be finished by then, as well as modest cabins. Half-day tram tours are expected to be about $50, full-day about $60. For more information, telephone or fax 225-8869; in the U.S., telephone (617) 239-3626, fax (617) 239-3610.

Bosque Lluvioso also offers a chance to walk in the rain forest—on five trails through some 86 acres (35 ha) of primary and secondary forest. It is open from 6 a.m. to 5:30 p.m. daily. Only 50 visitors are allowed per day, so make reservations. Telephone 224-0819 or 224-3820, fax 225-5646. An open-air restaurant serves breakfast from 7:30 to 10:00 a.m. and lunch from 12:30 to 2:30 p.m. The cost of a visit is $30 per person with lunch, $20 without. A self-guided trail and guides are also available. The entrance is east of Braulio Carrillo Park. Turn off the main highway at the Rancho Redondo road for about 2 miles (3 km) of unpaved road.

A turnoff to the north before Guapiles leads to Puerto Viejo via Las Horquetas. This is the jumping-off place for a visit to Rara Avis, a private nature reserve with glorious forest and an awe-inspiring waterfall—a trip for the adventurous. (See chapter 8.)

Past Las Horquetas, the road continues along the Puerto Viejo River to the town of Puerto Viejo. The pejibaye palm you will see is grown commercially for its fruit, which Costa Ricans love, and the heart (*palmito*), which is eaten raw or boiled. Try a palmito salad before you leave Costa Rica.

Northwest

Cloud forests, cattle ranches, miles of long beaches, deciduous dry forests—the area defined here as the northwest region contains fourteen national parks, reserves, and refuges, numerous privately owned reserves catering to the ecotourist, and more resort-type beach properties than any other section. This is the area with access off the Inter-American Highway north of Puntarenas, plus the Nicoya Peninsula.

Buses go to Puntarenas and all the way to Nicaragua and down into the peninsula; ferries cross the Gulf of Nicoya; scheduled domestic flights go to Tamarindo, Sámara, and Nosara; and taxis in many small towns fill in the blanks. (See Practical Extras.) Though the Inter-American Highway opens the biggest door, some travelers slip in the back way through the north-central region after a visit to the Arenal area.

From San José, the Inter-American Highway passes through pretty highland mountains and valleys of coffee, cows, and cane on the way to the warmer lowlands. A favorite stop of mine is just past the turnoff to San Ramón at a restaurant on the right called La Colina. The *gallo de picadillo de papa* (tortilla with a potato filling) or *gallo de arracache* is great for a snack, even for breakfast. Try agua dulce con leche, and do not miss the coconut *cajeta*— pure sugar and yummy. It is also fun to stop at roadside stands in Esparza to stretch your legs and give thanks for safely getting over the hair-raising stretch of winding road south of San Ramón that

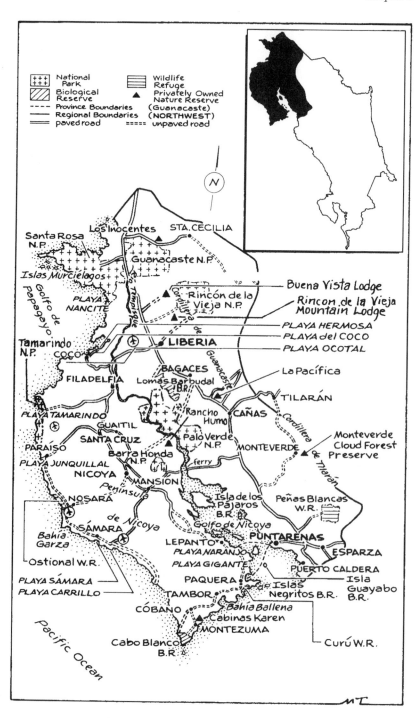

has yet to be widened. You will probably see some fruits you do not recognize, along with watermelons, pineapples, and avocados.

Puntarenas (population 38,274) is built on a narrow piece of land with an estuary on one side and the Gulf of Nicoya on the other. Its economy is based largely on fishing and tourism. You can get the car ferry across to Playa Naranjo here as well as a passenger boat or car ferry to Paquera, farther down the peninsula's coast.

Travelers who have never been to Costa Rica sometimes choose Puntarenas for their beach experience. This is the closest beach area to San José, but has had bad press because of polluted water and dirty beaches. However, the town has rolled up its sleeves to improve things—even buying a machine that regularly cleans the beaches. The waste treatment plant you see on the way into town has helped, as has a new aqueduct. Tests indicate that the water between the pier and the point is now OK. Whether you swim in the ocean or not, you can go to Puntarenas to experience a laid-back coastal lifestyle, walk along the oceanfront promenade, swim in a pretty hotel pool under a warm blue sky, and watch people, ships anchored offshore, and sunsets.

Among the most popular tours in the country are those offering a day on a yacht out of Puntarenas, cruising around islands in the Gulf of Nicoya (including the Guayabo, Pajaritos, and Negritos biological reserves), eating well, and swimming and snorkeling in the clear waters off the island selected for a lunch stop. Packages can include transportation from San José.

There are hotels for every budget. The generally cheaper rates in the low season, now called the "Green Season," may be even lower in beach areas. Puntarenas is popular with San Josefinos on weekends but is less crowded for midweek visits. The following are hotels you might consider.

Hotel Fiesta is the largest, with 191 rooms and suites. Rooms range from $112 for a standard single or double to $286 for the master suite. Credit cards are accepted. Rooms, some with ocean views, are spacious, with air conditioning and satellite TV. The hotel has a tour agency, casino, restaurants and bars, lighted tennis courts, Jacuzzi, volleyball courts, and a gym. It is located outside

Olive ridley turtle (Photo by Mayra Bonilla, courtesy of Audiovise, S.A.)

Puntarenas. Telephone 663-0185 or, in the U.S., (800) 662-2990 or (800) 228-5050; fax 663-1516.

Hotel Yadrán is in town on the tip of the peninsula at the end of Paseo de las Turistas. It has forty-three air-conditioned rooms, some carpeted and some tile, with satellite TV. Modern baths have central hot water, showers, and tubs. A single is $80, a double $95. Credit cards are accepted. There is a pool, restaurants, bicycle and car rental, and on-street guarded parking. Telephone 661-2662, fax 661-1944.

Hotel Porto Bello is along the estuary off the road from San José, not right downtown. The thirty-five rooms have air conditioning and fans, TV, in-room telephones, a large dressing table, and private baths with hot water (most with bathtubs). Each has a view of pretty tropical gardens. A single is $41, a double $55. Credit cards are accepted. There is a pool, mini-gym, and restaurant, and the hotel arranges yacht excursions in the Gulf of Nicoya. Telephone 661-1322 or 661-2122, fax 661-0036.

Next door is Hotel Colonial, with fifty-six rooms. Carpeted rooms have either a terrace or balcony, air conditioning, optional TV, large closets, and private baths, some with tubs and hot water. A single is $33, a double $56, breakfast included. Credit cards are accepted. There are pools, a tennis court, parking, a private dock, bar, restaurant, and disco bar. Telephone 661-1833 or 661-1834, fax 661-2969.

Hotel Tioga is downtown across the street from the palm-lined promenade and beach. (Beach umbrellas are gratis.) The forty-six rooms have air conditioning and private baths. Older rooms built around an interior courtyard with a pool do not have hot water. Singles are $30, doubles $38. Rates for newer, larger, rooms with hot water are $40 for a single, $50 for a double. Rooms with private balconies are $46 for a single, $57 for a double; breakfast is included. There is a wonderful selection of old photos in the hallways. The second-floor terrace cafe looks out on the ocean, the staff is friendly, and the on-street parking is guarded. Two-week packages for people older than 55 start at $1,050, not including airfare. Telephone 661-0271 or 255-3115, fax 661-0127 or 255-1006.

The two-story downtown Las Brisas Hotel has nineteen rooms and a small restaurant that serves excellent spaghetti along with salads, sandwiches, and other dishes. Bright rooms are in an L-shape building around the pool. There is no garden to speak of, but the promenade and beach are just across the street. A single is $35, a double $58. Credit cards are accepted. Private baths have solar and shower-head hot water. English, Italian, French, Greek, and Arabic also are spoken by the owners, the Saals. Telephone 661-4040, fax 661-1487.

Club de Playa San Isidro, off the road into Puntarenas, has forty-two rooms for up to four people for $52, with kitchenettes that include a hot plate, refrigerator, and dishes—but no hot water. Rooms have ceiling fans, and five are air-conditioned, A single is $42, a double $45, breakfast or lunch included. There is parking, and tours are arranged. Youth Hostel members get special rates when they make reservations through the Costa Rican Network of Youth Hostels in San José. The hotel has pools and a restaurant with a view of the ocean. Credit cards are accepted. Day visits cost $6 per person. Telephone 233-5027 or 223-0843, fax 221-6822.

If you are continuing on to the northwest, you will note vegetation changes as the Inter-American winds its way between the coastal zone and the mountains to the east.

Into drier Guanacaste Province, the question is not "When will the rains stop?" but "When will they start?" In the dry season, flowering red, white, pink, and yellow trees decorate a browner landscape. In any season, the national tree, the *guanacaste*, spreads its branches out like a great fan. Horses and cattle seek shade under its mimosa-type leaves in pasturelands.

The road to Monteverde turns right at the bridge over the Río Lagarto, at about kilometer 149. The bumpy 22-mile (36-km) route gives occasional breathtaking views of the lowlands below as you climb on roads that seem to hang by grace along the edge of the mountains. As you wind through thin clouds, cows across deep valleys look like brown and white dots scattered on the steep pastures. The slow going gives you plenty of time to enjoy it. An alternate route, also unpaved, leaves the Inter-American before Lagarto, going through Sardinal and joining the Lagarto road past Guacimal.

The progressive community of Monteverde is itself worth a visit. It was established in 1951 by Quakers from North America drawn by Costa Rica's disarmed environment. They set up a business that now makes some the finest cheeses in the country. The Quakers bought milk from neighboring farmers and invited them to become shareholders—today there are more than 400, including milk producers, employees, and neighbors. You can visit the modern dairy plant, La Lechería, Monday through Saturday from 7:30 a.m. to 4:00 p.m.; on Sunday, it closes at 12:30 p.m. Visitors may watch cheese-makers through a glass partition beside the sales room.

The CASEM gift shop sells locally handcrafted items, many with intricate embroidery or weaving. Save some of your souvenir shopping for here; the hand-painted cards and stationery make beautiful, easy-to-carry gifts. Designs used on the textiles and paper goods are drawn from the area's rich biological diversity: quetzals, bellbirds, golden toads. The craft cooperative, whose sales directly benefit local residents, is open from 8:00 a.m. to 5:00 p.m. Monday through Saturday, 10:00 a.m. to 4:00 p.m. on Sundays. Next door is Coope Santa Elena's coffee-roasting operation; stop in and try Café Monteverde.

The Monteverde Conservation League is a nonprofit conservation organization founded in 1986. It works in land acquisition, forest protection, reforestation, research, small-scale sustainable-development projects, information, conservation of flora and fauna, and environmental education. The league also operates tree nurseries and works with local schools and community groups. One of its most exciting projects is Bosque Eterno de los Niños, the first international children's rain forest. The league office, near the gasoline station, is open from 8:00 a.m. to noon and 1:00 to 5:00 p.m. weekdays, 8:00 a.m. to noon on Saturdays.

For $3, visitors can wander along a privately owned nature trail managed by the league, the Sendero Bajo del Tigre, which is part of the children's rain forest. Open from 8:00 a.m. to 5:00 p.m. daily, the trail goes through forest and around a beginning arboretum in an old pasture. The haunting notes of the long-tailed manakin and the raucous sounds of the bellbird sometimes predominate, and monkeys and coatis live here, too. The information booth at the entrance has material on league programs and gift items for sale. Ask about visiting other sectors of Bosque Eterno de los Niños.

There are a growing number of options for the nature traveler in Monteverde. See chapter 8 for information about the Monteverde Cloud Forest Preserve, a private biological reserve that has attracted visitors since 1972. A newer kid on the block is the Santa Elena Forest Reserve, which is also cloud forest habitat. It has 5 miles (8 km) of trails at an elevation of 5,600 feet (1,700 m). One of the trails has a view point where hikers can see Arenal Volcano—when the weather cooperates. Guided walks are available, and you can rent rubber boots. The reserve, 3 miles (5 km) northeast of Santa Elena, is open from 7:00 a.m. to 4:00 p.m. daily. The entrance fee is $5 per person; a guided walk costs about $7 more.

For a glorious experience with butterflies, visit the Monteverde Butterfly Garden. The entrance fee of $5 for adults and $3 for children entitles you to a walk with well-trained guides through a botanical garden that includes a host of plants from the area providing habitat for breathtaking butterflies. Afterward, you can have as much time as you want to walk along the paths or sit alone to watch or photograph the free-flying butterflies. It is a magical

INTERNATIONAL CHILDREN'S RAIN FOREST

Once upon a timle, there was a teacher from the United States who came to Monteverde, Costa Rica, to do biological research. Her enthusiasm for the rain forest and her concern about its destruction found its way into a small primary school far, far away in rural Sweden. There, a class of nine-year-olds wondered if there were something they could do to save the tall trees, the pretty waterfalls, and the many animals who made their homes in the tropical forest. With their teacher, they decided there was. The children wrote a play and presented it for their parents; they drew cards and sold them; they gave from their allowances. That money was sent to the Monteverde Conservation League, a group of people who were working hard to protect the threatened rain forest. It was enough to buy 15 acres (6 ha).

The idea of a rain forest saved by children for children spread to other schools in Sweden, to Maine where the biology teacher lived, to schools in England and Germany. Now, children in other European countries, in Japan, and in Africa —more than 37 countries in all— are lending a hand. They ask for donations instead of birthday presents, collect materials for recycling, and sponsor "green days." The result is Bosque Eterno de los Niños (the Children's Eternal Forest), the first international children's rain forest in the world.

Since it was established in 1989,

the children's rain forest has grown to cover thousands of acres of virgin forest. The Peñas Blancas River flows through this rugged land, whose steep slopes are unsuitable for farms or cattle. Living in this lush vegetation are quetzals, monkeys, bare-necked umbrella birds, ocelots, jaguars, and tapirs. Long vines trail to the forest floor. Some species of plants have yet to be identified.

As children learn about this piece of forest in Costa Rica and why it is important, they begin to think in a new way about their own environment. Often, their parents join in the campaign. One day, an educational center in Bosque Eterno de los Niños will bring together local children and children from around the world to learn more about natural history and each other. Research stations, where people learn about the tropical forest, are open already.

You can become a Rain Forest Partner with Bosque Eterno de los Niños. Long-term protection of the rain forest is more than buying land. It means patrols by forest guards, environmental programs in neighboring schools and communities, planting trees. Donations of any size can help. For $50, partners receive a certificate. Send contributions to:

Monteverde Conservation League
Apartado 10581-1000
San José, Costa Rica
Telephone 645-5003, fax 645-5104

place. Owner Jim Wolfe, a biologist, has lived in the area for years and is glad to share fascinating tidbits about insects, plants, and their relationships. The information center includes displays of butterflies and other insects—you can even look at butterfly wings under a microscope. You may get to see a butterfly emerge from its pupal case. There is a small gift shop; the shirts with the elegant butterfly designs are the work of Marta Iris, the other half of the ownership. The garden is open from 9:30 a.m. to 4:00 p.m. daily.

Other small reserves include Reserva Sendero Tranquilo, near the Monteverde Cloud Forest Preserve, which offers guided walks; Finca Ecológica, a 43-acre (17-ha) farm with forest and a view of a waterfall ($5), open from 7:00 a.m. to 3:00 p.m.; and Hidden Valley Nature Trail, past the butterfly garden, a mile-long (2 km) trail through a rainy-to-drier transition forest.

Some hotels and private guides offer night walks in the reserves. A 7:15 p.m. walk at the Monteverde Cloud Forest Preserve costs $12. Call 645-5118. The experience is dramatically different from daytime walks: nocturnal animals, glowing mushrooms, rain frogs, and a world of insects. Perhaps you will see the endemic golden-kneed tarantula, a beauty.

Gifts shops, restaurants, and pensions and hotels are located in and around Monteverde and Santa Elena and are strung along the road all the way to the Monteverde Cloud Forest Preserve. Art galleries include Sarah Dowell's studio (up the hill from the cheese plant) and the Hummingbird Gallery at the preserve (photographs by Michael and Patricia Fogden).

Check at one of the information centers in Santa Elena if you do not have hotel reservations, because hotels are small and scattered. The information centers are located near the bank, not far from where the buses pull in.

The Daiquiri restaurant in "downtown" Santa Elena has good food at a reasonable price, as does El Tucan, a block from the bank.

Santa Elena has a variety of lodging options. Just outside town is the Monteverde Lodge. The hotel has a fifteen-person Jacuzzi, a huge wood-burning fireplace in the bar/restaurant area, chandeliers, bathtubs, a good gift shop, and views of the surrounding forest through large windows. The gardens were designed to attract hummingbirds and other wildlife. Nature slide shows are presented several nights each week in a small auditorium. The hotel offers transportation to the reserve for $4 and bus service from San José on specified days for $35. Rubber boots are available for your walks in the cloud forest. The twenty-seven rooms are bright and comfortably furnished. Singles are $77, doubles $89. Credit cards are accepted. Meal plans are available. Ask about a three-day, two-night tour with a bilingual naturalist. Monteverde Lodge is owned by Costa Rica Expeditions. Telephone 257-0766, fax 257-1665.

A bit more than a mile (2 km) on the other side of Santa Elena is the Cloud Forest Lodge, eighteen rooms in nine guest houses on a 70-acre (28-ha) farm. The two rooms in each house are separated by a concrete wall to cut sound between them. Each has a good-sized tile bath with high windows for nice natural lighting. Rooms have natural-tone tile floors, a private terrace, and high wooden ceilings. The large, separate dining room/lounge area, made of wood and stone, has a grand balcony with a view of the Gulf of Nicoya and surrounding forest. A botanical garden is in the works, and there are about 2 miles (3 km) of forest trails for guests only— with no charge for ponchos and boots. The restaurant features international food; in the afternoon, guests are treated to complimentary pastries and beverages. No smoking is allowed in buildings or on trails. Room rates are $69 for up to two people. Credit cards are accepted. Telephone or fax 645-5058; in the U.S., telephone (415) 949-1064, fax (415) 949-1068.

Hotel Finca Valverde in Santa Elena has two-room wooden cabins set on a forested hillside, close to town but looking for all the world as if they are remote. Each of the ten pleasing rooms has a loft so it can comfortably sleep up to four—a very open feeling. Private baths have showers and tubs. Singles are $40, doubles $52. Credit cards are accepted. The restaurant/bar is open to the public.

Platforms some 100 feet (30 m) high in forest giants near the cabins allow canopy observation at $40 for four hours. The hitch is that you climb up there on ropes and move between the trees by cable. On a short forest trail on the property, one naturalist saw sixty species of birds in two days. A serpentarium is next door. Guests can even help pick coffee at harvest time—it is a farm, after all. The Valverdes offer tours to the Santa Elena reserve and will arrange transportation anywhere in the country. Tickets for the San José bus are sold here. Five Valverde brothers and one sister have a hand in the operation, which is on the farm where they were raised. Telephone or fax 645-5157.

Arco Iris Ecolodge, on one of Santa Elena's hills, must surely have good views of some of the spectacular rainbows (*arco iris* means "rainbow") that grace this high land. Owner Haymo Heyder is working to make the lodge a model of ecologically sound development. He uses natural concoctions rather than insecticides, is putting in solar hot water systems, and is developing an organic garden with his wife to supply produce for the small restaurant. The eleven rooms are in various buildings—one in a cabin at the edge of the forest and a small stream is called either the honeymoon or presidential cabin. It is special—windows on three sides and a porch facing the forest. All rooms have private baths with hot water, big towels, and ample windows. Prices range from $8.50 per person for bunk beds to $40 for a double. Credit cards are accepted. English, German, Dutch, and Italian also are spoken. Telephone 645-5067, fax 645-5022.

Pensión El Sueño, a block off the main street, has ten rooms with private baths and shower-head hot water. Furnishings are basic, but the atmosphere is friendly. The cost is $25 per person including breakfast and dinner. Credit cards are not accepted. Horse rental is $6 per hour, and transportation can be provided to the Santa Elena or Monteverde reserves as well as pickup from the Arenal-La Fortuna area. Rubber boots are available. Telephone 645-5021.

Just out of Santa Elena on the road toward Monteverde is El Sapo Dorado. Its twenty charming rooms in ten bungalows are tucked among fruit trees and gardens in a clearing surrounded by forest. Each room has a quiet, spacious feel to it, with a pretty table and chairs and two queen-size beds. Some have corner fireplaces, with wood provided. Newer bungalows have large terraces in front. The restaurant, open to the public, offers gourmet dining. Daily specials may include sailfish Nicoise, beef in peppercorn sauce, or chicken in olive sauce. A vegetarian dish is always available. Desserts are scrumptious. Doubles are $69, plus $13 for each additional person. El Sapo Dorado does not accept credit cards. Telephone or fax 645-5010.

Several hotels are in the Cerro Plano area between Santa Elena and Monteverde. Hotel Heliconia is a two-story hotel that started out as a small pensión, but its growth to twenty-one rooms has not diminished its friendly atmosphere. Curtains hand-painted with designs of local flora and fauna grace each room. The large downstairs lobby and lounge area has lots of comfortable couches for conversations before or after dinner. The pleasant rooms are carpeted; private baths have tubs and showers. A single is $44, a double $52. Credit cards are accepted. Floor-to-ceiling glass in the Jacuzzi room gives it a forest setting. There is a small conference room, and the dining room is open to the public, by reservation. The bar is new. The Heliconia runs afternoon and evening tours to Arenal Volcano for $80 per person. Transportation can be provided to or from anywhere in the country. Telephone 645-5109, fax 645-5007.

Next door is El Establo, a nineteen-room, two-story hotel with its own stables. Carpeted rooms have pretty comforters on beds with orthopedic mattresses, two stylized dressing tables with mirrors, lots of windows, and tiled baths with central hot water. A single is $52, a double $57. Credit cards are accepted. The restaurant is for guests only. Wonderful photos of the early Quaker settlement in Monteverde are in a comfortable downstairs lounge area with a fireplace. A three-day, two-night package from San José that takes guests to Poás and Sarchí on the way to Monteverde is $320 per person double occupancy, including transportation, lodging, meals, and taxes. Telephone 645-5110, 645-5033 or 225-0569, fax 645-5041.

Hotel de Montaña Monteverde has thirty-one rooms, a small conference room, an indoor Jacuzzi with a great view of forested mountains and the Gulf of Nicoya, a TV room, a lounge area with balcony and rocking chairs, and a bar, also with a gulf view. Doors to the rooms are decorated with painted butterflies and birds, and each room opens onto a terrace and pretty gardens with flowering plants. A single is $46, a double $69. The honeymoon suite ($126) has its own Jacuzzi and balcony. The dining room is open to the public. The hotel has a nature trail to a small lagoon, rents horses, and offers transportation to and from San José. Telephone 645-5046 or 224-3050, fax 645-6079 or 222-6184.

The Pensión Manakin has grown to twenty rooms, each with private tiled bath and hot water. Windows make rooms bright, and they are very clean. There is a family atmosphere: Mario and Yolanda and their four children are caring hosts. Good typical food is served in the dining room. A single is $12, a double $24. Credit cards are not accepted. Telephone 645-5080, fax 645-5042.

The Monteverde Inn is off the main road past the butterfly garden on a 28-acre (11-ha) farm. It has ten simply furnished rooms (a bit on the rustic side), eight with private baths and hot water. Hundreds of fruit trees attract birds and mammals, and the Hidden Valley Nature Trail starts here. Horses are $5 per hour. A room and meals costs $24 per person. Telephone 645-5156.

Cabanas Los Pinos' six bungalows have kitchenettes equipped with refrigerator, hot plate, and dishes, all spotlessly clean. One bedroom costs $32, two bedrooms $60, three bedrooms $80. Private baths have central hot water. No credit cards are accepted. The sound of the wind in the pines pervades the grounds; each bungalow is very private, set among the trees. Guests are free to explore the forest and the farm. Don Jovino, the owner, offers a horseback tour to the Santa Elena Reserve and to a view point overlooking Arenal, rents horses, and helps arrange transportation. Telephone 645-5005.

Farther along is the Hotel Belmar, up the road next to the gasoline station. The thirty-four rooms are in two Swiss chalet-type buildings with a commanding view of the slopes of the Tilaran Mountains going down to the Gulf of Nicoya. Guests have reported seeing monkeys and even a quetzal from the balconies. Rooms are large and tastefully furnished, with matching comforters and upholstered armchairs. Many have private balconies; all have private baths with central hot water. Singles are $46, doubles $57. No credit cards are accepted, but personal checks are. There is a lounge area in each building. Meals are served family-style in a large dining room. The hotel arranges transportation, horseback riding, guided tours to the forest (with rubber boots for rent), and laundry service. English and German also are spoken. Telephone 645-5201, fax 645-5135.

El Bosque Hotel and Restaurant are in Monteverde near the CASEM gift shop. The twenty-one rooms are in buildings curved around a clearing off the main road, surrounded by trees. Each opens onto a covered porch and has tile floors, rough white-plaster walls, a high wooden ceiling, and a private bath with hot water. Bright bedspreads add color. Singles are $20, doubles $28, Visa is accepted. The hotel has a small conference room and its own short nature trail. Guests get a 10 percent discount in the Bosque Restaurant, which has been a favorite in Monteverde for several years. The Vargas family will treat you well. Telephone or fax 645-5129.

Across the bridge and up the hill past the dairy plant is Pensión Flor Mar. Lodgings are on the rustic side in this friendly, family-run operation. Three of the thirteen rooms have private baths; several have bunk beds. The cost per person, including three meals, is $24 for rooms with shared baths, $28 for private baths. Credit cards are not accepted. The Flor Mar also has areas for tent camping, at $1.50 per person. Telephone 645-5009, fax 645-5088.

Past the main Monteverde community going toward the Monteverde Cloud Forest Preserve are two hotels. The Fonda Vela is on the 25-acre (10-ha) Smith farm. The twenty-eight rooms are in buildings situated to give maximum privacy, surrounding forest that offers ample opportunity for bird-watching without leaving the hotel—more than sixty species have been noted in a book kept at the reception desk. Guests can go on hiking trails through forest on the farm and on guided horseback rides ($8 an hour for one person, $7 each for two to five people).

Rooms are lovely, with several floor plans. Most are spacious, and have gleaming wood floors with area rugs, and nice bedspreads. Artwork by Paul Smith is on the walls and in the gallery. Single standard rooms are $55, doubles $63. Junior suites start at $71, double occupancy, suites at $80. Credit cards are accepted. Meals in the restaurant are $4.50 for breakfast, $6.50 for lunch, and $8.50 for dinner, plus tax. A big open dining room and bar addition has lots of glass—a small stage offers opportunities for musical presentations. There is a gift shop. Telephone 257-1413, 223-1083 or 645-5125, fax 257-1416, telephone or fax 645-5119.

Hotel Villa Verde has twenty-two rooms, all with private tiled baths and shower-head hot water. Singles are $41, doubles $52. Family suites starting at $75 have kitchenettes, a tub and shower in the bathroom, and a fireplace. Visa and MasterCard are accepted. Furnishings are simple. The hotel offers nature films in the conference rooms, horseback rides, and transportation, even to other areas of the country. Telephone 645-5025, fax 645-5115.

A number of small sodas along the road between Santa Elena and Monteverde serve good, inexpensive food: The Cerro Verde across from the gasoline station is one possibility. For restaurants, the Cascada has a varied menu (it is popular with locals on weekends, and has floor space for dancing), and it and El Bosque have both indoor and outdoor dining. Stella's Bakery and Coffee Shop is across from CASEM. Less than 2 miles (4 km) from Santa Elena is the rural community of Canitas and El Trapiche Sugar Mill and Restaurant—typical food at its best in a picturesque setting beside a sugar mill. On Saturdays, you can watch the operation (and buy fresh cane sugar) from 10:00 a.m. to 5:00 p.m., at $5 per person. Call 645-5271 to check. The small gift shop next door sells locally made handcrafts.

The schedule for the direct San José-Monteverde bus changes with the season, so check with ICT or call the bus company at 222-3854. The afternoon bus from San José, arrives after dark; bring a flashlight to find your way to the hotel from the main road. The driver will call out the name of your hotel so you will know where to get off. Though the bus passes in front of many hotels, others require a walk; ask about this when you make your reservation. For example, both El Sapo Dorado and the Belmar have uphill climbs from the main road. The bus stops first in Santa Elena before proceeding as far as the dairy plant in Monteverde. At this writing, a second company is starting direct service from San José, leaving Toruma Youth Hostel at 7:00 a.m. and Santa Elena at 2:00 p.m. Call 224-4085 or 645-5051 for information. Public buses from Puntarenas and Tilarán go only as far as Santa Elena, but taxis are available there. Walter Mendez, a thoughtful and delightful person, has a thirteen-passenger jeep that can take you around the area or elsewhere in Costa Rica. Telephone 664-5137. Again, if you are coming by bus and do not have a hotel reservation, it is best to make one at the information center in Santa Elena.

Back north on the Inter-American Highway, 11 miles (18 km) past the Monteverde cutoff at Río Lagarto is a sign pointing to the Tempisque ferry, which carries cars and passengers to the Nicoya Peninsula.

The next major town on the Inter-American is Cañas; 2.5 miles (4 km) farther is La Pacífica Ecological Center, which has a restaurant open to the public and offers day tours of its ranch and natural history areas. (See chapter 8 for specifics.) Next door is the Restaurant Rincón Coribicí on the banks of the Coribicí River, a river-rafting option. While dining on the open terrace facing the water, with a grand view of Tenorio Volcano, you can appreciate why birders like this area.

Also next door to La Pacífica is Safaris Corobicí, which offers a bird-watcher's special on the Corobicí: $35 for a two-hour float trip, $43 for three hours to the Catalina entrance of Palo Verde. There is also a five-hour family float trip for $60 per person. Children under 14 accompanied by an adult are half-price on all trips. A half-day salt-water estuary trip for $50 takes you by boat to the border of Palo Verde, into the Tempisque River. Telephone or fax 669-1091.

Another grand river trip is offered by Cata Tours on the Bebedero, which flows into the Tempisque just before it opens out into the Gulf of Nicoya. You will see crocodiles and birds galore, and probably monkeys, too. Three hours on the river with a bilingual guide is $45 from Cañas, $89 from San José; a full-day tour that follows the Bebedero to the Tempisque, Isla de Pájaros, and on to Palo Verde is $75 from Cañas, $103 from San José, including lunch. Telephone 296-2133, fax 296-2730, telephone or fax 669-1026.

The next town of any size along the Inter-American is Bagaces (population 7,431). The Miravalles geothermal project is east of town. Here is also where you turn west for Palo Verde National Park; a bit farther north is the road to Lomas Barbudal Biological Reserve. Both of these are wonderful natural history destinations. As a matter of fact, there is a back road that connects the park and the reserve, basically unmarked. I tried it and the beginning was marvelous: roseate spoonbills galore dotted the rice fields. Farther along, however, as night approached and the muddy ruts got deeper on what became little more than a track through isolated fields, I kept thinking, "This cannot be the road to Lomas Barbudal," and it wasn't. I had missed a turn. Perhaps you follow directions better than I do.

For good directions and information on either Palo Verde, Lomas Barbudal or Barra Honda National Park, stop at the office of the Tempisque Conservation Area in Bagaces, in a white house on the highway next to the gasoline station, just across from the road to Palo Verde. You can also call or fax the office for information, 671-1062 or 223-6963.

The big ditches you see are part of the government's ambitious Arenal-Tempisque irrigation project to supply Guanacaste farms with water. By the time the water gets to the lowlands, it has already generated electricity three times: at the Arenal, Corocibí, and Sandillal hydroelectric plants. The project benefits more than 1,000 farm families, providing water to almost 45,000 acres (18,000 ha) that otherwise would be dry for half the year.

Four miles (6 km) north of Bagaces, before the turnoff to Lomas Barbudal, is Albergue Las Sillas, a shady refuge under the Guanacaste sun. The small lodge is on a large cattle ranch with more than 2,200 acres (900 ha) of secondary forest populated by deer, tepezcuintle, howler monkeys, and more than thirty-five species of birds. It is a good base from which to visit Palo Verde, Lomas Barbudal, Miravalles Volcano, and Lake Arenal. Guests can go horseback riding, take a dip in two rivers on the ranch or in the swimming pool, or hike on forest trails. The five rooms are small and simply furnished (two shared baths and one private), but porches are expansive, with lots of chairs (*sillas*), and a few hammocks. The dining room and comfortable living room area have a spacious feeling. The double rooms with shared bath cost $30 for one person, $48 for two, with a sumptuous breakfast included. A room for four with private bath, but no hot water, is $72. Credit cards are not accepted. Lunch and dinner are $10 each. Telephone 671-1030, telephone or fax 221-2101.

Liberia, capital of the Province of Guanacaste, is 16 miles (26 km) north of Bagaces, 154 miles (248 km) from San José. Two of the volcanoes in the Guanacaste range break the horizon: Miravalles and Rincón de la Vieja. It is sometimes referred to as the White City because the early adobe houses got a coating of the area's abundant lime. Note the unusual architectural feature of old houses that have two doors on their northeast corners, with views of the rising sun and twilight, giving long hours of natural daylight inside. An information center at El Sabanero Museum, Casa de la Cultura, is in a house with these *puertas del sol*. Signs will direct you to the 150-year-old building three blocks from the park. It is open Monday through Saturday from 9:00 a.m. to 6:00 p.m., Sundays from 9:00 a.m. to noon. The small museum contains memorabilia related to the cowboy (or *sabanero*) and early life in this "Wild West" region. Friendly staff members can make reservations for you, and they have photos of many of the hotels and lodges in the area. Telephone 666-1606.

With a population of 30,191, Liberia is the commercial center and a transportation hub for the area. Perhaps planes will be landing at the new Tomás Guardia International Airport west of town

El Sabanero Museum and information center in Liberia (Photo by Ree Strange Sheck)

at Llano Grande by the time you arrive. There is a highway to the Nicoya Peninsula and beach resorts on the Pacific. Direct San José-Liberia buses run about every two hours during the day and take four hours.

Day trips to Santa Rosa, Rincón de la Vieja and Palo Verde national parks and Tamarindo wildlife refuge are possible from Liberia, as well as visits to beaches such as Ocotal, Hermosa, Coco, and Tamarindo. Three hotels near the highway arrange car rentals, help arrange tours, and accept credit cards.

Hotel Las Espuelas' forty-four rooms have private baths with hot water. Singles are $67, doubles $89. Polished floor tiles gleam along covered walkways leading from the lobby and restaurant/bar areas through landscaped grounds to wings of rooms named for nearby parks and reserves. Rooms are bright and air-conditioned, with cable TV. There is a large pool in the garden, and tennis courts. An in-house tour company with ecologically knowledge-able guides can get you to Santa Rosa and Guanacaste parks, Rincón de la Vieja, or Miravalles for $70, Tamarindo or Ostional for $60, and Arenal or Monteverde for $90. A float trip on the Corobicí is $60. Telephone 666-0144; in the U.S. and Canada, (800)-245-8420; fax 225-3987. Las Espuelas is now part of Costa Sol International.

Hotel El Sitio has fifty-two rooms opening onto landscaped grounds, a restaurant that serves both international and Costa Rican food, a pool, gift shop, gym, parking, and a rancho-style bar. Some rooms have air conditioning, and some have fans; all have private baths with shower-head hot water. A single is $63, a double $75. French, Italian, German and English, are also spoken. El Sitio rents bicycles, cars, and horses, and also offers riding lessons. Telephone 666-1211, fax 666-2059.

Right at the junction of the Inter-American with the road to the beaches is El Bramadero, a twenty-three-room hotel with a restau-rant that is popular with locals as well as travelers. Rooms with pri-vate baths are around a courtyard with a pool—both have had a face-lift, so if you have stayed here before, you will be pleasantly surprised. El Bramadero offers car and bike rental. Rooms with fans are $24 for up to two people; with air conditioning, they are

$34. Telephone 666-0203, fax 666-0371. The office of Guanacaste Tours, which offers natural history tours throughout the province, is in the Hotel Bramadero. (See chapter 9.)

Fourteen miles (23 km) up the road from Liberia to the head-quarters of Rincón de la Vieja National Park is a turnoff to Rinconcito Lodge, a small, rustic overnight option for visitors to the park. As my trustworthy 1977 Toyota and I lurched down the steep, incredibly rocky incline, I said to myself again, "This cannot be the road." But it was. The 1.8-mile (3-km) stretch is definitely four-wheel-drive. Better yet, let the owners transport you from Liberia for $30—an unqualified bargain considering the road. Five double rooms and two basic baths, without hot water, are in a house in a large clearing. No-frills rooms are $10 per person. Credit cards are not accepted. Lighting is by kerosene lamp, but a small hydro plant is planned. The small dining room down the hill serves typical Costa Rican food. (Breakfast is $4, lunch and dinner $6). A horseback trip to the park is $7. There is a river pool for swimming, a tree where keel-billed toucans hang out, and a chance to join in ranch activities. The lodge is also about 5 miles (8 km) from Miravalles Volcano. Telephone 666-0636 or 666-1889.

Just a little more than a mile (2 km) past the turnoff to Rinconcito is the ranger station for Rincón de la Vieja National Park. The drive from Liberia to the park entrance takes about an hour to an hour and a half. (See chapter 7 for what you will find there as well as at the entrance off the Inter-American Highway on the other side of Liberia, going through Curubandé.)

Two lodging possibilities exist between Curubandé and the park entrance. Eleven miles (18 km) past the turnoff to Curubandé is Hacienda Lodge Guachipelín, a 110-year-old ranch house with eight rooms, shared baths with no hot water, and a dining room. The ranch, with both dairy and beef cattle, also has primary forest where guests can enjoy forest walks. The lodge offers tours to the three main craters of the Rincón de la Vieja Volcano, the Jilgueros Lagoon, Las Pailas (the mud pots), sulfur springs, and the Hidden Waterfall. Horse rental is $15 for half a day, $22 for all day. Local guides are available. A single is $15, a double $35. Credit cards are not accepted. Breakfast and lunch are $6.50 each; dinner $8.

Transportation is available from Liberia. Telephone 441-6545 or 441-6994, fax 442-1910.

See chapter 8 for a description of another lodging possibility: Rincón de la Vieja Mountain Lodge, which borders on the park and has its own forest.

At the gate into the Hacienda Guachipelín, you will be charged about $2 whether your destination is one of the lodges or the park itself because the road is private.

Another park neighbor with a private reserve and lodging is the delightful Buena Vista Lodge, about 20 miles (31 km) from Liberia, turning off the Inter-American at Cañas Dulces. (See chapter 8.)

Santa Rosa and Guanacaste national parks are farther north. A paved road goes all the way to Santa Rosa headquarters and the historical La Casona. Guanacaste National Park has overnight facilities. (See chapter 7.) Visits to both are offered by nature tour companies and through hotels and private nature reserves in the area.

Near Cuajiniquil, which is off the Inter-American at the northern end of Santa Rosa, is Junquillal Recreation Area, an example of the integration of local communities into the management and use of natural resources. A restaurant operated by the people of Cuajiniquil puts money into the community, as do horse and boat rentals. Trails take visitors into the 1,248 acres (505 ha) of tropical dry forest. Junquillal Beach is down a dirt road passable without four-wheel drive; it is isolated, with tranquil waters, and forest. You can call the Guanacaste Conservation Area (695-5598) for information about Santa Rosa, Guanacaste, and Junquillal.

A delightful private nature reserve called Los Inocentes (see chapter 8) is east of the Inter-American, down a paved road from La Cruz. You can continue past Los Inocentes to Santa Cecilia and on to Upala.

Meanwhile, back in Liberia, some travelers choose the road southwest, Highway 21, for a visit to the beaches, historical towns, and nature reserves on the Nicoya Peninsula. Playa del Coco, the first beach area on that road, is a popular destination for ticos. A bus from San José and several from Liberia run daily to Playa del Coco. A number of rustic lodging places are right on the beach there.

Hotel Luna Tica has thirty-seven rooms. A single is $17, a double $20, breakfast included. Credit cards are not accepted. A restaurant, fans, and car and bicycle rentals are available, but there is no hot water. Telephone 670-0279, fax 670-0392.

Hotel La Flor de Itabo is not on the water, but it offers comfortable accommodations. It has eight rooms plus five bungalows with kitchens, and some large apartments, all with hot water. Doubles are $65, bungalows $85. Credit cards are accepted. The owners also speak English, French, German, and Italian. Facilities include a restaurant, casino, and pool. Some rooms are air-conditioned; others have fans. The hotel arranges scuba diving, fishing, and horseback riding trips and one-day excursions to nearby beaches, Palo Verde, the Tempisque River, Lomas Barbudal, the geothermal project at Miravalles Volcano, and Rincón de la Vieja. Telephone 670-0438 or 670-0011, fax 670-0003.

Just north of Playa del Coco is Playa Hermosa, where it is not uncommon to see dolphins in the bay or howler monkeys moving through the trees, especially in the dry season. There is a daily express bus from San José. A taxi from Liberia costs about $18. Here are several lodging possibilities; English is spoken at all, and car rental is available.

Hotel Condovac La Costa. A single or double is $120 in high season There are fifty-four rooms with air conditioning and fans, and 101 air-conditioned villas with bedroom, living room, bath, kitchenette, and terrace overlooking the bay. Credit cards are accepted. The hotel also has pools, tennis, a restaurant, disco, mini-market, tour agency, poolside bars, and beachfront. Motorized carts take guests around the hillside resort complex. Also available is transportation to parks and from San José, scuba diving (including classes), snorkeling, sport fishing, jet-skiing, waterskiing, sailboating, and boat tours, plus kayaking, windsurfing, tennis, and hiking. The hotel has a day trip to a secluded beach where guests can swim, explore, and enjoy a barbecue. Telephone 221-8949 or 233-1862, fax 222-5637.

Hotel de Playa el Velero, owned and operated by French Canadians, has twelve rooms. *Velero* means sailboat, and the hotel has one of its own for a variety of activities: a trip to Catalina Island with a gourmet lunch and cocktail for $45, scuba and snorkeling excursions (including scuba classes), and a sunset cruise. Tours go to Arenal/Coter Lake, Monteverde, or Palo Verde for $75, an ostrich ranch and Santa Rosa park for $65, or Rincón de la Vieja for $55. Rooms are light and airy, with nice closet space, tile floors, ceiling fans, and hot water in private baths. The restaurant is open to the public, and there is a bar at poolside in a garden setting. A single or double is $76. Credit cards are accepted. When I was there, music from the dining room drifted to the rooms, but it was nice music. The staff is helpful. Telephone or fax 670-0310.

Playa Hermosa Inn has eight rooms with fans plus two air-conditioned apartments with two bedrooms, kitchenette, and balcony. A single is $40, a double $46, including continental breakfast and private baths with hot water. The apartment is $86 for two. Credit cards are accepted. There is an air of quiet relaxation from the moment one enters the reception area with its comfortable furniture and view of the garden and beach beyond. A covered pavilion by the water has hammocks and chairs, and there is a grill where guests can cook their catch of the day. Only breakfast is served, but restaurants are nearby. Car rental and secure parking are available. Since the owner, Pioneer Tours, also has Pioneer Raft, rafting tours are easily arranged. There also are diving and snorkeling tours, fishing, and visits to nearby parks. Italian and French are spoken, too. Telephone or fax 670-0163, or in the U.S., (800) 288-2107.

Cabinas Playa Hermosa is a quiet, laid back place that has twenty rooms with private baths and shower-head hot water. The rooms are basic but clean, with tile floors and screened windows. Two white-faced monkeys roam the gardens, as does a pair of coatis —offering good photo opportunities. A single or double is $35, including breakfast and either lunch or dinner. Credit cards are not accepted. The restaurant is open to the public and specializes in Italian food. A small boat for up to seven people is available for fishing or tours. Horse rental is $7, with a trip possible to a nearby farm with tropical dry forest where you may see monkeys and trogons. Tours can be arranged to area parks. Telephone or fax 670-0136.

On Playa Panama a bit farther down the road from Playa Hermosa is Sula Sula Beach Resort, a large area along the coast with space for tent camping. The cost is about $4 per person, including latrines, showers, and picnic tables. Six cabins are scattered under the trees, with more planned. One that can sleep four is $46, and one that can sleep five is $60, both with furnished kitchenettes. Credit cards are accepted. The cabins, simply furnished, have ceiling fans, tile floors, private baths with hot water, and screened windows. Brightly colored mouthless crabs are abundant here. The thatched, open-air restaurant is open to the public. Telephone 670-0492.

Some new hotels in an ambitious government-directed project in the works since 1974 may be open by the time you arrive. The Gulf of Papagayo project along seventeen beaches, mainly on Culebra Bay, projects hundreds of hotel rooms, a marina, golf courses, vacation homes, and shopping centers. The project is considered a measuring stick for the government's commitment to environmentally responsible tourism.

Just 2 miles (3 km) from Playa del Coco is Ocotal Beach, small and beautiful. The tide pools are fascinating here. At the north end of the beach, caves shoot the water of the incoming tide back out with tremendous force. Big Guanacaste iguanas are almost always moving about at the edge of the sandy beach.

Hotel Ocotal has a spectacular view of coastline and sea from its rooms and restaurant on the cliff above the beach. Sunset from here is an occasion. Each of the forty rooms and three suites opens onto a terrace with a sea view—a table and chairs invite long looks. The tastefully furnished rooms have air conditioning and ceiling fans, telephone, room service, a small refrigerator, satellite TV, and king- or two queen-size beds. Private baths have central hot water. Rooms also are along the beach, and six duplex bungalows on the hillside going down to the beach contain forty rooms and three suites. Standard rooms are $91 for a single, $102 for a double. Meals in the dining room are a bit pricey: There is a full American plan—open menu—for $48, including taxes and tip. Credit cards are accepted. The hotel's Father Rooster Bar on the beach advertises a "barefoot atmosphere" for informal dining; prices there are lower. There are three pools, a Jacuzzi, lighted tennis court, a tour desk, and car rental. Transportation from San José can be arranged.

Hotel Ocotal offers sport fishing, surfing, tour boat cruises along isolated beaches and coastal islands, and scuba diving. A complete dive shop rents equipment, including cameras for underwater photography, and offers diving instruction. A $465 dive package, one of several available, includes five days and four nights, double occupancy, two days of boat diving, tanks, weights, guide, breakfast, taxes, and round-trip transportation from San José. Telephone 670-0321, fax 670-0083.

A charming ten-room bed-and-breakfast at Ocotal is Hotel Villa Casa Blanca. Janey and James Seip, who operate it, will probably join you for breakfast in a tropical garden setting in the rancho alongside a small swimming pool. Each room is different. Some have canopy beds, others have two beds for up to four people; all are nicely furnished and have private baths with central hot water. Staying here feels like being in the guest room of a very nice home. A single or double is $57 for rooms with fans, $63 for air conditioning, including an ample breakfast usually featuring eggs, fruit, bread, and some of the best pancakes around. Visa and MasterCard are accepted, but there is a 6 percent charge. There is a small gift shop and kayak, horse, and bicycle rentals. The staff arrange guides, scuba diving, boat trips to other beaches for snorkeling, and natural history tours. Only a few minutes' walk from the beach, the hotel has coatis that drop by, and there is good bird-watching in the gardens. The Seips also manage rentals of view houses and beach homes in the area. They will arrange transportation from Playa del Coco. Telephone 670-0448, fax 670-0273.

For the next cluster of accommodations along the beach, continue south on Highway 21 to Filadelfia, Belén, and Huacas, a junction where you can go north, south, or west to beach areas. Let's go north first. Signs to hotels at Conchal, Flamingo, and Pan de Azúcar (Sugar Beach) will guide you.

Hotel Condor Club overlooks the long curve of white sand beach at Conchal. The forty pleasant rooms have air conditioning as well as ceiling fans, satellite TV, telephones, and private baths with hot water. Floors of Spanish tile, wooden ceilings, and wicker furniture contrast with the white walls. Singles are $75, a double with twin beds is $80, and a room with king-size bed is $85. An

Beautiful Ocotal Beach from Hotel Ocotal (Photo by Ree Strange Sheck)

open-air restaurant and bar are in the main building, and the pool area has thatch-covered tables and lots of lounge chairs.

A four-minute shuttle ride away is the Condor's private beach club, where there is another pool, bar, grill, shuffleboard, and ping pong. There is a tennis court and areas for volleyball and basketball. Ridley turtles nest on the beach from February to April. You will see parrots and monkeys, too, but, no, those are not condors, as some tourists believe. They are buzzards, but it is nice to be in a place where even the buzzards seem regal. German and French are also spoken. Tours are arranged for guests. Telephone 231-7328 or 654-4050, fax 220-0670 or 654-4044.

The Flamingo Beach Hotel is now affiliated with the Holiday Inn in San José, so it is the Aurola Flamingo Beach Hotel. The 129 rooms, suites, and apartments are in two complexes, one on the beach. The hotel has a large pool, restaurants, bars, parking, a boutique, casino, disco, exercise room, tour agency, boat charters, and a diving instructor. Rooms are large and nicely furnished with air conditioning and fans; baths have both tubs and showers. Rooms begin at $126 for singles or doubles, with standards at $137 and suites beginning at $183. Credit cards are accepted. The hotel offers transportation from San José on Monday, Wednesday, Friday, and Sunday for $30. Telephone 233-7233 or 222-0090, fax 255-1036.

Also on Flamingo Beach is Villas Flamingo. The twenty-four two-bedroom, three-bath villas sleep up to six people. Downstairs are the living room, dining area, bath, and kitchen with a full stove—no hot plates here. The master bedroom upstairs has its own balcony. Lots of glass on the front afford views of the landscaped grounds, pool, and beach beyond. Villas Flamingo has no restaurant but there are a number nearby, and there is daily maid service. The rate is $100 for one or two people, $110 for three. Weekly and monthly rates are available. Telephone or fax 654-4215. There are daily buses from San José.

Farther up the road is beautiful Pan de Azúcar beach and Hotel Sugar Beach. The tranquillity always makes me want to linger—the curve of the small bay, the rocky headlands, the forest. There is a sense of intimacy with nature here. An uncrowded, white sand beach beckons; the hotel's large open-air restaurant invites leisurely dining. Twenty-two new rooms have windows on three sides, high ceilings, Spanish-tile floors, either hardwood or wicker furniture in the sitting area, a small refrigerator, air conditioning and ceiling fans, and private baths with central hot water—two with tubs. The rooms are $102 for up to four people. Some are accessible for the handicapped. The four older rooms have fans and shower-head hot water for $74. Credit cards are accepted. There is a swimming pool.

Hotel Sugar Beach can arrange guided trips to estuaries and offers half-day snorkeling, picnics, and sightseeing tours in a six-person boat (plus the captain) for $50 per hour. Guests can rent snorkeling equipment, boogie boards, sea kayaks, and horses. Air and bus service goes to Tamarindo, and a taxi from there is about $18. Telephone 654-4242 or 654-4239.

If you go west from Huacas instead of north, you come to Playa Grande and Tamarindo National Wildlife Refuge (also known as Las Baulas), which protects an important nesting site of the big leatherback turtle. Hotel Las Tortugas is a few steps from the beach where the leatherbacks nest from October to March, and turtles can be seen year-round. Owners Louis Wilson and Marianela Pastor have worked to protect this important wildlife area and educate guests on the do's and don'ts of turtle watching. Because turtles are sensitive to light, none of the eleven rooms has views to the south where the nesting beach is.

Each of the $85 rooms is different, though all have private baths, hot water, and air conditioning or fans. Credit cards are not accepted. There is a restaurant, small pool, and Jacuzzi. Las Tortugas offers estuary excursions by canoe or boat and deep sea fishing, and arranges horseback riding. Louis suggests that the express bus from San José to Santa Cruz is a good option if you do not have a car and do not want to fly. A taxi from the stand at the station to Playa Grande costs about $20; total time from San José is four and a half hours. Telephone or fax 680-0765.

Before you get to the beach, you will pass Cabinas Playa Grande. Some rooms are $35; those with kitchenettes are $48. Rooms are basic but clean, with fans and private baths. The restaurant serves typical Costa Rican food. Staff members will pick you up from the bus in Huacas or Matapalo. Telephone 237-2552, fax 237-1790.

The road southwest from Huacas goes through Villarreal to Tamarindo, a growing town that borders Tamarindo wildlife refuge (see chapter 7), an area important for turtles, birds, crocodiles, and mangroves.

SANSA makes the forty-minute flight from San José to Tamarindo five days a week. Travelair flies daily. The daily express bus takes about five hours. Here are some lodging possibilities:

On a hill above town is Hotel El Jardin del Eden, a complex of five Mediterranean-style villas, two swimming pools (one with a swim-up bar under a thatched roof), restaurants, and Jacuzzi. The beach is five minutes away. Each of the eighteen rooms has an ocean view, air conditioning and ceiling fans, refrigerator, wet bar, pretty rattan furniture, and private bath with central hot water. Most have a terrace or balcony. The least-expensive single is $86, double $98. Larger rooms are $103 for a single and $126 for a double. An ample buffet breakfast is included. There are two apartments with a full kitchen, dining room, and large terrace, costing $149 for two. Credit cards are accepted. The owners are Italian and French, a heritage reflected in the restaurant menu—fine dining. Herbs are grown on the property. Staff members will help arrange tours, and the hotel offers fishing packages. Telephone or fax 220-2096 or 654-4111.

Hotel Tamarindo Diría is on the beach. A large garden area stretches from the terraces to the sand. To diminish impact on nesting turtles, the hotel has special lights in the garden and does not illuminate the beach. The seventy rooms are tastefully furnished and have both air conditioning and ceiling fans as well as a small refrigerator and satellite TV. Private baths even have hair dryers. There is a large swimming pool, tennis, a gift shop, restaurant, and car rental. Standard singles are $98, doubles $115, including breakfast. Credit cards are accepted. A hotel microbus charges $70 from San José. Telephone 289-8616 or 654-4133, fax 289-8727 or 680-0652.

Six thatched octagonal bungalows above Tamarindo, Giapama Village Hotel, rent for $103 for two people, plus $23 for each additional person. MasterCard and Visa are accepted. The bungalows can accommodate up to six people. Downstairs is a furnished kitchen with a refrigerator and hot plate, as well as the living area. Sleeping space upstairs fits under the conical roof, with a ceiling fan for cooling. Private baths have shower-head hot water. The bungalows are full of light, with an airy feeling. Italian, French, German, and English also are spoken. Bungalows are situated around an inviting swimming pool. The owners have a microbus for tours in the area. Telephone or fax 654-4036.

Hotel Pasatiempo is downtown, about two blocks from the beach. Ten rooms are scattered in landscaped gardens, each with its own private porch. Baths have central hot water, and some have bidets. Reading lamps and good lighting on the mirrors are nice features. Cooling is with ceiling fans. There is a pool near the restaurant and bar area, and owners Ron and Dan will help you set up guided tours, horseback riding, snorkeling, or scuba diving. Rooms are $64 for one or two people. Credit cards are accepted. Fax 680-0776.

Hotel El Milagro is across the road from the beach. You can hear the sound of the waves as you go to sleep. The thirty-two rooms have high wooden ceilings, tile floors, and central hot water in private baths. Double wooden louvered doors open onto private porches to create a nice indoor-outdoor living space. English, German, and Dutch also are spoken. Be sure to talk with some of the young people waiting tables in the dining room. They are studying ecotourism and are enthusiastic about their work. The dining room is open to the pool and gardens. Staff members are helpful. A room for two with a fan is $46; with air conditioning, it is $58, buffet breakfast included. Visa and American Express are accepted. Telephone or fax 654-4042.

Cabinas Zullymar is at the center of town, with the restaurant on the beach and the hotel across the street. Note the pretty carved doors on each of the twenty-seven rooms, which are simply furnished and clean. The hotel offers parking and car rental, and arranges tours of the estuary, surfing, and snorkeling. The rate for one or two people in rooms with fans is $21; with fans and refrigerators, it is $26; with air conditioning, refrigerators, and central hot water in the baths, it is $41. Credit cards are not accepted. Manager Edwin Martinez is a happy, helpful man. Telephone 654-4140, telephone or fax 226-4732.

Sharing the road in the Nicoya Peninsula (Photo by Ree Strange Sheck)

As you drive over the back roads of the Nicoya Peninsula, you will see local residents looking for a ride; bus service is thin to nonexistent in some parts. You can meet some interesting people who just need a lift to the next town or crossroads. We once picked up a one-armed man waving a big saw; he turned out to be a deaf-mute, but he let us know where he wanted out. A few area hotels offer car rental, which allows you to get to the area initially by bus or air and then explore on your own. Road signs are far too sparse for strangers, though hotel signs help some. Four-wheel drive is advisable on some of the unpaved roads in the rainy season.

The Junquillal area is another popular beach destination on the Nicoya Peninsula. Four express buses a day go from San José to Santa Cruz, where you can get a bus or taxi connection. There is also bus service from Liberia. If you are driving, you can get to Santa Cruz on paved roads either from Liberia or by crossing over to the peninsula via the Tempisque ferry. Santa Cruz is a picturesque town (population 15,845) with streets of paving stones.

The nearby town of Guaitil is worth a visit for Chorotega Indian-style pottery. Someone at the community gift shop can probably tell you who is making pots that day so you can see the process. Pots are also sold in front of potters' houses, and the shop will pack pieces so they are safe for travel. The outdoor ovens are used not only to fire pottery but also to bake bread or cook a pig.

From Santa Cruz, get to the Junquillal area on the road passing through Ventisiete de Abril to Paraíso. (I wonder how many towns named "Paradise" there are in Costa Rica.) Hotel Iguanazul (watch for the signs) is a friendly place on Playa Blanca, 19 miles (30 km) west of Santa Cruz. The thirty-six rooms have a Southwestern U.S. flavor with white plaster walls, red brick floors, and exposed beams on the high ceilings. Each has a private bath with central hot water, TV, ceiling fan, and potted plants and is decorated with folk art rugs and wall hangings. A single is $55, a double $69. Credit cards are accepted. The hotel sits on a bluff above the beach with nothing else around. The overall impression is one of sky and sea. The hub of activity is the dining room/bar/pool area, which has a grand view of the Pacific—the setting sun is spectacular. The master of ceremonies, activities director Ron Klein, may sit down to chat with you at breakfast with a green iguana perched on his shoulder. If you want to do your own thing—or nothing—it's no problem, but Ron is there with suggestions if you want them.

In addition to horseback riding, surfing, snorkeling, fishing, mopeds, ping pong, billiards, volleyball, and the swimming pool, guests in high season may be treated to folk dances by schoolchildren from Paraíso or a typical night with marimba. Hotel Iguanazul is just one hour from the Ostional wildlife refuge, and beach walks from the hotel may bring you face to face with coatis, armadillos, iguanas, or monkeys. Ron has an excursion map he is happy to share. Ask about possibilities for hotel transportation from Santa Cruz or San José. Telephone or fax 680-0873.

Playa Junquillal is also south of Santa Cruz, just beyond Paraíso. The long, uncrowded, dark-sand beach invites long walks. A few turtles find their way here to lay eggs. Two hotels attractive for nature travelers are Villa Serena and Hotel Antumalal.

Villa Serena is nestled among the palms. Once as I ate a delicious lunch on the upstairs terrace looking out at the Pacific, a bird of the oriole family fed its young in a nest that seemed to hang by a thread from the tip of a palm branch. It is one of those terraces where you could probably sit happily for two or three years. The ten rooms are in the main two-story building and bungalows around the pool. Each has a fan and a large private bath with central hot water and dressing area; some have refrigerators. The $120 cost for two includes meals with a set menu. Credit cards are accepted. A candlelight dinner with classical music and the sound of the ocean in the background brings each day to a restful close. The German owner has added a honeymoon suite, a round tower-like room—even the bathroom has a view to the sea. There is an ice machine—not common in small hotels in Costa Rica.

Guests at Villa Serena can star-gaze at night—the telescope stands ready—and are welcome to use the library. Table games are available in comfortable lounges near the dining terrace. There is a tennis court and horse rental. Staff members can arrange transportation from the airport at Tamarindo or from Santa Cruz. Telephone or fax 680-0737.

Hotel Antumalal is a piece farther down the road. It is beautifully situated in lush tropical gardens. The open-air restaurant and some

Gardens down to the sea at Hotel Antumalal (Photo by Ree Strange Sheck)

rooms are on the gentle slope that descends to the sea. The rest of the twenty-three rooms are in bungalows tucked in gardens going down to the pool next to the beach. The high-ceilinged rooms are large, with red brick floors and rough-plastered white walls. Windows on two sides provide good ventilation, and there are ceiling fans. Each room has a porch with a hammock and table and chairs for dozing, reading, or watching the birds attracted to the flowering plants. Private baths with central hot water also have bidets. Singles are $80, doubles $92. Credit cards are accepted.

Guests can hike around a rocky headland at low tide to walk along the beach to an estuary for good bird-watching, or take a road there through dry forest. I was delighted to spot a colorful member of the trogon family. Tide pools along the mostly unpeopled beaches invite exploration. You will hear howler monkeys, some of whom spend most of the day in trees near the dining area and upper rooms. I photographed a troop, including several babies, after breakfast, and when I checked by after a late lunch, they were still dozing. The hotel can arrange tours and has a tennis court and horse rental. From November to May, diving is offered. Telephone or fax 680-0506.

I drove during the rainy season through the coastal hills from Junquillal all the way south to Playa Carrillo. Some of the stretches are gutbusters, and there are rivers to ford, but the landscape is interesting. Four-wheel drive is recommended; count on many 25-mph (40-kph) stretches. Places along this road may be reached more easily from Nicoya and Mansión or by flying to Sámara or Nosara. A word of rainy season caution on this coastal route: there are two large, as-yet-unbridged rivers, one between Junquillal and Ostional and the other between Ostional and Nosara. Ask at your hotel and in villages along the way whether they are passable.

Near Nosara is Ostional Wildlife Refuge. (See chapter 7.) Along with Nancite Beach in Santa Rosa, it is among the world's important nesting sites for olive ridley turtles. During the day, there is good bird-watching along the estuary. If you are there on an evening when the turtle *arribadas* begin, you may see horses with sacks of turtle eggs slung over them tied up at the local cantina. These eggs were taken legally in a managed harvest by the turtle cooperative that patrols the beaches against poachers.

South along the coast from Ostional is Nosara (population 3,328). Travelair flies there daily, SANSA five times a week. There is now a daily express bus from San José and also a bus from Nicoya.

Hotel Playas de Nosara is one of those gracious beach hotels in harmony with its natural surroundings. Though many rooms offer a view of the sea, it is hard to spot the hotel among the trees from the beach just below. Expansive vistas of sky, sea, and shoreline from the open-air dining room would surely bring a bit of balance to even the most restless mind.

Rock outcroppings on the beach create wonderful pools at low tide for exploration, swimming and snorkeling. The hotel arranges turtle nesting tours, river trips for birding, horse rentals, and a day trip to a nearby ranch, led by local guides. There are trails on the property. English, French, German, Greek, and Italian also are spoken by owner John Fraser.

The twenty rooms are in several buildings set among flowered gardens. Each is large, with brick floors, a ceiling fan, louvered doors to the balcony, decorative wall hangings, table and chairs, and private bath with central hot water. With a sea view, singles are $68, doubles $85; without the view, singles are $57 and doubles $75. Credit cards are not accepted. From a spacious observation area above the dining room, one has a panoramic vista of the coastline, the pretty swimming pool below (which surely will be finished by your arrival), and forest and gardens. Telephone or fax 680-0495.

Just a half-block from the ocean is Estrella del Pacífico, a twenty-four-room hotel. There is a tennis court and pool, and staff members can arrange tours, including a three-hour trip to the mangroves for $25. Rooms have white tile floors and are cooled by both air conditioning and fans. The blue tile bathroom seems soft, like the sea. Pretty rattan furniture with colorful cushions brightens the open dining room. Singles are $68, doubles $92, bungalows for four people $100, with continental breakfast included. Credit cards are accepted. Telephone 680-0763, fax 680-0856.

Estancia Nosara, on a shady street a short walk from the beach, has eight rooms around a kidney-shaped pool. Each sleeps up to four people and has a kitchenette, dining nook, and private bath with shower-head hot water. Rooms have high wooden ceilings and Spanish tile floors. There is a pool and tennis court; bikes can be rented for $7 a day, and horses for $8 an hour. A tour to Ostional is $25, as is a crocodile/bird tour on the Nosara River. There is a rancho bar and large open-air dining room. Telephone or fax 680-0378.

Rancho Suizo Lodge is just down the road. Eleven rooms are in thatched bungalows, each with its own porch. Rooms are bright, with high ceilings, fans, and private baths with shower-head hot water. Singles are $29, doubles $40. Credit cards are not accepted. The Swiss owners, René and Ruth, are gracious hosts, and can help you out in English, French, Italian, and German as well as Spanish. The restaurant, open to the public, includes dishes from their homeland, and the decor has flags from the Swiss cantons. A tour to Ostional for turtle-watching is $20 per person, to the Nosara River for bird-watching $25. Horse rental is $10 per hour. Other tours include hiking and snorkeling. The beach is close enough to hear the sound of the surf. Telephone 255-0011 or 255-2155, fax 685-5004.

Parrots and parakeets are among the many species of birds that help travelers forget the rough and sometimes dusty routes from many of these beach areas to another. Howler monkeys rest in tree branches hanging over the roads.

Between Nosara and Sámara is Bahía Garza. Thatched bungalows and a towering thatched restaurant lend an exotic, romantic flavor to the Villaggio La Guaria Morada hotel. Located between the coastal hills and the sea, with forest along the beach stretching to Punta Guiones, the hotel arranges tours to the Ostional refuge, horseback riding, and sport fishing. It also can arrange transportation from the Nosara airport, and the San José-Nosara bus passes in front. Sounds of a group of howler monkeys, which the manager says are almost domesticated, drift to the bungalows at night and in the early morning. In this tranquil, natural setting, the hotel's casino and discotheque seem out of place. A large swimming pool is next to the restaurant/bar. The thirty rooms are in well-ventilated bungalows with French doors that can open up one side of the room onto private terraces. Rooms have walls of rough white plaster, red-clay tile floors, bamboo ceilings, dressing room areas, louvered windows, large closets, fans, and private baths with showerhead hot water and bidets. The rate is $124 for a single or double. Visa and MasterCard are accepted. Telephone 680-0784 or 233-2476, fax 222-4073.

Sámara (population 2,462), along with Nosara and Tamarindo, offers travelers access by air as well as direct bus from San José. (See Practical Extras.) The 22 miles (35 km) from Nicoya to Samara should be paved by the time you read this.

There are some modest-looking places in town, but Hotel Las Brisas del Pacífico is a quality hotel on the beach. Some of its thirty-six rooms are in bungalows close to the beach; others offer fantastic views of the ocean from an addition above the original complex. The pleasant, bright bungalows have louvered doors to the porches, baths with bidet and hot water, ceiling fans, and table and chairs. Suites are large, with balconies and air conditioning. If you can't get one with its own Jacuzzi, you can take advantage of the whirlpool beside the swimming pool and the open restaurant/bar (good food), surrounded by trees and tropical plants. The ocean is steps away through the hotel's gate to the beach. Las Brisas has parking and rents horses, boats, and equipment for windsurfing and water skiing. Inquire about tours. A single or double is $60; suites are $109. Credit cards are accepted. German and English also are spoken. Telephone or fax 233-9840, telephone 223-8685.

Hotel Marbella is a two-story hotel with fourteen rooms facing an inner courtyard with a small pool. The rooms are light, with ceiling fans and private baths with central hot water. A single is $38, a double $42. Six one-bedroom furnished apartments are $55 for up to three people. A small restaurant upstairs serves breakfast, and there are nearby restaurants to choose from for other meals. The hotel arranges tours and is the SANSA agency in Sámara. English and German also are spoken. Telephone or fax 233-9980.

A few miles from town is Villas Playa Sámara, seventy-three classy villas on the beach. Motorized carts go through landscaped grounds from the reception area to the villas. Each red-tile-roofed villa has a fully equipped kitchen, tasteful furnishings in the living room, dining room, and bedrooms, and ceiling fans. Rattan chairs with colorful cushions make the large terraces a comfortable outdoor living area. There is a large pool, children's pool, water slide, Jacuzzi, and restaurant. Some of the baths also have tubs. Villas Playa Sámara offers snorkeling, surfing, water skiing, and scuba diving, and also arranges tours. English and French are spoken as well. A one-bedroom villa is $143; two-bedroom, $223, three-bedroom $275. Credit cards are accepted. Telephone 233-0223, fax 221-7222.

About 4 miles (6 km) south of Sámara is Playa Carrillo and the beautiful Guanamar Resort. There are forty-two rooms in villas above the ocean and a mile-long (1.5 km) white-sand beach, with free shuttle from the resort to the beach. The pool, surrounded by a wooden deck, is at the edge of the bluff above the blue of the Pacific. Broad, shaded wooden walkways with white railings connect the areas of the resort. White wicker furniture with bright cushions stand out against the rich wooden floors and ceiling of the restaurant/bar, which is also open to the view of the sea and forest-covered hills. The restaurant is open to the public. Spacious, airy rooms are carpeted, with balconies or terraces, satellite TV, room service, air conditioning, fans, and fresh flowers on the table. Some baths have tubs as well as showers, all with central hot water. Rooms without a sea view are $126 for up to two people; with the view, they are $137. (Children under twelve are free.) Suites are $286, and some have balconies at treetop level for a closeup view of canopy wildlife. Monkeys have been known to drop by the reception area.

In high season, there is live entertainment at Guanamar, and there also is a casino. The resort, which has more than 1,000 acres (470 ha) of land, offers trail walks with local guides, horseback riding, mountain biking for $7 per hour, kayaking, snorkeling, water skiing, boat rental, and sport fishing (catch and release). Ask about special transportation possibilities by boat or air charter. The resort is part of Costa Sol International. Telephone 239-2000 or 239-4500, or in the U.S. and Canada, (800) 245-8420; fax 239-4839.

Nicoya is a pretty town (population 23,726) with a picturesque colonial church. Though most tourists just pass through on their way to somewhere else, it can be a pleasant destination, giving a flavor of small-town life on the Nicoya Peninsula.

Hotel Curime at the edge of town has twenty-six rooms in units scattered among landscaped gardens. It is a tranquil place with a resident parrot (uncaged) who hangs out near the large swimming pool alongside the open-air restaurant. Most of the larger rooms have air conditioning (a single is $24, a double $48), and the smaller ones have fans (singles are $12, doubles $20). Both have refrigerators, a living room area, and TV. Private baths have central hot water. The staff is extremely helpful. Zelmira called her dad to help me change a flat tire one Sunday morning, and he was good enough to tell me I was driving around with a broken spring! That was not the end of helpful people in Nicoya—I was back on the road within a few hours. Call the Curime at 685-5238, fax 685-5530.

Southeast of Nicoya is Mansión, and just about five blocks (500 m) north of the Mansión junction on the main highway is a delightful little restaurant called Los Girasoles, owned by Marcial Flores. He loves to have a satisfied customer and says, "We cook with the heart, not in the kitchen." For us, he put together a dish of grilled chicken, shrimp, and beef that would have been fit for a fine city restaurant. We ate it in the thatched rancho in a large flowered garden as we watched parakeets in the trees. Los Girasoles is open from 11:00 a.m. to 10:00 p.m. daily. Tell Marcial hello for me.

From Mansión, you can head northwest for the ferry across the Tempisque River or a visit to Barra Honda National Park. At the entrance is a community ecotourism project—Barrio Cubillo— with a restaurant (typical dishes) called Las Delicias and three clean, simple rooms with private baths but no hot water. They cost $11 per person. Credit cards are not accepted. Electricity may arrive at the park by the time you get there, but if not, there are candles. Fourteen camping areas, with latrines and water, are spaced in a forest frequented by howler monkeys. The cost is about $2 per person. You can also see deer and tepezcuintle projects. Guides lead three-hour trips to the caves in Barra Honda for $35 for up to five people (with a minimum of two), and half-day hikes for about $10. There is a small grocery. A handcrafts area has ceramics and carved gourds for sale. Call 685-5580 for reservations for rooms or tours.

A new private reserve at Puerto Humo, with both a modern hotel that has a view of Palo Verde park across the river and a more rustic thatch and bamboo lodge, is off the road to the ferry. (See Rancho Humo Ecotourism Center in chapter 8.)

The road east of Mansión soon heads south for Playa Naranjo. When the pavement stops, it is slow going—plenty of time to take in the countryside and a character or two. One rainy afternoon, I noticed an old, bearded man on the bank along the road, half-hidden as he squatted in the tall grass. As the car approached, he rose slightly, carefully aimed his machete, and fired. Hilarious. In the rear-view mirror, I watched as he resumed his station, presumably waiting for the next passerby.

When you get close to Lepanto, notice the salt beds. Then it is Playa Naranjo and the dock where the car ferry from Puntarenas comes in five times a day now. (See Practical Extras.) This is where some travelers begin their journeys on the Nicoya Peninsula.

Oasis del Pacífico is a small resort and marina not far from the dock. Hotel transportation meets each ferry. The thirty-six rooms have ceiling fans and private baths with hot water. They face the hotel's gardens on 12 acres (5 ha) and the Gulf of Nicoya. Singles are $45, doubles $59. Credit cards are accepted. The restaurant is surely one of the few in Costa Rica where you can get biscuits and country gravy for breakfast and eat it to the sounds of pet macaws and parrots.

Ranchitos with hammocks by the water and swimming pools are conducive to staying right at the hotel, but you can also rent horses ($10 for the first hour, $5 after that), charter a boat, or go on a fishing trip ($275 a day for up to three people, including tackle, food, and drinks). Oasis de Pacífico has its own 260-foot (80-m) pier. Half-day trips to San Lucas Island, a former penal colony, are $125 for up to six people. Day trips in the Gulf of Nicoya are tailored to what people want, according to owners Lucky and Agie, two of the world's truly nice people. They also own the Piano Blanco Bar next to the Hotel Balmoral in San José, and you can sometimes find Lucky there. Telephone or fax Oasis del Pacífico at 661-1555. For those who want to cross on the ferry but have no time to go farther, a day rate at the hotel lets visitors use the pool and showers.

Hotel el Paso is a motel-type establishment at the edge of Playa Naranjo on the way to Nicoya. (The Nicoya bus passes in front.) Some of the fifteen rooms, all neat and clean, have private baths (but no hot water) and air conditioning. Single is $40, a double $45. Rooms with fans and shared baths are less. Credit cards are accepted. There is a small pool and a restaurant that serves a delicious chicken sandwich and good gallo pinto. Telephone 661-2610.

The road from Playa Naranjo to Cabo Blanco (paved to Tambor) goes up and down through the hills, with lots of birds and occasional magnificent views of the coastline.

Hotel Bahia Gigante, under new ownership, sits on a bluff above the bay of the same name. It provides pickup service at the ferry 5.5 miles (9 km) away and will arrange transportation from San José. It is a friendly place. The large, pleasant dining room, open to the public, is screened and has a pitched thatched roof. You can dine on typical dishes, catch-of-the-day, cracker-crusted fried chicken, fresh vegetables, pastas, smoked barbecue pork chops, and specialty sandwiches. Rooms are large, and most face the pool. There are private baths, which should get hot water this year. Furnishings are simple. A single is $32, a double $40.

The hotel owns a chunk of surrounding property with 5 miles (8 km) of road and numerous trails through forests and along the beach. Tree species are marked on an interpretive trail. As many as 256 species of birds have been counted, and about as many butterfly species. You may see howler or capuchin monkeys, armadillos, and deer as you hike. There is an estuary for bird watching, tours to the Gitana, San Lucas, Tortuga, and Negritos islands, and a guided horseback adventure for $5 an hour to a waterfall with three large pools and a natural water slide. Scuba, snorkeling, and sport fishing equipment is for rent. There is a dock on the beach, and Bahia Gigante has supplies, fuel, and fresh water for yachts. Telephone or fax 661-2442.

The twice-a-day launch from Puntarenas comes in at Paquera (see Practical Extras), where a bus waits to take passengers as far as Montezuma.

South of Paquera is Curú National Wildlife Refuge, but access is through private property and you will need arrangements and directions beforehand. (See chapter 8.)

Bahia Ballena, which means Whale Bay, is down the road a piece. Waters lap on a long, curved beach with a very gentle slope. At sunset one July evening, two dogs and I were the only ones on the beach near the town of Tambor. A roseate spoonbill perched in a tree at the mouth of a stream, kingfishers darted back and forth, and howler monkeys sounded just out of sight. The 400-room Playa Tambor Hotel, opened in 1993, reduces the possibility that you and the dogs and the wildlife will have the beach to yourself, but the last time I was there, it was still a tranquil setting.

The luxury resort complex built by the Barcelo hotel chain has helped focus the debate in Costa Rica about the impact of tourism on the physical and social environment. What kind of tourism does the country want? What is its market? What can it support? How can environmental safeguards be enforced? And what tradeoffs are acceptable? As a visitor, your vote counts. You can write to ICT. (Address in Practical Extras.)

The focus of this book is on smaller hotels, but if your taste runs to large, full-service beach resorts, Hotel Playa Tambor's telephone number is 661-2039, fax 661-2069.

Hotel Dos Lagartos is on the beach in the town of Tambor. The twenty-three rooms are neat and simple with ceiling fans. Only four have private baths. A single is $12, a double $24. For those who share, there are about three rooms per bath. A single is $8, a double $13. There is no hot water, and credit cards are not accepted. The small restaurant serves breakfast and sometimes other meals. Cristina's, around the corner, is a typical restaurant that can fill in. Dos Lagartos rents bicycles and has a small launch for tours in the bay or to Tortuga Island, Isla Gitana, Montezuma, or Curú and can also transport guests from Puntarenas. Telephone 661-1122, extension 236.

Tango Mar Beach Resort and Golf Country Club, past Tambor, offers the traveler deluxe surroundings and a full range of activities. Resident naturalist guides lead sailing trips to Curú Wildlife Refuge and Tortuga Island and offer estuary tours especially for birders. Turtles come ashore to nest on the beach in front, with the largest arrivals in October and November. There is a pool with natural mineral water, a restaurant, a gift shop, a ten-hole golf course, and tennis courts. The hotel rents mountain bikes, horses, cars, and equipment for tennis, golf, diving, and fishing, and you can get a massage. San José is twenty minutes away by air taxi service. The 125-acre (50-ha) complex includes pastures, primary forest, and beachfront. A 40-foot (12-m) waterfall graces one end of the property, and at low tide, there is a great natural pool at the bottom for swimming.

Large, elegantly simple rooms have cool floors of reddish-brown polished tiles, two queen-size beds (two rooms have a king-size bed), rattan furniture, including a desk and long benches, folk art and original paintings, fresh flowers, satellite TV, reading lamps, ceiling fans, and an ample closet area with space for luggage. Baths have central hot water—and big towels. Each room opens onto a private balcony facing the sea. For the sixteen rooms, singles are $137, doubles $150. Villas start at $205. Credit cards are accepted, and package tours are available. The food is excellent. Telephone 223-1864, 255-3128 or 661-2798, fax 255-2697. Tango Mar is about two miles (3 km) from Tambor.

At Cóbano, turn left (dirt road all the way) for the interesting little beach town of Montezuma. In the past, it could not seem to decide whether to dress up and go for big-time tourism or just hang out and take what came. Now some in the community have organized to combat some of the problems that did come, such as unregulated camping anywhere someone decided to pitch a tent.

Specified camping areas with latrines and water are a positive result. You can pitch in and help on Saturday beach cleanups. New small hotels are going in, and older ones are being spruced up. The beaches are spectacular—some to the north have loads of gorgeous shells. You can go horseback riding, hike to a waterfall, snorkel, visit the Cabo Blanco reserve farther down the road, bird-watch, or just hang out. The town is waiting for more phone lines. Most now have extensions, which makes it difficult to accept credit cards.

The Sano Banano, a macrobiotic restaurant, serves delicious food with a flair. It has not only a frozen yogurt machine but also a slush machine and serves fresh popcorn, too. Lenny and Patricia Iacona, the owners, also show nightly movies on a big TV screen. They own Cabinas El Sano Banano, ranging from $30 to $50, some with equipped kitchens. The cabins are in the forest near the beach. Telephone 661-1122, extension 272, or stop by the restaurant.

Hotel El Jardín is one of the newcomers. Its ten rooms are very clean, with refrigerators, floor or ceiling fans, and private tiled baths. From the upstairs balcony, there is a view of the sea—the beach is less than a four-minute walk away. An outside shower lets guests rinse off beach sand before going in their rooms. A room for up to two is $46. Reservations can be made through Monte Aventuras, a tour and information center next door. Telephone or fax 661-2320.

Some of the tours offered through Monte Aventuras are to Cabo Blanco for $20, an overnight to Malpais, or to various beaches. Bus and ferry schedules are posted along with happenings in Montezuma. English and Italian also are spoken.

Hotel Los Mangos is past the town center on the way to Cabo Blanco, across the road from the sea. More than 200 mango trees shade the grounds, their fruit drawing birds and animals. Anteaters have been known to visit. New, pleasant, raised, thatched bungalows with pyramid ceilings have private baths with central hot water, lots of windows, ceiling fans, a full-length mirror, and rockers on the porches. The cost is $75 for up to three people. Some of the ten older rooms have private baths, at $52 for up to three people. Rooms with shared baths are $40 for two. Visa is accepted. A pretty pool with a view of the ocean and forest is next to the restaurant/bar, which is open to the public and specializes in Italian food. English, Greek, Italian, and Polish also are spoken.

Los Mangos rents horses, bicycles, and motorcycles and offers tours on a catamaran—for example, a one-day trip to Tortuga or Malpais or three days around the area. Forest covers the hillside behind the hotel, and you are likely to hear the sounds of the howlers and perhaps spot white-face monkeys. Telephone 661-1122, extension 259.

Hotel Montezuma Pacífico has twelve rooms, all but two with both air conditioning and fans. All have private baths, and most have hot water. The two least expensive rooms are $20, with fans. The others range from $32 to $43. The restaurant menu includes vegetarian dishes. Telephone 661-1122, extension 200, or telephone or fax 222-7746.

The Amor de Mar is family-oriented: owners Doris and Richard Stocker welcome children. Eight of the rooms have private baths with shower-head hot water, at $46 to $52 for a double. Rooms with shared baths are $35. There is also a casita with a private bath and kitchen for $52. English, German, and French also are spoken. The two-story hotel has the sea in front and the river on one side. Hammocks are strategically placed in the garden. The restaurant serves full breakfasts all day—marvelous homemade bread and natural fruit juices—and snacks, even milk shakes. Telephone 661-1122, extension 262.

Hotel Montezuma, downtown on the beach, has rooms from $8 per person (with shared baths) to $13 for a single and $20 for a double with private baths. There are ceiling fans but no hot water. Rooms across the street from the restaurant are quieter. The hotel rents bicycles, motorcycles, and horses and will help arrange transportation to Cabo Blanco and Tortuga Island. Telephone 661-1122, extension 258.

Karen Wessberg has a small nature reserve up the beach with cabins—but no electricity. (See chapter 8.) She also runs Cabinas Karen (with electricity) in Montezuma, at $10 per person. There is no telephone.

Another possibility in Montezuma is the Hotel Aurora, with clean, basic rooms from $24 with shared bath to $28 for private bath but no hot water. There also is no telephone.

Before coming down the hill to Montezuma, you will see a sign saying "Juan's." This is short for Hermanos y Hermanas de la Madre Tierra, which offers rustic lodging on 250 acres (100 ha) of regenerating pastures and primary and secondary forest. The restaurant focuses on vegetarian food, using produce from its organic garden, but you will find dishes with Thai, Spanish, Indian, and Mexican flavors. Guided nature tours can take you on forest trails to waterfalls, springs, and the river, either walking or on horseback. Accommodations run the gamut from a room with private bath to dormitory-style sleeping with communal toilets and baths in a separate building. There is no hot water. Howlers come every morning; morphos drift by. Telephone 661-1122, extension 291. Actually, the "Juan's" sign is for owner Juan Cielo. Local people call it Juan's place.

The village of Mal Pais is another option on the Pacific side near the tip of the Nicoya Peninsula. Access is from Cóbano via a dirt road. Mar Azul offers simple lodging and an area for camping. Some of the eleven rooms have private baths. Rates range from $12 to $29. The restaurant serves seafood and typical meals. Telephone 661-1122, extension 300.

The road to the Cabo Blanco Strict Nature Reserve is worth the trip. It eventually narrows to a one-lane track that can be quite muddy in the rainy season. There is one large river to cross. When I got out of the car to photograph a thatched house with a television antenna atop a bamboo pole, a small child ran up to advise me not to venture too close to the water. "There are crocodiles in there," she said. Spiny pochote trees and gumbo-limbo trees, in Spanish called *indio desnudo* (naked Indian), with their peeling reddish bark, form living fences along the road. A huge strangler fig stands at the road's edge. (See chapter 7 for information about the reserve.)

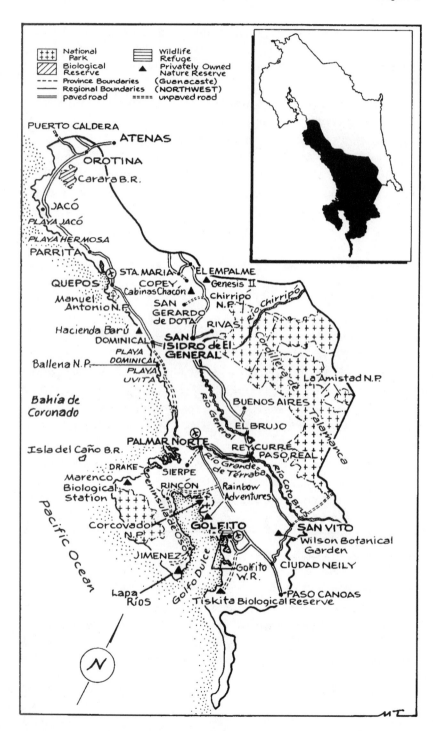

Legend:
- National Park
- Biological Reserve
- Province Boundaries
- Regional Boundaries
- paved road
- Wildlife Refuge
- Privately Owned Nature Reserve (Guanacaste)
- (NORTHWEST)
- unpaved road

PUERTO CALDERA
ATENAS
OROTINA
Carara B.R.
JACÓ
PLAYA JACÓ
PLAYA HERMOSA
PARRITA
STA. MARIA
QUEPOS
COPEY
Cabinas Chacón
Manuel Antonio N.P.
SAN GERARDO de DOTA
Hacienda Barú
DOMINICAL
PLAYA DOMINICAL
Ballena N.P.
PLAYA UVITA
EL EMPALME
Genesis II
Chirripó N.P.
Río Chirripó
RIVAS
SAN ISIDRO de El GENERAL
La Amistad N.P.
Bahía de Coronado
BUENOS AIRES
EL BRUJO
Isla del Caño B.R.
PALMAR NORTE
REY CURRÉ
PASO REAL
Río General
Cordillera de Talamanca
DRAKE
SIERPE
RINCÓN
Marenco Biological Station
Rainbow Adventures
Río Grande de Térraba
Río Coto B.
Corcovado N.P.
Península de Osa
Pacific Ocean
GOLFITO
SAN VITO
Wilson Botanical Garden
CIUDAD NEILY
JIMENEZ
Golfito W.R.
Lapa Ríos
Golfo Dulce
Tiskita Biological Reserve
PASO CANOAS

N

South

The Talamancas, the highest mountains in the country, are in the region we are looking at here, along with beautiful mid- and southern Pacific beaches; plantations of pineapple, African palm, and bananas; virgin forest; and some lands that knew only indigenous peoples and a trickle of pioneers until the Inter-American Highway to Panama pushed back the frontier in the 1950s.

Travel into the region from San José is mainly along the Inter-American Highway through the highlands or the old Spanish road through Orotina and then south along the coast. Some of the largest and some of the smallest national parks are here, along with biological reserves, wildlife refuges, and some private nature reserves.

The Highland Route

An early start is recommended for a trip on the Inter-American Highway south from San José. Fog or rain become likely at higher elevations as the hours pass. After you pass through the colonial capital of Cartago and turn at the sign for San Isidro de El General, the road begins to climb out of the Central Valley. Fields of agave plants called *cabuya* (hemp) grow on hillsides. Then small farms with dairy cows dominate the landscape.

About an hour out of the capital is Bar y Soda Los Angeles. If you did not have breakfast, a typical one awaits you here: gallo pinto and coffee or agua dulce, or you can order a papusa or *gallos* (tortillas filled with beef, cheese, or chicken). Several small roadside restaurants through here offer the same typical atmosphere. At kilometer 60, you'll find Chesperito, another one I like. If these places seem too rustic, Las Georginas on the other side of Cerro de la Muerte has good food. Buses stop there, and it has a buffet.

Near the gasoline station at El Empalme, a road to the right takes travelers along what is called the Route of the Saints, visiting Santa María de Dota, San Marcos de Tarrazú, San Pablo de León Cortés, and San Cristóbal Sur. Four-wheel drive is recommended if you venture south of Santa María de Dota to Copey, where there is a graceful waterfall and a lake, plus rose nurseries. Inquire about the roads at ICT if you are interested in this day trip.

On the left near kilometer 58 on the Inter-American Highway is the little yellow church of Cañon. For a taste of the Talamanca cloud forest and a stay at the private nature reserve called Genesis II, take the unpaved road beside the church for about 2.5 miles (4 km). Genesis II is as intriguing as its name; read about it in chapter 8.

Albergue de Montaña Tapantí, named for nearby Tapantí Wildlife Refuge, is at kilometer 62, just before La Trinidad. The albergue has six apartments, some for up to five people, and four double rooms. A single or double costs $63. Each has heaters (the elevation is close to 10,000 feet, or 3,048 meters) and a private bath with hot water; furnishings are comfortable. There is a conference room, lounge with fireplace, library, table games, and restaurant. You can go trout fishing or seek out the quetzal for $12 per person, or have a tour in the páramo for $24. Telephone or fax 232-0436.

If the day is clear when you get to Cerro de las Vueltas, you can see the peaks of Cerro de la Muerte ahead. Near kilometer 78 is a lake in a depression near the highway at Jaboncillo (park in a safe spot and take a look from the road or walk down a trail to the water). Nineteen miles (30 km) south of El Empalme, at kilometer 80, is the turnoff for San Gerardo de Dota, famous among natural history travelers in the know for its cloud forests and a chance to see the resplendent quetzal. Six miles (10 km) from the turnoff is Albergue de Montaña Savegre, known everywhere as Cabinas Chacón. It is a delightful private nature reserve. (See chapter 8 for specifics.)

Just before the turnoff to San Gerardo de Dota, watch on the left for the ruins of a refuge that once sheltered travelers on the trail through these mountains. Cerro de la Muerte got its name, Mountain of Death, because of the storms and frigid nighttime temperatures This is the northernmost true páramo in the hemisphere, and its plants are associated with Andean climes. At this top-of-the-world vantage point, when conditions are right, it is possible to see both coasts.

The next part of the road offers one of the most spectacular drives in the country. In a distance of 28 miles (45 km), the road

BANANAS

Bananas are in practically every back-yard, sometimes planted between rows of coffee, and in huge plantations in the coastal zones. More than 91,000 acres of land (37,000 ha) are devoted to bananas. Costa Rica is the second-largest exporter of bananas in the world, after Ecuador, and bananas are the number two foreign exchange earner.

Bananas originated in India, Malaysia, the Philippines, and other parts of Asia and were brought to the New World in the fifteenth century. Both bananas and the United Fruit Company got their start in Costa Rica in the 1880s. United Fruit was formed by Minor Keith, the builder of the railroad from Limón to San José, and his associates. Under the name of Chiquita Brands, it continues as a major foreign company in the banana business in Costa Rica, along with Standard Fruit and Bandeco (which belongs to Del Monte).

Each trunk in a banana plant produces one bunch (a raicimo), and then it dies. But a continuous supply of new trunks emerge from the plant's base. Look at a banana plant in a commercial operation, and you will see the major trunk and two smaller ones. When the major trunk has fruited and been cut, trunk number two takes over, and another shoot at the base is allowed to grow. This way, production from a plant is continuous.

It generally takes about nine months from the start of a trunk to the cutting of the fruit, three months from flowering to harvesting of a bunch. On a plantation, there may be 2,000 plants for every 2.5 acres (1 ha).

Blue plastic bags are put on a bunch at about two weeks, though this varies some. The bags concentrate heat so that the fruit gets fatter and longer more quickly, and they are also impregnated with insecticide and fungicide.

At harvest time at the plantation I visited, a cutter in the field removes the still-green stalk of bananas from the trunk and places it on the shoulder of another worker, who carries it to a cable that goes to the packing plant. When twenty-five bunches are hanging on the cable, a runner pulls the "train" to the packing plant. (Some places use tractors now, pulling up to 100 bunches.) The plastic is removed, and workers cut "hands" of bananas from the bunch, tossing them into water, where they stay at least eight minutes to let latex drain out of the cut stem. The fruit that survives the selection process is washed again and stacked on trays in forty-two-pound lots (the amount that goes in each box), a fungicide is sprayed on, and each banana gets a label (Chiquita in this case). Bananas from a tray are loaded into a box lined with plastic and put aboard a container, which holds 800 to 900 boxes. Government inspectors check at the boxing stage, because once the container's doors are closed, they are not opened until they reach their destination. Containers are then trucked to the port for shipment by boat.

Costa Rica's bananas go mainly to the United States, with other important markets in Germany, Belgium, Italy, and the Netherlands.

The banana industry has come under attack from people concerned about the cutting of forests for plantations and about the ecological impacts of pesticides and the plastic bags, which sometimes end up in rivers and oceans.

drops from its highest point at 10,938 feet (3,334 m) to 2,303 feet (702 m) at San Isidro de El General. You pass from páramo vegetation to a forest with red bromeliads shining in the sun and then to tree ferns, vines, and sombrilla del pobre—walls of greenery on both sides of the road. As the vista of the General Valley opens up, you may catch a whiff of heliotrope from plants growing along the road.

Just below the statue of Christ above the highway on the right, there is a *trapiche* (sugar mill) on the left. If it is in operation, you can see oxen turning the press to extract liquid from the sugarcane. Roadside stands sometimes offer wooden *bateas* for sale. You can occasionally still see a woman washing clothes on one in the countryside, but these small versions make beautiful trays or centerpieces loaded with fruit or flowers.

San Isidro de El General (population 38,729) is the commercial center of this rich agricultural area. It can easily be a hub for travelers as they visit Chirripó, Cerro de la Muerte, the Wilson Botanical Garden at San Vito, hot springs at Canaan de Rivas, the Savegre Caverns, or beaches at Dominical. Buses run frequently between San José and San Isidro, a distance of 85 miles (137 km).

San Isidro is a pleasant place to wander around in for the flavor of a small Costa Rican town. I stumbled onto a double wedding in the church on the plaza one evening. Shortly after, a dog ambled in through the open door, made its way down the aisle, sniffing and looking, and then ambled out again. Nobody got upset or even paid any attention. Since church doors stand open everywhere, it is not uncommon to see a bird flying above the altar or to hear chirping from the ceiling in the quiet of the day.

This valley will be familiar to those who have read books by one of its most famous residents, naturalist and ornithologist Alexander F. Skutch. (See Practical Extras, Recommended Reading.) His farm and nature reserve a few miles from San Isidro is open principally to nature tour groups but not to the general public.

Lodging in town is rustic to modest, but Hotel del Sur is a comfortable hotel 2.5 miles (4 km) from the city center heading south on the Inter-American. On clear days, you can sit by the large pool and gaze at the impressive Talamanca Mountains above the trees.

uaria morada orchids, national flower of Costa Rica, in a typical painted ox cart
hoto by Ree Strange Sheck)

▲ Mural at Hacienda Doña Martá near Orotina (Photo by Ree Strange Sheck)

▼ Hotel Los Mangos in Montezuma (Photo by Ree Strange Sheck)

▲ Folk dancing at Cañitas, near Monteverde (Photo by Ree Strange Sheck)

▼ Unique bungalows at Cabañas Escondidas (Photo by Ree Strange Sheck)

▲ Golfito from the Golfo Dulce (Photo by Ree Strange Sheck)

▼ Santa Elena Forest Reserve, Monteverde (Photo by Ree Strange Sheck)

▲ Author (a tall person) next to tree buttresses at Hacienda Barú near Dominical (Photo by Jack Ewing)

▼ Tango Mar on the Nicoya Peninsula (Photo by Ree Strange Sheck)

▲ The Pacific from Marenco Biological Reserve on the Osa Peninsula
(Photo by Ree Strange Sheck)

▼ Villa Casa Blanca at Ocotal (Photo by Ree Strange Sheck)

▲ Escazú ox cart parade (Photo by Ree Strange Sheck)

▼ Blue-crowned motmot (Photo by Ree Strange Sheck)

▲ Drake Bay Wilderness Camp, between the forest and the sea
(Photo by Ree Strange Sheck)

▼ Steam rises from hot waters at Tabacón near La Fortuna
(Photo by Ree Strange Sheck)

The fifty-seven rooms are on two floors around a pretty garden with a fountain, and ten cabins for up to five people are farther back on the property. All have private baths with hot water and either air conditioning or fans; some have telephones and TV. In addition to the pools for adults and children, there are facilities for tennis, volleyball, and soccer, and a small game room with ping pong and billiards. The hotel is a popular destination for Costa Rican families on weekends and holidays and has a nice tico flavor. There is a gift shop. Singles are from $31 to $46, doubles $46 to $64. The suite is $84 and the cabins $69. Credit cards are accepted. Telephone 771-3033, fax 771-0527.

The entrance to Chirripó National Park is just a few miles east of San Isidro, at San Gerardo de Rivas. (See chapter 7.) You can do the trip to Chirripó on your own, of course, but tour companies also make arrangements. One is Camino Travel, which runs a three-day trip. The first day gets you from San José to base camp in a park refuge at 11,155 feet (3,400 m), requiring an eight- or nine-hour hike of 10 miles (16 km). Day two is the trek to the peak, San Juan Lagoon, and Los Crestones. The return to San Gerardo de Rivas on the last day takes only four hours, which gives you an idea of the terrain. The cost is $330 for transportation, meals, guide, cook, park entrance fees, and a $5 donation to the park. You need your own backpack and sleeping bag. The minimum number of people is two or three, depending on the time of year. Telephone 225-0263 or 234-2530, fax 225-6143.

Just 22 miles (35 km) west from San Isidro via a paved road are Dominical and lovely Pacific beaches. This route allows the traveler to make a loop that joins up with the southern coastal route discussed later in this chapter, a way to get to the middle Pacific without returning to San José.

Many choose the highland road to get to Dominical, combining a mountain experience with the coast. Near Dominical are approximately 30 miles (50 km) of sandy beaches with names like Matapalo, Barú, Playa Hermosa, and Uvita. This is really supposed to be the year that the famous Costanera Sur, envisioned since 1963, is completed—an all-weather road offering an alternative to the mountainous Inter-American Highway from San José to

Panama. Lack of bridges has made travel south much beyond Dominical difficult if not impossible; the bridge over the Barú at Dominical was just completed in 1986. When finished, the road will allow you to go all the way to Ciudad Cortés and connect with Palmar Norte on the Inter-American. The sections of wide graveled road already done south of Dominical are great.

Dominical is still very small—everybody knows everybody else. There are a handful of restaurants and a growing number of places to stay. Dominical is earning a name for itself in Costa Rica as a community concerned with protecting the environment.

Hacienda Barú is a private nature reserve a few minutes north of Dominical on the road to Quepos. It covers a variety of habitats, from beach to coastal range primary rain forest, offering day visits and overnight facilities, both in tent camps in the forest and in the new Cabanas El Ceibo near the beach. Jack and Diane Ewing are marvelous hosts. (See chapter 8 for details.)

The Ewings' Selva Mar Tours focuses on ecological tourism in the Dominical area. A day of canopy exploration in the tropical wet forest, up to 130 feet (40 m) high, is an option for the physically fit who have a yen to climb tree giants. The company also books for most of the lodges and reserves in the area. (Radio communication is the order of the day here because of the lack of phones.) Telephone or fax 771-1903.

In Dominical proper, Ann and Richard Dale are charming hosts at Albergue Willdale, also known as Cabinas Willy. Among the trees alongside the Barú River, Albergue Willdale has seven very clean and simply furnished rooms—cement floors painted red, bright sheets, some lovely purple heartwood, fans, and private baths with shower-head hot water. The cost is $30 for two people. There are bikes, an inflatable paddle boat, and kayaks. A floating dock on the river is great for bird-watching. A stem of bananas is always out for guests.

The Dales also have a two-bedroom mountain villa, Cabeza de Mono, for those who seek solitude in beautiful surroundings. A spectacular view stretches from Punta Catedral in Manuel Antonio to Isla de Caño and Corcovado. The two-bedroom villa has a swimming pool and comes furnished with food for two meals per day.

It costs $125 a day or $800 per week. Visa and MasterCard are accepted only if absolutely necessary. You can also contact the Dales about a friend's house in Dominical, which sleeps up to four in one bedroom for $40 a day. Telephone or fax 771-1903 at Selva Mar.

Hotel Rio Lindo is an attractive, ten-room, two-story hotel with rooms priced at $46 for up to three people. They are airy, with ceiling fans, bamboo furniture, screened windows, and private baths with central hot water (some with huge showers). The Maui Restaurant next door also belongs to the hotel. Telephone 771-2009, fax 771-1716. Credit cards are not accepted.

South of Dominical are a number of destinations for nature travelers. Bella Vista Lodge above Punta Dominical lives up to its name—there is a gorgeous view of forest and sea. Woody and Lenny Dyer have turned the old farmhouse made out of hand-cut hardwood into a rustic, delightful place to get away from it all. A wide veranda surrounds the heart of the house. The four rooms are off a central hallway that is open to catch the breeze. There are two shared baths, but no hot water, though Woody says the water tends to be warm naturally. A single costs $25, a double $35. A tiny independent room, the Tiki House, is $10. There are no power lines here, so it is candle or battery power at night. You will get a full breakfast for $2.50, lunch for $3, and dinner for $5. Do not anticipate a strict rice and beans diet—some gourmet dishes come along with the candlelight. A number of horseback tours are available for overnight guests and day visitors: the rain forest-waterfall tour is $35, beach rides $30. There also are walking trails in the forest. Transportation from Dominical can be arranged—the road requires four-wheel drive and an experienced chauffeur. Woody also oversees rental of two houses near the lodge for up to ten people, at about $45 for two plus $5 for each extra person. Telephone or fax 771-1903 at Selva Mar).

Cabinas Punta Dominical is situated high on the point at Punta Dominical, with the sea on both sides—a lovely retreat for nature lovers. Four cabins of tropical hardwood built up off the ground are among the trees and have tremendous views of the ocean, which you can also enjoy from a hammock on your own porch.

Rooms are big, with louvered floor-length shutters on three sides, polished wood floors, ceiling fans, screened windows, and private baths with hot water. The place is peaceful and private. A single is $35, a double $45. The thatched, open-air restaurant, open to the public, has excellent food—and it is worth a trip just to sit here and drink in the panorama of sea and coastline, with Ballena National Park at center-stage. Cabinas Punta Dominical is just five minutes south of Dominical by car. Telephone or fax 771-1903 at Selva Mar.

Ten minutes south of Dominical on the road to Uvita is Cabañas Escondidas. Each of the very private cabins is unique: Rancho Bamboo has sliding screen doors, Japanese-style; Rancho Ambrosia is next to cacao trees; Treehouse seems to be in the branches of the trees. There is no electricity, so night lighting is by candles or flashlight—nothing to dim the starlight. Cabins are $35 for up to two people, plus $10 for each additional person. Food is gourmet vegetarian; the continental breakfast is complimentary, a full one is $3, lunch $5, dinner, $10. Owners Gailon West and Patricia Mitchell have created beautiful gardens of native plants and trees around the cabins and dining room, but 80 acres (32 ha) are in natural forest. Guided nature walks are $20 for two and a half hours. There are mountain bikes, horses, and Tai Chi or Chi Gong classes. A walking path leads to a secluded beach with tide pools for safe swimming. Three beach cabins are in the works. Telephone or fax 771-1903 at Selva Mar.

Oro Verde Private Biological Reserve above Uvita, managed by the Duarte family, offers day visits as well as overnight stays in rustic cabins with private bath. A visit involves a horseback ride and a hike in. It is a cultural as well as an ecological tour, with a chance to experience something of life on the Duarte farm. Day tours are $35, cabins about $10 per person and another $10 a day for meals. Inquire at Selva Mar; telephone or fax 771-1903.

Check out Reel 'N Release in Dominical for fishing, diving, or snorkeling options. A boat trip to Isla de Caño or Ballena National Marine Park is $275 for half a day, $425 for a full day for up to four people—including equipment for fishing or diving, food, juice, and soft drinks. Owner Steve Wofford is also running a Corcovado Sea

Shuttle that makes a run from Quepos, Dominical, and Uvita, to Drake's Bay and Corcovado. Telephone or fax 771-1903 at Selva Mar.

Public buses are an option for travel to Dominical. Two a day go between San Isidro and Quepos, passing through Dominical. A San Isidro-Uvita bus can get you to points south of Dominical.

For those continuing south from San Isidro, the Inter-American Highway goes through farm and ranch country and then into mile after mile of pineapples. In less than an hour, you can be in the Buenos Aires area, where there is a Pindeco pineapple processing plant. The chamber of commerce in San Isidro can give you information on tours of the plant. Try fresh pineapples at a roadside stand.

Past El Brujo (where there is a guard checkpoint and a large restaurant), a few miles on the right, is a lovely waterfall that Indians in the area believe has a special quality. Healers use the water in medicinal preparations. Just before the Inter-American Highway reaches the Río Grande de Térraba is the junction to Paso Real and the road to San Vito and the Robert and Catherine Wilson Botanical Garden, operated by the Organization for Tropical Studies. (See chapter 8.) A bridge is being built over the mighty river, but in the meantime, cars and buses to San Vito cross by ferry. The paved road passes through beautiful country, where travelers can come across cowboys and cows going down the road along with the usual menagerie of bicycles, dogs, chickens, and pedestrians. The Talamanca Mountains in La Amistad Park, an international biosphere reserve, rise up to the east. A four-wheel-drive vehicle is recommended to reach the park headquarters at Las Tablas.

Though I have not had the opportunity to stay there, lodging does exist in the Amistad Biosphere Reserve. Perhaps you can try it before I do. La Amistad Lodge, in the Las Tablas Protected Zone, has a maximum capacity of twenty people in six rooms, sharing three baths with hot water. A single is $35, a double $50. Meals are $7 for a buffet breakfast and $12 each for lunch and dinner. Entrance to the reserve is $10 per person, and guided nature walks cost $40 per group. La Amistad is 20 miles (32 km)—about an

hour—from San Vito. Call Tropical Rainbow Tours for more information, including details on a four-day, three-night package that
also includes a visit to the Wilson Garden. Telephone 233-8228 or
221-5371, fax 255-4636.

Italian immigrants helped settle the area around San Vito, arriv-
ing in the early 1950s to clear and farm the land. In this town of
11,779 people, you will find several Italian restaurants and hear the
language spoken on the streets. (There is a gas station.)

Hotel El Ceibo has thirty-eight modest rooms, all but eleven with
private baths. The single rate is $12, double $21. MasterCard and
Visa are accepted. There is a large, pleasant dining room/bar and
ample parking. Telephone or fax 773-3025. Lodging is also available at the Wilson Botanical Garden, ten minutes from San Vito.

Just 2 miles (3 km) east of San Vito are the San Joaquín Marshes,
a habitat that includes more than 100 species of plants and 100
species of resident and migratory birds as well as fish, snakes, and
insects that live only in aquatic environments.

The road from San Vito to the Wilson Botanical Garden continues on through the mountains and then drops spectacularly to the
lowlands, Ciudad Neily, and the Inter-American Highway, where
one can go south to Panama or head back north for Golfito or San
Isidro.

For those who continue on the Inter-American rather than taking
the Paso Real cutoff to San Vito, the road winds along the Térraba
River. At the Indian village of Rey Curré, pull off for a visit to the
local craft cooperative across from the school. If it is closed, go to
the house next to the school. Children and adults carve plants, animals, and indigenous designs on gourds. It is much more fun to
buy the gourds here than in San José. At the cooperative, each
gourd has the name of the person who made it and the price he or
she wants for it—very inexpensive. Sometimes there are woven
purses for sale. If you buy at the house by the school, where the
chickens have more bravado than feathers, check to be sure there
are no ants living in the gourds. You do not want to be cooped up
in a car when the creatures decide to come out.

Palmar Sur, where both SANSA and Travelair flights land daily, is
often the route for travelers heading to the Sierpe River or Drake

Bay. These destinations are described in the Osa Peninsula section after Golfito. About 40 miles (65 km) south of Palmar on the Inter-American is the turnoff for Golfito, some 14 miles (22 km) farther. From San José, by air, the trip takes about 50 minutes; by bus, almost eight hours.

Golfito (population 19,727) is a port town on the Golfo Dulce and was a busy center for banana exportation when the Bananera Company, a subsidiary of United Brands, was operating in the area from 1938 to 1985. African palms have replaced bananas on much of the land, though bananas are being planted again now. The biggest news in Golfito in the last couple of years, however, has been the "duty-free" shopping complex known as the *depósito* which opened in 1990. People come from around the country to shop there, especially on weekends. The town itself is a narrow strip of about 4 miles (6 km) between the water and the mountains. If you fly in, you may wonder as you approach where there is enough level land for a runway.

Driving in, one of the first hotels encountered is Las Gaviotas. There is a pleasant open-air restaurant—with fresh flowers on the tables—attractive swimming pools for children and adults next to

Golfito—rusting rail cars in background remind one of an earlier era (Photo by Ree Strange Sheck)

the Golfo Dulce, looking across to the Osa Peninsula, and a small gift shop. Each of the eighteen rooms and three bungalows has private baths with hot water, and they open onto pretty gardens that reach to the shore. Rooms, a bit dark because they open onto covered individual porches, are brightened by quilted bedspreads. Each contains a desk and chair. Bungalows have two bedrooms and a living room/kitchen area with a hot plate and refrigerator. Rates for a single or double range from $30 to $38, depending on whether cooling is by air conditioning or fans. Bungalows go to $75. Credit cards are accepted. Near the shore are the remains of a minesweeper used in World War II, which now often serve as a picturesque roost for land and sea birds. Telephone 775-0062, fax 775-0544.

At the opposite end of Golfito, near the duty-free facilities, are two other lodging possibilities. Hotel Sierra, between the airport where the daily flights from San José land and the depósito, has seventy-two tastefully furnished rooms, each with a private bath with hot water and both air conditioning and ceiling fan. Furnishings include two double beds with bright bed coverings, a pretty wood dressing table and big mirror, remote-control TV, telephone, and a table and chairs. Floors are a pretty, cooling green tile. In the landscaped courtyard between the two wings of rooms are swimming pools for children and adults, the latter with a wet bar. There is a restaurant/bar, lounge, and conference room, plus secured parking. Singles are $68, doubles $82. Credit cards are accepted.

The hotel offers guided half-day hiking tours for $30 to $40 in the Golfito Wildlife Refuge next door, a $60 day-tour to Zancudo Beach, a $16-an-hour half-day jungle expedition on horseback, and a day trip to Wilson Botanical Garden, which costs $65 to $85 depending on whether the trip is by hotel van or taxi. Fishing is offered on the Coto or Esquinas rivers. Ask about tours to Corcovado. In San José, telephone 233-9693, fax 233-9715; in Golfito, telephone 775-0666, fax 775-0087.

Hotel Golfo Azul is in a residential area, the American Zone of United Fruit days, with well-kept wooden houses. The hotel's twenty-five simply furnished rooms, of varying sizes, have nice private baths with hot water and either air conditioning or fans. Rates for rooms with a fan range from $24 to $39, with air conditioning

Boat travel is common out of Golfito to nearby beaches and hotels (Photo by Ree Strange Sheck)

from $26 to $45. There is a restaurant and secured parking. Credit cards are accepted. Telephone 775-0871, fax 775-0832.

Getting around in Golfito is no problem. Taxis constantly run the major street from one end of town to the other, picking up passengers for less than $1, and the public bus is even cheaper. Across from the downtown dock is Restaurante Luis Brenes where you can get typical, inexpensive food—Luis speaks English and seems to have answers to most questions about how to get where. Samoa del Sur, with its huge, distinctive thatched roof is another restaurant possibility. It is north of downtown by the waters of the gulf.

Forty-five minutes by boat north of Golfito is lodging at secluded, captivating Rainbow Adventures, a private reserve with a mix of sea and forest. South of Golfito is the Pavones Bay area, which draws surfers and nature travelers alike—surfers for the big waves and nature travelers for Tiskita Lodge, a biological reserve and experimental station where exotic tropical fruits are grown. (See chapter 8 for descriptions of both of these private reserves.) A private botanical garden, Casa Orquídeas, is on Playa San Josecito, north of Golfito. A two-hour morning tour costs $5, but it is closed

Friday and Saturday. Access is by boat only; ask about a trip at your hotel or at the local dock.

Both the Golfito Wildlife Refuge, which practically surrounds the town on its landward side, and Corcovado National Park across the gulf are good options for nature travelers. (See chapter 7.) For those who want to cross the Golfo Dulce to Corcovado, Puerto Jiménez, and other destinations on the Osa Peninsula, the daily launch leaves Golfito at noon. The $3 trip takes less than an hour and a half. Passengers are often treated to views of dolphins who keep company with the boat for a ways. Boats between Golfito and Puerto Jiménez can be chartered.

Puerto Jiménez is where you find an office for Corcovado National Park and the Osa Conservation Area. Lodging in this small town is modest. Hotel Manglares has ten rooms and a restaurant; six of the rooms are next to the street and restaurant, and four are behind in a pleasant garden. A thatched rancho with hammocks offers a place for guests to enjoy the tropical flowers and the birds. Watch for the resident crocodile and scarlet macaw. Each room has a private bath—but no hot water—and fans. Singles are $25, doubles $30. Credit cards are accepted. The hotel offers a boat trip in the gulf, horseback riding, and tours to Corcovado. Telephone 735-5002, fax 735-5121.

Two other clean, small establishments with lower rates are Cabinas Marcelina and Cabinas Puerto Jiménez.

Heading south of town toward the tip of the peninsula are two private nature reserves well worth a visit. (See chapter 8 for descriptions of charming Bosque del Cabo and architecturally distinctive Lapa Rios.)

About 9 miles (14 km) north of Puerto Jiménez off the main road to Rincón is Albergue Ecoturistico El Tigre, near the border of Corcovado park. The project belongs to a group of farmers who are working in tourism, farming, and conservation. The albergue has six rooms with private baths, a restaurant, craft shop, and 500 acres (200 ha) of forest. Guests can visit Corcovado for a day for $22 or the community's gold mine, with the promise that finders are keepers, for $24. The way is clearly marked with signs for El Tigre. Telephone 783-3937.

Waterfall in Bosque Eterno de los Niños (Photo by Ree Strange Sheck)

This unpaved road from Puerto Jiménez to Rincón goes on to join the Inter-American, opening up the eastern and southern parts of the Osa to road travelers. Access to the western shores of the peninsula can be by air, by boat from other Pacific ports, or by road for 7 miles (11 km) from Palmar to Sierpe and then by boat on the Sierpe River to Drake Bay and points south.

The trip on the Sierpe River can be fascinating, with an opportunity to see kingfishers, tiger-herons, crocodiles, turtles, parrots, monkeys, blue herons, muscovy ducks, perhaps even a roseate spoonbill. But how much you actually do see may depend on the speed at which you travel. Some boat captains seem to view the river pretty much as a highway, a means of getting from one place to another as fast as possible. Others, like Mike Stiles, owner of the Río Sierpe Lodge, slow down for wildlife viewing and explore some of the estuaries, enjoying the trip as much as his guests. A hard rain in the mountains had brought an avalanche of water hyacinths downriver on my return trip with him, transforming the water into a floating garden—beautiful but tricky for navigation. The mouth of the Sierpe can be treacherous at times—be sure to go with a seasoned boatman.

The Río Sierpe Lodge is 15 miles (24 km) from Palmar by boat. At that point, the river is more than a half-mile (1 km) wide and 50 feet (15 m) deep. Along the opposite shore are some of the tallest mangroves in the world.

The lodge, on a narrow piece of land between the river and the mountains, consists of eleven rooms with private bath, some in the main house and others a few steps away. All have private baths with passive-solar hot water. Rooms are plain but comfortable, with thoughtful touches such as mirrors in both the bathroom and bedroom. Electricity is from a generator, and battery-powered reading lamps function after the generator goes off at night. Windows are screened, and there is a wall fan. Rubber boots and snorkeling equipment are free for guests. Food is plentiful and tasty, with lots of fruits, vegetables, and seafood—Mike serves a mean spaghetti. Rates of $65 per person, double occupancy, include lodging, meals, transportation between Palmar and the lodge, and taxes. Guests can be picked up at Quepos, Dominical, or Playa Piñuela—at added cost.

Tours with local naturalist guides include Corcovado or Caño Island for $55, an overnight hiking trek for $65, an overnight horseback trip for $125; a half-day excursion to Violin Island for $25, or a Laguna Sierpe boat trip for $50. Hiking trails near the lodge are free. A four-day, three-night package costs $295. Mike also offers scuba diving and fishing trips, and there are archaeological ruins to visit and beaches where you can swim, snorkel, or marvel at huge sand dollars and other sea shells.

The lodge has a reference library, including bird books to help you identify the myriad you will see. Some 175 species are spotted regularly, including the mangrove hummingbird, which Mike says often comes at breakfast, and the Baird's trogon. Telephone 220-1712 or 220-2121, fax 232-3321.

The Sierpe River is also the gateway for many travelers headed for Drake Bay, named for Sir Francis Drake, who sailed these waters more than 400 years ago. Though the area is remote, accessible by charter flights or boat, a growing number of nature tourism sites exist between the Sierpe and Corcovado National Park. Three are a short hike from the village of Drake Bay. Remember that boat landings on beaches will be wet, so come prepared with suitable shoes and clothes.

The closest lodging to the village is the newest, Aguila de Osa Inn, an upscale, fourteen-room complex of rooms, open-air restaurant, and dock. On a bluff overlooking the bay, the rooms have hardwood floors, screened windows, ceiling fans, carved doors, and private tiled baths with hot water. Some bathrooms have sunken tubs, and a two-bedroom bungalow with a conical roof has windows on three sides. Singles are $75; doubles range from $80 to $125, including meals. Transportation from Palmar to Sierpe is $15 each by taxi, and from Sierpe to the Aguila de Osa, it is $30 each by boat. A horseback tour is $55, a jungle hike in Corcovado $55, diving at Caño Island $110, snorkeling at Caño $55. Telephone 296-2190, telephone or fax 232-7722.

Just across the Agujitas River is the Drake Bay Wilderness Camp, a relaxing, laid-back kind of place where one soon settles into tropical time, pausing to delight in the antics of two squirrel monkeys who spend a lot of time in the fruit-laden gardens (they even play with a domestic cat), making a date with a spectacular sunset, lounging in hammocks. At low tide, one of the prettiest natural tide pools I have been in beckons.

Part of the wilderness camp is on the point between the river and the Pacific; the rest faces the ocean, backed by forest. Nineteen rooms with private baths, most with solar hot water, are in seven buildings scattered on the property. Newer units have tile floors and tile baths. All, simply furnished, have ceiling fans, brightly flowered sheets, luggage racks, even washcloths. Four ten-by-ten-foot oceanfront furnished tents (with electricity) offer an alternative, with occupants sharing a two-shower, two-toilet communal bath. Rates are $66 per person, double occupancy, in the rooms, $44 in tents, meals included.

A four-day, three-night package that includes lodging, meals, day trips to Corcovado and Caño Island, bilingual guide, and airplane and boat transportation from San José is $498 for a single, $488 each for doubles. Pickup and dropoff at Quepos can be arranged. Credit cards are accepted, at an additional charge. Good food is served family-style in a separate dining room. Complimentary bocas at 5:00 p.m. in the thatched, open-air lounge bring most guests together to talk over the day's adventures.

A horseback tour along beach and through forest is $35, and the Corcovado or Caño tour ranges from $35 to $50, depending on the number of people. I treasure the memorable morning I had on the $35 Río Claro tour. Walking on beach and forest trails with Fernando, a knowledgeable naturalist guide, was a treat. We saw twelve scarlet macaws feeding in distant trees, a white hawk (which Fernando explained follows white-faced monkeys, waiting for the chance to take a young monkey—and then we saw the monkeys). We watched a spectacular blowhole and a "walking beach" alive with hermit crabs. River otters were playing in the Río Claro. Guests swim up the beautiful river, outfitted with life vests and fins, and float back down with the gentle current. Tall trees of primary forest are on both banks; kingfishers fly by. It is special. You can snorkel in a lagoon if you like, or maybe visit a waterfall. I recommend it.

The owners and hosts at Drake Bay Wilderness Camp, Herbert and Marleny (Marleny's family homesteaded this land), will help you work out the details of your visit. Ask about scuba diving at Caño Island, either for the day or as part of a package. Fishing is also available. Telephone or fax 771-2436 at the camp itself, or telephone 285-4367 in San José.

Do not miss the hanging bridge over the Agujitas River between Drake Bay Wilderness Camp and the Aguila de Osa Inn. It is on the traditional path that villagers and travelers have walked for years connecting the town of Drake Bay with areas farther down the Osa Peninsula. Continuing toward the south on this path from the wilderness camp is delightful La Paloma Lodge, owned by Mike and Sue Kalmbach. The hilltop retreat has spectacular views of the Pacific and landscaped gardens that provide a rich setting for the tropical birds that abound in this area. Fiery-billed aracaris were feasting regularly on *almendro* trees when I was there. Their calls mixed with those of chestnut-mandibled toucans, parrots, and macaws in appropriate jungle melodies, blending nicely with distant sounds of the sea.

The centerpiece of the complex is a large, thatched-roofed structure that contains the dining room, bar, lounge area, a small library with reference books and magazines, and a marvelous veranda along the ocean side with lots of chairs for sunset-watching at complimentary boca time before dinner. Food is served family-style, and it is excellent. Homemade bread is on the table at every meal, and nighttime brings rich desserts. Do not be surprised if Mike sits down with you at dinner. Sue is generally the one who helps with arrangements by phone or fax.

There are five rooms and five thatched, two-story ranchos to house guests. The comfortable, simply furnished rooms open onto a big veranda with hammocks. The ranchos have private porches, with beds and bath downstairs, and a marvelous, spacious bedroom upstairs open between the waist-high walls and the overhang of the tall thatched roof. The views are of forest and sea. Both rooms and ranchos have private tiled baths, though no hot water. There are no electric outlets, so don't bother bringing your plug-in appliances. Electricity for lighting is from a generator. Rates per person for double occupancy, with meals, are $68 for the rooms, $85 for the ranchos. A four-day, three-night package is $520 for the rooms, $570 for ranchos, including round-trip air and boat transportation from San José, meals, and guided tours to Corcovado and Caño Island.

Accompany Pedro, an experienced naturalist guide, and you may see and learn about toucans, manakins, scarlet macaws, parrots, monkeys, sloths, herons, and iguanas. Have him tell you about the *vaca* tree. For pure pleasure, go on a gentle canoe or kayak trip on the Agujitas River, taking a dip in the cool water—a contrast to the warmer water of the bay—and enjoy bird-watching. You can go with the guide or alone. The beach is a short walk down the trail.

La Paloma Lodge offers guided day trips to the Río Claro (by horseback) or Corcovada for $55 and to Caño Island for $65. The half-day on the Agujitas River is $25. Ask about sport fishing and diving rates. Telephone or fax 239-0954.

A bit farther along the trail is Cocalito Lodge. Rustic rooms in the main lodge and cabins with decorative bamboo house up to twenty-five people. Each unit has a private bath. A small hydroelectric project provides lighting for bathrooms and kitchen, but there are no electric outlets. The restaurant serves organic produce along with seafood and pastas—by candlelight in the evening. There is traditional music and dance after dinner. Rooms are $20 per person, cabins $35 per person (quadruple occupancy). Meals are $30 per day. Cocalito Lodge, on the beach, offers guided tours to Caño, Corcovado, or the Río Claro for $50 each, a waterfall hike for $15, and an overnight trip to Los Planes for $100. There is also fishing and scuba diving. Ask about packages. Fax 786-6150 or 786-6335. In Canada, telephone (519) 782-4592.

Corcovado Adventures Tent Camp is also on the beach. Each tent, on a base that also provides a private porch, is furnished with a single and a double bed, night stand, and battery-powered lamp. The dining room and kitchen are powered by solar panels. In the communal bath houses are five toilets and five showers. The cost is $60 per person for lodging and meals. Corcovado Adventures offers a full-day trip to Caño or Corcovado with a local guide for $60 and horseback riding to the park or snorkeling in park waters for $55. Ask about sea kayaking, fishing, and transportation from Quepos or San José. Telephone 238-2726 or 233-6868, fax 260-4434.

The trail farther south continues to wind through forest and along the beach to Marenco Biological Station, a private nature reserve. (See chapter 8.)

Coastal Route through Orotina

Part of this route was the old Spanish trail from San José to the Pacific. From the capital, take the highway for the international airport and head for Atenas, a town founded in the sixteenth century. This area is known for the quality of its fruits; ticos travel to Atenas and Garita on weekends just to buy them. As you travel along the mountain road to Orotina, you pass through picturesque villages, farms, coffee fields, and patches of forest. Notice the "living fences." A branch cut off a tree of certain species is stuck in the ground, and it grows there. Besides serving as fence posts, the trees are windbreaks, and some of them offer fodder for cattle. *Madero negro* and *poró* (showy red flowers) are two of the species used. Sometimes the indio desnudo is chosen. Photosynthesis can take place through the bark of this species.

Other trees with bright blossoms on this route are the *llama del bosque*, "flame of the forest" (with red flowers), and *cortesa amarilla* (with yellow flowers).

While you are in Costa Rica, you may hear talk of a dry canal, referring to a land route from coast to coast that Costa Rica can offer as an economical alternative to the Panama Canal. There are rail and road possibilities here and farther north through Guanacaste. As a matter of fact, the one here is functioning already with containers trucked between Puerto Caldera on the Pacific and Moín, near Limón on the Caribbean. The missing highway segment that will streamline the route is between Ciudad Colón and Orotina, a straighter route farther south than this one.

Descending toward Orotina on the historic route, notice the almost perpendicular hillsides cleared for pastures. The terracelike appearance is created by the horizontal trails of grazing cows. Past Orotina is a turnoff northwest to Puntarenas and the Caldera dock, where cruise ships stop regularly.

Two delightful destinations for nature travelers are between Puerto Caldera and the junction to Orotina: Dundee Ranch Hotel and Hacienda Doña Marta Lodge. Watch for road signs. Both offer nature tourism on a working ranch; guests have a chance to explore this tropical dry forest-moist forest transition zone and to work alongside ranch hands.

Dundee Ranch Hotel has a large reception/lounge/dining room building, a sparkling swimming pool, a seventeen-room lodge, and a small conference/bird observation structure across a shallow lagoon connected to the rest of the complex by a wooden walkway. Colorful northern jacanas, egrets, and black-bellied whistling ducks were enjoying the water when I was there. The hotel has a nice list of some 100 birds compiled sporadically over a four-month period at the ranch, and another for the nearby estuaries, giving each its scientific, English, and Spanish names. You may see the crested caracara, hummingbirds, trogons, kingfishers, hawks, and cuckoos. Other animals include monkeys, crocodiles, coatis, and anteaters.

The comfortable rooms are bright, with red clay tile floors, colorful bedspreads, big closets, table and chairs, air conditioning and ceiling fans, and modern baths with hot water. The rate is $87 for one or two people, including continental breakfast. Visa and MasterCard are accepted.

Optional tours include horseback riding in the Valley of the Monkeys for $28, Rainbow Safari aboard Cricket (a tractor-tram) to a lagoon for $75, and an estuary and mangrove boat trip for $75. Transportation from San José is $15 per person. Dundee belongs to Alvaro and María Batalla, who also have Hotel Chalet Tirol in the Central Valley. Telephone 267-7371 or 428-8776, fax 267-7050.

Hacienda Doña Marta, just down the road from the Dundee, belongs to another branch of the Batalla family. Part of the fun of doing this book is discovering a totally unexpected delight to share: Hacienda Doña Marta made my day. The hacienda house has been restored to include a small dining room and lounge area for guests. Details of decoration in each of the six rooms creates the impression that one is visiting a fine hacienda and has been put up in a family bedroom. My favorite is the "hat room" with a wonderful collection of hats hanging on a long wall rack. Trophies for horseback riding, old family photographs, and fine antiques make each room distinctive and personal. The headboard of one bed is made of decorative metal gates with a landscape painted on the wall behind. Original art is in the private bathrooms—which have hot water. There are high bamboo ceilings, ceiling fans, and screened windows. Singles are $57, doubles $69. Breakfast is $5, lunch $10, dinner $14, plus tax.

Guests can swim in the pool, ride with cowboys, go horseback riding, take trails in the forest, or visit rivers.

The farm has cattle for milk and meat production (the stables and corral are near the main house), a pochote reforestation project, and mango groves. Telephone 234-0853, fax 234-0958.

Just ten minutes from these two lodges is the Tarcoles River and Carara Biological Reserve. Get out your binoculars for a stop near the bridge over the river. Crocodiles usually bask in the mud along its banks; birds enjoy the waters. You might see a wood stork, blue heron, or American egret. Early and near sundown, watch for scarlet macaws flying overhead. Restaurant Los Cocodrilos is beside the bridge.

Because of one-day nature tours from San José, Carara has become a popular natural history destination. Seeing it with a guide is recommended. One disappointed young woman told me she had gotten off the public bus at the entrance to Carara and walked on the trail without seeing anything spectacular. I think she had expected the birds and animals to come out and greet her. Guides know animal territories, which trees are in fruit, and what to look for. They can point out orchids that a visitor might not even spot. (See chapter 7 for information on Carara and chapter 9 for some tour possibilities.)

Area lodges and hotels also offer Carara tours. Hotel Villa Lapas is next door to Carara, on a former cattle ranch whose pastures have been returning to forest for six years now. The forty-eight-room modern hotel is built in the forest along the Tarcolitos River—the sound of its waters lull one to sleep at night. Coatis roam the garden area unafraid, black-bellied whistling ducks (called *piches* in Spanish) sometimes wander into the pretty open-air dining room, and scarlet macaws may squawk in a nearby tree as you eat. One birder spotted more than seventy-five species of birds in a half-hour period.

Large rooms with high ceilings are in nicely spaced units facing the river. Nice touches include a desk with storage drawers, a large mirror, an ample closet (in the bathroom), and one of the best hot showers in the country—the water flow is perfect. Most rooms have ceiling fans; some have air conditioning. There is a small conference center, a gift shop, a library, table games, and facilities for badminton and ping pong as well as a swimming pool. A single or double is $84. Credit cards are accepted.

Service and food are good in the dining room: the freshly made tortillas are excellent—go for them instead of bread at least once. Try the banana flan. The restaurant is open to the public, and it is only five minutes from the park station at Carara. Guided tours in the Villa Lapa forest (by foot or horseback) last from two hours to a full day, one going to a spectacular three-tiered waterfall. Trails are well-maintained, but there are rivers to cross. Tours to Manuel Antonio and Carara are available. Call about day visits. Telephone or fax 293-4104.

In the little town of Tarcoles, about 1 mile (2 km) from Carara is Cabinas Carara, quite basic but clean accommodations. Singles are $10, doubles $20; cabins for up to six are $28. There is a small restaurant and pool. Visits to Carara can be arranged. Telephone 288-3429 or 255-3993.

Farther down the road is Tarcol Lodge, geared to birders and naturalists. At high tide, the five-bedroom, two-bath lodge at the mouth of the Tarcoles River is almost surrounded by water. At low tide, guests may see as many as 2,000 birds on the sand flats. The rooms in the thirty-year-old, two-story house are simply furnished. The food is good. The rate is $85 per person, including round-trip transportation from San José, meals, laundry, and lodging. There is a three-day minimum stay.

With your binoculars, in the evening you might be able to see thirty to forty pairs of scarlet macaws in a tree across the river. Possible tours include Carara, horseback riding on the beach, turtle watching at Playa Hermosa, or an estuary trip. Some tours are included in your stay, depending on its length. The owners of Tarcol Lodge are the Erbs, who also have the private nature reserve Rancho Naturalista near Turrialba. Telephone or fax 267-7138.

From Carara, the road drops down to the coastal lowlands, with tantalizing views of the Pacific. Architectural variations appear, the most striking being the sharply pitched, thatched roofs on huts and open-air ranchos.

Jacó, on the beach, is popular with Costa Ricans, and tour companies often take tourists there, too. There are hotels, cabins, restaurants, a disco, car rental, and rental of surfing and other water-sports equipment. Swimmers and surfers should read the tips on water safety; riptides are not uncommon. ICT or Info can give you information on lodging possibilities in town, where there always seems to be a lot of activity for a place with only 2,500 people. Here are three that, for me, offer a sense of place.

Hotel Club del Mar is tucked away on a peaceful cove at the south end of Jacó Beach. Light, nicely furnished rooms nestle among the trees and tropical gardens, with the Pacific only a few steps away. The view of the surf and headland is fantastic. The fourteen rooms and a villa offer a cool, soft respite from the coastal sun—all have ceiling fans, some have air conditioning. A lovely sea-green floor tile adds a peaceful air. Carved wooden lintels, floor to ceiling louvered doors, rattan furniture with deep cushions, and balconies or porches are among the attractive features. Doubles range from $69 for budget rooms, $76 for standard, and $88 for superior rooms to $114 for the villa. Credit cards are accepted. There is a sparkling swimming pool and a library.

Philip and Marilyn Edwardes, owners and hosts, help guests with custom trips. The hotel offers a float trip on the Tulín River, turtle walks during the egg-laying season, a horseback trip into the forested mountains with a member of the Madrigal family, and a picnic at a hidden waterfall. They speak English, French, and various African languages. If you cannot stay at Club del Mar, stop by for a gourmet meal at its Las Sandalias restaurant. Telephone or fax 643-3194.

Just off the mountain side of the highway at Jacó is Hotel Hacienda Lilipoza, a twenty-room class hotel with prices to match: singles for $137, doubles $162, breakfast included. Arrangements of fresh tropical flowers are even in the bathrooms—big bathrooms with larger-than-life bathtubs, a shower, two sinks, and a bidet. Lovely, individually decorated rooms are huge, spacious enough for two full beds and a sitting area, with space to spare. Cushioned wicker chairs and wicker desks and tables vary from ornate styles in natural tones to a more traditional white wicker. The rooms are air conditioned and have TV and direct-dial phones. The high, pitched wood ceilings add to the open feeling.

The Lilipoza has a swimming pool, tennis court, boutique, shuttle to Jacó, car rental, and tour desk. Owner Lili Neale oversees personalized service for guests, helping arrange boat trips to see the dolphins, a sunset cruise, horseback riding, or an excursion on the Tulín River for excellent birding. Breakfast and lunch are served in an open-air restaurant/bar next to the pool, while dinner is served in a more formal restaurant. The vegetables are garden-fresh; this is fine dining. Credit cards are accepted. Telephone 643-3062, fax 643-3158. (By the way, Gerard Depardieu and the rest of the cast booked the entire hotel for the filming of the movie about Columbus, *1492*.

Terraza del Pacífico is a forty-three-room hotel just 3 miles (5 km) south of Jacó where Playa Hermosa begins. Rooms in the two-story hotel open onto porches or balconies facing the swimming pool and garden, looking toward the ocean. Hand-painted birds and butterflies decorate the curtains. The air-conditioned rooms have a TV, telephone, and private bath with hot water and tub. Singles are $92, doubles $105. Credit cards are accepted. There is daily transportation from San José, and car and horse rental. Tours can be arranged. Specialty dishes at the restaurant reflect the Italian ownership. Telephone 643-3222 or 643-3444, fax 643-3424.

Leaving the Jacó area and continuing south along the costanera, roadside signs advertise other lodging on Playa Hermosa, which is a favorite with surfers and also is a sea turtle nesting site. Next is Esterillos Beach and the Hotel Delfín. All fifteen rooms have a balcony with a sea view, and nice tiled baths with hot water. Some have ceiling fans, others air conditioning. A beautiful curved staircase leads from the large restaurant, open to the ocean, to the rooms upstairs. There is a small pool and a nearby beach with lots of shells to enjoy. Nothing much else is here, just a few houses—a sensation of being just you and the sea. Staff members can meet the bus at the highway and provide tours to Manuel Antonio,

Carara, and a nearby estuary. A single is $80, a double $97. Credit cards are accepted. Telephone or fax 771-1640.

Going on south, waving fields of rice for a nearby processing plant draw birds. Near Parrita, groves of African palm appear.

In 1945, the Bananera Company started the first commercial palm plantation in the area, replacing banana plantations that had been badly affected by Panama disease. By 1965, African palm plantations reached as far south as Golfito. Oil extracted from the plant is used not only for fat, margarine, and cooking oil but also in soaps and perfumes. Be alert for one-lane bridges.

The town of Quepos, 110 miles (177 km) from San José, is the gateway for visits to Manuel Antonio National Park. Express buses from San José make the trip in about three and a half hours, and SANSA has twenty-minute flights six days a week. If you come by bus, you can get off at Quepos and make reservations for your return trip before continuing to Manuel Antonio. There are also buses to Quepos from San Isidro de El General and Puntarenas. (See Practical Extras for schedules.) Car rental is available in Quepos and Manuel Antonio.

Quepos (population 12,444) was named for the Quepo Indians who once roamed these parts. Artifacts turn up in surrounding pastures and fields. Mogote Island, a sheer-sided land with a crown of thick vegetation visible from Cathedral Point in Manuel Antonio National Park, was Quepo ceremonial ground. Today, Quepos is the center of an agricultural area where cattle are raised and rice, beans, sorghum, papayas, and mangoes are grown.

The Buena Nota gift shop, which also serves as an informal information center for the area, is run by Anita Myketuk. It has a second location near the Karahé Hotel on the road to Manuel Antonio. Along with handcrafted items, including originally designed clothing and beachwear, Anita has maps, books, English-language newspapers, and the patience to answer tourists' questions. A North American, she has lived here almost twenty years. She also has two houses for rent near the Mariposa Hotel, with a gorgeous view of Manuel Antonio: The one-bedroom is $400 a week, the two-bedroom $600. La Buena Nota is open Monday through Saturday from 8:00 a.m. to 6:00 p.m., half-day on Sundays. Telephone 777-0345 in

Quepos or 777-1002 for the new store on the road to Manuel Antonio.

Quepos is a bustling town with lots of small shops that serve local residents as well as the growing number of tourists. One of the small restaurants I like on the street facing the beach is El Gran Escape (the Great Escape), open from 7:00 a.m. to 10:00 p.m. but closed Tuesdays. Restaurant Isabel just down the street is also good. At the far end of the road into town is Nahomi, a tourist spot with restaurant and swimming pools.

Michael Lynch, the owner of Lynch Tourist Service in downtown Quepos, can fix you up with a whole range of ecoadventure tours, including snorkeling, bird-watching, a tour of a vanilla farm, or hiking to a waterfall in the rain forest, for $45 each; white-water rafting for $75; sea kayaking or scuba diving for $65; and a nature tour of Manuel Antonio park for $25. Lynch's is the SANSA ticket agent. Telephone 777-0161 or 777-1170, fax 777-1571.

Rain forest Expeditions & School has an office at Lynch Travel Service. It runs adventure-based education programs basically for students over age fifteen, though there are some older participants. Courses can involve cave exploration, backpacking, rafting, surfing, biking, and basic rock climbing, along with a home-stay and conservation projects. For information, fax 777-0279.

Two other tour operators are located on the road to Manuel Antonio. Eqqus Stables (777-0001) has guided horseback tours. Its beautiful stables make it kind of a horse heaven. Ríos Tropicales (telephone 777-1262, fax 777-0574) offers sea kayaking tours with professional, bilingual guides to the Damas Island estuary, great for seeing birds and perhaps even crocodiles and monkeys—lunch is aboard La Tortuga floating restaurant. Or you can kayak to the park along its ocean side. A one-day rafting trip (class III) on the clear, beautiful Savegre River takes you into a world of birds, monkeys, gorgeous trees, iguanas, a snake or two, and butterflies.

Here are two hotels in Quepos. The three-story Kamuk Hotel has twenty-eight rooms that range from $57 to $85 for a double, depending on the size of the room and whether it has a balcony. Credit cards are accepted. Each tastefully furnished room is air-conditioned and has TV, telephone, and private bath with hot water.

There is a restaurant, bar, gift shop, and snack bar. Telephone 777-1079, fax 777-0258.

The two-story Hotel Sirena has fourteen double rooms with air conditioning, private bath, and hot water. The pleasant rooms are simply furnished and open onto a courtyard with the pool and bar/restaurant. A single is $50, a double $65, breakfast included. Credit cards are accepted. The conservation-minded owners have put together interesting tours. On the $60 Savegre River horseback venture, travelers may see crocodiles, white-faced monkeys, and some of 150 species of birds as well as habitats that include mangrove, primary forest, beach, and river. A look at local agriculture—cattle, rice, and African palm—is included. Two-night, three-day packages can include horseback riding, park tour, bilingual guide, lodging, and breakfasts for $158; or horseback riding and a tour in a yacht equipped for fishing and diving for $224. Telephone 777-0528, fax 777-0171.

For a less-expensive option, contact Cabinas Ana in Quepos. Telephone 223-5567 or 777-0443.

About 4 miles (6 km) outside Quepos on the road to the airport is Hotel Rancho Casa Grande, fourteen rooms and ten one- and two-bedroom bungalows, swimming pool, tennis courts, whirlpool, and a restaurant that is open to the public. Rancho Casa Grande has its own walking paths through a humid tropical forest frequented by squirrel monkeys *(monos tití)*, some seventy species of birds, and thirty-three of butterflies. The large, pleasant rooms have ceiling fans and air conditioning, cable TV, telephones, hair dryers, coffee makers, and a small refrigerator. The bungalows also have a living room, dinette, and kitchenette with a microwave. Rancho Casa Grande is the ticket agent for Travelair and also has a tour agency. Guests can go horseback riding, rent motorcycles or cars, go on a guided nature walk, and visit Playa de Rey or Manuel Antonio. Baby-sitting is arranged. Rooms are $109 for a double; the one-bedroom bungalow is $126, the two bedroom $143. Credit cards are accepted. Telephone 777-0330, fax 777-1575.

The town of Manuel Antonio and the park are less than 5 miles (7 km) south of Quepos. A proliferation of small sodas in the town has unfortunately diminished its appeal and raised questions about pollution, but the park itself continues to be a small jewel. It protects beautiful beaches as well as the flora and fauna of the tropical forest. Visitors must wade across an estuary to reach the entrance, an adventurous introduction to the special experience ahead. A bus between Quepos and Manuel Antonio passes every hour or two in front of the hotels sprinkled along the road.

The following hotels in the Quepos-Manuel Antonio area are listed according to rates and location. Remember that many of them have considerably reduced rates during the "winter" months of May to November.

Makanda by the Sea is as elegant as its name. Located about halfway between Quepos and Manuel Antonio down the road that passes the Hotel Mariposa, it is surrounded by tall forest. Squirrel monkeys like it here, and sloths come to call. The secluded beach is down a short trail through the trees. Each of the seven studios and villas has an ocean view. Colorful purples and greens contrast with slate-gray tile. Louvered doors open up rooms to the natural world. Cushiony sofas, king- or queen-size beds, kitchenettes or full kitchens, ceiling fans, hot-water showers, balconies or terraces, hammocks and lounge chairs, individual Japanese gardens—these are some of the features. The large pool and Jacuzzi are in a forested setting. Studios are $114 and $143, villas $195. Credit cards are accepted. No children under sixteen. Telephone or fax 777-0442.

Something about Hotel La Mariposa seems to suspend time, so that the most important thing is simply being, and being there. Maybe it is because the view of forest, sea, and white-sand beach curving out to Cathedral Point touches the eternal in each of us. Ten villas, refined in their simplicity and tasteful decor, are woven into the greenery of the hillside: Spanish-style clay tile red roofs, white walls, bright colors in art and fabrics, bathrooms that incorporate tropical gardens (hot water, of course), big windows, ceiling fans, balconies that open off comfortable living rooms. The restaurant in the main building serves excellent international cuisine (it is open to the public, but dinner is with reservation only) and there is a poolside bar. English and French also are spoken. Tours can be arranged. No credit cards accepted; no children under fifteen. Rates include breakfast and dinner. Villas are $150 for a single, $206 for a double. The penthouse is $126 for a single and $189 for a double. Shuttles to the airport and beach are provided. Telephone 777-0355 or 777-0456, fax 777-0050. In the U.S., telephone (800) 223-6510; in Canada, (800) 268-0424.

Hotel El Byblos advertises "a touch of class in the jungle," and indeed it is. Each of the seventeen rooms is distinctively decorated. They are large and light, with private baths and hot water, cable TV, air conditioning, telephone, and small refrigerator. Tall trees and graceful tropical plants surround the pool and adjoining snack bar. The main restaurant, in a separate open-air building with an impressive ceiling of tropical wood, is known for its French cuisine; it is open to the public. El Byblos has a yacht for cruises to the park, Caño Island, or Corcovado, and for sport fishing or diving if you are certified. There also are guided tours to Manuel Antonio. A double room is $156; add $40 for breakfast and dinner. Credit cards are accepted. Telephone 777-0411 or 777-0217, fax 777-0009.

Hotel Arboleda has thirty-two rooms plus two family units with kitchenettes, living area, two bedrooms, and private bath, built on a hillside going down to the beach. There are two restaurants, a pool, gift shop, and kayak rental at $7 per hour, or $40 for a guided tour to Manuel Antonio. The hotel also has a half-day tour to Isla de Damas. Beds are large and long for king-size guests, sheets are bright. Some rooms are in a two-story building, others in bungalows. Private baths have shower-head hot water. Air-conditioned rooms are $109 for one or two people; rooms with fans are $97. Credit cards are accepted. Airport pickup is available. Ask about the rustic cabins at the mouth of the Naranjo River. The Barahonas, owners of the Arboleda, make them available to people doing research or who are interested in helping protect the turtles that nest there. The cabins have no electricity or hot water. Telephone 777-1056, fax 777-0092.

Bahias Hotel, closer to Quepos than Manuel Antonio, has ten rooms (two with indoor Jacuzzis) built around a garden. The rooms vary in decor and size, each with tiled baths, air conditioning and small porches or balconies. There is a poolside bar and a pleasant restaurant beside the road. Most rooms are $86; those with Jacuzzis are $105, and breakfast is included. Credit cards are accepted. Telephone 777-0350, fax 777-0549.

Hotel Divisamar about halfway between Quepos and Manuel Antonio, has twenty-four air-conditioned rooms and suites with private baths and hot water. The master suite has a refrigerator, wet bar, and coffee maker; superior rooms are large, with big windows and tasteful furnishings. The hotel has a swimming pool set in a garden, a whirlpool, bar, and restaurant. The standard double room is $82, superior $110, suite $150. Visa is accepted. Divisamar offers a three-hour park tour for $30 and an all-day waterfall tour for $70. Its hand-out information includes helpful maps of Quepos and the area from Quepos to Manuel Antonio as well as the bus schedule between the two. Views from the hotel are of tropical plants and trees, not the ocean. Telephone 777-0371, fax 777-0525.

Hotel y Villas Mogotes has eight rooms and four one- and two-bedroom villas, some with ocean views and kitchenettes. The bright, modern baths have hot water. Bamboo accents are found in the furniture and lamp shades. The rooms have ceiling fans, and there is also a swimming pool. Double rooms are $80, villas $114. Credit cards are accepted. A half-day guided tour is available to the park and to Isla de Damas, with lunch on a floating restaurant. Telephone 777-1043, fax 777-0582.

The Karahé Hotel has small villas and rooms tucked away in gardens up a hillside and air-conditioned rooms in a two-story addition near the beach. The newer ocean-front rooms, light with large windows and pretty quilted bedspreads, open onto balconies or terraces that overlook an attractive pool and whirlpool, and the sea beyond. The separate river-stone villas involve some climbing on paths through pretty gardens. Each has a private porch, kitchenette with a refrigerator but no stove, louvered windows with screens, and a large nicely furnished room. Villas for one or two people are $80, rooms $92, and beach-front rooms $114, breakfast included. Credit cards are accepted. Telephone 777-0170, fax 777-0152.

Costa Verde has a special feeling about it. It has wide tiled balconies with classy rocking chairs, terraces, gardens, big sliding wood-framed glass doors, tití monkeys moving through the trees, and a panoramic view of forest, sea, and Cathedral Point. The openness of the thirty rooms built on the hillside above Manuel Antonio connects them with the forest just outside the door. Some have kitchenettes, king-size beds, and small refrigerators. All have ceiling fans and private baths with hot water. The turquoise color of the swimming pool contrasts with the red brick terrace around it. There is a poolside bar and an attractive open-sided restaurant with a sea view—the food is pleasing to both the eye and the palate. You may want to try the new beer garden. Costa Verde rents kayaks by the hour and also offers guided kayak tours and a mangrove tour. A single or double room is $90. Credit cards are accepted, but there is a fee. Telephone 777-0584, fax 777-0560; in the U.S. and Canada, telephone (800) 231-RICA. The Costa Verde in Manuel Antonio is affiliated with the Costa Verde Inn in Escazú, just outside San José. Telephone 228-4080.

Hotel El Lirio has nine rooms, some with a Southwestern U.S. flavor: rough plastered white walls, tile floors, and a splash of color from the bedspreads. Rooms are large, with queen-size beds, ceiling fans and private baths with hot water. Four are in the two-story house next to the road; five are across a pretty garden where orchids bloom. A garden breakfast gazebo restaurant is next to the swimming pool. Rooms are $65. Credit cards are accepted. Telephone or fax 777-0403.

Ylang Ylang is a small, charming alternative to larger hotels. Each of the three units is different—you can choose the largest, with a full kitchen and a wooden deck, or one of the smaller ones, which also have balconies, ocean views, ceiling fans, reading lamps, large windows, and private baths with hot water. The rooms come complete with books and games. The largest is $80; the others are $60 for double occupancy. Credit cards are not accepted. Telephone 777-0184, fax 777-0594.

The ten bungalows at El Colibrí have the forest of Manuel Antonio park as a neighbor. They are pleasing and private. Louvered doors open onto terraces with a table and chairs for eating out and lounge chairs or a hammock just for relaxing and enjoying the landscaped gardens of tropical flowers and trees, pools, and fountains. Pleasant paths lead through the gardens to the swimming pool. Each room has cooking facilities, private bath with hot water, a ceiling fan, barbecue grill, and high wooden ceilings; some have king-size beds. A single is $57, a double $69; Visa is accepted. El Colibrí does not accept children under age eight. Telephone or fax 777-0432.

Plinio Hotel attracts people from all over the world. It is the kind of friendly place where you hear, "If you are ever in Sweden, look me up." The restaurant is a favorite with locals and visitors alike—cooking with a European flair. A wide variety of sleeping accommodations is available. There is the Jungle House with a king-size bed plus a queen-size in a loft, living area, kitchen facilities, a deck and a bath with a tub, for $86. Or there are three-story family suites with a rooftop sun deck, a big living room, a balcony overlooking the swimming pool, beds, and sofa beds for $105. There are two-story ocean-view studio suites for $86 and rooms from $69 to $75, double occupancy. All the units have hot water and ceiling fans or air conditioning. Those red, red bathroom fixtures are from Germany, the tiles from Italy. Plinio also has three miles of nature trails through its forested mountain slope, one that leads to a 45-foot (14-m) wooden outlook tower that lets you see canopy level and above—on clear days to Talamanca, Dominical, and the Nicoya Peninsula. Plinio is closer to Quepos than to Manuel Antonio. Credit cards are accepted, but there is a surcharge. Telephone 777-0055, fax 777-0558.

Hotel Villa Oso is high on a hill with a good view of the ocean—and the spectacular sunsets. Four rooms and one apartment each have a large terrace with hammocks, table, and chairs, a private bath with hot water, ceiling fan, and cooking facilities. The apartment has a full kitchen. The beds have orthopedic mattresses. The rates for doubles range from $57 for standard rooms to $69 and $80 for larger rooms and $97 for the apartment. Credit cards are not accepted. Bjorn Sanbech, the Norwegian who will be your host, has information on house rentals and also helps with tours and reservations elsewhere in Costa Rica. Telephone or fax 777-0233.

La Quinta consists of four pleasant, peaceful cabins above Manuel Antonio, all with a balcony or porch and an ocean view, and private baths with hot water; some have cooking facilities. There is a pretty pool in a landscaped garden, and an outdoor terrace where breakfast is served. English, French, and Hungarian also are spoken here. Cabins are $80 with kitchenettes, $57 without. Credit cards are not accepted. Telephone 777-0434.

The following hotels are in Manuel Antonio:

Hotel Villa Bosque has sixteen rooms in a two-story modern building set among the trees. Each opens onto a terrace or balcony that runs the length of the structure. They also have air conditioning and ceiling fans, private baths with hot water, and carved wooden doors with palm motifs. A bamboo-framed mirror, soft green floor tile that suggests the sea, and lots of potted plants are nice features. A room is $91 for up to two people. Credit cards are accepted. The attractive restaurant is in a separate building across a landscaped garden. A bilingual local guide leads four-hour tours to the park for $25. Telephone 777-0463 or 777-1152, fax 777-0401.

Los Almendros has expanded to twenty-one rooms. The newer units have hot water in the bathrooms and are air-conditioned; the older units have ceiling fans. Porches and balconies with lots of chairs look out on a palm-studded garden. A spacious open-air restaurant is across the garden—its music flows to the rooms. The older rooms are $50 for up to three people, the newer ones $60. Credit cards are not accepted. Telephone or fax 777-0225.

Cabinas Espadilla has also added new units, a pleasant two-story annex across the street from the original ones. All the newer rooms and some of the older ones have kitchenettes. All thirty-one rooms are air-conditioned and have hot water in private baths. Rates for one or two people are $34 for the rooms with fans, $47 for air conditioning; Visa is accepted. Telephone or fax 777-0416.

Hotel Vela Bar adjoins the protected forest of Manuel Antonio. There are nine rooms with balconies or terraces that are furnished with hammocks and open onto a pretty tropical garden. (I once found an exquisite hummingbird nest on the branch of a tree by the path.) Some rooms have fans, others air conditioning. Singles range from $11 to $48, doubles from $20 to $48. Credit cards are accepted. A one-bedroom casita for up to three people is $63, and a one-bedroom apartment for two is $49. A local bilingual guide leads a morning park tour for $25. Telephone 777-0413, fax 777-1071.

Hotel Piscis has twelve rooms that share six baths, and six newer cabins with private baths. The older rooms are a bit dark and open onto a long shaded porch, but they are immaculate, and there are fresh flowers on the table. The newer cabins are brighter. All the units have fans. The restaurant is in a separate building. A single or double is $20 with a private bath; the shared baths are cheaper. Credit cards are not accepted. Telephone 777-0046.

In addition to the hotel restaurants mentioned, others I like are Karola's, the Barba Roja, and La Brise.

From Quepos, it is about 28 miles (45 km) farther along the coast to Dominical, where the road to San Isidro de El General comes in, offering an alternative route back to San José or south on the Inter-American Highway. The private nature reserve Hacienda Barú just before Dominical is an easy day trip from Quepos or Manuel Antonio. (See chapter 8.) This area is mentioned in the earlier highland route section.

Caribbean

The Atlantic Coast is shorter than the Pacific and has a more extensive coastal plain. The area offers long, uncluttered beaches, high forested mountains, coconut palms, plantations of cacao and bananas, national parks and wildlife refuges, sleepy villages, and a commercial port.

The newer highway through Guapiles and Braulio Carrillo National Park cuts travel time to two hours by road from San José to Limón. Even when you have left the park, though, keep your eyes peeled for sloths in the trees. If you are driving, be careful of heavy fog and landslides, especially through the park, and also of speeding drivers.

The old highway through Cartago and Turrialba, mentioned in the Central Valley section, requires about four hours of travel time. The large pipeline you notice in places carries petroleum products from the port at Limón, following the old road to Siquirres. The famous Jungle Train from San José to Limón was discontinued in 1991, but some local lines persist in the coastal banana areas. Steel rails and both highway routes come together at Siquirres, where you are definitely in banana country. Signs point to towns whose names tie them to the railroad: Linea B, 28 Millas. Many short lines provided transportation in this area, some with rail cars pulled by burros until the 1950s.

The main line took from 1871 to 1890 to build, with Chinese and West Indians brought in as workers. To help finance the project, bananas were grown for export (and to feed the workers), and that brought in more blacks from British colonies, many from Jamaica. That is how the United Fruit Company got its start in Costa Rica. Though only about 2 percent of the country's residents are African-American, the percentage in the province of Limón is about one-third. Their cultural influence adds to the flavor of the Caribbean zone and, because many speak English, broadens communications for monolingual English-speaking tourists.

Limón, or more correctly Puerto Limón (population 69,728), is the capital of the province. Christopher Columbus dropped anchor offshore near Uvita Island in 1502. Around October 12—a holiday commemorating Columbus and his discovery that ticos celebrate as Día de la Raza—Limón throws a big party that draws about 200,000 people. It may not be Río, but this carnival is five days of music, parades, dancing, bullfights (the bull is never killed in this nation of peace), and local arts and crafts.

During the rest of the year, Limón is a center of commerce (with deep-water docking facilities at nearby Moín), of fishing, shipping, agriculture, and tourism. If sloths have so far eluded you, go to Vargas Park near the seawall, where several live. If you cannot spot the well-camouflaged mammals, a passerby will usually help. If you go to the Municipal Market, stop by one of the food stands to try rice and beans, or a fried cake, or *agua de sapo*, literally "toad water" but actually a kind of cold agua dulce with lemon.

In Limón and south, you still see a few signs of the April 22, 1991, earthquake that walloped the region, though reconstruction of buildings and damaged roads and bridges has whittled away at the physical evidence. The quake, which registered 7.4 on the Richter scale, raised the Atlantic coast about 5 feet (1.5 m) at Limón, diminishing to about a foot (30 cm) farther south at

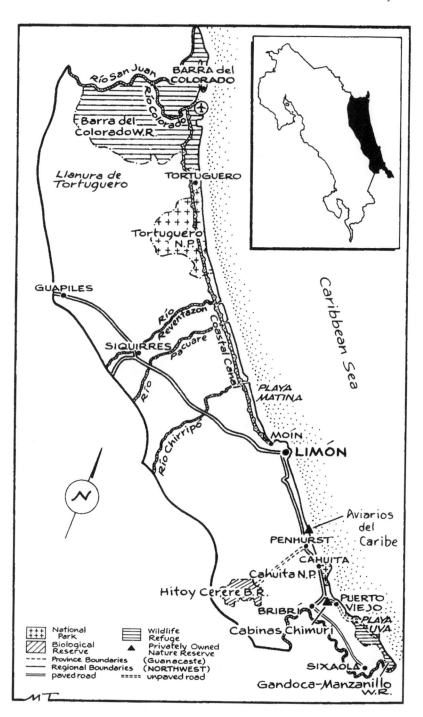

National
Park
Biological
Reserve
----- Province Boundaries
Regional Boundaries
paved road

Wildlife
Refuge
▲ Privately Owned
Nature Reserve
(Guanacaste)
(NORTHWEST)
===== unpaved road

Río San Juan
BARRA del COLORADO
Río Colorado
Barra del Colorado W.R.
Llanura de Tortuguero
TORTUGUERO
Tortuguero N.P.
GUAPILES
Río Reventazon
SIQUIRRES
Pacuare
Río
Río Chirripo
Coastal Canal
PLAYA MATINA
MOÍN
LIMÓN
Caribbean Sea
Aviarios del Caribe
PENHURST
CAHUITA
Cahuita N.P.
Hitoy Cerere B.R.
BRIBRI
PUERTO VIEJO
PLAYA UVA
Cabinas Chimuri
SIXAOLA
Gandoca-Manzanillo W.R.

Gandoca near Panama. So you will note some changes along the beaches. A positive note is that scientists predict no major earthquake here for about another 100 years.

Though there are several hotels in and near Limón, my pick would be the Maribú Caribe on the ocean, where the sounds are of the sea; La Matama in the forest, where birds break the silence; and Hotel Acón downtown, where the sounds are of the city. The first two are on the road to Portete, just north of downtown.

At Hotel Maribú Caribe, a single is $74, a double $85. Fifty-four air-conditioned rooms are located in fourteen upscale thatched bungalows, some with ocean views. The hotel has a restaurant specializing in French food, a snack bar, swimming pools, bike rental, a gift shop, and parking. Credit cards are accepted. It offers tours to watch turtle-nesting during the season plus one-day tours to Tortuguero for $65, and visits to Cahuita National Park for snorkeling at $60 and diving at $85. If you do not have time to go all the way to Tortuguero, you can take a three-hour tour on the canals for $35. The hotel is situated on a hill, with grassy grounds going down to the Caribbean. Hotel transportation from San José to Limón is $35. Telephone 234-0193, 758-4543 or 758-4010, fax 758-3541 or 234-0193.

At Hotel Matama, a room for one or two people is $74, plus $15 for each additional person. The open-air restaurant/bar and rooms in scattered bungalows are nestled among the trees. Some of the bathrooms have small tropical gardens growing under their skylights. The sixteen rooms are nicely furnished; cushioned wicker chairs add color. There is also a pool, air conditioning, car rental, and parking. Credit cards are accepted. The hotel offers a half-day walk on its own jungle trail for $30. Javier, the bilingual naturalist guide, knows just where the spectacled owl is likely to be and where a boa constrictor hangs out. The first part of the walk goes through a coconut plantation, where you can drink the liquid from a green coconut, or *pipa*. Passing by cacao trees, you can see where chocolate comes from. You may spot a black-cheeked woodpecker, yellow-tailed oriole, or three species of tanager, as well as a sloth, coati, or anteater. Trips to Tortuguero and Cahuita can be arranged. Telephone 758-1123 or 758-4200, fax 758-4499.

At thirty-nine-room Hotel Acón, a single is $23, a double $29. The hotel has a restaurant, private baths with hot water, air conditioning, TV, and a discotheque and arranges trips to Tortuguero. Telephone 758-1010, fax 758-2924.

Express buses for Limón depart hourly during the day from San José at Avenida 3, Calles 19/21, near the National Park.

Tortuguero and Barra del Colorado national parks on the northern Caribbean coast are popular destinations for nature travelers. SANSA and Travelair offer air options. The most convenient way to get to either is by taking a prearranged tour. From San José, package tours include transportation by bus and boat or airplane, hotel, and meals. Some offer guided exploration of the waterways off the main canal. (See chapter 9 for specifics.) Hotels and travel-related businesses from Limón south also arrange tours to Tortuguero, many with one-day tours. You can do the trip yourself, too, arranging boat transportation from Moín outside Limón, finding your own lodging, and hiring a boat and local guide once you arrive at Tortuguero or Barra del Colorado.

Green, leatherback, and hawksbill turtles nest in the area, with heavy concentrations on a long beach at Tortuguero. This is the home of the Caribbean Conservation Corporation started by the late Dr. Archie Carr to carry out turtle research.

The canals that run parallel to the sea were built in the 1970s connecting existing rivers and lagoons to provide an 80-mile (129-km) inland waterway from Moín, just north of Limón to Barra del Colorado. Roads have yet to connect some of this area with the rest of the country, so this lifeline of canals and rivers is the highway for canoes loaded with bananas and coconuts, logs that are floated south, and barges carrying supplies north. Families travel in tiny dugouts. Sometimes the narrow canals open into wide lagoons; signs give distances and directions. A trip on these waters is fascinating, and one notes a courtesy in traffic lacking in San José. Large boats propelled by motors slow down when small craft appear to avoid swamping them. When our boat died between Tortuguero and Barra del Colorado, the first boat by took us on, luggage and all.

CACAO

Cacao trees were cultivated in Costa Rica before the Spaniards arrived. The plant, whose seeds provide us with cocoa, chocolate, and cocoa butter, is native to tropical America. The name it was given in Latin, Theobroma, means "food of the gods."

Spanish explorers found cacao fields at Matina in 1540. During colonial times, it was the most important cash crop until coffee was introduced, and cacao beans were even used as money up to the late 1700s. Climatic conditions continue to make the Atlantic lowlands the major region for cacao plantations; you will see them on the road south from Limón to Puerto Viejo and between Braulio Carrillo park and Limón.

Cacao is a short tree, about 26 feet (8 m) in height. It has some interesting biological peculiarities. Leaves are both green (mature ones) and red (young ones). They go from a horizontal to a vertical position depending on the amount of sunlight—the more intense the sun, the more they droop. The fruits or pods (called mazorcas*) grow directly from the trunk or branches, hanging like ornaments.*

As the pods ripen, they change from green to yellow or red. As many as sixty seeds—the commercial cocoa beans—can be in the oval-shaped fruit. The one opened for me had forty-three, all covered in a slippery, soft pulp that is quite tasty.

Harvest is year-round, but it peaks in April and May and from October to December. Mature pods are hand-picked and cut open. The seeds are fermented for a few days and then dried, either in the sun or mechanically. They are then shipped to factories—there are three large ones in Costa Rica—for processing. If you take a side road off the main highway in the Penhurst area, you will see platforms with cacao spread out to dry.

Costa Rica was once Central America's leader in cacao export, but disease damaged many trees in 1978. Gradually, production has increased since then. CATIE, the agricultural research center at Turrialba, has worked with disease-resistant strains and distributes hybrids.

Most of the cacao crop exported from Costa Rica goes to the United States, France, and Germany.

Fishing draws visitors to this area as well, especially for snook and tarpon. There is a fishing camp at Barra del Parismina and others at Barra del Colorado.

South from Limón you can travel by road all the way to Panama. The direct bus from San José to Sixaola at the border will take you by Cahuita National Park and to the Indian village of Bribrí. It does not go all the way in to Puerto Viejo. There is a direct San José–Puerto Viejo bus, however, and there are buses from Limón to Cahuita and Puerto Viejo. (This is Puerto Viejo de Limón.) Several tour companies now offer nature-oriented tours to the southern Caribbean region, and lodges and hotels in the area arrange visits to the parks and reserves.

With the Caribbean on the left and forest remnants and farms on the right, there is much to take in. Some fields contain coconut palms, banana plants, and cacao trees together. The mix of Indian and black culture in the area is unique in Costa Rica.

About 20 miles (30 km) south of Limón, just before the Estrella River, is a delightful destination for nature travelers: Aviarios del Caribe. Luís and Judy Arroyo own and operate this refuge. (See chapter 8.)

At Penhurst, a road west goes through miles of cacao plantations. Platforms are covered with seeds spread out to dry. You may see *guanábana* fruit covered with the same blue plastic bags impregnated with insecticide that you have noticed over bunches of bananas. The size of the guanábanas is astounding. Follow this dirt road through big banana plantations to the Hitoy-Cerere Biological Reserve. Little visited, it holds treasures for those who reach its forests.

Back on the main road, a few miles farther is the town of Cahuita and Cahuita National Park. A pedestrian entrance to the park lies at the edge of town.

Cahuita, 27 miles (44 km) south of Limón, has only about 3,400 people. Though hotels and lodges are still small, tourism is increasingly big business here. There is a thriving tour company, Cahuita Tours and Rentals, telephone or fax 758-0652, telephone 758-1515, extension 232 or 266. It is a full-service operation where you can send a fax; exchange money; buy newspapers, handcrafts, or postage stamps; make reservations; and find a public telephone. Owner Antonio Mora can also recommend good restaurants. Snorkeling equipment is available, as well as bikes and scuba gear. For $20, you can spend four hours in a glass-bottomed boat viewing the marvels of the coral reefs offshore. Other tours include

Hotel Jaguar at Cahuita (Photo by Ree Strange Sheck)

late-afternoon guided nature walks, a half-day visit to the Bribrí Indian reserve, and visits to Manzanillo and the Gandoca-Manzanillo refuge and to Tortuguero National Park. A tour to Hitoy-Cerere Biological Reserve with a bilingual local guide is about $35 per person, with a minimum of three people.

Here is a sample of some of the hotels:

Chalet y Cabinas Hibiscus is by the sea. Three bungalows for two people and two two-story, two-bedroom houses are scattered on palm-studded grounds. Private baths with hot water feature showers lined with smooth river stones. Lace curtains cover the windows, and mosquito nets are draped over the beds, though owner Graf Thomas, who has lived here twelve years, says they are more for show than necessity. The houses have a balcony, sitting room, and completely furnished kitchen—the larger one is $120 for up to six people, the smaller $90. Bungalows are $50 and $60. Credit cards are not accepted. English and German also are spoken. The Hibiscus has no restaurant, but one is nearby. Fax 758-0652.

The Hotel Jaguar has forty-five rooms across the road from the beach on the north end of town, close enough to go to sleep to the sound of the surf. The building design incorporates cross-ventilation and thermo-siphoning, resulting in passively cooled rooms that have queen-size beds with orthopedic mattresses and private baths with hot water. Louvered shutters cover screened windows. Just outside the front door are lounge chairs on long porches facing the beach. A variety of fruit trees draw birds to the hotel grounds. Watch for the flash of the scarlet-rumped tanager and listen to the parrots. Junior suites are $40 for a single, $70 for a double, including breakfast; standards are $30 for a single, $55 for a double. A standard room with breakfast and dinner is $40 per person. Visa and MasterCard are accepted.

Paul and Melba Vigneault own the hotel and are creators of a menu fit for a gourmet, true elegance by the sea, with such delicacies as avocado omelets for breakfast and Basque-French cooking that uses fresh herbs and spices in ten sauces served with fish, beef, or chicken. The sea bass with heart of palm sauce is memorable. If you cannot stay at the Jaguar, stop by for a meal. The restaurant is open for breakfast beginning at 7:30 a.m., and dinner is served until 9:00 p.m.

Nature trails on the 18 acres (7 ha) offer hotel guests the possibility of seeing a crocodile, armadillo, sloth, kinkajou, agouti, or colorful frogs. Trips can be arranged to Tortuguero for $50, to Punta Uva, Puerto Viejo, or the Bribrí reserve for $25, and to Aviarios del Caribe or, for the hardy, Hitoy-Cerere and Gandoca-Manzanillo. A rental shop has boogie boards, beach mats, fins, and snorkeling equipment as well as books and souvenir items. Telephone 226-3775 or 758-1515, extension 238. Transportation from Cahuita is available if you come on either the direct bus from San José or Sixaola or one from Limón.

The Magellan Inn, tucked away on a street back from the beach, has six delightful rooms. Original oil paintings adorn the white walls. There are big closets, a long desk, and beautiful woods in carpeted rooms. Each room has French doors that open onto a terrace facing the pool and a tropical garden colored by bright bougainvillea and hibiscus flowers as well as avocado, guava, orange, and lime trees. There are ceiling fans not only in the rooms but also on the terraces, which has cushioned rattan furniture. The dining room and bar, for guests only, is also open to the garden. Classical music sets the tone for breakfast, quiet jazz for dinner.

Toucans, parrots, parakeets, and hummingbirds like the place, and sloths are not uncommon here. A garden path by the pool leads down to a coral hole that was once under the sea. Owner Elizabeth Newton offers guests an exclusive half-day canoe trip on a river where even a manatee has been spotted—but no promises. Perhaps you can be content seeing monkeys, birds, and crocodiles. The cost is $25 for two people. The rate at the Magellan Inn is $44 for a single, $56 for a double, continental breakfast included. Fax 758-0652.

El Atlántida has thirty rooms, each with its own porch separated by a cane division from adjoining porches and fringed with a thatched-roof overhang. Rooms have cement floors, ceiling fans, reading lamps, cane furniture, wooden shutters over screened windows, and private baths with hot water. The single rate is $45, the double $50, full breakfast included. Credit cards are accepted. There is an open-air restaurant, pool, parking, and a tour desk in the reception area—don't miss the antique crank cash register at the reception desk. A chestnut-mandibled and a keel-billed toucan are kept in a large enclosure, but there is a free-flying parrot. Tours can be arranged, including a river trip near Panama. Telephone 758-1515, extension 213, telephone or fax 228-9467.

Cabinas Vaz in downtown Cahuita offers simple accommodations (a single is $14, a double $18) and a restaurant. The fourteen rooms have fans and private baths; some with shower-head hot water. Telephone 758-1515, extension 218. Owner Charles Wilfred Vaz has another place at Playa Blanca, fifteen rooms with private baths costing $12 for a single, $15 for a double. Telephone 758-1515, extension 284. No credit cards at either.

Farther south on a slow road is the tiny town of Puerto Viejo de Limón, a mecca for surfers. There is now a direct bus from San José to Puerto Viejo as well as buses from Limón.

Autotransportes Manzanillo also provides service in nine-passenger vans. The trip from San José includes a stop in Braulio Carrillo and Río Sucio, a look at Moín and Limón, and if you are going to Puerto Viejo, a drive through Cahuita, at $30 per person. Travelers can also be picked up in the Arenal area for the trip to the Caribbean for the same price. Telephone 224-4139 or 234-9665. You can call the same numbers for information on four tours with local guides run by Talamanca Express: the Bribrí Indian Reserve including a boat ride on the Sixaola River, at $50 per person for five hours; a $50, four-hour hike in Cahuita National Park; a $30 half-day beach and Gandoca-Manzanillo refuge tour; and a two-day trip to a marine refuge in Panama for $160. Note: U.S. residents need a visa to Panama for this trip, but Canadians and Europeans do not.

At the edge of town is Pizote Lodge, which has its own nature trails plus tour options that include a boat trip to Punta Uva and a barbecue there, a venture on the Sixaola River, and a day trip on the Bananito River to the site of pre-Columbian graves, at $45 per person. You can rent bicycles or horses for $7 per hour, and the lodge arranges scuba diving with professional divers.

A restaurant in the main building serves breakfast and dinner. Housing is in eight rooms in a U-shaped wooden building with shared baths, or in six bungalows with private baths. Neither have hot water, but the baths are otherwise modern with the delightful feature of high windows so you can do some bird-watching in the tall trees while you shower. There are bright bedspreads, screened windows, cane ceilings, and ceiling fans. There is also a two-bedroom casita for up to three people for $114. Visa and MasterCard are accepted. Telephone or fax 229-1428.

If you have not yet tried *patacas*, fried plantains, stop by Stanford's and order a plate of them. The person who serves you will probably be moving to the beat of the music.

For a thatch-and-bamboo experience, try Cabinas Black Sands near the entrance to Puerto Viejo; turn at Pulperá La Violeta and go along the road parallel to the beach. Owned by Diane Applebaum and Ken Kerst, this rustic retreat has grounds sprinkled with banana, papaya, and other fruit trees, pineapple, and palms. There is an outhouse with a flush toilet, and the outdoor shower is open enough to let you watch the birds while you bathe. A cabin consists of three rooms and a kitchen. The cost is $12 for one person, $20 for two. Telephone 758-3844 and leave a message.

The privately owned Cabinas Chimuri nature reserve is near Cabinas Black Sands. Owner Mauricio Salazar, a Bribrí Indian, leads nature tours into the Indian reserves. (See chapter 8.)

Mauricio is a prime mover in a grass-roots organization, ATEC, that promotes ecologically sound tourism and small-scale, locally owned businesses. Try to get a copy of *Welcome to Coastal Talamanca*, published by ATEC, a booklet describing the history, traditions, and natural history of the area. The group has cultural and natural history offerings from Cahuita to Gandoca: birding walks, visits to Indian reserves, rain forest hikes, snorkeling, fishing, night walks, and multiday adventure treks. The ATEC office is in Puerto Viejo across from Soda Tamara. You can call 758-3844 and leave a message or fax 253-7524 for information on costs and reservations.

Heading south out of Puerto Viejo you will see a red-tile-roofed complex called Villas del Caribe, twelve two-story villas for up to six people each; doubles are $114, plus $12 for each additional person. Credit cards are accepted. The sitting room and fully equipped kitchenette downstairs open onto a private terrace with lounge chairs and an outdoor shower for rinsing off when coming in from the beach. Upstairs balconies have hammocks. Bedrooms are large, with hardwood floors, ceiling fans, desk, and occasional tables and chairs. Bathrooms have plants in the shower area under a skylight; there is central hot water. The view is through scattered coconut palms and gardens that go right to the Caribbean. Enjoy the fragrance from the heliotrope hedge.

Villas del Caribe rents horses for about $6 an hour, and guests can ride on roads in a 125-acre (50-ha) forest. There is a motorboat with an English-speaking guide for trips along the coast, and you can rent surfboards, boogie boards, bicycles, and snorkeling equipment. Nearby is an old-fashioned *trapiche*, so you may have a chance to see sugar extracted from cane with oxen power. Telephone 233-2200, fax 221-2801. By the way, there is a *pulpería*, or small grocery, near the entrance.

As you make your way south toward Uva Beach, one of the most beautiful on the coast, you will probably glimpse the brilliant flash of scarlet-rumped tanagers as they fly across the road.

Less than 3 miles (5 km) south of Puerto Viejo is Hotel Punta Cocles, an inviting place from which to explore the nearby parks and reserves or just sit and watch the toucans and parrots fly by. The complex of sixty rooms, restaurants, and good-sized pool is surrounded by tall trees, with several well-maintained nature trails through forest on the 25-acre (10-ha) property. Watch for small, brightly colored frogs, but do not touch them. Those bright colors usually warn of strong toxins. Guests can make one- to two-hour self-guided forays into the lush forest. A checklist of birds found in the area list 326 species in 55 families.

Trails from the hotel lead across the road to golden sand beaches, with a seaside rancho where drinks and snacks are sold. Other hotel amenities include a Jacuzzi and ice machines. Rooms are in bungalows connected to the restaurant and pool area by covered walkways. Each has its own terrace, private bath with central hot water, and both fans and air conditioning. Five bungalows have furnished kitchens. A single is $80, a double $91; bungalows with kitchens, for up to five people, are $170.

The hotel helps arrange tours, including one to the Bribrí reserve and a two-day visit to the San Blas Islands in Panama. It also rents binoculars—a nice feature—as well as bicycles, rain ponchos, boogie boards, snorkeling equipment, and cars. Hotel Punta Cocles will pick up guests who take the direct bus to Puerto Viejo. The Limón to Manzanillo bus passes in front, and the hotel is also served by Autotransportes Manzanillo. Telephone 224-3926, or in the U.S., (800) 325-6927; fax 234-8033.

At Playa Chiquita, Miraflores Lodge, a bed-and-breakfast, has eight rooms for up to twenty-five people, some with shared bath. They cost $40 to $50. Pamela Carpenter Navarro, the owner, is raising tropical flowers on an old cacao farm. She takes guests on trips to the Bribrí reserve and by boat to Panama and the Gandoca-Manzanillo reserve, and arranges visits that help guests learn about local culture. English and French also are spoken. Telephone 233-5127, fax 233-5390.

Nearby is Playa Chiquita Lodge, which definitely has a jungle feeling to it. Wooden buildings seem to rise out of the abundant plant life. A thatched rancho serves as dining room and central gathering place. The eleven rooms have forest views even out of the bathrooms (there is no hot water), screened windows, and ceiling fans, and there are rocking chairs on the porches for bird-watching and relaxing to the sound of howler monkeys.

Guests can rent bicycles, snorkeling equipment, boogie boards, and surfboards. Tours go to Gandoca, Punta Mono, and Cahuita, and boats are available for fishing. Singles are $32, doubles $58. The Limón-Manzanillo bus passes in front. Telephone 233-6613, fax 223-7479.

The Gandoca-Manzanillo Wildlife Refuge begins between Puerto Viejo and the town of Manzanillo, literally "the end of the road." Punta Uva at Manzanillo is one of the prettiest beaches on the Caribbean. Tours to the refuge are offered by a number of hotels and local agencies from Limón south.

7
National Parks, Biological Reserves, and Wildlife Refuges

After a breathtakingly beautiful multimedia presentation in which images of Costa Rica's flora and fauna inundated our senses from a giant screen, with three projectors going simultaneously, the ranger at Poás National Park asked if anyone in the audience had a comment. A middle-class Costa Rican in his fifties, there with his family, rose slowly from his seat. Persuaded by what he had just seen, he said, "With all the beauty and resources in this country, it must be the responsibility of every citizen to protect them."

In growing numbers, citizens of Costa Rica and the rest of the world feel the same. Today 12 percent of the country's land is in parks, refuges, and biological reserves; another 16 percent is legally set aside as forest reserves, protected zones, and Indian reserves.

Natural history travelers today follow in the footsteps of naturalists and explorers who have been drawn to the biological diversity of this small country since the mid-1800s. Five percent of all the plant and animal species known on the planet exist here, in a space that takes up three ten-thousandths of the Earth's surface. The protected areas are showplaces for the wealth of species found in Costa Rica. The National Biodiversity Institute, which is at work on an inventory of all plant and animal species in the country, so far has these numbers: mammals, 209 species; birds, 850; reptiles 220; amphibians, 163; freshwater fish, 130; and arthropods (insects, spiders, and crabs with segmented bodies and jointed limbs), 350,000. Among the 13,021 species of plants discovered are 1,500 trees and more than 1,400 orchids.

A new wrinkle in the conservation framework is an overlay of specific areas to facilitate regional protection of ecosystems and cultural resources. These conservation areas include national parks, refuges, and biological reserves as well as private reserves. The sites, which retain their names and identities, are incorporated in the following protected areas:

Amistad: La Amistad, Cahuita, Chirripó, Gandoca-Manzanillo, Hitoy-Cerere, Tapantí. Telephone: Atlantic sector 758-3996, Pacific sector 771-3155.

Arenal: Alberto Manuel Brenes, Arenal. Telephone 222-4161 or 695-5908.

Central Volcanic Range: Braulio Carrillo, Guayabo, Irazú Volcano, Juan Castro Blanco, Poás Volcano. Telephone 224-8215 or 224-9096.

Guanacaste: Guanacaste, Rincón de la Vieja, Santa Rosa. Telephone 695-5598.

Tempisque: Barra Honda, Curú, Lomas Barbudal, Ostional, Palo Verde, Tamarindo. Telephone 671-1062.

Osa: Ballena, Caño Island, Corcovado, Golfito. Telephone 735-5036.

Tortuguero: Barra de Colorado, Tortuguero. Telephone 710-7673.

Today both public and private organizations recognize the importance of coordinating their efforts to preserve biodiversity, not only within Costa Rica but perhaps also in links reaching from Mexico to Colombia. Biological corridors that connect protected sectors help create areas large enough for survival of tapirs, cats, and birds that migrate altitudinally, such as the quetzal, and help ensure survival of the biodiversity that is jeopardized in isolated units—the philosophy of "the whole is greater than the sum of its parts."

Emphasis since the park service was set up in the sixties has been on preserving areas before they are destroyed. Though money is still needed to purchase the approximately 12 percent of the park land still privately held, more attention now can be directed toward better protection of those areas and amenities for visitors, which up to now have been quite limited.

No monorail systems transport people through this fantastic kingdom of plants and animals; only a few parks offer roads, waterways wind through a handful, and maintained trails exist in a growing number. Only Guanacaste National Park has overnight lodging built with nature travelers in mind, though visitors can sometimes stay in a park or refuge station when space permits and in facilities built for researchers when there is an empty bed, such as at the Palo Verde Field Station or at the Sirena station at Corcovado. You usually need to bring your own bedding, towel, and soap; rangers are not in the hotel business. Some areas do allow camping. Housing from humble to fine may be available nearby. For day visits on your own, take food and drink; generally, there are no restaurants or souvenir shops selling candy bars.

VOLUNTEERS IN PARKS, RESERVES, REFUGES

If you are open for a different kind of vacation—a working vacation—are eighteen years of age or older, and speak at least basic Spanish, the National Parks Service may have a deal for you. As a volunteer in the parks, you can work alongside rangers or in the San José office. The minimum time to volunteer is two months.

Depending on your skills and interests, you could be a lifeguard at park beaches during the high tourist season, work on an archaeological dig, help fight forest fires, protect nesting sea turtles, cook, or maintain trails. Extra hands and minds are always needed in environmental education and assisting visitors.

The work can be hard, the hours long, and living conditions rustic. You pay for your food (about $5 a day) and transportation. You wash your own clothes in a pila. *Some stations have no electricity, with the only outside contact by radio phone. Bring your own sheets. Both men and women are welcome, and there is no upper age limit.*

What does a volunteer get out of all this? A rare opportunity to experience Costa Rica's parks in a way no tour or day visit can offer, to learn, and to contribute to conservation efforts in a real way. Parks are understaffed and for the most part work within severe budget constraints.

If you are interested, write to ASVO, Servicio de Parques Nacionales, Apartado 11384-1000, San José. State when you are coming—writing in Spanish may speed up your answer. You will receive information and an application. Allow at least three months for the exchange of letters to arrange your stint. Telephone 222-5085, fax 223-6963. The office is in the same building as the park information office, Avenida 21, Calles 25/27.

The men and women who work in the parks are delightful to know and will help you get oriented. However, the staff is usually shorthanded, so do not expect a personal guided tour. If you call the park service or wildlife office in advance, tours with off-duty rangers can sometimes be arranged. You may be able to buy a printed trail guide; if not, a map of the trails is usually posted where you pay admission.

Even parks where you will see the most people, like Poás or Manuel Antonio, may not be crowded on weekdays except at Easter or Christmas. Your group may meet no one else on a trail through pristine country. Your chances of seeing the wildlife, of course, depend on you. Proceed quietly, be patient, and be alert. For safety's sake and to minimize impact, keep on the trails.

Hours vary a little, but most of these protected areas are open at least from 8:00 a.m. to 4:00 p.m. Admission is less than $1.50, but some parks sell a voluntary $5 Gold Pass if you would like to contribute more. Guidelines for public use are being established for each park.

There is no fee for taking photos, so you can share your vacation with friends or family back home, but there is a hefty fee of about $175 for filming in the nationally protected areas. Though the charge is aimed at commercial filming, park administrators do not yet seem clear on the point. If asked why you have not paid the fee, explain the reason you are filming and keep your fingers crossed.

The information center for the National Parks Service is in San José, about a block east of the National Museum, a few doors down from Apartotel San José, Avenida 2, Calles 25/27. Hours are 8:00 a.m. to noon and 1:00 to 4:00 p.m. weekdays. Telephone 222-5085. The center has postcards, posters, pamphlets on the parks and biological reserves, and some charming lapel pins for 18 of the areas (costing less than $4 each). You may want to buy brochures there about the parks you are going to visit in case none is left when you get there.

To contact individual parks and biological reserves about overnight space or the availability of guides or horses, call the radio room at park headquarters in San José, 233-4160, or the appropriate conservation area. For general information on parks and biological reserves, call the park ecotourism office at 257-0922, extension 316. The National Park Service is next to the Ministry of Natural Resources, Energy, and Mines, Calle 25, Avenidas 8/10.

For information on wildlife refuges, call Vida Silvestre (the national wildlife department) at 233-8112. The entrance fee at refuges is also less than $1.50; the camping fee is about $2 per person. The wildlife office in San José has no street address, but any taxi driver can find it with these directions: behind the Santa Teresita Church, go 100 meters south and 150 meters east. There is a sign in front. Fax is 221-2617.

In contrast with national parks, which by law belong to the government, wildlife refuges can also include areas either partly or completely in the hands of private owners. The state can authorize farming, homes, recreational activities, businesses, research, and industries in those areas.

The region of the country where each park, reserve, or refuge is located is noted in parenthesis, so you can read about accommodations and the surrounding area in chapter 6 or look up nearby private reserves that offer accommodations in chapter 8. Look for specifics in chapter 9 on companies specializing in nature tours.

The brief descriptions here tell you how easy or difficult it is to get to the site, what visitor facilities are available, and highlight some of the magic you will encounter.

Parks and Biological Reserves

La Amistad Costa Rica-Panama International Park (South)

La Amistad means "friendship," and the international park was created with an understanding that a counterpart park would be established across the border in Panama.

La Amistad is a gigantic national park, 479,199 acres (193,929 ha), big enough to sustain a healthy population of animals that require large areas for hunting and reproduction, such as the tapir, jaguar, puma, and harpy eagle. Probably the largest population of resplendent quetzals in the country resides in this refuge of rain forest, cloud forest, and páramo, along with at least 400 other bird species. Epiphytes abound in the tall cloud forests, where you can see oak, elm, magnolia, and sweet cedar. More than 130 varieties of orchids have been found in the southwest corner of the park alone. There are 263 species of amphibians and reptiles. Spread across the rugged Talamanca Mountain Range, the highest in Costa Rica, the park protects not only endangered plants and animals but important watersheds as well.

You will have to bring more than your binoculars to enjoy this fantasy land of geology and wildlife. This is backpacker territory. Much of the park has yet to be explored; trails are limited and unmarked. If you are staying in the area (San Isidro, San Vito), a day trip would be a way to get a taste of it.

Elevation ranges from about 328 to 11,644 feet (100 to 3,549 m), and temperatures vary accordingly, with upper altitudes rainy and sometimes cold.

The park administration office is at Las Tablas, about 25 miles (40 km) northwest of San Vito de Coto Brus. When you call the parks office in San José, also ask about the condition of the road to La Amistad. The highway is good to San Vito, which is about five hours from San José near Panama.

Alberto Manuel Brenes Biological Reserve (North Central)

Created at the end of 1993, the reserve was formerly the San Ramón Protected Zone. There are no facilities for visitors.

Arenal National Park (North Central)

Created in 1991, Arenal National Park is in a zone whose waters drain into Lake Arenal and are used to produce hydroelectric energy and supply irrigation projects. No tourism facilities exist.

Ballena National Marine Park (South)

Created in 1990, the Ballena park was established to protect marine resources. It encompasses 13,282 acres (5,375 ha) of ocean and 272 acres (110 ha) of land. The coast is about 6 miles (10 km)

Anteater (Photo by Ree Strange Sheck)

long between Punta Uvita and Punta Piñuela along the Pacific
south of Dominical, an area rich in well-preserved mangroves.

Ballena Island and the smaller rocky protrusions called Las Tres
Hermanas are nesting sites for frigate birds, pelicans, and boobies.
The park gets its name from the humpbacked whales that visit
from December to March. Dolphins are common here.

Park personnel have worked with local residents to change their
fishing methods to protect the resources. It is the first marine park
in Costa Rica to involve a fishing community. There is a guard station, but the park is not developed for large-scale tourism. Visitors
can, however, snorkel around the coral reefs, dive in the protected
area or visit by boat. Visits can be arranged from Dominical.

Las Baulas National Park
See Tamarindo National Wildlife Refuge.

Barra Honda National Park (Northwest)
The main attraction at Barra Honda is a network of caves through a
peak that once was a coral reef beneath the sea. Located just west

of where the Tempisque River flows into the Gulf of Nicoya, Barra Honda still holds many secrets. Of the forty-two caves discovered, only nineteen have been explored. The human remains and pre-Columbian artifacts discovered have yet to yield their stories. But the exploration has revealed several large caverns adorned with stalactites, stalagmites, pearls, soda straws, columns, popcorn, and other intriguing formations. Nature's underground artistry is most profuse in the Terciopelo (fer-de-lance) Cave, so named because early speleologists found a snake of this species smashed on its floor. Terciopelo contains the Organ, a columnar formation that resounds with different tones when gently tapped. This is the only cave open to the public. The deepest cave, Santa Ana, is almost 790 feet (240 m) beneath the surface.

The shafts into these caves are mostly vertical, and there are no elevators to carry you down or caverns lit with colored lights. Descending into the caves is not for the fainthearted or infirm: straight down a metal ladder almost 90 feet (27 m) and back up the same way. Arrangements should be made at least four days beforehand by calling 685-5580. A local community association, Barrio Cubillo, conducts the tours. A guide and caving equipment costs about $35 for up to five people. The maximum time in the cave is forty-five minutes, though the tour is three hours. Besides offering tours, the association maintains the trails and helps with park protection.

For noncavers, the 5,673-acre (2,296-ha) park offers trails that lead to a view point overlooking the Gulf of Nicoya and Chira Island, a tall evergreen forest, and waterfalls over natural travertine dams. The summit of Barra Honda Peak at 1,312 feet (400 m), pocked with large and small holes and decorated with sculptured rock, hints of the artistry in the caves below. Los Laureles Trail, about 3.5 miles (5.5 km) long, is open to the public. The first forty minutes are uphill, but then it levels off. Bring water (it is hot), and keep to the trail. Two tourists became lost and died here in 1992. Half-day guided tours are $10. Trail visits are limited to five hours.

Belowground wildlife includes bats, insects, blind salamanders, fish, and snails, while aboveground visitors might see the white-faced monkey, Amazonian skunk, long-nosed armadillo, white-nosed coati, coyote, and orange-fronted parakeet. The vegetation of the tropical dry forest, moist province transition zone, is mostly deciduous.

The average annual rainfall ranges from 59 to 79 inches (1,500 to 2,000 mm), and the average temperature is 81°F (27°C). The highest elevation is 1,886 feet (575 m).

The Cubillo community organization has clean cabins and campsites in the forest next to the park entrance. (See chapter 5 for details.) Monkeys move through the trees around the small campsites. This project is an example of park neighbors helping with and benefiting from a protected area.

To get to the park from San José, turn off the Inter-American Highway about 6 miles (10 km) before Cañas and take the Tempisque ferry. Go through Quebrada Honda and Tres Esquinas to Barra Honda. Two streams you need to cross can rise rapidly with rains, so inquire in the village of Barra Honda if in doubt. The road deteriorates past the town. From Liberia, take Highway 21 south and turn north just before the town of Mansión to get to the park. There is a bus from Nicoya, 9 miles (14 kilometers) away, to Santa Ana, a little more than a mile (2 km) from the entrance. You can call the parks office in San José for information or the Tempisque Conservation Area in Bagaces, 671-1062; tour guides are arranged by calling 685-5580.

Barra Honda is open from 8:00 a.m. to 4:00 p.m. daily, but visits to the caves are allowed only from 8:00 a.m. to 1:00 p.m.

Braulio Carrillo National Park (Central Valley)

Braulio Carrillo is a symphony in green. Waterfalls, deep canyons, and raging rivers lend their tones. The exciting part is that the concert begins only twenty minutes from San José—and on a paved road.

While roads through virgin forest usually spell ecological disaster, this particular road spurred creation of a national park that now encompasses 113,416 acres (45,899 ha) of majestic beauty. Braulio Carrillo was born out of the conflict between the need for a new highway to the Atlantic and the determination to preserve the largely primary forest it would pass through. The park was established in 1978, and the road through this rugged, largely untouched land opened in 1987. Most of the traffic between San José and Limón now passes on a ribbon laid down through this awesome landscape. Be alert for landslides.

The park offers many levels of enjoyment; just driving through it is a thrill. View points provide safe places to pull off. A five-minute trail I know leads from highway to primeval beauty, complete with waterfall and morpho butterflies that flutter up and down above the sparkling stream. A *tepezcuintle*, the wonderful name used in Spanish for the paca, once jumped from a cave hidden by vegetation into the pool where we had just been quietly swimming and disappeared behind the waterfall. It is a timeless, hushed place—one of nature's gifts. A park ranger told me about the trail. If you find it, I trust you will treat its delicate beauty with respect.

As for established trails, there is one of about a half-mile (1 km) from the main ranger station at Zurquí, thirty minutes from San José. A trail at Barva gives you an other-worldly view of a volcanic lagoon. Two trails take off from the Carrillo station close to the Limón end of the highway: Botarrama (which takes about two hours) and the longer La Botella. Camping is permitted.

Special permission is required for a multiday trek from Barva Volcano, one of two volcanoes in the park, through a protected zone added in 1986 to join Braulio Carrillo with land protected by the Organization of Tropical Studies' La Selva Biological Station, all the way to Puerto Viejo de Sarapiquí. The journey goes from 9,514 feet (2,900 m) to 112 feet (34 m), so perhaps how long it takes depends on which end of the trail you start at. This is the only place in the country where an altitudinal variation of this magnitude is protected, which is extremely important for species that migrate, including some of the 515 bird species identified so far.

Braulio Carrillo is one of the beneficiaries of the Foresta project funded by the U.S. Agency for International Development in 1989 to help develop and improve the protection of some of the parks in the Central Volcanic Mountain Range. With proximity to the burgeoning population in San José and nearby towns, the park offers a valuable environmental education opportunity for residents and tourists alike.

LIFE IN A CECROPIA TREE

Discovery of relationships between trees, other plants, insects, and animals opens a window on understanding the intricacies of life in the tropical world. One such symbiotic relationship has evolved between the cecropia tree, called guarumo *in Spanish, and Azteca ants.*

The cecropia tree, a member of the mulberry family, grows throughout the country at elevations up to approximately 6,500 feet (2,000 m). It is called a pioneer species because it is among the first to come back on cleared land or to grow when forest is opened up by the fall of a big tree. It grows rapidly and requires a lot of light. You will notice it along road cuts. Look for a tree with a ringed trunk that resembles bamboo; leaves are large and lobed, resembling hands.

Because it is a relatively short-lived tree, maybe twenty years, the cecropia has not developed chemical protection such as toxic leaves, which longer-lived trees tend to have. However, its hollow stems are home to some species of aggressive Azteca ants, which tend to live in large colonies and swarm out over the tree at the slightest disturbance,

attacking unsuspecting caterpillars, other ants, and even a lightly placed hand on the tree. Aztecas do not seem to bite birds, who eat the fruits and scatter the tree's seeds, but they zero in on epiphytes and vines—chewing off any vine that starts up the trunk. In return, the tree provides glycogen-rich food at the base of each leaf stalk for the ants to feed on and hollow stems for them to live in.

But the ant patrols are not effective against all predators. Sloths are among the animals that like cecropia leaves and fruit. You are more apt to spot them in a cecropia tree than others they feed on because of the openness of its growth. Apparently, their heavy fur gives sloths some protection. Howler monkeys also eat in cecropia trees.

Countless symbiotic relationships exist in the natural world. Some we know about; others remain to be discovered. Even in this tree-ant relationship, all the answers are not in on why the tree has developed lodging and food to attract these ants or the degree of protection the ants actually give.

Try to reach the park early to reduce the chance of fog narrowing your views. Dropping into the lowlands, you may see a sloth in a tree alongside the road. Watch the *guarumo* (cecropia) trees in particular. Other animals that live in the park include three species of monkey—also frequently spotted at lower elevations—tapir, jaguar, kinkajou, deer, and ocelot. In all, there are 135 species of mammals here. The resplendent quetzal knows these forests, as do eagles, umbrella birds, trogons, hawks, curassows, and guans. Bromeliads and orchids, among the 6,000 species of plant life found here, adorn the trees. This is a good place to see the poor man's umbrella (*sombrilla del pobre*), a plant whose leaves grow up to 7 feet (2 m) across. People caught out in the rain in the countryside have used them for protection. If you are caught driving in the rain, which averages 177 inches (4,500 mm) a year, enjoy the waterfalls that pour down the roadside and keep your eyes open for landslides.

Because of the topography and range of elevation within the park, temperatures can go from 59°F (15°C) at Zurquí and Barva to 86°F (30°C) in the Atlantic lowlands, where rainfall can be 315 inches (8,000 mm) a year.

Primary access to Braulio Carrillo is at the stations at either end of the highway through the park (Zurquí and Carrillo), though some people start at the Barva Volcano station near Sacramento. Nature travel companies in San José offer hiking on Barva and day visits to the park. Two other stations exist, but access to them is difficult.

Remember to stay on trails and to check in at the ranger station before setting out. Vegetation is extremely dense in this rugged region. Experienced hikers have gotten lost; as one Costa Rican put it, the forest has eaten several small planes and a few people.

Cabo Blanco Strict Nature Reserve (Northwest)

Cabo Blanco Strict Nature Reserve is important historically as well as biologically. It was set aside as a protected area in 1963 before Costa Rica had a park service largely through the efforts of Olof and Karen Wessberg, who had come to live on the Nicoya Peninsula in 1955. Because of their love of nature and concern about rapid destruction of the forest on the tip of the peninsula—plus personal commitment and a good measure of persistence with funding sources and bureaucracy—this forest and sanctuary for seabirds exists today. You will see a memorial plaque honoring Olof at the reserve entrance. Doña Karen is still writing letters and knocking on doors, looking for funds to enlarge Cabo Blanco.

The reserve is a treasure. Visitors often see howler monkeys and an admirable assortment of birds and butterflies before even leaving the picnic area next to the ranger station at the entrance. The reserve claims 119 tree species and possibly the larget pochote tree in any park. It is 115 feet high (35 m) and almost 10 feet (3 m) in diameter. Predominant species are gumbo-limbo, lemonwood, frangipani, dogwood, trumpet tree, and cedar.

Though the land portion of the park is only 2,896 acres (1,172 ha), wildlife is plentiful: deer, white-faced and howler monkeys, agoutis, pacas, margays, ocelots, coyotes, coatis, tamanduas, and raccoons. Birds are abundant, too—one birder counted seventy-four species in four hours. Land species include manakins, woodpeckers, trogons, crested caracaras, parakeets, and chachalacas. The reserve also protects 4,423 acres (1,790 ha) of marine habitat.

Cabo Blanco (White Cape) got its name from the small island a short distance off the point, though there is dispute about whether the name comes from deposits of bird guano or a white cliff or the light-colored soil. Pelicans, frigate birds, and brown boobies hang out there. The area is rich in marine life: octopus, starfish, sea cucumber, lobster, giant conch, and fish such as snapper and snook.

Look in at the small museum before setting off on one of the well-maintained trails. An hour-and-a-half trek through low mountains, steep in places, leads to Cabo Blanco Beach, a sandy spot on a mostly rocky shoreline Though visitation has increased, you may still have the beach practically to yourself for a bit except for colored crabs and seabirds.

To protect this small, fragile place, no camping is allowed, and the number of visitors is being monitored. Plans call for guided walks. Remember that this is a small reserve, a place that could be loved to death. Safeguards are aimed at preventing that. Park hours are 8:00 a.m. to 4:00 p.m.

Montezuma, 7 miles (11 km) away, offers hotels, restaurants, and tour possibilities; some small lodges are closer to Cabo Blanco. The road from Montezuma piddles down to one lane just before the Cabo Blanco reserve. It is a muddy track in the rainy season, and since you must also ford a river en route, a four-wheel-drive vehicle is recommended for those months. There is no bus between Montezuma and Cabo Blanco, but taxis are available, along with bike and horse rentals. (See chapter 6, northwest section, for area facilities.)

Cahuita National Park (Caribbean)

Take white sands, coconut palms, a coral reef, the wreck of an eighteenth-century slave ship just offshore, and clear Caribbean waters; add to these at least 123 species of fish, an abundance of bird life, and an assortment of other animals from monkeys to caimans. The winning combination is known as Cahuita National Park, 27 miles (44 km) southeast of Limón. One entrance is in the town of Cahuita, and another is at Puerto Vargas, a few miles farther down the main road toward Puerto Viejo.

The 1,483-acre (600-ha) reef encircles Cahuita Point, forming a rich undersea garden of thirty-five species of varicolored coral some 1,640 feet (500 m) from shore. Brightly colored fish such as rock beauty, blue parrotfish, and angelfish swim among the formations. There also are sea urchins, barracudas, moray eels, sharks, lobsters, sea cucumbers, and green turtles, which feed on the expanse of turtle grass.

But there is trouble in paradise. Increased erosion from deforestation in the Talamanca Mountains has brought silt carried by the Río Estralla that is affecting the reef, a vivid reminder of the distance trouble can travel from a mismanaged forest.

Snorkeling and scuba diving are allowed, but the park does not rent equipment; tours in glass-bottomed boats are available at Cahuita. Though the Puerto Vargas area was closed after the 1991 earthquake, camping and hiking are once again possible there. A 4-mile (7-km) nature trail lets visitors experience the exuberance of tropical moist forest vegetation. The abundance of land and sea birds makes it a bird-watcher's delight. Troops of up to twenty-five howler monkeys roam the area, and coatis and raccoons are abundant. You might also encounter a three-toed anteater, an otter, a four-toed armadillo, or a three-toed sloth. The park encompasses 2,639 acres (1,068 ha) of land and about 55,350 acres (22,400 ha) of sea.

The colors of the sea on a sunny day run from almost transparent near the white sand to bright green, turquoise, and aquamarine. At some points, you can wade quite a distance from shore without getting wet above your knees. Some areas have strong currents where swimming is not safe. In general, the first 400 meters after the park entrance are dangerous,and there is another very dangerous area at the Puerto Vargas entrance. Pay attention to the warning sign.

The park receives a little less than 118 inches (3,000 mm) of rain a year, and the distinction between the wet and dry seasons is not as clear as in the Central Valley. Visibility around the reef, however, is better from December to April.

Tour companies in Cahuita and San José offer both day trips and multiday options. You can hire a local guide trained by the nonprofit Talamanca Association for Ecotourism and Conservation. Lodging is available along the route from Limón through Cahuita to Puerto Viejo and farther south. (See chapter 6.)

Caño Island Biological Reserve (South)

Located 12 miles (20 km) west of the Osa Peninsula in southern Costa Rica, Caño Island is of interest largely as an archaeological site and for its marine life. About 494 acres (200 ha) rising to 361 feet (110 m) above the Pacific, the land contains tall evergreen forest, a prehistoric cemetery, and mysterious round stones sculpted by the Indians who once walked here. Unfortunately, many graves were plundered before the island came under the protection of Corcovado National Park. The most abundant pottery dates from A.D. 220 to 1550.

The crystalline waters are a snorkeler's delight. Five coral reefs, containing fifteen species of stony coral, create a marine wonderland that almost made me forget my fear of being so far from shore in deep waters. Lobster and giant conch live here, as do eels, octopuses, sea urchins, brittle star, and countless fish—jacks, grunts, and triggerfish. Manta rays, sailfish, sea turtles, humpback whales, and dolphins have been seen near the island. Snorkeling and diving are limited to the sea in front of the ranger station. In all, the reserve protects 6,672 acres (2,700 ha) of marine habitat.

Wildlife on the island is scarce, consisting mainly of pacas, opossums, boa constrictors, a few species of bees, moths, butterflies, beetles, frogs, bats, rats, lizards, and ants. Among the birds are ospreys, brown noddies, brown boobies, terns, and egrets.

The forest is largely made up of locusts, wild figs, rubber trees, wild cacaos, and milk trees, which exude a white latex that can be drunk as milk.

Rangers are stationed on the island, and a trail climbs through the forest to points of archaeological interest. High cliffs rise from the coastline, with only a few small, sandy beaches that largely disappear at high tide.

Most visitors to Caño Island arrive as part of a tour. Private nature reserves in the area offer optional day trips to the island, as do several coastal hotels. (See chapters 6 and 8.) Advise Corcovado National Park in advance to arrange an independent trip, limited to twenty people at a time. Telephone 735-5036.

Carara Biological Reserve (South)

You can spot the Carara Biological Reserve before you see any sign as you come from San José through Orotina toward the Pacific coast. Its green forest stands tall against the eroded hillsides—land whose soil, once the trees were cut, tired out quickly when turned into fields for crops or pastures for cattle. In a transition zone between the dry north Pacific and the more humid south, Carara has an average rainfall as high as 126 inches (3,200 mm) in the interior and as low as 79 inches (2,000 mm) near the coast. A large lagoon and rivers and streams supply life-giving moisture.

The reserve has archaeological importance, with Indian sites dating from 300 B.C. to A.D. 1500. Artifacts include gold objects, pottery, and large rectangular stones.

Most of the 11,614-acre (4,700-ha) reserve is in primary forest, with regal giants that spread their branches in a tall canopy. Some plants live up in the trees and send their roots to the ground; vines wind up trunks toward the light. Epiphytes, ferns, and palms soften the setting.

Because of the lush vegetation and relative ease in seeing the abundant wildlife, Carara Biological Reserve can be an excellent choice for a traveler's first experience in a tropical forest—especially when accompanied by a naturalist guide. I had crossed the Tarcoles River there a dozen times and never knew crocodiles wallow in the mud along its banks until the guide pointed them out. Naturalist guides know where the wildlife is, which trees have fruit to attract animals, and when the orchids are blooming.

Let me share with you what we saw in about three hours: a fiery-billed aracari, blue-gray tanager, spectacled owl, boat-billed heron, crested guan, anhinga, brown jay, white-tailed kite, wood stork, blue heron, orange-bellied trogon, roseate spoonbill, yellow-headed caracara, chestnut-mandibled toucan, dotted-winged antwren, blue-crowned motmot, great kiskadee, scarlet macaws, crocodiles, white-faced monkeys, iguanas, squirrels, leaf-cutting ants, and lizards. We did not see the snakes that live there, the morpho butterfly, nor a sloth, coati, agouti, peccary, porcupine, anteater, coyote, or howler or spider monkey. Perhaps you will. Near sundown, dozens of red, blue, and gold scarlet macaws fly from the reserve over the Tarcoles River to nighttime resting places in mangroves along the ocean—a spectacular sight.

Visitors should go first to the Quebrada Bonita ranger station to pay the admission fee and arrange for a walk on one of the trails. The Las Aráceas Trail leaves from there, with a maximum walking time of one hour. Only guided walks are allowed on the Laguna Meándrica Trail which starts between the Tarcoles River and Quebrada Bonita. If you are traveling alone, check with the rangers about joining up with a guided group. A maximum of sixty people at a time is allowed on each trail. Carara is open from 8:00 a.m. to 4:00 p.m. No camping is allowed, but there is a picnic area, latrines, and water.

The dry season is from December to April. The terrain is hilly, and though the maximum altitude is only about 3,576 feet (1,090 m), you may find yourself huffing and sweating. Average temperatures are from 77° to 82°F (25° to 27.5°C). Take it easy.

A parataxonomist working with the National Biodiversity Institute was collecting insects at Carara the last time I was there. He showed me cases of insects so tiny they can barely be seen, as well as flashy butterflies and bizarre-looking beetles. This multiyear project aims to identify all the species in this biologically diverse country.

Carara is 56 miles (90 km) from San José along the old Spanish highway. No camping is allowed. It is an easy day trip from the capital or a stopping place on the way to Jacó or Quepos. A number of hotels all the way from Puntarenas to Quepos arrange tours to Carara. (See chapter 6. Chapter 9 lists some tour companies that offer trips.)

Chirripó National Park (South)

Geologists, botanists, mountain climbers, biologists, adventure seekers, and just plain nature lovers make their way to Chirripó National Park, 94 miles (151 km) south of San José near San Isidro de El General. The park contains the highest peak in the country, Chirripó Peak at 12,529 feet (3,819 m), glacial lakes, rivers, and habitats ranging from mixed forests, fern groves, and swamps to oak forests and páramo.

On a clear day, visitors can see both oceans from the peak. There are cloudy and clear days throughout the year, but the driest time is February and March. Annual rainfall is between 138 and 197 inches (3,500 and 5,000 mm). Some longtime visitors say that they cannot resist trips in the rainier times when the exuberance of the vegetation defies description.

At whatever time of year, take warm clothes. Though maximums in the 80s are possible, count on cold at night in the upper elevations. There can be strong winds. Extremes between day and night can vary by 43°F (24°C); the lowest temperature recorded is 16°F (-9°C). You may wake up to a frosty world, finding ice on lakes and stream banks.

Marked trails traverse the 123,921-acre (50,150-ha) park. Refuges offer bunks with foam mattresses, a wood-burning cook stove, and a table for hikers. Bring a warm sleeping bag, and be sure to carry enough liquids. While the ascent to the summit appears daunting, it is not so difficult if taken slowly and carefully. Allow at least ten hours to get to the top. If you are going to the Crestones Base, you must leave the San Gerardo ranger station no later than noon. Tent camping is generally not allowed, nor are open fires—you will see signs of a huge forest fire that raged here in 1992.

Endangered species protected at Chirripó include the margay, puma, ocelot, jaguar, tapir, and quetzal. Birds and animals are more abundant in the forest zones, though there are hummingbirds even in the high páramo. Plants seem to cover every inch of trees in the cloud forest: orchids, bromeliads, mosses, and ferns. On the way to the summit, you pass through seven distinct forest types. The higher you climb, the more stunted the vegetation.

Names like Savanna and the Lions, Valley of the Rabbits, and Moraine Valley hint of what early explorers found when they scaled these heights (the lions being pumas). Discovery awaits today's visitor to Chirripó National Park, a place where you can look down on rainbows.

The entrance to the park is 9 miles (15 km) northeast of San Isidro at San Gerardo de Rivas, where there is a ranger station. Buses run from San Isidro to San Gerardo. The hardy inhabitants of San Gerardo have been known to actually run up the mountain and are often sought out as guides. If you are going independently, call the park service for information about guides or pack horses and to reserve space in a shelter. The San Gerardo de Rivas station is open from 5:00 a.m. to 5:00 p.m.

Coco Island or Isla de Coco (South)

A small green island in the Pacific more than 370 miles (500 km) off Costa Rica, Coco was an early haven for explorers, privateers, pirates, and whalers because of its abundant fresh water and its coconuts; *coco* is Spanish for coconut. Today, it attracts treasure hunters, divers, scientists, and natural history travelers.

More than 500 expeditions have uncovered only a few tantalizing pieces of three treasure caches believed to lie hidden on Coco Island. Some believe that stories of these treasures fired the imagination of Robert Louis Stevenson for his *Treasure Island*.

Scientists and tourists come in search of other riches: Many endemic species—those that occur nowhere else—have evolved on this isolated piece of land; its wild beauty encompasses both spectacular inland waterfalls and others that plunge into the sea, dense vegetation, and underwater caves and coral gardens. Seventy of the 235 plant species identified so far are endemic, two species of lizards, sixty-four of the island's 362 species of insects, and four of the eighty-five bird species. There is an endemic palm named for Franklin D. Roosevelt, who visited the island four times. Coco is an important nesting site for seagulls, noddies, and boobies. Another nesting bird is called in Spanish the *Espíritu Santo*, or Holy Spirit. A small white bird, it often hovers in the air, unafraid, a few feet above a visitor's head. Its more prosaic name in English is white tern. Eleven species of shark move through the island's waters, including huge whale sharks, hammerheads, and white tips, among 200 species of fish.

A fragile environment maintains this living laboratory for the study of evolutionary processes. Species introduced by people, such as pigs, deer, rats, coffee, and papaya, endanger the delicate ecological balance. Fishing and increased tourism also are having an impact on this special place, as is its extreme popularity with divers. Historically, the island's isolation minimized human impact; its inclusion in the park system is aimed at protecting it in a shrinking world.

The rugged coastline of high cliffs makes access possible at only two bays, Chatham and Wafer. Inscriptions dating to the 1600s on the rocky coast at Chatham provide evidence that sailors sought safe harbor here. Though the island is only 4.7 by 2 miles (7.5 by 3.3 km), its rugged terrain and dense vegetation call for caution. In 1989, a tourist became separated from her group and has never been found.

A park station on Coco Island has radio contact with the mainland. Permission from the parks service is necessary for a visit. Most travelers come as part of an organized tour. There are no overnight facilities for visitors.

Rainfall averages up to 276 inches (7,000 mm) a year. The highest point on the island is Iglesias Peak at 2,080 feet (634 m), and upper elevations are covered by cloud forest; epiphytes abound. Of volcanic origin, the island contains rocks that are 2 million years old. It is the only outcrop of the Cocos Ridge, a chain of volcanoes reaching from Costa Rica almost to the Galápagos Islands. The park contains 5,930 acres (2,400 ha) of land and 240,268 acres (97,235 ha) of coastal waters.

Corcovado National Park (South)

Corcovado, on the Osa Peninsula in southwest Costa Rica, is a remote park. It is a big park—134,766 acres (54,539 ha) of land plus 5,930 acres (2,400 ha) of marine habitat.

The administrator of the park told me he had once counted 150 scarlet macaws flying in two groups near the Madrigal River. I sat at the Sirena station one morning and watched two of these large members of the parrot family preen their brilliant red, yellow, and blue plumage, eat, and gracefully glide from treetop to treetop.

Herds of white-lipped peccaries have sometimes treed visitors along the trails. Five hundred species of trees, one-fourth of all those found in Costa Rica, live here, including probably the tallest in the country, a ceiba or kapok tree that soars to 230 feet (70 m). Eight habitat types exist: montane forest, cloud forest, alluvial plains forest, swamp, palm forest, mangrove, and rocky and sandy vegetation.

You are likely to encounter scientific researchers studying everything from how jacamars know not to eat toxic butterflies to the life habits of the squirrel monkey to why some South America species are found here but not in Panama or on the Atlantic side of Costa Rica. Researchers often work out of the Sirena station, which is where overnight tourists generally lodge on a space-available basis. If you are on trails in the park, you may not see anyone else. Six trails from Sirena offer 1- to 2-mile (2.5- to 3.5-km) forays into the forest.

The beach along the Pacific adds a marine component to the park. Sperm whales have been sighted offshore, and marine turtles nest on its beaches. There is a live coral reef at Salsipuedes. Among endangered species protected at Corcovado are five species of cats (including the jaguar), giant anteaters, sloths, and the harpy eagle, the largest bird of prey in the world (last seen in 1977). Identified so far are 367 species of birds, 500 species of trees, 104 of mammals, and 117 species of amphibians and reptiles. Visitors sometimes actually see the elusive tapir. On one of my trips, a fellow traveler spotted one at the Río Claro.

Though its remoteness and heavy vegetation protected the area now encompassed by the park, Corcovado does have some interesting human history. Local lore holds that Cubans trained along its beaches before the Bay of Pigs landing and that Sandinistas sought its isolation for training for a brief period before President Anastasio Somoza of Nicaragua was overthrown in 1979. Miners invaded its confines to pan for gold in the 1980s but were evicted in 1986. Small farms and forestry operations had made inroads in the virgin forest before the park was established in 1975.

Much of the terrain is hilly, rising from sea level to 1,932 feet (782 m). December through March are the driest months; rainfall is 197 inches (5,000 mm) a year in the mountains. The average temperature is 77°F (25°C).

You can get information about Corcovado at the Osa Conservation Area office in Puerto Jiménez (telephone or fax 735-5036) as well as from the park service office in San José. If you plan to stay overnight, you will need written permission, obtained at either the Osa office or the ranger station where you enter. Permits are based on the availability of space in the park refuges or, for camping in designated areas next to the refuges. Reservations for overnight camping are not accepted more than a month in advance. Bring mosquito netting.

Public trails in the park go between several ranger stations, basically between Sirena and La Leona, Los Patos, and San Pedrillo (from December to April only). They range from 4 to 12.5 miles long (6 to 20 km). Shorter trails fan out from the ranger stations at Sirena, Los Patos, La Leona, and El Tigre. A $1 booklet of information and maps is available at the Osa office.

Puerto Jiménez is accessible by air, land (turn off the Inter-American Highway toward Rincón), and sea (across the Golfo Dulce from Golfito). From Puerto Jiménez, the closest ranger station is Los Patos, which involves getting a ride to La Palma and then about a two-hour trek by foot.

Several private nature reserves and lodges in the area offer day tours of the park, visiting sites along the Pacific side of the park. (See chapters 6 and 8.) Tour companies also offer overnight trips to Corcovado.

Guanacaste National Park (Northwest)

Established in 1989, Guanacaste encompasses dry tropical forest and rain forest and stretches from lowlands along the northern Inter-American Highway to the mountains of the Guanacaste

Range. It contains 80,337 acres (32,512 ha), and is a crucial piece in the puzzle of ecological interdependence being fitted together in northwestern Costa Rica.

Preservation and restoration of one of the last remaining tropical dry forests, protected in adjoining Santa Rosa National Park, was an impetus for forming Guanacaste National Park. Tropical dry forests once stretched along the Pacific from central Mexico to Panana, but most have fallen prey to agricultural and residential use. Studies at Santa Rosa on the forest's seasonal patterns, distinct life forms, and interactions between plants and animals helped determine the size and habitats necessary to sustain healthy populations of species. Seasonal migration of some of the animal life from Santa Rosa to rain forests in mountains to the east meant protecting those forests as well. Animals are crucial to the life cycle of the forest as seed dispersers. Even the place of insects in the food chain cannot be overlooked.

The idea began as preservation and grew to regeneration, allowing the original dry forest to reinvade large areas cleared for agriculture and pasture, a long-term project its initiators will not see completed in their lifetimes. But they and natural history visitors can measure the progress of this innovative experiment with each season. Environmental education programs for visitors, who range from local schoolchildren to foreign travelers, communicate what is being learned.

Guanacaste is big enough to maintain the needed habitats for plants and animals that have historically lived in the area and to open up places for intensive use by visitors and researchers. The good news for nature lovers is that three biological stations in the park offer accommodations for tourists as well as researchers on a space-available basis.

Cacao Biological Station sits in cloud forest at 3,609 feet (1,100 m). Cacao Volcano, at 5,443 feet (1,659 m), looms above. Sleeping quarters are in one of the station's three wooden buildings: four rooms for eight people each, costing $9 per bunk, blanket included. A panorama of forest and distant coastline unfolds from the long covered porch. The station is rustic: no electricity, cold-water showers. The other small buildings house a kitchen (there is a fee for its use) and a laboratory or meeting space. Virgin forest behind the buildings holds tapirs, cats, bellbirds, orchids, and bromelidads. Howler monkeys announced the day when I was there. Hiking back out in the afternoon, we saw howlers and spider and white-faced monkeys within a hundred yards of each other. There is a trail to the Maritza Biological Station, about three hours away by foot, and one to the top of Cacao. Getting to Cacao is a trip—you can go only so far on the bad roads and then it is foot or horseback. The trail is not well marked, so a local guide is recommended.

Maritza is also accessible by a road that is best covered in four-wheel-drive vehicles. I can attest to that personally, having slid the entire 11 miles (18 km) after a serious downpour. Maritza lies on the skirts of Orosí Volcano in a windier, cooler area. A more modern facility, the station can house thirty-two tourists and researchers. Lodging is $9 a day with shared baths. Meals can be arranged if requested in advance. Research on aquatic insects has been going on here for several years.

In forests around the rivers, wildlife is abundant: toucans, bellbirds, peccaries, sun bitterns, monkeys. Jaguars have been known to kill cattle in the area. I arrived too late to see a band of fifteen peccaries that had appeared on the trail near the laboratory that morning. Coatis frequently visit the station. Less than two hours from Maritza by foot is Llano de los Indios, an open pasture with petroglyphs carved in volcanic stone. The more than eighty pieces of rock art are both abstract and representational.

In the Atlantic watershed, Pitilla Biological Station can hold thirty-two people. Both the facilities and the road leading to it are rustic; there is no electricity, and four-wheel drive is necessary. (Enter via Santa Cecilia.) Lodging is $9 per day, plus a fee for kitchen privileges. Views from Pitilla include the Lake of Nicaragua, Orosí Volcano, and the rain forest around it.

All three biological stations have radio contact with other places, and horses are usually available at $5 per hour. The fee for camping is less than $1 a day. Telephone or fax the Guanacaste Conservation Area at 695-5598. Transportation can sometimes be arranged from Santa Rosa National Park.

The nearest lodging outside the park is at Liberia or some of the private nature reserves in the area. Some one-day tours are offered by hotels in Liberia and along the north Pacific coast, and nature tour companies in San José also offer Guanacaste trips. Access is via the Inter-American Highway north of Liberia. Several buses a day run from San José to Liberia, a trip of about four hours; the bus from San José to La Cruz passes by. However, you will not see much from the highway. There is no separate visitor center for the park. Contact is through the Guanacaste Conservation Area at Santa Rosa National Park. Telephone 695-5598. Trails for visitors are limited to those connected with the biological research stations.

Guayabo National Monument (Central Valley)

Guayabo is the blue morpho butterfly, the yellow flash of a Montezuma oropendola flying through the tall trees, flowing water, patches of profuse pink impatiens, and ancient carved stones. It is the quiet of centuries-old ruins hidden in the rain forest.

The only archaeological park in the country, Guayabo protects the remains of a city that flourished and disappeared before the Spaniards arrived. People may have occupied the area as early as 1000 B.C.; at its peak, Guayabo is estimated to have had as many as 10,000 people. Small rural villages perhaps supplied labor and revenue to this religious and political center. There was little new building after A.D. 800, and the site was abandoned by 1400.

Visitors today see cobbled roads (*calzadas*), stone-lined tanks to store water, open and covered aqueducts that carried water through the site (many still in use), and mounds (*montículos*) with stone-covered bases. Information signs at the park depict conical houses believed to have been built on the mounds out of wood and palm leaves. Trails lead past covered and open tombs, plundered before the park was established. Stylized forms of a jaguar and caiman decorate a striking monolith. Sixty-three petroglyphs picture birds and animals as well as art whose meaning has yet to be deciphered.

A five-year conservation and excavation project begun in August 1989 may shed light on some of the mysteries of people and place. The project will increase the excavated area to half of the almost 50-acre (20-ha) site.

Carved monolith at Guayabo National Monument (Photo by Ree Strange Sheck)

Among items found in the area are golden bells, carved stone tables, roasted corn kernels, beautiful pottery, a copper and gold frog, and a sacrificial stone. Some of the works of art are exhibited at the National Museum in San José. In 1991, four fragments of Nicoya pottery were discovered that were precisely dated, A.D. 1359. According to park administrator and archaeologist Rodolfo Tenorio, the find indicates a contact between Guayabo and Nicoya at that time that perhaps went beyond commercial interchange. One hypothesis is that the contact was at a diplomatic/political level.

In addition to the archaeological site, Guayabo protects the only remaining primary forest in the province of Cartago, accounting for 22 percent of the park's 538 acres (218 ha). More than 80 varieties of orchids and other epiphytes adorn the trees; toucans are present, as are chachalacas, woodpeckers, and brown jays (ticos call them *piaspias* and say they are the scouts of the forest, their warning cries signaling that an intruder is near). Notice the abundance of long, hanging nests built by oropendolas. Mammals include sloths, coatis, rabbits, squirrels, and armadillos.

Guides have been trained to accompany visitors on Sendero de los Montículos, the interpretive trail that leads through the archaeological site to a mirador with a fantastic view of the ruins below, the valley where Turrialba lies, and mountain peaks. Their English is limited but their enthusiasm and knowledge about natural history and the ruins come across in any language. Guayabo is open from 8:00 a.m. to 3:00 p.m. daily. A new trail lets visitors watch excavation of a road that ran from Guayabo to an outlying area. On weekdays, you will see archaeological work in progress. Visitors can walk alone on the nature trail, which makes either a short loop or a longer one down to the river. It can be muddy in the wet season. Rainfall averages 138 inches (3,500 mm), and the average temperature is 68°F (20°C). The highest point in the park is 3,609 feet (1,100 m).

Do not miss the visitor center across the road from the park entrance. The nearby camping area has been revamped to provide ten camping sites scattered among the trees and one group camping area. There are bathrooms and potable water.

The nearest lodging outside the park is a ten-minute walk away in the town of Guayabo; hotels in Turrialba 11 miles (19 km) away can be reached in thirty minutes by paved road. Tour companies in Turrialba and San José offer trips to the park. Bus service from San José to Turrialba is frequent and takes less than two hours to cover the 40 miles (65 km). There also is bus service from Turrialba to Guayabo. Taxi fare between the two runs about $11 one way.

Guayabo, Negritos, and Los Pájaros Biological Reserves (Northwest)

These four small islands in the Gulf of Nicoya are havens for large populations of resident and migratory birds, mainly seabirds. No visitor facilities exist; in fact, along with protection of the birds, another reason for making them biological reserves was to avoid their "development" for tourism or other purposes—to keep at least some of the gulf islands in a natural state.

Guayabo welcomes peregrine falcons in the winter and holds the largest of the country's four nesting colonies of brown pelicans. Located 5 miles (8 km) southwest of Puntarenas near San Lucas Island, Guayabo is also home to brown boobies, frigate birds,

MONKEY BUSINESS

Four species of monkeys live in Costa Rica: the white-faced capuchin (called cara blanca *in Spanish), the howler (congo), spider (mono colorado or araña), and the squirrel (tití or ardilla). The word for monkey in Spanish is* mono. *Howlers, the most abundant, are fruit and leaf eaters, as are the acrobatic spider monkeys, while the capuchins and squirrel monkeys eat everything from fruits to insects to lizards.*

The small squirrel monkey, or tití, is found only in the southern Pacific lowlands. At Manuel Antonio National Park, Grace Wong of the wildlife management program of the National University of Heredia is studying the titís in the area, which are a subspecies endemic to Costa Rica. Another subspecies farther south is endemic to Costa Rica and Panama, though few remain in Panama.

Grace has identified fourteen troops totaling about 681 individuals, with six of the troops, varying from fifteen to sixty-five individuals, ranging mainly inside the park

From May to October, when fruit is abundant, the titís have more time to rest and play, but by November, they spend most of the day looking for food. They are up at 5:00 a.m. and retire for the night about 6:00 p.m.

The young are born from the end of February to the end of March, one birth per pregnancy. Females have young every two years. Babies are carried for their first three months, with other adults taking turns helping the mother. In Grace's study group, there are four male adults and six females adults, and the rest are young.

When food is scarce, there is some competition between capuchins and titís. Grace says that when they clash, the smaller tití leaves; she has seen a capuchin grab a tití and throw it to the ground. When food is plentiful, they eat together. In Manuel Antonio, natural enemies of the tití are mainly boa constrictors and tyras, minklike animals.

Though human activity does not seem to drive titís away, Grace is concerned. The increase in tourists and tourism infrastructure has reduced the habitat of monkeys and other animals living outside the park, in some cases destroying corridors that forest monkeys move through and isolating troops. Another impact of tourism is that monkeys near a trail or road where people stop to observe them spend more energy on guard and less time foraging.

Tropical storm Gert in 1993 also influenced habitat in the park. About 60 percent of the canopy, or upper layer of the forest, was affected, reducing sites where the monkeys look for insects and fruits. Though short-term effects of this natural destruction are negative, Grace says that in the long-term, it can be beneficial because of the mosaic of different types of forest that will regenerate.

laughing gulls, lizards, and crabs. It has cliffs, a small beach, and sparse vegetation.

Two islands make up the Negritos, separated by a narrow channel that harbors whirlpools. Brown pelicans, frigate birds, boobies, and gulls live here, too, along with parrots, doves, raccoons, and iguanas. Artifacts indicate that Indians have been to the islands, either to live or bury their dead. Coral reefs make access difficult, but the waters support dolphins, giant conch, and oysters. Forests of palm, cedar, gumbo-limbo, and frangipani survive. The Negritos are almost 11 miles (17 km) south of Puntarenas near the Nicoya Peninsula. The Guayabo and Negritos reserves cover 355 acres (144 ha).

Isla de los Pájaros means "island of the birds." Less than 550 yards (500 m) from the coast, 8 miles (13 km) north of Puntarenas, it has some low-growing forest and fresh water. Again, seabirds, mainly pelicans, are the predominant species. It is the smallest of the four islands at 10 acres (4 ha).

There are no facilities at these reserves, camping is prohibited, and permission is required to visit. Look at them as you pass by on one of the popular day cruises of the Gulf of Nicoya.

Hitoy-Cerere Biological Reserve (Caribbean)

Visitors are welcome at the Hitoy-Cerere reserve, but so few actually go that park guards are really glad when they see a new face, though area hotels and businesses are beginning to promote tours that bring more people.

Off the beaten path, Hitoy-Cerere is not a stopping-off point on the way to somewhere else but a destination in itself. The most recent map I have does not even show a road in, but there is one, passable even in the wettest months. The reserve is 37 miles (60 km) southwest of Limón, an hour and a half from Cahuita.

The real adventurer will be thrilled to know that parts of this rugged portion of the Talamanca Mountains have yet to be explored. We do know some of the animals that live on its 22,622 forested acres (9,155 ha): tapirs, jaguars, peccaries, pacas, porcupines, weasels, white-faced and howler monkeys, agoutis, anteaters, armadillos, kinkajous, sloths, squirrels, otters, and deer.

Among the 276 bird species identified are the blue-headed parrot, keel-billed toucan, squirrel cuckoo, spectacled owl, green king-fisher, and slaty-tailed trogon. Frogs, toads, insects, and snakes have not been counted. Perhaps you will spot one of the remarkable Jesus Christ lizards, so named because they can walk on water. Their secret is quick movement and large hind feet with flaps of skin along each toe that allow them to skip over the surface of streams and ponds.

The forest canopy hovers at about 100 feet (30 m), but some species protrude through the top, reaching more than 160 feet (50 m). Buttresses from the trunks of these giants widen their base of support. Some trees begin as high as 7 feet (2 m) above the ground and have a horizontal reach of almost 50 feet (15 m). There are black palms with spiny stilt roots, tree ferns, orchids, and bromeliads. Mosses and lichens cushion trunks and branches.

Trails in this perpendicular place are difficult and not well marked. One researcher found it easier to stick to the rivers, though moss-covered rocks make streambeds slippery. (The reserve is surrounded by legally protected Indian lands.)

Water flows through the reserve. "Hitoy" in Bribrí refers to moss- and algae-covered rocks in the river of that name, "Cerere" to another river's clear waters. Pools surrounded by exuberant vegetation invite a solitary dip, while waterfalls almost 100 feet (30 m) high inspire awe. Bring rain gear—there is no defined dry season. Yearly amounts average 138 inches (3,500 mm). Humidity is high year-round; temperatures average 77°F (25°C). Elevation goes from about 328 to 3,363 feet (100 to 1,025 m).

To stay overnight, check with the park service about space at the ranger station. Day trips can be made from lodging in Limón, Cahuita, Puerto Viejo, or spots in between. Parks can also tell you the current road status. The bus from Limón to Valle de Estrella comes within 6 miles (10 km) of the entrance to Hitoy-Cerere. (Stay on until the end of the line at Finca Seis, one of several stops on a big banana plantation.) A taxi from there costs about $12. Taxi fare from Cahuita to the reserve is about $30 one way. If you stay overnight, you may want to arrange with the driver to pick you up for the return trip.

Irazú Volcano National Park (Central Valley)

Irazú Volcano has a history of showing off. Its awesome power is evident long before one reaches its impressive craters. Near Cartago, notice the devastation from the most recent major eruptions, from 1963 to 1965. Whole areas were buried in mud, floods were significant, and volcanic rock still peppers the countryside. But as you travel along the paved road to the park, give the volcano credit for the rich soils that now produce cabbages, potatoes, onions, and grasslands for dairy cows.

The highest peak in the Central Volcanic Range, Irazú reaches 11,260 feet (3,432 m). It has been known to send ash as far away as the Nicoya Peninsula; steam clouds have billowed 1,640 feet (500 m) high, and debris has shot up 984 feet (300 m). The rumbling giant tossed boulders weighing several tons from its innards in 1963 and send tremors to rattle buildings miles away.

Today, with Irazú in a sometimes-restless resting phase, visitors can ride right to the top of a lunar landscape that muffles its fiery nature. But thin streams of steam or gas and occasional tremors remind us that it is not dead; it only sleeps. People can walk along the rim of the main crater, peering down into a bright green lake almost 1,000 feet (300 m) below. Volcanic grays and blacks are highlighted by swatches of reds and oranges in the steep sides. The diameter is 3,445 feet (1,050 m). There are four other well-defined craters: Diego de la Haya, Playa Hermosa, La Laguna, and Pioroclústico.

Tenacious plants dot the largely empty areas around the craters, some bravely sporting bright flowers. On slopes, where the green of secondary growth gives testimony to nature's powers of recovery, old, barren branches rise like ghostly fingers above the new forest.

Animal life is scarce at the park as a result of both human activity and the eruptions. Where cougar and jaguar once thrived, today you may see rabbits, coyotes, armadillos, or even a tiger. Hummingbirds are numerous, and you might also spot a volcano junco, mountain robin, ruddy woodcreeper, or ant-eating woodpecker.

For clearest views and a chance to see both oceans, go early. I have a memory of Irazú at sunset, however, that I would not trade. Buffeted by a cold wind, I stood on a narrow path between two

Seemingly lunar landscape at Irazú Volcano National Park (Photo by Ree Strange Sheck)

craters and watched as the setting sun lit swirling clouds of mist with rich tones of orange and gold.

Whatever time of day you visit, take a jacket and something for rain, just in case. The average temperature is 45°F (7.3°C), with a lowest recorded temperature of 26°F (-3°C). When it is cold, it is very, very cold. Frost is possible from December through February.

The annual rainfall is 85 inches (2,158 mm) in the 5,706-acre (2,309-ha) park.

Irazú park protects rivers born here that flow into some of the country's major rivers: Chirripó, Reventazón, Sarapiquí, and Río Grande de Tárcoles. The name given it by the Indians who lived on its slopes was Iztarú, which means mountain of trembling and thunder.

Irazú Volcano Park, open from 8:00 a.m. to 3:30 p.m., is an easy hour-and-a-half drive from San José. Take the main highway to Cartago, then watch for signs telling where to turn. Up on the mountain, there is a pleasant view point with picnic facilities where you can safely pull off the road and drink in the expansive view of the valley below and peaks beyond. Most San José tour companies offer trips to Irazú, some in conjunction with a visit to the Lankester Gardens, Cartago, or the Orosi Valley.

Juan Castro Blanco National Park (North Central)

Created in 1992, Juan Castro Blanco National Park protects important water resources and primary forest. Its 35,232 acres (14,258 ha) encompass Platanar Volcano. It is east of the road from Zarcero to Ciudad Quesada. There are no facilities for visitors.

Las Baulas de Guanacaste National Park (Northwest)

See Tamarindo National Wildlife Refuge.

Lomas Barbudal Biological Reserve (Northwest)

My impression of Lomas Barbudal was birds—birds everywhere, so many to peer at through binoculars that we could hardly make progress driving along the dirt road. The species list is up to 180; the sheer quantity is overwhelming. Three species particularly important because they are disappearing in other areas are the king vulture, great curassow, and yellow-naped parrot. The man on the street will tell you that yellow-naped parrots are the best talkers in the parrot family. Trapping is no doubt a factor in their disappearance, along with loss of habitat. Curassows make for good eating.

Enthralled with the birds, we had little time for the bees, one of the reserve's claims to fame. About 250 species are thought to live

Encounter a coati (*pizote*) at Manuel Antonio National Park (Photo by Ree Strange Sheck)

here, some found nowhere else in the country. About sixty species of moths and butterflies and wasps are also abundant. Congo and white-faced monkeys move about the reserve, as do coatis, peccaries, white-tailed deer, armadillos, and raccoons.

Four species of endangered trees survive here, only three of which are familiar to most people: mahogany, Panama redwood, and rosewood. Deciduous forests make up 70 percent of the 5,631-acre (2,279-ha) reserve. One of the species that flowers profusely in the dry season, when its branches are bare of leaves, is the yellow cortez, *cortesa amarilla*. With a profusion of yellow blossoms, the trees resemble giant bouquets. Flowers in a single tree last only about four days, but it may bloom two or three times during the dry season. A curious tree is the cannonball. You will know it when you see it. The fruit looks like big balls hanging on strings down the trunk and on lower branches.

Water sources are plentiful in this region, which is classified as tropical dry forest. Rainfall averages 59 to 79 inches (1,500 to 2,000 mm). Rivers such as the beautiful Cabuya flow year-round;

its natural, sandy-bottomed pools are ideal for a swim under the big trees along its banks, where monkeys and birds escape the afternoon heat. There are more than twenty natural springs.

Lomas Barbudal, which means "bearded hills" in Spanish, is three hours from San José on the Inter-American Highway toward Nicaragua, or half an hour south of Liberia. Turn west 6.8 miles (11 km) north of Bagaces and continue about 4 miles (6 km) to the visitor center, which is operated in conjunction with Friends of Lomas Barbudal. Inside the reserve are picnic areas, trails, a lookout, and a place to swim in the river. Lodging is available in Liberia or at nearby privately owned nature reserves. For more information, stop by the Tempisque Conservation Area office in Bagaces or call 671-1062.

Manuel Antonio National Park (South)

This park is special. White-faced monkeys leap from tree to tree along the beach in dazzling displays of aerial skill. Shier squirrel monkeys, found only in this area and the Osa Peninsula, peek from behind leaves along trails. Slow-moving sloths turn a lazy look at visitors from their high vantage points. I had my first close-up look at a coati and an agouti in the wild on the forest trail in Manuel Antonio. Large iguanas rustle through leaves on the forest floor or sun themselves on logs along the beach.

The warm waters of the Pacific are home to a variety of marine life; snorkelers, divers, and even watchers at the tide pools see brightly colored fish. Do not miss the tiny bright blue ones in pools among the rocks at the western end of Manuel Antonio Beach. Whales pass by, and dolphins swim offshore. There are ten species of sponge, seventeen of algae, seventy-eight of fish, nineteen of coral, and twenty-four of crustaceans.

Researchers have identified 184 species of birds and 109 species of mammals, more than half of which are bats rarely seen by visitors. Among marine birds are brown pelicans, magnificent frigate birds, and brown boobies. Land birds include parrots, Baird's trogons, green kingfishers, gray-headed chachalacas, and golden-masked tanagers.

The fun begins at the entrance to the park, reached by wading across an estuary that can be waist-high on a short adult at high tide or barely cover the feet at low. There is no bridge, so wear shoes and clothes you do not mind getting wet. Carry whatever you want to eat or drink.

Once inside the park, you can choose a wide trail through the tall forest or walk along South Espadilla Beach. Toward the far end of the beach, you can enter the forest and cross over to gentler Manuel Antonio Beach or take the path to Cathedral Point, which separates the two beaches. From Cathedral Point, you can see Mogote Island—one of twelve included in the park—rising up sharply from the sea, its high cliffs crowned with vegetation. Both Mogote and Cathedral Point were sites of prehistoric Indian activities.

These two white sand beaches are lined with lush vegetation almost to the high-water line. The clear waters are warm. Espadilla is steeper with bigger waves.

Playa Escondida, rockier, not as kind to the feet, lies farther down a trail through the low mountains. Its beach disappears at high tide. Check with rangers before you start out. Guided walks on the trail to Puerto Escondido and a lookout point are limited to groups of no more than fifteen, with a total of forty-five people allowed on the trail at a time.

Allow time for a leisurely walk along the short Perezoso Trail, named for the sloths you may see there. No more than thirty people at a time may be on this trail.

At Manuel Antonio Beach, face the sea and look at the far right end near the rocks for a prehistoric turtle trap built by the Quepo Indians. Most easily visible at lowest tides after a full moon, the trap is a semicircular rock barrier that forms a pool at the beach's edge. Low and high tides vary about 11 feet (3.4 m) here. Female turtles would come in on high tide over the rock wall, but some would be caught in the pools when they tried to return to the sea as the tide went out and the water level dropped below the barrier. Both green and olive ridley turtles lay eggs here, though not in mass nestings.

The park, which covers 1,687 acres (683 ha) of land, does have a dry season from December to March, but rains are possible even then, and clear days, especially mornings, in the rainier months permit hours of quiet enjoyment on the beach. The annual rainfall is 150 inches (3,800 mm); the rainiest months are August, September, and October. The average temperature is 81°F (27°C). The park also protects 135,905 acres (55,000 ha) of marine habitat.

In addition to primary and secondary forest and beaches, there are marshes, a mangrove swamp, lagoons, and woodland. Warning signs point out the manzanillo tree along the beach; its leaves, bark, and applelike fruit secrete a white latex that stings the skin and is toxic.

The park is open from 7:00 a.m. to 4:00 p.m. It is crowded at Easter, Christmas, and during the two-week school vacation in July. Even though it is one of the most-visited parks, it is sometimes possible on a midweek visit to have the beach practically to yourself. No more than 600 people are admitted at a time during the week, 800 on weekends.

To protect both vegetation and animals in this small park, camping is no longer allowed. Accommodations are available in the adjacent town of Manuel Antonio and along the road to Quepos, less than 5 miles (7 km) away.

Daily express buses travel between San José and Manuel Antonio. The trip takes about three and a half hours. There are daily scheduled flights from San José to Quepos. (See Practical Extras at the end of the book.)

Palo Verde National Park (Northwest)

Palo Verde National Park, which includes what was formerly known as the Dr. Rafael Lucas Rodríguez Wildlife Refuge, covers 41,523 acres (16,804 ha). Lying along the east bank of the Tempisque River above where it empties into the Gulf of Nicoya, the area encompasses lakes, swamps, grasslands, savanna woodlands, and forest—probably fifteen habitats in all. It is one of the most important sanctuaries for migrating waterfowl in Central America. Along with the thousands of migratory birds that arrive every year, there are many resident species. Up to 279 species of birds have been counted, but it is believed that as many as 300 are here because other species have been seen nearby.

Herons, ibis, ducks, storks, and jacanas are among those that descend on the lowlands to feed and mate. The rare, endangered jabiru stork nests here. The largest stork in the world, the jabiru has a white body, gray neck and head, and a rose-red necklace. The only scarlet macaws left in the tropical dry forest of the Pacific live in this area.

In the rainy season, flooding of the plains is widespread. In the dry months of November through April, some waterholes disappear, and those that remain attract both birds and other wildlife, allowing the patient visitor a good chance to see them. An observation tower open to visitors is near a marsh.

Approach the mango trees near the Organization for Tropical Studies (OTS) station quietly for a chance to see some of the many mammals that make their home in the region. Peccaries, iguanas, deer, monkeys, and coatis feed on the fruits. The white-tailed deer who watched us while we watched him did not seem the least bit frightened. The park is home to 177 species of mammals.

Because OTS has a biological station at the park, a good trail system takes visitors into the forest past flowing springs that attract wildlife, past a natural cactus garden, to a superb lookout over the Tempisque floodplain, through a marsh (a printed guide recommends this as the best place to see a tropical rattlesnake or boa constrictor), through second-growth forest that is reclaiming pastureland, and to virgin tropical dry forest.

Friendly park staff greet visitors at the entrance stations. On my last visit, the ranger on duty rushed from the forest to urge me to come with him quickly—he had just come across a snake eating a frog and wanted me to see it. You can go to the Catalina sector of the park or continue to the OTS station and Puerto Chamorro on the banks of the Tempisque, where you will surely see huge iguanas foraging. Signs point to the Sendero Pizote (Coati Trail), Sendero Venado (Deer Trail), and others.

Isla de los Pájaros in the Tempisque River is an important nesting site for some spectacular birds. The small island seems covered with birds. On river trips past it, you can see the lovely color of the roseate spoonbills as they nest and fly overhead. There are wood storks, glossy ibis, anhingas, and great egrets. Many boas inhabit the island, feeding on bird eggs and nestlings. The river has a 13-foot (4-m) rise and fall with the tide. Sometimes it flows backward. Crocodiles can often be seen along the banks.

At the park, you may see cattle grazing; it is part of a management plan to keep the marshes open. Nearby farmers lose more of their crops than they like to birds, who do not recognize boundaries, so now automatic cannons help keep them from the fields.

The elevation ranges from 33 to 689 feet (10 to 210 m) above sea level. The annual rainfall is 90 inches (2,295 mm), and the average temperature is 81°F (27°C).

In the dry season, most trees lose their leaves to conserve water, but many wear bright flowers. The palo verde tree which gave the park its name, has pretty yellow flowers that adorn its green, thorn-clad branches. Temperatures can reach 105°F (41°C) at midday, but nights and early mornings are cool. While it is windy in the dry season and insects are scarce, the rainy season brings humidity, little breeze, and mosquitoes and gnats: Pack the repellent.

Camping is allowed in the park. If the rustic Palo Verde Biological Station belonging to OTS is not full up with researchers, tourists can stay there. The cost is about $25 a day without meals, $50 with meals (available when kitchen help is there for a student group). Make reservations at OTS. Telephone 240-6696, fax 240-6783.

The main land route is by the Inter-American Highway to Bagaces, between Liberia and Cañas. Turn west at the sign just across from the Tempisque Conservation Area office. The pavement ends, but the road is passable year-round. Just follow the signs. Keep your binoculars and cameras handy, because birds are everywhere. The 17-mile (28-km) trip from Bagaces can take a while, depending on how often you have a binocular stop. You can get from San José to Bagaces on one of the frequent buses that go on to Liberia. From Bagaces, you will need to hire a taxi.

The second route is to turn off the Inter-American and take the Tempisque ferry; once across the river, head for Puerto Humo. There you can hire a boat to take you along the meandering Tempisque to a dock at the park. It is a little more than a mile (2 km) by foot to the park headquarters. Tour companies and hotels offer both land and water trips to Palo Verde. Boat trips on the Tempisque to Isla de los Pájaros are attractive for natural history travelers—some tours include shore time for lunch and hiking. There is now a private reserve with lodging at Puerto Humo just across the river from Palo Verde. (See chapter 8.)

Poás Volcano National Park (Central Valley)

At Poás Volcano, you can stand at the edge of a multicolored crater almost a mile (1.5 km) in diameter, look down 984 feet (300 m), and watch geyserlike eruptions that leave no doubt this mountain still has something to say.

Its message was so clear in 1989 that the park was temporarily closed. The intensity of eruptions, the gases, and the ash made visits inadvisable. Forests and agriculture, especially coffee grown on the slopes below, suffered from acid rain. Some nearby residents were evacuated. Today the park is open from 8:00 a.m. to 4:00 p.m. No camping is allowed. You will see evidence of the acid rain.

Volcanologists cringe when they hear Poás called the largest geyser in the world, but the fact that it is not takes nothing away from the beauty and power of this 8,884-foot (2,708-m) giant. There are actually five craters on the mountain, but two get the most attention from visitors: the newer active crater responsible for the recent lava, rocks, ash, and steam, and an extinct one that now cradles Botos Lake, a twenty-minute easy climb through dwarf forest from the active crater.

From the view point constructed along the edge of the active crater, you have a spectacular view of the greenish hot-water lake. The earlier you go, the better chance you have of an unimpeded look. Clouds that drift in as the day progresses can completely obscure the bottom. While waiting for a column of mud and water to shoot into the air, notice the fumaroles, and look for small measuring devices scattered around the crater. Costa Rica has a fine Volcanological and Seismological Observatory at the National University in Heredia; its staff keeps a close watch at Poás and other sites around the country. Depending on the wind direction, you may get a good whiff of sulfur.

The park, with 13,838 acres (5,600 ha), has more to offer, though, than volcanic craters. Trails lead through shrubs, dwarf forest, and cloud forest covered with epiphytes. Because of volcanic activity, hunting, and deforestation outside the park, few mammals remain. Coyotes, rabbits, frogs, and toads are common, and at least 79 bird species are at home here. A park ranger told me he has seen resplendent quetzals fly over the road between the park entrance and administration building in early morning.

POETRY ON THE ESCALONIA TRAIL
POAS VOLCANO

I am light and shadow
Shining sun
Cold kiss of clouds
Fertile home of ancient trees
Of flowers just born
And of the red-green hummingbird
All pass their days
In my arms
Free
I am the cloud forest
That crowns Poás
We have much to share.

Poetry on the Escalonia Trail, Poás Volcano National Park (Photo by Ree Strange Sheck)

Hummingbirds are easy to see, and if you take some of the less-traveled trails, you might spot an emerald toucanet, brown robin, black guan, or masked woodpecker.

The trail to Botos Lake, named for the Botos Indians who lived on the north slope when the Spaniards arrived, begins near the view point. At this altitude, take your time, enjoy the tangled vegetation, and try to figure out the birds you are hearing but may not be able to spot.

My favorite is the Escalonia Trail, which begins at the picnic area. Trees soar overhead, bromeliads are everywhere, and trail markers full of poetry do justice to the forest's magnificence. They are only in Spanish; I have translated one of them for you.

The visitor center is being repaired—acid rain takes its toll on buildings, too. If it has reopened by the time you arrive, ask about audiovisual presentations. The multi-screen slide show of Costa Rica's flora and fauna is beautiful. There is a gift shop at Poás.

Bring a jacket and rain gear. Rainfall is 138 inches (3,500 mm), and though temperatures average between 48°F and 55°F (9°C to 13°C), a minimum of 21°F (6°C) has been recorded. On a bright, sunny day, it can be 70°F (21°C).

Poás lies about an hour and a half from San José through Alajuela and San Pedro de Poás. The drive is spectacular, through coffee farms, nurseries where ornamental plants are grown for export (under those huge expanses of black shade cloths), strawberry fields, and dairy farms. If you are going by tour, check to see if it gets to Poás by 9:30 a.m. at the latest and how much time it allows there. Some give you thirty minutes, barely enough time to peer into the crater. Other nature tour companies offer more time or even a naturalist guide to take you on a day trip to the area.

Public bus is not the easiest way to get to Poás. The only direct bus is on Sunday, and it is crowded. Daily buses go from Alajuela to San Pedro de Poás, and you can hire a taxi there. If several people are going, you can hire a taxi from San José and split the cost.

Rincón de la Vieja National Park (Northwest)
From the porch of the century-old ranch house that now houses park rangers, an exhibit room, and an administrative office at Rincón de la Viejo park, I watched a doe and fawn at the edge of

the clearing. They walked without fear. On the way up the mountain, a morpho butterfly had fluttered across the road; four species of this brilliant butterfly live in the park. Tapirs roam here, as do howler, capuchin, and spider monkeys. The armadillo is so abundant it could practically be the symbol of the park. Peccaries are common, and there is evidence that jaguar and puma stalk this 34,801-acre (14,084-ha) preserve.

The white-fronted Amazon parrot and spectacled owl are among 257 species of birds. Doves are everywhere; you have a good chance of seeing the curassow at lower elevations. The park ascends from 1,968 to 6,545 feet (600 to 1,995 m). There are kites, toucans and toucanets, redstarts, and motmots. A small cicada with the voice of a frog lives under the ground, its imitation fooling even the experts.

The park, 14 miles (23 km) northeast of Liberia in the Guanacaste Mountain Range, is the source of thirty-two rivers. As much as 197 inches (5,000 mm) of rain falls at higher elevations, practically year-round. The park's forests are important not only in preventing rivers that flow to the lowlands from disappearing in the dry season but also in keeping them from flooding in rainy months. The area's importance as a water source is one reason the park was established.

Two volcanoes crown this mountain mass: Rincón de la Vieja, which is active, and Santa María, which is dormant. In fact, Rincón de la Vieja has two craters; the dormant one has a crystal clear cold-water lake, while the lake in the other crater steams. The best time to climb to the craters is in the driest months, February through April.

Visitors have access to the scenic beauty and geologic attractions of the park through two entrances, both on bad roads. The ranch house, or *casona*, entrance on the slopes of Santa María is 16 miles (25 km) from the center of Liberia. (Jeep taxi from Liberia is about $35 one way.) The Enchanted Forest Trail begins here, and indeed, a walk through that fairyland of tall trees, delicate orchids (the national flower, the *guaria morada* orchid, thrives in the park), ferns, and mosses touches a primeval chord within. A small waterfall makes it picture perfect.

A shorter Sendero Colibrí (Hummingbird Trail) or a walk to a mirador with a view of Liberia and Miravalles Volcano are other possibilities. Less than 2 miles (3 km) away are sulfur waters that many say are medicinal. A 5.6-mile (8-km), three-hour trek takes you to Las Pailas, a magic land of bubbling mud pots, pools of hot water, and steam and gas vents at the other entrance to the park.

The second entrance is reached by turning off the Inter-American Highway about 3 miles (5 km) north of Liberia and continuing 12 miles (19 km) through the village of Curubundé to the park. After checking in at the ranger station, visitors can hike on forest trails to Las Pailas. The walk starts out by crossing a river—no bridge— which was about knee-deep when I waded across one August.

Various trail possibilities exist from this entrance also, including the climb to the craters. Camping is permitted in designated areas. Bring rubber boots for hiking. The average temperature is 59°F to 79°F (15°C to 26°C)—it can get cold at night.

Contact the park service in San José or the Guanacaste Conservation Area (telephone or fax 695-5598) for information. If you drive from Liberia to the *casona*, you may have to wait for the river at the edge of Liberia to go down after a hard rain before you can get across—there is no bridge.

Hotels and tour companies offer visits to Rincón de la Vieja. There are some small lodges and private reserves near park entrances. (See the northwest section in chapters 6 and 8.)

Santa Rosa National Park (Northwest)

In times past, Indians have walked this land, and hunters, woodcutters, cowboys, and soldiers, too. Footprints today belong mainly to researchers, park rangers, and nature lovers. What had been virgin tropical dry forest, cleared pastures, and a battlefield now is Santa Rosa National Park, a piece of property where history is still being written.

The historical significance of Santa Rosa was the primary reason it was protected by the government, first as a national monument and then as a national park. Soon, however, the ecological importance of its flora and fauna and of the habitats that exist in this dry Pacific region was recognized.

It is the ecological battle that is making history now, an effort not only to protect but also to restore some of these habitats. Research at Santa Rosa is shedding light on plant and animal inter-relationships and how forests regenerate themselves—discoveries that make a difference here and around the world.

A young park ranger told me that most Costa Ricans who visit Santa Rosa National Park come initially because of its history, but they leave excited about the intricacies of nature. She carries the park's environmental education program to nearby village schools, and walks with the children when they come on tour.

The historical drawing card is the site of the Battle of Santa Rosa on March 20, 1856, which pitted a well-trained and well-armed invading army against a ragtag band of Costa Rican peasants who had become soldiers overnight. The patriots won, routing the forces of adventurer William Walker in fourteen minutes. The battle took place around La Casona, the house at Hacienda Santa Rosa. Visitors today can walk through the big house and see the historical displays, stand on the wide wooden veranda and look toward the 300-year-old stone corrals, or step into the kitchen and see where cheese was hung over the wood stove to preserve it.

A stately Guanacaste, the national tree of Costa Rica, stands nearby. Its wood is good for construction, and its ear-shaped fruit, which gives the tree its English name of ear fruit, has been used to wash clothes and is food for horses, cows, and small forest mammals.

Climb the short view-point trail behind La Casona or take the short, well-marked nature trail. Keep your eyes open: I was within spitting distance of a handsome 5-foot (1.5-m) boa constrictor before I could discern it draped over a tree root by the path. Its natural camouflage is remarkable. The trail is called Indio Desnudo for the gumbo-limbo tree. You can identify it by its reddish-brown bark, which inspired the popular name—*indio desnudo* means "naked Indian." Since the reddish skin has a tendency to peel, ticos sometimes irreverently refer to it as the "tourist tree." Look for Indian petroglyphs along the trail.

Two of Santa Rosa's beaches are famous as sea turtle nesting sites: Naranjo, about 8 miles (12 km) from park headquarters, and

History-filled La Casona at Santa Rosa National Park (Photo by Ree Strange Sheck)

Nancite, 11 miles (17 km) away. Though three species come ashore to lay eggs, it is the hundreds of thousands of Pacific or olive ridley turtles on small Nancite Beach that get the most attention. From July to December, mass nestings, called *arribadas*, occur periodically, while single turtles come ashore every night in this peak season. The other two species are green and leatherback turtles. Nancite is in a study area, so permission to visit is required.

The park does have a pronounced dry season from November to May. Rainfall for most of the park's 91,719-acre (37,118-ha) land surface is about 63 inches (1,600 mm). Average temperature is 79°F (26°C). The park also protects some 193,000 acres (78,000 ha) of marine habitat.

Entrance to this part of Santa Rosa, which also includes the park headquarters, is 22 miles (36 km) north of Liberia via the Inter-American Highway, paved all the way to La Casona. At the entrance booth, you can buy a map of the park, and the ranger can help you decide what you can see in the time you have.

Entrance to the Murciélago section of Santa Rosa is farther north on the Inter-American, turning off to Cuajiniquil at the rural guard station. If you do not see a sign for Murciélago when you get to the village, ask for directions. The road is unpaved, and a couple of rivers must be forded to reach the ranger station. I did it in the rainy season in a standard pickup, but I would have worried less in four-wheel drive; there is lots of mud.

Stop along the narrow road and take a close look at the acacia tree for a lesson in plant and animal relationships. The tree provides food for acacia ants, and the ants protect it from animal predators and foreign vegetation. They even keep a circle cleared around the tree. Find the small hole near the base of one of its thorns and watch what happens when the tree is disturbed. Do not get your fingers in the way of the ants rushing out: Their stings are painful. If you unwittingly brush against an acacia branch along a trail, you will find out for yourself.

Murciélago ("bat" in English) belonged to Anastasio Somoza when he was president of Nicaragua. Talk to the delightful cook at the ranger station there; she can share stories from those days. She can also tell you about the coyotes and monkeys that come into the yard. You can travel on to the coast at Playa Blanca or Santa Elena Bay or walk on the trail to the Pozo El General, which has water year-round, and is important for animals in the dry season.

Santa Rosa National Park has capuchin, howler, and spider monkeys, deer, armadillos, coatis, raccoons, and even some cats—155 species of mammals in all, about half of them bats. Studies have identified 3,140 species of moths and butterflies among more than 10,000 of insects. Magpie jays and parrots make lots of noise, while some of the 253 species of birds get attention with their coloring: Look for orange-fronted parakeets, elegant trogons, and crested caracaras.

Santa Rosa park now includes Bolaños Island, formerly a wildlife refuge. Located up the coast from mainland Santa Rosa west of the town of La Cruz, Bolaños is in a small bay whose waters lap on both the Costa Rican and Nicaraguan shorelines. Rising 266 feet (81 m) out of the Pacific, this rocky mound protects seabirds. Magnificent frigate birds and American oystercatchers nest here, and this is one of four nesting sites in the country for brown pelicans.

Winds seem to be an important factor in determining where frigate birds build a nest: They need help landing and becoming airborne because of their small bodies, short feet, and long wings and tails. The wind on Bolaños during the dry season—nesting time—is consistent and strong. There are as many as 1,000 of these birds, called *tijeretas* (tea-hay-RAY-tahs) in Spanish because of their scissorlike tails. During mating season, the male blows out a bright red throat pouch to attract a female, who then lays a single egg. No facilities for visitors exist at the bird sanctuary, but watching through binoculars at a tactful distance is not against the rules. The island is less than 3 miles (5 km) from Puerto Soley.

No lodging is available in Santa Rosa park, but there will be eventually. Camping is allowed at specific sites. Hotels in Liberia, as well as at some private nature reserves, offer day trips to Santa Rosa. Several nature tour companies have trips to the park, and it is easy to find on your own if you are driving. Buses to Peñas Blancas or La Cruz will let you off at the park entrance, though you will have a 4-mile (7-km) walk to the headquarters. Or you can hire a taxi from Liberia for a day trip to the park. Santa Rosa is four and a half hours from San José. The information booth at the entrance is open from 7:30 a.m. to 4:30 p.m. Telephone or fax 695-5598.

Tapantí National Park (Central Valley)

"Dripping forest" is not a scientific term, but for me, it describes the Tapantí National Park in the Talamanca Mountain Range. Inside the forest, raining or not, the air is moist, plants seem wet, the earth smells fresh. The sound of running water can be pervasive: 150 rivers and rivulets run here, important sources for hydroelectric projects.

Reports give an average rainfall of about 256 inches (6,500 mm), though it has on occasion totalled 315 inches (8,000 mm). Even in the drier months of January through April, wise travelers bring rain gear. The average temperature is 70°F (21°C).

A number of marked trails near the entrance lead through the extravagance of rain forest vegetation. Tree crowns form a leaky umbrella under which grow delicate ferns (including 18 species of tree ferns), orchids, bromeliads, lianas that tempt one to take a swing, mosses, and multicolored lichens. Along the road and on forest slopes grows a plant with immense leaves and a tall reddish flower that Costa Ricans call "poor man's umbrella." I have seen its leaves used in the countryside by people caught in the rain.

Tapantí is a favorite with bird-watchers. Among the more than 260 species identified here are the ones everybody wants to see: quetzals, exotic hummingbirds, toucans, parakeets, parrots, great tinamous, and squirrel cuckoos. Endangered mammals live here, too: jaguar, ocelot, tapir. Animals you are more likely to see are squirrels, monkeys, raccoons, opossums, coyotes, agoutis, and red brocket deer: forty-five species of mammals. There are porcupines, silky anteaters, otters, and lots of toads. Butterflies are everywhere. Your day may be blessed by the appearance of a blue morpho.

An exhibit room at the entrance is a good starting place to orient yourself and talk with a friendly ranger. A map and booklets on forest fauna published by the wildlife service (in Spanish) can be purchased here. About half a mile (1 km) from the ranger station is the Oropendola Trail, which has covered picnic shelters, popular swimming spots in the frigid river water, and a place designated for fishing. Two and a half miles (4 km) farther is a vista point marked by a sign with a large eye. Climb the short trail for a splendid view of a waterfall in the densely forested mountains across the river. In all, the refuge covers 15,024 acres (6,080 ha). There are covered shelters at a picnic area.

The gravel road is excellent because the Costa Rican Electric Institute (ICE) has a dam about 9 miles (15 km) from the entrance. You can continue along it for views of magnificent virgin mountain forest. The Río Grande de Orosí which flows here produces hydroelectric energy and helps supply San José with water.

Tour companies offer day trips to Tapantí. If you go by the Orosí-Río Macho bus from Cartago, you still end up more than 5 miles (9 km) from the refuge entrance, though you can hire a taxi to go the rest of the way. You may want to consider a taxi from Cartago or Paraíso, where they are more plentiful. If you are driving, take the highway to Cartago, and continue to Paraíso and Orosí, taking the bumpy road for Purisil. Watch for the Tapantí sign. The park is open from 8:00 a.m. to 4:00 p.m.

Tortuguero National Park (Caribbean)

With very little imagination, you can see yourself as Hepburn or Bogart on the *African Queen* as you wind your way through the rivers and canals to Tortuguero National Park on the northern Caribbean coast. Flora, fauna, and the condition of the boat may differ, but the feeling is there—you and the water, vegetation, and wildlife in an intimate and solitary encounter.

If you travel to Tortuguero by boat from Limón, the contrast of settled lands along the water with these protected lands vividly portrays the difference a park can make. From the air, the park is a mass of greens from the coastal plain to the Sierpe Hills, broken only by narrow ribbons of water.

However you get there, to explore Tortuguero is to discover a crocodile along the bank, a small turtle sunning on a trunk in the water, a monkey or sloth asleep in a tree, vultures peering down from a lofty perch. Perhaps a river otter will slip into the water as the boat approaches. Water and land birds keep your binoculars busy: At least 309 species live here. Watch for green macaws, herons, egrets, parrots, kingfishers, oropendolas (notice their large, hanging nests), tanagers, toucans, and bananaquits.

Tortuguero is tall forest and palm groves, lianas trailing into the water, and floating gardens of water hyacinths. The endangered West Indian manatee feeds on these and other aquatic plants. This large sea cow can be 13 feet (4 m) long and weigh about 1,300 pounds (600 kg).

Tortuguero is also beaches, important nesting sites for the sea turtles (*tortugas*) that gave the place its name. Green, leatherback, hawksbill, and occasionally loggerhead turtles return to these beaches every year to lay eggs. Some come in massive arribadas, others singly. Though you could see a turtle any night, there are peak times. The best time to see hawksbills is from July to October, leatherbacks from February to July with a peak in April and May, and green turtles from early July into October, peaking in August. Rangers from other parks are brought in to help patrol the beaches during the busiest months to prevent eggs from being stolen. Researchers at the nearby Caribbean Conservation Corporation have been tagging nesting turtles since 1955. The female green turtle comes ashore to lay eggs an average of two or three times during her season there, staying not far offshore in between. It may be up to four years before she returns to Tortuguero.

There are many crustaceans (prawns feed under the water hyacinths), eels, fifty-two species of freshwater fish (including the gar, considered a living fossil because species of that genus lived 90 million years ago), and sharks.

Trails take off from ranger stations on the water at either end of the park. On foot in this tropical wet forest, perhaps you can spot some of the small, brightly colored frogs that live here. Some of the mammals include peccaries, raccoons, kinkajous, ocelots, pacas, cougars, and skunks. The park protects more than fifteen endangered mammal species, including the tapir, jaguar, giant anteater, and three species of monkeys. Rain gear and rubber boots come in handy.

Rainfall averages about 197 inches (5,000 mm), but it can go up to 236 inches (6,000 mm) in parts. Elevation reaches from sea level to 1,020 feet (311 m) in the Sierpe Hills. It is hot and humid, with an average temperature of 79°F (26°C). The park covers 46,818 acres (18,947 ha) on land and also protects 129,147 acres (52,265 ha) of marine habitat.

Camping is allowed in the park. The nearest lodging is in the village of Tortuguero, at the northern end. It is possible to visit Tortuguero park in a day trip, but being there overnight allows for an after-dark boat ride to see nighttime animal life on the river, a chance to see the turtles, or simply more time to savor the flavor. You can also make your own arrangements for boat and hotel, but you save yourself that hassle by going with a tour company leaving from either San José or a site on the Caribbean. Tour companies offer boat or plane trips or a combination of the two. (See chapter 9.) Some lodges in the north central area offer boat trips to Tortuguero via the San Juan River.

Canals sometimes get low, and boats have to proceed slowly. I have heard tales of passengers getting out to push; I myself have seen the captain do it. If you do not take a tour, you can hire a small boat or sometimes get a ride on a cargo boat. There is daily air service.

Wildlife Refuges
(Administered by National Wildlife Directorate)

Barra del Colorado National Wildlife Refuge (Caribbean)

The Barra del Colorado refuge is as far north as one can go on Costa Rica's Caribbean coast. On the other side of its northern border along the San Juan River is Nicaragua. Access within the park is by its waterways. Virtually no land trails exist. Part of the western region has yet to be explored.

What is happening on that western edge illustrates the pressures on protected areas in Costa Rica. Logging and roads to bring the trees out are cutting into the virgin forest. It is a remote area, and the wildlife staff is spread too thin to control it.

Travelers get to Barra del Colorado by air or by boat. Boats come through Tortuguero park or the Sarapiquí-San Juan-Colorado River route. There is plenty to see from the network of rivers, channels, and lakes in the reserve. Among the endangered species are the West Indian manatee, tapir, cougar, jaguar, ocelot, and jaguarundi. Species you are more likely to see are caimans and crocodiles, white-faced and howler monkeys, red brocket deer, and sloths. Birds include the great green macaw, great curassow, herons of various kinds, the red-lored Amazon parrot, great tinamou, cormorant, and keel-billed toucan.

A very wet rain forest, the area averages from 158 inches (4,000 mm) of rain on the western edge to 221 inches (5,600 mm) at the town of Barra del Colorado. However, my two-day visit in one of the rainiest months was sunny and beautiful. Go prepared for rain, but take your sunscreen just in case.

You will see swamp forests, swamp palm forests, and mixed forests growing above the swamps in this 242,158-acre (98,000-ha) refuge. *Caña brava*, a wild cane, grows mainly along the rivers. Its stiff, solid stems are used to make decorative ceilings and prop up banana plants. Another forest species with commercial value is cativo, which is used in plywood. If you come via the canals, you may see lumber being floated down to Moín; supposedly, it is all being cut outside the park lands.

THE RESPLENDENT QUETZAL

The name is exotic. The bird is exotic. A member of the trogon family, the resplendent quetzal was a symbol of freedom and independence to some indigenous Central American peoples. It thrives in Costa Rica. Travelers are more likely to see it here than in Guatemala where the quetzal is the national bird because of the protected forests at the elevations where they live: 5,000 to 10,000 feet (1,524 to 3,048 m) in the Central and Talamanca ranges, above 4,000 feet (1,219 m) in the Tilarían Cordillera.

Though Monteverde Cloud Forest Preserve is the more famous site for seeing this fantastic iridescent bird with its blue-green head, neck, and body and its crimson belly, Braulio Carrillo, Poás, and Chirripó national parks are also home to the quetzal as well as other forests in the Talamanca Mountains. Some birders say the easiest place to see it is near San Gerardo de Dota off the Inter-American Highway before Cerro de la Muerte. Dr. Alexander F. Skutch, who wrote a classic descriptive account of the natural history of the quetzal, lives near San Isidro de El General. He says that in the 1970s, he often saw quetzals at 7,000 to 8,000 feet on the road from San José to San Isidro.

The birds are endangered because of the destruction of their habitat. Though they eat many kinds of fruits and other things

such as insects and lizards, they depend heavily on fruit from the laurel family, a relative of the avocado. At Monteverde, quetzals move seasonally, apparently following the fruiting patterns of the different species and migrating from Monteverde to unprotected land. As reserves such as Monteverde become isolated by deforested land, the survival of migrating species is endangered.

Not only do quetzals depend on laurels but laurel trees also depend on the quetzals to distribute their seeds. Swallowing the fruit whole, the bird coughs up the seed after digesting the nutritious part.

The breeding period is from March to June, peaking in April and May. This is the easiest time to see quetzals because they come down lower in the trees to nest, making do with a hole already hollowed out by a woodpecker or excavating space in rotting limbs or dead tree trunks. The female generally lays two blue eggs, which hatch about eighteen days later. As soon as the first babies fly away, she lays eggs again. Both male and female take part in building the nest, incubating the eggs, and feeding the young. The end of the male's longer tail streamers can sometimes be seen protruding from the hole when it is his turn on the nest.

The main predators of the eggs and chicks at Monteverde are short-tailed weasels and perhaps snakes.

A variety of fish live in the lakes, rivers, and estuaries, among them snook, tarpon, mackerel, snapper, gar, and *guapote* (a tropical rainbow bass). The area draws many sportfishermen.

Lodging is available inside the reserve at private hotels near the town of Barra del Colorado. Tour companies offer one-day or multi-day trips to the reserve. You can easily combine a trip to Tortuguero and Barra del Colorado, either with a tour or by hiring a boat to take you from one to the other. Scheduled airlines fly from San José to Barra del Colorado in thirty minutes; the canal trip to Barra from Moín takes six hours.

Caño Negro National Wildlife Refuge (North Central)

The centerpiece of this 24,633-acre (9,969-ha) refuge for resident and migrant birds is Caño Negro Lake, which covers some 2,225 acres (900 ha) with up to 10 feet (3 m) of water in the rainy season. As the dry season progresses, it diminishes to a few pools, streams, and an arm of the river that feeds it. I have only visited the refuge in wet times, but in the drier months from January to April, the lake turns to pasture, and birds and animals come to the shrinking waterholes to drink.

The largest colony of neotropic olivaceous cormorants in the country are found here, and it is a good place to see the roseate spoonbill, wood stork, species of ducks you never imagined existed, snowy egrets, five species of kingfisher, and green-backed herons. Seventeen of the huge jabiru storks are sometimes here.

During a few magical hours on a boat, I saw some of these birds plus jacanas, two groups of spider monkeys, three of howlers, a red-lored parrot, a black-bellied whistling duck, anhingas with their wings spread to dry, caimans, iguanas, great egret, and, for the thrill of the day, a common potoo looking for all the world like a part of the branch on which it was perched. I do not know how the boatman ever spotted it.

A number of endangered mammal and reptile species live at Caño Negro: tapir, jaguar, ocelot, cougar, and crocodile. Other animals include white-faced, howler, and spider monkeys, sloths, river otters, peccaries, white-tailed deer, silky anteaters, bats, and tayras. What is a tayra? you ask. It looks like a large mink, colored chocolate brown to black, with a long, furry tail. It lives in a den under the ground but searches for food both on the ground and in trees. Tayras probably include bird eggs and nestlings in their diets. In the dry season, visitors who wait patiently and discreetly in sight of the remaining waterholes can watch a variety of animals come to drink.

From January to April, less than 4 inches (100 mm) of rain falls. Since the year's total rainfall averages 138 inches (3,500 mm), you can see that the other months are damp. South and west of the lake, where the land rises from the plain abruptly to the Guanacaste Mountain Range, rainfall can reach 158 inches (4,000 mm) a year.

One aim of the wildlife refuge is to help improve the economic well-being of those who live in and around it. Under an agreement with the local development association, the wildlife department allows grazing of cattle on the dry lake bed in summer. Cattlemen pay less than a dollar a head for grazing rights, with eighty percent of the income going to community projects and the rest to conservation. A tree nursery established with area families provides trees to reforest parts of the refuge and the basin of the Río Frío, with some sold for profit. Fresh-water turtles are being raised—thirty percent are released and the rest sold.

There are two main entrances to the Caño Negro refuge. The headquarters is at the town of Caño Negro, accessible by road from Upala, San Rafael de Guatuso, and Los Chiles, near Nicaragua (the latter by very bad road). The other entrance is by boat from Los Chiles on the Río Frío. Many organized tours take the river route but do not go all the way to the headquarters. Hotels in the north-central section offer one-day tours. (See chapter 6.)

A visit to the refuge could be combined with a trip to Arenal or Guananaste parks and private nature reserves, using the Upala route. There are buses from Upala to Caño Negro and from Ciudad Quesada to Los Chiles.

Camping at the refuge costs $2 per person, and limited overnight space in rustic facilities is $7 per person. Bring your own sleeping bag. Call 460-1301 for overnight reservations. In the dry season, visitors can explore on foot or rent horses, but in the rainy months, boat rental at $4 per person is necessary—no motorboats.

Ask about the availability of a local guide. The refuge is open from 8:00 a.m. to 4:00 p.m.

Curú National Wildlife Refuge (Northwest)

The Curú refuge has a deserted island kind of feeling, even though it is on the Nicoya Peninsula. Perhaps the reason is the coconut-strewn beach, or the mangrove swamp, or the jungled hills rising up at the end of the bay. Walking through the tall forest behind the palm-fringed beach, one senses the wildness of the place.

Boa constrictors are at home here, as are paca, agouti, ocelot, white-faced and howler monkeys, rattlesnake, iguana, white-tailed deer, mountain lion, and margay (a small, spotted cat with a long tail). Waters along the beach host giant conch, lobster, and oyster—there is good snorkeling. Hawksbill and olive ridley turtles come ashore to nest. The magnificent frigate bird soars overhead. Parrots squawk. Hummingbirds, trogons, hawks, swallows, egrets, motmots, tanagers, roseate spoonbills, and fish eagles are among the 115 species of birds.

Small islands jut up in the Pacific in front of Curú Beach, one of three sand beaches in the refuge. On the distant horizon is the mainland.

Creation of the Curú refuge was the doing of Federico and Julieta Schutt, who established Curú Hacienda in 1933 for commercial logging, reforestation, and agriculture. When squatters took over more than 980 acres (400 ha) of the farm in 1974, the Schutt family looked for ways to protect habitat and wildlife. Refuge status was secured in 1983 for 208 acres (84 ha) of fragile marine and beach habitat, leaving the surrounding Schutt farm with 2,698 acres (1,092 ha), two-thirds of which is forest and one-third pasture.

Visitors can explore ten trails with names like Mango, Killer, Laguna, and Río, rated from very easy to difficult. On some, the scientific names of plants are marked. The Finca de los Monos (monkey farm) trail has a printed guide, with lists of trees, birds, and mammals.

Besides running the farm, the family manages Curú as a living laboratory for students on directed projects. To walk with Doña Julieta or her children is to walk with the best guides around.

Doña Julieta took me to the corral to see baby white-tailed deer. Captured by a nearby landowner on private property, they were brought in to be cared for until they can be relocated on protected land. Doña Julieta had predicted that white-faced monkeys would be at the corral at that time of day to get bananas, and they were. We climbed a ladder to the second floor of a barn to look at a makeshift museum of shells, bones, rocks, and other research projects. Near the forested mountain, she told of a leader of the Costa Rican conservation movement who got lost overnight in the dense jungle; he shall remain nameless.

Walking with daughter Adelina, I received an introduction to the forest, to the swamp, to the life she has in this wonderland, where boas can be found in bedrooms and dinner can be for just family or for hungry hordes of researchers. Adelina has spearheaded environmental education programs, leading more than 750 students from sixteen area schools on walks and giving talks. The naturalist guides who have been trained to lead trail walks are from Valle Azul, the town begun by the squatters of twenty years ago. The town is also opening a naturalist gift shop.

Though the rustic cabins along the beach at Curú are primarily for researchers, space may be available for a overnight stay. Meals, served family-style, are ample and tasty. Lodging and meals cost $25 per day; day tours are $5. Doña Julieta requests a call in advance, even for a day visit: 661-2392 or 226-4333.

The entrance to Curú is about 4 miles (7 km) south of Paquera off the main road to Cóbano. Buses to Cóbano and Montezuma pass by. The refuge is a mile and a half (2.5 km) from the highway. Several area establishments offer day tours.

Gandoca-Manzanillo National Wildlife Refuge (Caribbean)

Gandoca-Manzanillo, which touches the border with Panama on the Caribbean, is a mixed-management reserve. That means its goal is not only to conserve the rich biological resources but also to work with the community in sustainable use of those resources to promote economic development. Tourism is one of the components in the development formula; a number of hotels and lodges exist on private land within the refuge.

Nature has spread a visual feast there. Go and enjoy. Take the road south from Limón past Cahuita and Puerto Viejo. Since the tourism institute and roads people are adding more signs, perhaps there will be one to tell you where the refuge starts. If not, know that you are already in the refuge when you get to Punta Cocles. Maybe an administration building at Manzanillo will be open by the time you arrive.

Some call the beaches around Punta Uva the most beautiful on Costa Rica's Caribbean coast. They are often pictured on post-cards. And gorgeous they are: white sand, graceful palms with jungle-looking vegetation beneath, just the right amount of logs and coconuts washed up on the shore. Coral reefs about 650 feet (200 m) out create a snorkeler's paradise: blue parrotfish, green angelfish, white shrimp, red sea urchins and long-spined black ones, anemones, sea cucumbers, lobsters, sponges. Turtle grass sometimes attracts Pacific green turtles that feed on it.

Explore the land portion of the refuge by foot from Manzanillo or take a boat to a more southern shore and then go by foot. It is about a four-hour hike to the Gandoca Lagoon. Terrain in the refuge ranges from flat to rolling country with small, forest-covered hills. You might discover a freshwater marsh, the only natural banks of mangrove oysters in the country, or the place where tarpon fish larvae grow to adulthood. Endangered species protected there include the manatee, crocodile, and tapir. There are also pacas, caimans, opossums, five species of parrots, sloths, ocelots, margays, otters, bats, falcons, hawks, frigate birds, pelicans, chestnut-mandibled toucans, and collared aracaris.

As for weather, forget the Costa Rican rule of thumb for wet and dry seasons. Rain falls year-round, though the driest months are March, April, May, September, October, and November. Expect cooler temperatures with wind and rain in December and January. The temperature averages 82°F (28°C). The total area of the refuge is 23,348 acres (9,449 ha).

Check with the wildlife office about camping. Consider Limón, Cahuita, Puerto Viejo, or places along the road linking them for lodging. Buses and taxis will get you to Manzanillo. Several hotels, lodges, and tour agencies along the Caribbean coast offer tours to the refuge.

Golfito National Wildlife Refuge (South)

Virgin forest covers most of the 3,336 acres (1,350 ha) of Golfito National Wildlife Refuge. Preservation of that forest is the reason the refuge was created, not only for the species of plants and animals that live there, some of them endangered, but also for the community of Golfito it surrounds. The tall evergreen forest on this rugged terrain safeguards water sources for today's population and future generations while it also reduces the danger of landslides that would affect the town.

Rainfall is heavy in this area of southwestern Costa Rica, almost 196 inches a year (4,976 mm), and temperatures are warm, averaging 82°F (28°C). The combination creates a marvelous tropical wet forest where mosses, lichens, bromeliads, and thirty-one species of orchids make a veritable greenhouse on the limbs of a single tree. Heliconia plants splash their exotic, showy flowers of red, orange, and yellow against the vibrant greens of the understory. Eleven of the thirty or so species of heliconia found in the country are here. Pollinated by hummingbirds, their berry fruits are food for many birds. Indigenous peoples used the bananalike leaves medicinally and for building, thatching and wrapping food.

Some tree species reach almost 165 feet high (50 m). The purple heart tree grows at Golfito; you see its beautiful purple wood made into salad bowls and earrings in souvenir shops. There is manwood, whose wood can lie on the ground for more than thirty years without decomposing, ceiba, and bully tree, whose red leaves stand out against the canopy.

Among the 146 bird species identified so far are the endangered scarlet macaws, great tinamous, parrots, herons, pelicans, ibis, owls, parakeets, and trogons. All four species of monkeys found in Costa Rica (including the squirrel monkey, or tití) live in the Golfito refuge, as do cats such as jaguarundi and margay, anteaters, bats, pacas, and agoutis. A number of trails, short and long, crisscross the refuge. A visit to the other side of the airport may allow you to see monkeys who come to eat the exotic fruits planted here by the banana company. It will certainly allow you to see a variety of birds.

The driest months are January through March, but bring your rain gear even then. Check with the wildlife office in San José

The cougar, or mountain lion, *puma*, one of six wild cats in Costa Rica (Photo by Omar Coto Loría)

about camping in the refuge. Since it is at the edge of the town of Golfito, lodging is nearby. Some Golfito hotels offer guided tours to the refuge. By bus from San José, the 213-mile trip (342-km) trip takes eight hours. There is daily airline service between San José and Golfito.

Ostional National Wildlife Refuge (Northwest)

The night was very dark. A young man led us across the beach of the Ostional National Wildlife Refuge to the high-tide line, where a Pacific or olive ridley turtle was patiently digging a hole in the sand with her back flippers. She dug as far as the flippers would reach, flinging sand out behind her shell.

Practically as soon as the flying sand had settled, soft eggs began to drop into the hole—one, two or three at a time—plopping on top of each other until there were about a hundred. Once the egg-laying began, the guide could briefly use his flashlight without dis-

SEA TURTLES

Six of the eight species of sea turtles in the world nest on Costa Rica's coasts. Though it is possible to see a turtle laying eggs on a beach somewhere in the country almost any night of the year, there are times when turtles arrive in large numbers (arribadas) at particular sites. Some of the most important nesting sites are in protected areas at the Tortuguero and Santa Rosa parks and Ostional and Tamarindo wildlife refuges.

*The turtle species and their Spanish names are green (*verde*), leatherback (*baula *or* canal*), hawksbill (*carey*), olive ridley (*lora *or* carpintera*), Pacific green (*negra*), and loggerhead (*cabezona*). The Pacific green, green, hawksbill, and leatherback are found on both coasts, while the ridleys are only on the Pacific. The loggerhead is mainly in the Caribbean. Hawksbills, loggerheads, and leatherbacks usually are solitary nesters; the greens come ashore to lay eggs in concentrated colonies; and the ridleys come singly, in small colonies, or in massive arribadas.*

The most important nesting beaches are listed here.

Tortuguero: Green turtles nest from early July to October, with August the peak month; hawksbills are also easiest to see here at this time, though they nest year-round on both coasts.

Playa Grande in Tamarindo National Wildlife Refuge: Peak nesting for leatherbacks, the largest sea turtles, is from October to March,

though there are turtles year-round.

Ostional Wildlife Refuge: July to December are peak months for olive ridley turtles, though there are nesting turtles or hatchlings almost all year.

Santa Rosa Park: July to December brings arribadas of olive ridley turtles, especially on Nancite Beach. Leatherbacks and Pacific greens also nest at Nancite and Playa Naranjo.

Barra de Matina Beach, north of Limón: Leatherbacks come ashore from February to July, with peaks in April and May; green turtle nesting peaks from July to September; hawksbills also come ashore.

Green turtles are prized for their meat, especially in the Caribbean area. Hawksbills are hunted for their shells (from which tortoise-shell jewelry is made) along both coasts. While eating turtle meat is not a tradition on the Pacific, the eggs are prized as aphrodisiacs. Turtle protection and conservation programs in Costa Rica range from patrolling beaches and public education to egg hatcheries, controlled harvesting of eggs at Ostional, and setting of legal catches of turtles to be sold for meat near Limón.

Practice proper turtle-watching etiquette.

Stay still and low when a turtle is coming onto the beach—movement may scare it back into the water. Light disturbs the turtles, so restrict the use of flashlights. Do not use a flash camera. Wait until turtles are laying their eggs before drawing near. Be quiet!

turbing the creative process. We could hear the whishing of sand off to the left, another hole begun.

Within twenty-five minutes, the digging and laying were done, and the turtle began methodically pushing sand back in, using both front and back flippers. Then she pounded her body against the surface to pack it down and moved around in a circle, scattering sand, leaves, and beach debris over the spot to obliterate any evidence of her buried treasure. Within an hour of emerging from the sea, she was back in it.

Nesting turtles can be found on this beach practically any night of the year, though massive arrivals, called *arribadas*, peak from July to December, when as many as 120,000 ridleys nest over four- to eight-day periods. Arribadas are usually about two weeks apart, but they can stretch to a month apart.

Harvesting of turtle eggs for food (there is a popular but apparently false idea that they are aphrodisiacs) along with the killing of adults for their meat or the leather trade threaten these and other species of sea turtles around the world. The Ostional refuge, on the west coast of the Nicoya Peninsula, was set up to protect the nesting sites of the ridleys, leatherbacks, and occasional green turtles that also come ashore. In an innovative program, local residents, who once plundered the nests and now live mainly off subsistence agriculture, harvest some of the eggs from the first arrivals on the beach and then patrol it to prevent illegal egg taking. About 30 percent of the eggs deposited during an arribada are lost anyway when turtles dig up eggs laid earlier, so everybody is happy with the arrangement. Visitors who come for the nesting should join a guide from the turtle cooperative at the rancho at the upper edge of the beach. An administrative station for the refuge is scheduled to be built in 1994.

Ridley eggs hatch in about fifty days, with many hatchlings picked off on their way to the water by vultures, crabs, or frigate birds, while others become food for predators in the water, including other turtles. Survival rates are low, making the protection of eggs all the more important. Ostional and Nancite in Santa Rosa Park are the major nesting sites for olive ridleys in Costa Rica.

The 395-acre (160-ha) refuge also has a few patches of forest that contain howler monkeys, kinkajous, coatis, and basilisks. The estuary of the Ostional River offers good bird-watching—190 species have been identified.

You may notice a sign for a University of Costa Rica laboratory at Ostional. Under an agreement between the university and the refuge, scientists are conducting turtle research as well as carrying out education programs on the rational use of eggs.

Rainfall averages almost 67 inches (1,700 mm) a year; the temperature averages 82°F (28°C). Unpaved roads are slow going and rough. Your best bet is to rent a car or take a tour to Ostional. If you plan to come from Sámara or Nosara, inquire about the road—there are rivers to cross. (See chapter 6 for lodging.)

Tamarindo National Wildlife Refuge (Northwest)

Fortunately the mangroves and big leatherback turtles (*baulas*) that this area was set up to protect do not give a diddly what the place is called. It began life as a government protected area under the name of Tamarindo Wildlife Refuge, but in 1991 the area was enlarged and decreed to be Las Baulas de Guanacaste National Marine Park to give it a higher status of protection under the law. The legislative assembly has not approved the decree, and the issue is complicated by the fact that the expanded area includes expensive private lands that it will be difficult for the government to purchase. National parks are theoretically government owned, while wildlife refuges can be mixed ownership. So the area is currently back to being a wildlife refuge administered by the wildlife department. You will hear it referred to as both Las Baulas and Tamarindo.

Whatever its eventual name, it encompasses beaches that attract one of the largest populations of leatherback turtles in the world. The peak nesting months in the refuge are October through January, when as many as 200 females may come ashore per night. Smaller but noticeable numbers continue to arrive until March, but there are actually turtles there year-round. Each nest contains from seventy to a hundred eggs, and the babies hatch in about seventy days. Warmer temperatures in the nest produce females; cooler temperatures, males.

The baula is the largest sea turtle living today. The female can be 6 feet (1.8 m) long and weigh more than 1,300 pounds (590 kg). The species has a tough skin or hide instead of a true shell—hence the name.

The major dangers to survival for these sea creatures are not only loss of habitat, egg poaching, and accidentally being caught by fishermen but also plastic pollution. Plastic resembles jellyfish in the water and may be ingested by the turtles, who love the jellyfish that most sea animals steer clear of: the Portuguese man-of-war.

Olive ridley turtles also sometimes come ashore on Tamarindo's beaches to lay their eggs, though not in the massive arribadas experienced at Nancite in Santa Rosa park or at Ostional Wildlife Refuge.

To see the protected mangrove, you can take a boat. All five species that live in Costa Rica thrive here: black, white, buttonwood, tea, and the red, with its stilt or prop roots. You may be surprised to see what can decorate the woody plants: orchids, bromeliads, termite nests.

Tamarindo is a good bird-watching area. Lowlands attract the wood stork, white ibis, jacana, roseate spoonbill, and American egret—at least 174 species of birds have been identified. There are estuaries where the American crocodile can be found, and there is a fragment of tropical dry forest. A large pochote tree at Langosta is 9 feet (2.8 m) in diameter. Crabs abound: ghost crabs, hermit crabs, and mouthless crabs, those garish creatures with black bodies, orange legs, and purple pincers.

Access to the wildlife refuge is easiest at Tamarindo and Playa Grande. Lodging exists at each (see chapter 6), and several hotels and tourist businesses in the region operate tours. Boats can be rented for trips in the estuaries. There is daily bus and air service between San José and Tamarindo. (See Practical Extras.) The bus trip takes five and a half or six hours, depending on the route.

8
Privately Owned Nature Reserves

Privately owned nature reserves catering to natural history tourists are springing up around the country. These are more than just hotels. They encompass tracts of protected ecosystems that range from large areas of virgin forest to river habitats to ribbons of primary and secondary forests surrounded by pastures. These reserves offer not only a chance to spend the night where monkeys live and toucans fly but also to learn about the ecosystems on guided walks or horseback rides. Some have bilingual biologist guides, others use local people with varying commands of English who are naturalists by life experience. Accommodations range from bunk beds and "bring your own gear" to comfortable lodges with hot water and fine dining. Some provide transportation; others help arrange it from San José or other locations.

Some people thrive on adventure: tromping along muddy trails through a jungle miles from nowhere is bliss. Others prefer to view plant and animal life from a shady veranda or to stroll along a quiet beach. The privately owned reserves run the gamut. There is something for everyone. This chapter tells you which offers what, with details on how to get there, costs, and some idea of what you may see. Reserves are listed in alphabetical order in each region. Only those visited personally are described. Others are mentioned in chapter 6.

If you call or fax from outside Costa Rica to make reservations, first dial the international area code (011) and then the country code (506); for example, 011-506-000-0000. Places that accept credit cards are noted; most do not. I no longer include mailing addresses because service can be very slow. I recommend using phone or fax.

Central Valley

Rancho Naturalista

Fields of cane and coffee spread out below the mountain retreat of Rancho Naturalista, while Irazú and Turrialba volcanoes dominate the skyline to the northwest across a vast valley. Tropical forest is steps away from the lodge. Tranquillity is the key word.

Located 1.7 miles (2.8 km) southeast of Turrialba up a dirt road from the village of Tuis, the ranch belonging to the Erb family caters strictly to nature travelers. "Anybody else would probably be bored," said John Erb. Boredom does not seem likely, however.

Daughter Lisa is an enthusiastic, knowledgeable guide on the trails and farm roads that visitors may take to look for the birds, butterflies, and moths that abound. More than 345 species of birds have been seen within two miles of the lodge. Lisa likes to help visitors start a bird list and is extremely patient with beginning bird-watchers who find it difficult to spot birds in the dense forest foliage, much less zero in on them with binoculars. With her encouragement, neophytes experience the thrill of seeing something first—maybe even a rare bird. Noticing a blue-crowned motmot, she points out the telltale tick-tock motion that motmots make with their racket-tipped tails. You are likely to see toucans, manakins, trogons, tanagers, and a world of hummingbirds. Perhaps you will also spot a scarlet-thighed dacnis or a green honeycreeper.

If you have yet to see the gorgeous morpho butterfly, this could be your chance. Several of the six Central American species of this butterfly live near the lodge. The blue flash of one of these against the green of the forest is a treasure that glows forever in the mind's eye.

The Erbs don't claim to have all 12,000 species of moths found in Costa Rica, but they believe they have enough to keep you occupied. Just ask, and they will put up a sheet and plug in a lamp outside at night to attract them. The variety is awesome. Guided night walks are available.

A neighbor down the road has a trapiche, the old-style sugarcane press. Horses are available at no extra charge, and you may want to explore along roads in the 125-acre (50-ha) farm or outside the farm on neighboring roads or along the Tuis River.

If you stay a week, the Erbs offer you a complimentary all-day field trip to an area with a different elevation, so you may see different flora and fauna. Popular choices are the Tapantí National Park, Irazú Volcano, or the Siquirres area to see poison dart frogs. Tours can be arranged to volcanoes, beaches, or national parks at an additional cost, as well as white-water rafting on the nearby Reventazón River.

The two-story main house has six large, comfortable bedrooms, one a suite. Three of the bedrooms have private baths; the others, a shared bath. There is great birding from the upstairs balcony and the long porch off the downstairs living room. A one-bedroom and a two-bedroom cottage with private baths are nearby. All the baths have central hot water, some with tubs.

Meals are family-style, and the food is plentiful and delicious, ranging from filet mignon to Mexican food, with some Costa Rican cuisine as well. The Erbs are gracious hosts who have lived in Costa Rica for many years and are pleased to share their knowledge with you.

Because of Rancho Naturalista's personal service, a minimum stay of three days is required. The Erbs say most guests stay at least a week. Laundry service is part of the package, at no extra charge.

The lodge is at 2,953 feet (900 m) and is in the transition zone between premontane wet forest and premontane rain forest. Daytime temperatures are usually in the 70s (21°-26°C), nights in the 60s (15°-20°C). Afternoon rain is common, especially from May through November. Rubber boots are recommended. Four main trails on the ranch are well-maintained and not difficult. You will find shelters and benches along the way where you can sit and wait for nature to reveal its treasures. A cable car crosses above a waterfall on one trail.

A stay of a week or more can be split, for the same rates, between Rancho Naturalista and the Erbs' other location, Tarcol Lodge near the Pacific, not far from the Carara Biological Reserve. Cathy Erb oversees that operation. (See chapter 6.)

Transportation: Transportation to and from San José is provided as part of the package, but you can arrange for pickup at the airport or elsewhere instead. There is a moderate transportation charge on optional tours.

Rates: From November through April, costs are $99 a day per person or $603 a week double occupancy; from May to October, they are $88 per day, $499 for a week. Rates include meals, lodging, guided walks, horseback riding, laundry, and transportation to and from San José.

Reservations: Telephone or fax 267-7138.

North Central

Arenal Observatory Lodge

At 4:30 in the morning, a thunderous explosion brought us from our bunks to the door in one swift leap. Outside, the cone of Arenal Volcano, about 1.2 miles (2 km) away, was sharp against the dark blue of the night sky. Stars were brilliant. From the crater, red rocks and thin streams of lava began to make their way down the slopes.

Arenal Observatory Lodge has a front-row seat for viewing eruptions of one of the most active volcanoes in the world. Built in 1987 as a laboratory and base for scientists carrying out long-term geological and biological research, the facility is now also open to non-scientific visitors.

The small group I was in had already jumped up twice during dinner to pay homage to the spectacle in a steady rain. Later, two of us sat patiently on the elevated, covered observatory platform trying to elicit a command performance, but Arenal seemed uninterested in our schedules. The real show began after everyone was

Liana sculpture (Photo by Ree Strange Sheck)

in bed. In all, I jumped up for four explosions—and saluted two rumbles from underneath the covers.

The rooms are simply furnished but comfortable. Twenty have private baths, and five have two shared baths.

Some rooms have large windows that let allow one to watch an eruption from the bed. I had one of these on my latest visit, but each explosion brought me to my feet—the power and beauty somehow demanded it.

In the dining room, guests sample fruits from the area and such typical meals as *olla de carne* (a meat and vegetable soup) or *arroz con pollo* (chicken and rice) from a set menu. Huge windows face the volcano, so diners will not miss an eruption.

After a four-hundred-year dormancy, Arenal devastated more than 4 square miles (10 sq km) in the last three days of July 1968. It has been continuously active since then. The flow comes from a horse-shoe-shaped crater—one of four—that is open to the northwest, west, and southwest. Fortunately, the observatory is to the south. Arenal is young as volcanoes go—about four thousand years young—and relatively small—5,358 feet (1,633 m) high. It is in the Tilarán Mountain Range.

Scientists from the Smithsonian Institution stay at the observatory while monitoring the volcano, and Earthwatch groups have used it as a base.

When you are not watching eruptions, you can turn your eyes to the tranquillity of Lake Arenal, just down the hill, site of Costa Rica's largest hydroelectric project. Visitors may want to arrange optional tours for fishing in its waters or a three-hour boat motorboat tour, including guide, for $75.

Visitors to the observatory have access to almost 300 acres (120 ha) of primary forest reserve on the property, a 185-acre (75-ha) reforestation project of pine and eucalyptus, and almost 250 acres (100 ha) in a macadamia nut plantation. Trails through the lush forest lead to Cerro Chato, an extinct crater near Arenal and its green-colored lagoon, or to a lovely waterfall. Trails as well as roads through the farm offer excellent bird-watching as well as a chance to see the spectacular morpho butterflies. Walking is easy around the farm and along the roads, but the trail to the crater is for the physically fit. It is steep. But incredibly beautiful forest lures one on step after step, even when it is bathed in cloud or washed by rain.

The farm also offers a firsthand look at agricultural operations. You can watch macadamia nuts being harvested and husked, or you can rent horses to explore the area, at $5 per hour.

Elevation at the observatory is 2,428 feet (740 m), and annual rainfall is 197 inches (5,000 mm). The drier months are from December through May, but rain can occur anytime, so bring your gear.

A one-day trip from San José operates Tuesday, Thursday, and Saturday, leaving at midday so you will also see the volcano at night. If time and weather permit, the tour includes a dip in a nearby hot springs.

Transportation: If you are driving, you can go through either Varablanca or Zarcero to La Fortuna, or head north from San Ramón to La Tigra and La Fortuna. From the west, you can head around Lake Arenal from Tilarán. Four-wheel drive is recommended in the rainy season—there is a river to ford. Drivers who want to leave the last 6 miles (9 km) of gravel road and river crossing to someone else can take a jeep-taxi from Fortuna, as can bus travelers. Tours include transportation.

Rates: The eleven-hour Arenal Volcano night tour from San José is $70 per person, including dinner. A two-day, one-night tour, including transportation, specified meals, and guide, ranges from $165 to $195 per person, depending on whether you have a bilingual naturalist guide. A three-day, two-night tour includes a visit to Caño Negro for $310 to $395, Monteverde for $325 to $375, or La Pacífica for $345. Rooms for those not on a tour are $46 for a single and $56 for a double. Breakfast is about $6, lunch about $8.50, and dinner a bit less than $10. Ask about the American plan.

Reservations: Telephone 255-2112 or 695-5033, fax 255-3529. Sun Tours, which owns the lodge, is at Avenida 7, Calles 3/5 in San José.

Eco-Lodge, Lago Coter

You will learn about such things as flying sticks and why some tropical trees shed their bark (to keep epiphytes from getting a hold). You can see a huge mound built by busy little leaf-cutter ants and marvel at the free-form sculpture of a vine called monkey ladder.

On the thirteen marked trails that wind through the Eco-Lodge property, bilingual, well-trained naturalist guides can help guests appreciate that tropical forests are more than monkeys jumping from branch to branch, than coatis darting across a trail, than the turquoise flash of a scarlet-thighed dacnis as it flies against the rich greens of the trees and plants. It is these things, but it is also the tiny flower almost hidden among fallen leaves, an insect disguised as a dried leaf, an animal track in the mud, the elegant tree fern, thousands of species of plants and animals intertwined in a web of life.

In the distance, Arenal Volcano rumbles. It seems to rise out of Lake Arenal from some vantage points on the property Though it is not visible from the lodge, it is from a covered observatory and bungalows.

Eco-Lodge is a comfortable place from which to wander forest trails or go horseback riding, bicycling, fishing, windsurfing, canoeing, or sailing either on Lake Arenal or Coter Lake. Those who want to can plant a native tree in an ongoing reforestation project. The lodge can be the base for trips to the volcano, to caverns at Venado 90 minutes away, to Ocotal beach, to Palo Verde or

Caño Negro, or for rafting on the Corobicí. Rubber boots, flashlights, and rain ponchos are provided.

Eco-Lodge has a spacious living/recreation area with a big fireplace, conversation areas, television with a supply of videos, billiard table, bar, and restaurant. Ample meals are served buffet style. The twenty-five rooms are in two wings off this area, with a maximum capacity of fifty people (No one under twelve is allowed.) Each wing has a bath for women and another for men, among the nicest shared baths I have seen: sparkling clean, light, and with a degree of privacy.

Interesting photographs of an earlier Costa Rica adorn the hallways. Probably one of the most intriguing photographs is of a flying saucer near Arenal Volcano. The friendly staff can show you books commenting on the authenticity of the photo.

Twelve nicely furnished rooms have been added in six bungalows within a five-minute walk from the lodge. The rooms are larger than in the lodge, with high ceilings and a glass wall that faces the porch and the volcano, Arenal and Coter lakes, and the nighttime lights of Nuevo Arenal. Each room has a table and chairs both inside and on the porch. Baths are private with central hot water.

Guests are invited to record the animals see and where. More than 350 birds have been sighted. Leafing through the book, one finds monkeys, brocket deer, keel-billed toucans, the bare-necked umbrella bird, squirrel cuckoo, and coatis, among others.

The dry season is not as pronounced here as in some other places in the country: rainfall amounts to about 152 inches a year (3,857 mm). The elevation varies, but the lodge is at about 2,329 feet (710 m). The forested slopes have characteristics of both rain forest and cloud forest.

Transportation: Eco-Lodge is 17 miles (28 km) from Tilarán above the northwest section of Lake Arenal near the kilometer 46 marker. Buses between Tilarán and Ciudad Quesada (San Carlos) pass by on the highway less than two miles (3 km) below. Transportation can be arranged from San José or Tilarán for a minimum of four people.

Rates: A single in the bungalows is $56, a double $75, with private bath; rooms in the lodge, with shared bath, are $46 for a sin-

gle and $55 for a double. Breakfast is $6, and lunch and dinner are
$12 each. Here is a sample of prices for activities: half-day moun-
tain biking, horseback riding, hiking (with guide), or canoeing,
$20; sailing, $50; full-day trip to Ocotal or Palo Verde, $69.
Packages include lodging, meals, and some of the activities. For
example, the two-night, three-day tour ($325 each double occu-
pancy in the lodge or $345 in the bungalows) includes hiking,
horseback riding, biking, one water sport, and an Arenal Volcano
and hot springs tour. Credit cards are accepted.

Reservations: Telephone 221-4209, fax 221-0794.

La Laguna del Lagarto Lodge

Spider monkeys moved through tall treetops, sometimes with
spectacular leaps. I would swear I saw one slide down a long liana.
Sitting on a bench across a small pond from them, I watched as
they hung from their tails to feed on fruits in the tall forest. Flock
after flock of noisy parrots and parakeets flew in, stayed for a bit,
and moved on. Jesus Christ lizards skittered across the water. On
the short walk to the pond from the lodge, I had stopped to watch
white-fronted parrots, a Montezuma oropendola, and squirrels eating pejibayes. This was all before breakfast.

La Laguna del Lagarto, 93 miles (150 km) north of San José, is
a trip. It is a watery world—lagoons, rivers, swamps—but also a
place of striking forest. Owner Vinzenz Schmack has almost 250
acres (100 ha), and a neighboring forest of 1,000 acres (400 ha)
extends the habitat for such species as white-faced, howler, and
spider monkeys, tepezcuintle, the great currasow, aracaris, chestnut-mandibled and keel-billed toucans, and great green macaws.
With luck, Vinzenz says, one can see the scarlet macaw.

Ten miles (6 km) of trails open the forest for exploration. The
tiny red frogs with blue legs, known as poison dart frogs, can be
easily seen on the forest floor. The small green frogs with black
spots are more elusive—I saw only one. A highlight of the hike
was finding the track made by a tapir.

A different habitat can be explored by canoe. Moving silently
through a swamp lagoon, with only the sound of the oar dipping
into the water, brings one close to the spirit of the place. The

green-backed heron made several appearances, kingfishers flashed by, and a lineated woodpecker perched on a lifeless trunk standing in the water. Vinzenz pointed to another trunk where small sleeping bats made a dark line down the tree. Orchids and bromeliads abound.

A nighttime walk with a good flashlight can reveal the bright eyes of caimans along the edge of the lagoons. Caimans, or *lagartos*, are also visible during the day, and gave the place its name.

Guests at the lodge can go horseback riding along the edge of the forest ($10 for two hours) or take a boat down the San Carlos River to the San Juan ($18 for four hours). I longed for more time just to sit on the veranda and bird-watch. Local guides are available, but a trained naturalist guide can be arranged with prior notice. Languages spoken also include English, French, and German.

Eighteen rooms are distributed in several buildings, newer ones with private baths but no hot water. In the original building where the open-air dining room is, every two rooms share a bath. Furnishings are simple. Each room has ceiling fans, and the newer ones have movable louvered shutters. Windows are screened, with reason. Bring your repellent.

Food is a mix of Costa Rican and European. Pineapple, papaya, oranges, yuca, tiquisque, and pejibaje are grown near the lodge. The pejibaje also supply heart of palm—you can watch it being cut fresh for your meal. Black pepper is another crop.

The lodge is about 330 feet (100 m) above sea level, and temperatures range from 68°F (20°C) to 95°F (35°C). February to mid-May are the driest months, but for rainy times, boots and ponchos are available.

Transportation: La Laguna del Lagarto Lodge is 23 miles (37 km) of gravel road north of Pital, 4 miles (7 km) from Boca Tapada. The lodge provides round-trip transport from San José for $35. There are buses from San José and Ciudad Quesada to Pital, and a bus twice a day from Pital to Boca Tapada, with lodge pick up from there. A taxi from Pital is about $21.

Rates: A single is $63, a double $60 each, including meals. Credit cards are not accepted. Unguided trail walks and canoe rides are included in the price. Reservations are recommended.

Reservations: Telephone 231-4299, telephone/fax 289-5295.

La Selva Biological Station

La Selva Biological Station near Puerto Viejo de Sarapiquí offers a marvelous opportunity to see a variety of habitats: Besides the virgin tropical wet forest, there are swamps, creeks, rivers, pastures, agricultural lands, and secondary forests in various stages of growth. Dr. Leslie R. Holdridge, a tropical biologist, began La Selva as an experimental farm in the fifties and sold his plantation of peach palm (*pejibaye*), cacao, and laurel along with virgin forest to the Organization for Tropical Studies (OTS) in 1960. The primary use of La Selva is for biological research and education. Many of the leading tropical biologists in the hemisphere have studied or worked there.

Visitors are guaranteed to taste the area's diversity even if they never get farther than the main dining hall. The panorama from the porch may include flocks of parrots flying overhead or the red flash of a scarlet-rumped tanager. As you sway across the long suspension bridge over the Puerto Viejo River, look down. Machacas leap up to grab leaves floating down to the water's surface. You could be lucky enough to see a caiman or a river otter. La Selva is home to more than 100 species of mammals, including the howler, spider, and white-faced monkey, peccary, agouti, coati, sloth, jaguar, and tapir. There are more than 2,000 species of plants in this tropical rain forest, 410 species of birds, and thousands of species of insects.

The *bala*, or giant tropical ant, is one species it pays to look out for. Researchers tell tales of its powerful sting. It is the largest ant in Costa Rica—up to an inch (33 mm) long—and really looks big when you see it on a leaf next to you.

Brightly colored poison dart frogs may jump in the leaf cover at the side of trail. Toxins secreted from their skin glands were used by Colombian Indians to poison blowgun darts—hence the name. Because of their toxic skin, these frogs have no need for drab coloration; in fact, their colors warn predators. As the life history of these tiny creatures is being discovered, we learn that they lay eggs on the ground, with adults transporting the tadpoles on their backs to water. Studies of one genus show that the female feeds the tadpoles unfertilized eggs.

Trails meander through the 3,707-acre (1,500-ha) reserve. Don't miss the arboretum, where a keel-billed toucan perched patiently while a group of us drew near, admired his splendor, and photographed him. We spotted a purple-throated fruitcrow, collared aracari, crested owl, and yellow-billed cacique within a few yards. Armed with a trail map and a delightful printed guide (written by Beth Farnsworth and Héctor González) to the natural history trail, one can set out for an experience in a tropical forest in relative safety. Snakes do live in the tropics, however, and can appear as you make your foray into their world. As the trail guide suggests, watch where you walk, stay on the trail, and give any snake you see plenty of breathing room. The trail takes about an hour.

La Selva is open for day visits from 6:30 a.m. to 5:00 p.m., but reservations are necessary because the number of visitors per day is limited. Local naturalist guides have been trained in an intensive natural history course at the biological station. The charge is $7 for a half day, $14 for a whole day. Bilingual guides cost $21 for a group of up to 10 people, but all of the trained guides receive enough English instruction to enable them to communicate the essentials. These guides have formed a cooperative whose activities include environmental education in the communities, ongoing education for members, and conservation and sustainable management of natural resources in the area. The project is an example of an ecotourism-related activity around a forest reserve that involves the community and presents an alternative to deforestation and unemployment.

Overnight facilities are open to visitors as space permits. The new buildings have four beds per room, with a shared bath, with hot water, between two rooms. Each bed has its own reading lamp, and there is a ceiling fan. Since the rooms are primarily for researchers who may stay awhile, there is ample storage and closet space. There also are two-bedroom houses complete with kitchen, which sleep up to six each.

In the modern dining room, set up for cafeteria service, you may find yourself rubbing elbows with leading tropical scientists. Mealtime conversations are fascinating, but don't expect these researchers to lead you on a tour; their time in the field is precious.

A small gift shop in the dining hall has a great selection of T-shirts, and there also is a visitor center with exhibits.

More than 4 inches (100 mm) of rain falls even in the drier months, from February to April, and the yearly total is almost 158 inches (4,000 mm). The average temperature is 75°F (24°C). Elevation ranges from 115 feet (35 m) to 656 feet (200 m). The reserve is adjacent to Braulio Carrillo National Park.

Transportation: La Selva has van transportation from San José three times a week, but space is not always available. You can take the public bus from San José through Braulio Carrillo and Las Horquetas to Puerto Viejo (tell the driver you want to get off at La Selva) or through Varablanca and Chilamate to Puerto Viejo, and then a taxi to La Selva.

Rates: For a bed and three meals per day, the charge for natural history visitors is $88 per day. A day visit costs $18.

Reservations: Individuals who want to visit for the day have two choices: If you contact the OTS office in San José (telephone 240-6696, fax 240-6783, open Monday through Friday) lunch is provided and you may go on your own with the trail guide and maps instead of walking with a naturalist guide. If you reserve through La Selva (telephone 710-6580, fax 710-6481, open daily, forty-eight hours advance notice), a naturalist guide will accompany you on the trails; lunch is not provided. For overnight stays, contact the office in San José.

Magil Forest Lodge

Tenorio Volcano looms behind. In front is an incredible panoramic view stretching from Arenal Volcano to the Caño Negro National Wildlife Refuge. Sometimes it is possible to see Lake Nicaragua from this mirador on the hills above the lodge at Magil.

In the 700 acres (283 ha) of rain forest in this private nature reserve live monkeys, ocelots, aracaris, raccoons, keel-billed toucans, three-toed sloths, tayras, and tapirs. There are orchids, heliconias, ferns, mushrooms, and tall, tall trees.

Once it was home to Maleku Indians, and the traces of their life here include strange rock formations, burial tombs, jade pieces, arrowheads, metates, and pottery fragments. Today it belongs to Dr. Manuel Emilio Montero, who has had it for more than 25 years and who developed the Magil Forest Lodge. The property also includes about 300 acres (120 hectares) of ranchland for horses and cattle.

The rustic lodge contains eleven rooms with private baths but no hot water. Each room has single or bunk beds, a desk, a large mirror, and a porch off the back where a small creek rushes by. The sound of the water almost drowns out the hum of the hydro-electric generator. The porch is a good place for bird-watching in the early morning—there are lots of red-rumped tanagers.

Rooms open off the dining room, which has a long table fit for kings made from a single log. There is a set menu, with cooking on a wood stove. You can look forward to fresh orange juice (trees on the property), cheese empañadas (the lodge makes its own cheese), gallo pinto, and other typical dishes. Food is tasty and plentiful.

Across a covered patio is a pleasant bar with a small television. A short walk away is a rancho with chairs and hammocks. There is even a telescope available for star gazing.

Guests have many activities to choose from. The $20 half-day tour to the 100-Waterfalls Trail is by horseback and foot, taking in the mirador and passing by an enormous, solitary ceiba believed to be 1,000 years old. It stands as sentinel over the pasture and surrounding forest. White-faced monkeys moved through the trees while I climbed along the river trail, and a blue morpho butterfly made my day.

A $35 full-day trip, also by horseback and foot, goes to the place where the waters turn blue in the Tenorio Forest Reserve. Hot springs are an added treat. With a minimum of six people, the lodge offers a full-day trip, at $35 each, to the Venado Caves, hot springs, and Arenal Volcano. With a minimum of four people, you can take a car and boat trip, for $35 each, to a farm where caimans are raised and see the gaspar fish and crocodiles ($35).

On your own, you can walk down to the bridge you crossed coming in and bathe in clear pools in the river, play in small waterfalls in the good company of birds and butterflies, and soak up the healing green of the lush forest around you.

Magil Forest Lodge is 117 miles (189 km) from San José. It can be reached either from Ciudad Quesada, La Fortuna, Tilarán, or Upala heading for San Rafael de Guatuso. From San Rafael it is dirt road, with four-wheel drive recommended. Turn left after crossing the suspension bridge and go 12 miles (19 km) to Río Celeste. From there, Magil is less than 2 miles (3 km).

Transportation: Magil offers transportation from San José for groups of four to eight, at $100 per person round-trip.

Rates: A single is $73, a double $116, meals included. A two-day, one-night trip from San José is $190, including passing by Poás Volcano, Angel Waterfall, and La Marina zoo on the way in and Arenal Volcano and Venado Caves on the return The tours leave San José every Wednesday and Saturday. Credit cards are accepted.

Reservations: Telephone 221-2825, 233-5991; fax 233-3713.

Rara Avis Rainforest Lodge and Reserve

Visiting the beautiful Waterfall Lodge for the first time, a local tour operator remarked to Amos Bien, founder of Rara Avis, "You know, Amos, most people would have put the road in first." But Amos Bien is not most people, and Rara Avis is not your ordinary country inn.

Actually there is a road of sorts that allows your adventure to start at Las Horquetas. The 9 miles (15 km) into Rara Avis from there can be a horseback ride plus a 2-mile (3-km) walk, taking about five hours, or four hours in a tractor-pulled cart, fording two large rivers and lurching along the miles of slippery clay, mud, and corduroy road. There is a chance to see the great green macaw as you bump along, to hear about a nearby achiote plantation (the plants are grown in Costa Rica as both ornamentals and as a source of red dye), to observe the pasture lands clear-cut from tropical rain forest, and to see reforestation projects and secondary forest. Amos spins tales about a horse who died along the way and a budding student of the tropical world who later lugged the bones for miles in the belief that they represented a giant tapir.

Amos himself first came to Costa Rica in 1977 as a biology student. He returned to found Rara Avis, not only for nature/adventure tourism but also as a biological research center and a conservation proving ground to show his neighbors they can make more money by maintaining the forest than by clearing it for ranches or farms.

The road leads to Albergue El Plástico, a former prison colony barracks rehabilitated into a rustic lodge with seven rooms containing bunk beds for thirty people and shared baths with hot-water showers. Guests sit at dining tables on a hard-packed dirt floor where the prisoners sent in to cut the forests once ate. Lighting is by kerosene lantern. There is good bird-watching from the upstairs porch/library, and a rushing stream down the open slope invites a dip on sunny days. At the edge of the clearing, forest beckons on all sides.

Two miles (3 km) farther into that forest is the impressive, two-story Waterfall Lodge, built of beautiful tropical hardwoods. Each of the eight spacious rooms is a corner unit with chairs and a hammock on a wraparound balcony and a private bath complete with both shower and tub. A longtime birder saw five birds he had never seen before from his balcony one afternoon. A breathtaking 180-foot double waterfall is a two-minute walk away. The dining room is in a separate structure, where a spectacular variety of hummingbirds feeds on flowers at the porch rail.

Two new cabins near the main dining room, with private baths with hot water, have balconies facing the river canyon, also an excellent site for bird-watching. Food, served family-style, is tasty and includes typical black beans and rice as well as more exotic fare such as fried chicken or tuna croquettes. Miles of trails go through the virgin rain forest, with emphasis on the rain. There is virtually no dry season at Rara Avis; rubber boots are essential. A fellow visitor, after an hour on the wet slippery trail between El Plástico and the Waterfall Lodge, commented, "This must be the only trail in the world with an undertow." In a four-day period, we explored Rara Avis in 4.5 inches (114 mm) of rain. The annual rainfall is from 200 to 300 inches (5,080 to 7,614 mm).

A working biologist, bilingual in English and Spanish, guides visitors on the trails, spotting such exotic birds as the slaty-tailed trogon and the keel-billed and chestnut mandibled toucans (more than 330 bird species have been identified), and the home of a tent-making bat, who cuts the leaf of a wild plantain on either side of the midrib and bends it to form a tent to sleep under in the daytime. Howler, white-faced capuchin, and spider monkeys are very

A trail at Arenal Observatory leads to magical waterfall (Photo by Ree Strange Sheck)

common, as are pacas, coatis, vested anteaters, and brocket deer. Tapirs, jaguars, collared peccaries, agoutis, and three-toed sloths live here, but you probably will not see them.

On a walk with Amos in the forest, you hear about the possibilities for sustainable production of forest plants that he hopes will convince his neighbors to harvest rather than destroy the forest, proving there is more profit in managing it than they could ever make by clearing the land for crops or cattle. An understory palm once thought to be extinct but found here could provide seeds for export as an ornamental plant; the roots of a species of philodendron can be harvested for wicker products; selective cutting of wood instead of clear-cutting can provide income while preserving rain forest habitat and biological diversity.

The two miles of corduroy road between the two lodges are excellent for bird-watching on your own or for a relatively safe chance to have some solitary time in a tropical rain forest. People from two to eighty-six years of age have found their way to this remote spot, but access and trails can be rough for those who are not in good physical condition. There are few mosquitoes. The elevation is about 2,000 feet (600 to 700 m).

Transportation: On a paved road from San José to Las Horquetas, it is 48 miles (77 km) by way of Braulio Carrillo National Park, taking about an hour, or some 120 miles (193 km) via Poás Volcano, taking about three hours. The Rara Avis office can advise you on bus schedules or the cost of hiring a taxi from San José. At Río Frío—$15 and about twenty-five minutes by taxi from Las Horquetas—there is an airstrip for charter planes. All visitors to Rara Avis leave from Las Horquetas, with the tractor-driven cart starting the trip at 9:00 a.m.

Rates: El Plástico Lodge is $45 per person per night. At Waterfall Lodge, a single is $85 per night, a double $75 per person, triple $65 per person. Prices include meals, a naturalist guide, and round-trip transportation from Las Horquetas to Rara Avis by cart. Youth hostel members should make El Plástico reservations at La Toruma in San José.

Reservations: Telephone/fax 253-0844.

Selva Verde Lodge

Dusk along the Sarapiquí behind the lodge at Selva Verde. The only sound is the rushing water; green forest that gave Selva Verde its name guards the river. Brilliant blue morpho butterflies flutter along the forest's edge above the water. Dusk becomes darkness, the magic moment is gone, and yet it lives forever.

Images of time spent at Selva Verde Lodge near Chilamate, less than three hours north of San José, crowd in. The delightful day on a river trip down the Sarapiquí was arranged at the lodge. We saw river otter, crocodile, white-crowned parrot, kingfishers, keel-billed toucans, parakeets, blue herons, aracaris, a three-toed sloth, anhingas, egrets, flycatchers, a bananaquit, oropendolas, turtles, a scarlet-rumped tanager, trees full of vultures, and iguanas draped on limbs high above the water. We observed children playing along the river, women washing, men riding on horseback along a high bank. We passed ranches, farms, forests, and lush river vegetation.

Selva Verde has a reserve of its own across the Sarapiquí River, 529 acres (214 ha) with trails that reveal the wonder of a tropical lowland forest. You can go with Selva Verde's own bilingual guide or follow a trail map. Eight well-marked trails offer walks ranging from easy to somewhat steep. Benches along the way provide a place to rest or a place to wait and see what the forest will reveal. It could be a coati, sloth, raccoon, kinkajou, brocket deer, anteater, or maybe a tiny lizard or frog. There are more than 2,000 species of plants, 700 species of butterflies, and 400 species of birds. The most commonly seen birds are tanagers, honeycreepers, oropendolas, trogons, and chachalacas. You can add what you see to a book in which previous guests have already recorded species such as agoutis, tayras, river otters, kinkajous, toucans, and monkeys. A natural history guide leads private tours, charging $15 per person for four hours. The Sarapiquí River boat trip is $20. At the tour desk, you can also arrange horseback riding, at $20 for up to four hours, canoeing, river rafting for $45, and a visit to a banana plantation for $25.

The River Lodge consists of forty rooms in a series of modules built on stilts and connected by walkways covered with thatch. One has the sensation of walking on a bridge through the forest. Construction is of beautiful tropical woods. Each double room has

Heliconia (Photo by Ree Strange Sheck)

a small desk, reading lights at each bed, convenient closet space, lots of windows with louvered shutters, and large towels in the private baths with hot water—even washcloths!

A large dining room that accommodates one hundred people also has an outdoor deck on the river side, great for sitting and soaking up the beauty of the natural world. There is a set menu, served cafeteria style. Near the bar is a delightful outdoor area with an old-fashioned wood-fired bread oven where guests can help prepare *bocas* for happy hour if they wish. Next to the highway is the older Creek Lodge with a few rooms and shared baths; is less expensive and subject to availability. Five bungalows in the butterfly sanctuary across the road are simply furnished, with four beds in each and private baths.

The butterfly sanctuary is the work of Peter Knudsen, a physicist, mathematician, and lifelong student of butterflies. He has created a flowering garden tucked among the trees on a forested hillside that both attracts butterflies and provides host plants for larvae. He is rearing thirty species there, including five species of morpho: four blue and one green-brown canopy species. Peter's collection of native plants makes it a botanical garden as well; one section focuses on medicinal plants and endangered local species. The garden is open from dawn to dusk, free to guests at the lodge, $5 for others, with guided walks on the 2.5 miles (4 km) of easy trails. Peter's rearing house will assure a reliable source of butterflies for the enclosed area, and some butterflies will be released to rebuild local populations.

Selva Verde has a commitment to community involvement. The Sarapiquí Conservation Learning Center has been built on Selva Verde property for use by guests and members of the community. It has a library, auditorium, and work rooms where local people study German or English, attend natural history classes, or work on handcrafts for the hotel gift shop. The manager of the shop, Betty Ann Knudsen, tries to use as many natural, renewable resources as she can in developing new products with the artisans. The shop also has a nice selection of nature books at reasonable prices, as well as tropical forest posters, basketry, belts, primitive carvings, jewelry, and lots more.

Transportation: You can take a public bus to Puerto Viejo through Braulio Carrillo and Las Horquetas (a taxi from Puerto Viejo to Selva Verde is less than $4) or a longer route toward Río Frío through Varablanca. Tell the driver to let you off at Selva Verde. The trip by taxi from San José is about $70.

Rates: In the River Lodge, singles are $83, doubles $72 each; in bungalows, doubles are $72 each, triples $60. Children under 12 sharing a room with their parents are free. Prices include meals.

Reservations: In the United States, call Holbrook Travel in Gainesville, Fla., at (800) 451-7111. In Costa Rica, call 766-6077 or fax 766-6011.

Villablanca Hotel and the Los Angeles Cloud Forest

As one approaches Villablanca, it appears to be a small village, and that is just what it was built to resemble, an 1800s colonial settlement centered on the *casa grande*, or big house, which would have belonged to the family that owned the land. The landowners in this case are former president of Costa Rica Rodrigo Carazo and his wife, Estrella, who bought the farm in 1989.

The individual *casitas* (little houses) where the workers would have lived serve as charming guest cottages. They have the look and feel of adobe, rough white plaster with blue trim. Some are suites with a separate sitting room. All have a corner fireplace with *bancos* extending out on each side, rocking chairs pulled up in front of the hearth, and a writing desk. Colorful comforters on the beds and bright rugs lend a cozy look. Nights can be cool here, so the comforters and fireplaces are not merely decorative. Each private bathroom has both a shower and a tub, with a large, well-lit mirror in a small dressing area.

The big house contains the dining room, bar, small library, and sitting areas. Upstairs are five rooms, handy for those who prefer to be in the same building as the dining room. There is also a dormitory-style building with shared baths for student groups. To finish out the village, plans call for a small church that will offer Sunday mass for guests and nearby residents as well as a curate's house that can be used as a conference room or for parties.

Meals are buffet style, with breakfast at 7:30 ($5 plus tax), lunch at 12:30 ($8), and dinner at 7:00 ($8). Complimentary coffee and tea are available from early to late.

The casitas have little gardens in front and a 2,000-acre (800-ha) forest out back. The Los Angeles Cloud Forest is wet, exuberant, and green. There is a trail of a little more than a mile (2 km) and a shorter trail very near Villablanca. Walkways are wooden planks covered with wire to prevent slipping. It is home to more than 230 species of birds, including the bare-necked umbrella bird, hummingbirds, the black guan, the great curassow, and chachalacas. There are three species of monkeys, sloths, raccoons, squirrels, tepezcuintles, ocelots, and snakes, though you probably will not see a snake. The tree ferns are magnificent.

From a mirador about a mile from the main house one can see Arenal Volcano, Lake Nicaragua, and the Plains of San Carlos on a clear day. Though there are clear days, go prepared for rain, and for the clouds. The driest months are March to May according to Geovanny Bello, a resident biologist guide who leads guided walks into the cloud forest, which is about 3,600 feet in elevation (1,100 m).

In addition to the nature reserve area, the farm has cultivated land with coffee, sugarcane, and vegetable crops, and pasture for dairy cows that provide milk and cheese for the dining room. Ask about availability of a guided agro-ecology tour for $21.

Horses, at $9 an hour, and mountain bikes can be rented for exploring the farm. There is a two-hour horse trail in the forest. Villablanca also offers a full-day trip to the Tabacón hot springs, La Fortuna, and Arenal for $120 for up to four people. A one-day tour to Zarcero and Sarchí is $90 per person. After dinner, free videos with ecological themes are shown in the library.

Transportation: Villablanca will bring you from San José for $30 or from San Ramón for $15. If you are driving, the turnoff is at the guard station just past the kilometer 8 marker from San Ramón.

Rates: Rooms in the main house are $57 for singles, $79 for doubles. In the casitas, singles are $74, doubles $96. There are special rates for student groups staying in the dormitories. Credit cards are accepted.

Reservations: Telephone 228-4603, fax 228-4004.

Northwest

Buena Vista Lodge

A rushing cold mountain stream, bubbling mud pots, steam escaping from open fissures in the earth and drifting up from pools of hot water to play hide-and-seek with the tall trees of the primary forest. Standing here one cannot help but think of the Earth in formation, of creation, of beauty, of the power of natural forces, of so much that we do not yet know or understand.

Here on the slopes of Rincón de la Vieja Volcano, next door to the national park that protects wonders such as these, Gerardo Ocampo and his wife, Amalia, and their four children carefully share and quietly conserve nature's bounty. Buena Vista Lodge is both a private nature reserve and a working farm. Visitors are invited to hike forest trails, bird-watch, help ranch hands working with the cattle, bathe in thermal waters or mountain streams, go to the site of an Indian cemetery, watch the milking or cheesemaking, and walk or go by horseback to waterfalls—with six large ones to choose from. All of this is on the 3,950-acre, (1,600-ha) farm, but there is also the option of a tour to Rincón de la Vieja National Park less than 2 miles (3 km) away.

An intriguing sign points the way to a spa about half an hour by horseback from the lodge. A spa? Indeed it is. Enjoy the sauna, a simple wooden house built over one of the *pailas*, or mud pots. The steam flows up through the floor. A short distance away is a concrete and stone "hot tub" fed by a mix of hot mineral waters and cold water from the mountain stream alongside, set among the verdance of tropical rain forest. Along the trail, notice the rich pink fruit of the *pitaya*, a cactus-looking plant.

Trails in the forest just behind the lodge are well maintained and easy to walk. Five trails wind through the almost 100 acres (40 ha) of primary forest. A troop of white-faced capuchin monkeys fussed at me as I explored at dusk. You might see a paca, peccary, deer, river otter, macaw (either the scarlet or the green), toucan, oropendola, or agouti. Perhaps you will hear a coyote concert or the sound of the howler monkey. One of the forest trails displays tree names. On the drive up to the lodge, just past a wooden bridge in magnificent forest, I spotted a spider monkey in trees near the road, golden red hair shining on its back, while a motmot posed for pictures on the other side of the road. I also saw quail and cuckoos.

The lodge consists of fifteen rooms, with those in the main house built around a lush tropical garden. Two have private baths. Doña Amalia presides over the dining room and kitchen. Cooking is on a wood stove, and the food is ample, varied, delicious, and visually pleasing. There is a set menu.

A second building contains a conference room/entertainment center, with television, games, small library, and insect collections. Rooms with bunks for larger groups are here. A thatched rancho with tables, chairs, and hammocks (plus many large frogs in the evenings) completes the complex, all set in landscaped grounds.

Buena Vista means "good view." There are quite a few: an almost touchable view of Rincón de la Vieja Volcano, a more distant look at Orosí Volcano, and the lights on a clear night of Bagaces and Liberia down below.

The rainy season from about May 15 to November 30 brings about 6.5 feet (2 meters) of rainfall. The elevation at the farm ranges from 1,300 to 3,940 feet (400 to 1,200 m); at the lodge it is 2,428 feet (740 m). Gerardo says the best time to visit the crater at Rincón is March to May and July or August. The temperatures average 82° to 86°F (28° to 30°C), but in the early morning in December, it has gotten down to 64° (18°).

Drinking water comes from a spring and energy comes from a hydroelectric plant. There is no hot water for showers. The rooms are of dark wood, cozy. Gerardo is thinking of adding a few more with extra privacy—especially for honeymooners, he says.

Transportation: Buena Vista is 19 miles (31 km) northeast of Liberia. From the sign at kilometer 247 on the Inter-American Highway, it is about 12 miles (19 km), paved to Cañas Dulces, mainly gravel afterward. Round-trip transportation from Liberia can be provided by Buena Vista for $40 round trip for up to four passengers. (Check Practical Extras for information about buses to Liberia.)

Rates: Rooms with two beds and shared bath are $20 per person; rooms with a double bed and private bath are $45. Bunk-bed rooms with shared bath are $15. Breakfast is $6, lunch and dinner $8 each. Credit cards are accepted. Two- to three-hour guided tours to the spa are $15 by horseback, $5 on foot. A half-day horseback trip to the waterfalls is $28; the ranch tour is $15. An all-day visit to the park is $38.

Reservations: Telephone or fax 695-5147.

Cabinas Karen

Karen and Olof Wessberg came to the Nicoya Peninsula in 1955 in search of a primitive life. On land 1 mile (1.6 km) from Montezuma, they built a palm-leaf cottage near the sea, their determination to live from the land without damaging it inspired by Fairfield Osbourne's *Our Plundered Planet*.

Soon, however, they became deeply disturbed by the widespread destruction of virgin forest. Karen said they could look across the water and see the spreading patches of brown on Cabo Blanco at the tip of the peninsula, 7 miles (11 km) away. Olof began an arduous campaign to raise money to save that bit of tropical moist forest. Today, Cabo Blanco Strict Nature Reserve stands in tribute to their efforts.

Though Olof was killed in 1975 on a visit looking into the possibility of conserving a part of the Osa Peninsula now known as Corcovado National Park, Karen continues their conservation work—investigating and reporting the illegal entrapment of tropical birds to sell in San José, opposing the country's electrical company when it proposed putting lines through original forest, protecting her own 170-acre (69-ha) reserve, and trying to raise money to expand Cabo Blanco.

A taste of the primitive life the Wessbergs sought is still possible on that reserve. Some visitors have called it a piece of paradise. There is no electricity; candles glow at night. Water is piped from a pure source high on the coastal mountain; the reserve stretches from shoreline to mountaintop. There is a shared open-air kitchen for the three cabins and a shared cold-water shower and outhouse. Bedding is provided. Views from the cabins are idyllic, with the

blue of the Pacific shimmering through the greens of lush vegetation. The one-room wooden cabins have big shutters that open on
three sides to let the jungle in. For at least one guest, that has
meant the casual passing through one night of a kinkajou, a small,
bright-eyed mammal related to the coati and raccoon. White-faced
and howler monkeys are common, and there is a chance of seeing
a paca or an agouti. Bird songs punctuate the stillness.

Trails lead to the highest point of the reserve, where there is a
simple shelter for any guest who wants to spend the night under
the stars, and go past a small waterfall. The reserve is open only to
those housed in the cabins. A panoply of colored rocks and shells
fills a section of beach stretching northeast.

Doña Karen's reserve is a thirty-minute walk from Montezuma
along the shore. Guests must carry in their own gear and food.

If you get to Montezuma, do not miss the chance to visit with
doña Karen. She also speaks her native Danish as well as Swedish
(her husband's language), Spanish, and English. A conservationist
through and through, she is adamant that we must offer alterna-
tives to cutting the forest. She believes, for example, that we need
more studies on the nutritional content of leaves that animals eat
with an eye to harvesting them for the human diet. She often eats
leaves the monkeys consume and says they make her feel fantastic.

Transportation: Puntarenas is the primary departure point. Cross
the Gulf of Nicoya on the car ferry (see the schedule in Practical
Extras) and drive to Cóbano and Montezuma. By public transportation, take the launch to Paquera and then a bus to Montezuma.
Paving proceeds bit by bit, but the unpaved sections are passable
without four-wheel drive.

Rates: $10 per person per night.

Reservations: There are no reservations; there is no phone. It is
first-come, first-served. Look for the Cabinas Karen sign as you
enter Montezuma. She also has two rooms at a house in town, with
shared bath.

La Pacífica

Pacífica means peaceful or tranquil, and indeed the traveler who
pulls into La Pacífica senses a serenity to the place. Actually it was

named for the woman who designed the Costa Rican flag early this century, but why quibble. The name fits.

The purpose of the ecological center also fits with the growing concern throughout the country that conservation and development proceed together. La Pacífica has been set up as a model for economic self-sufficiency and protection of natural resources.

Scientific researchers have been coming to "Finca La Pacífica" since the sixties. The rich diversity of habitats that continues to draw researchers—tropical dry forest, river habitat, swampland, pastures—also makes the center attractive to today's natural history tourists.

Thirty-three rooms are located in buildings scattered over spacious grounds. Newer units closer to the swimming pool—what a treat that pool is on a hot Guanacaste day—have modern, tastefully decorated rooms with large windows that open onto gardens dotted with ferns, flowers, and trees. Older bungalow units are tucked beneath tall trees. All have private baths and hot water. The restaurant is a favorite with local folks as well.

Guests can follow the roads and trails on their own or go with a bilingual naturalist guide. Watch for informational signs along the trails. About one-third of the almost 5,000 acres (2,000 ha) is covered with natural forest, windbreaks, and reforested areas, including tree species such as the increasingly rare *cocobolo* (rosewood), the *caoba* (mahogany), and the spiny pochote. Bird life is abundant, with 26 percent of the species found in the country seen here; 68 species are migratory. The lagoon and rivers on the property lure water birds. You may spot boat-billed herons, blue herons, trogons, manakins—La Pacífica has bird and tree lists for sale. Forest animals include armadillos, squirrels, tamandus (anteaters), deer, and monkeys. Studies on the howler monkey at Pacífica go back some twenty years.

The far-sighted Swiss agronomist who preserved the deciduous forest as part of his working ranch put the rest of the land in pasture, rice and sorghum fields, and vegetable crops. He used windbreaks that still stand to fight erosion and increase productivity; he pioneered many experimental practices in dairy farming, crop breeding, and livestock management. The current owners, also Swiss, continue to see La Pacífica as a model for the tropical Pacific lowlands. Visitors are welcome to tour the agricultural operations, including a modern dairy and an organic garden. In addition to beef and milk products, the ranch produces mangoes and cashews. Visitors can watch a reforestation project—using native species—as it develops. An hour by foot from the hotel complex, near the Tenorio River, is a restored farmhouse with artifacts from the past century. A library at the entrance to La Pacífica focuses on the dry tropics. Of the thirty-nine archaeological sites on the property, five have been excavated.

The beautiful Corobicí River, popular with rafters, forms part of the center's boundary. Staff members can arrange rafting trips as well as river trips on the Bebedero to Palo Verde. Horseback riding and bicycling are also available. Visit Laguna de los Piches on the farm, a lake where the black-bellied whistling duck nests in dry season.

If you happen to be at La Pacífica when a group is there, you may have a chance to hear typical Guanacaste marimba music in the large, outdoor rancho used for cookouts.

La Pacífica is in the transition zone between tropical dry and moist forest. The annual rainfall is about 66 inches (1,674 mm). the average high temperature is around 91°F (33°C), the average low 73°F (23°C).

Transportation: The center is about 3 miles (5 km) north of Cañas on the Inter-American Highway toward Liberia, 108 miles (173 km) from San José. You can take the bus for Liberia or buses going to La Cruz or Peñas Blancas. Ask the driver to let you off at La Pacífica, or get off in Cañas and take a taxi.

Rates: Singles are $46, doubles $77. Credit cards are accepted. Guided walks with the biologist are $10 for a half-day. Guided horseback tours with a local guide are $10 per hour.

Reservations: Telephone 669-0266, 669-0050; fax 669-0555.

Los Inocentes

There's something special about waking to the dawn's early light and the bass-toned barks of the howler monkey. When you open the big windows of your south-facing room at Los Inocentes, Orosí Volcano looms big enough to touch. Teak floors, polished wood, wide L-shaped verandas both upstairs and down—the hacienda is so inviting that nothing less than those intriguing barks from the forest down by the river spur one to get dressed and leave it for an early morning horseback ride.

Los Inocentes is a working ranch as well as a naturalist lodge for travelers looking to experience a bit of life and nature in Guanacaste. Perhaps that accounts for horses that are a pleasure to ride. Don't worry if you are not an expert horseman. Dennis Ortiz, your guide for the nature tour, will have you riding like a pro. We found the howlers and the white-faced monkeys. Dennis patiently tracked the shier spider monkeys three times so I could get a perfect camera angle. He tried not to laugh when a tree and I got tangled up while I was juggling cameras, lenses, and binoculars. If horses are not your thing, manager Jaime Víquez has a tractor-driven cart to take you to the forest.

The forest generally follows the *quebradas* (ravines) and the riverbeds. Bird-watching is excellent in the open pastures. We heard the laughing falcon before we saw it. Both white-fronted and yellow-naped parrots are common, flying overhead in pairs or flocks. Even the elusive king vulture is among the 119 species of birds officially recorded on ranch property. Orange-fronted and orange-chinned parakeets, several species of hummingbirds,

Los Inocentes (Photo by Ree Strange Sheck)

Montezuma oropendolas, and pauraques (nightjars) are among the birds seen regularly. Animals to watch for include white-tailed deer, coatis, raccoons, sloths, tapirs, and peccaries. Los Inocentes is less than 1,000 feet (280 m) above sea level in premontane moist forest.

All nature tours are escorted. The guide knows not only where and what to look for in flora and fauna but also the boundaries of the ranch. Bird-watchers who want a solitary trip can go to the nearby river, and the veranda offers good viewing for those who cannot tear themselves away from the charm of the house. The hacienda was built in the last century and was remodeled with an eye to maintaining the integrity of its architecture. Stone corrals also witness to the age of the property. A small swimming pool has been added, and guests can also swim in natural pools in the river.

On the south, Los Inocentes approaches Guanacaste National Park. Maybe you really do want to touch 4,879-foot (1,487-m) Orosí Volcano. You can visit one of the park's biological stations located on its slopes. Staff members can arrange transportation for a number of other day trips: to the beaches on the bays of Salinas and Santa Elena, to Murciélago (a section of Santa Rosa National Park), to Las Pailas and its bubbling mud at Rincón de la Vieja National Park, to Santa Rosa. For a different kind of tour, with

Gray fox (Photo by Ree Strange Sheck)

advance notice you can visit the two-room school on the property that workers' children from the ranch and nearby farms attend. Local children perform traditional dances if requested beforehand. A guided night walk in the forest is another possibility. At night, turn your eyes to the heavens for a bit of stargazing, there may be new constellations for you in Guanacaste's vast sky. And don't forget to ask Dennis about when it "rains fish."

Meals are something to look forward to. Not only the milk that is fresh, but the ranch also makes its own cheese and brings fresh fish in from a few miles away. Fruit trees near the house include limes, mangoes, guavas, nances, and passion fruit.

The main house has eleven nicely decorated rooms with large closets. Each has its own bath—with solar hot water—but the bath does not adjoin the room. Day visits are welcome.

Transportation: By car, go north from Liberia to just south of La Cruz and turn right toward Santa Cecilia. Los Inocentes is almost 9 miles (14 km) on paved road from the Inter-American Highway. You can also approach it from the east through Upala. Bus service is available to La Cruz, and taxis are available from La Cruz or Liberia. When making reservations, ask about transportation; ranch personnel can sometimes pick you up in La Cruz.

Rates: The cost for room and meals is $58 a day per person. The horse and guide service cost $11 for three hours. The day trip is $27, including lunch and a horseback tour. Credit cards are accepted.

Reservations: Telephone 265-5484 or 679-9190, fax 265-6431.

Monteverde Cloud Forest Preserve

The flash of a resplendent quetzal above a waterfall made every bump on the road to the Monteverde cloud forest worthwhile. It was a rainy day, and the guide's search for the bird at familiar haunts had turned up nothing. Then suddenly, appearing almost a turquoise color against the rich, dark green of the forest behind, the red and emerald bird with its magnificent tail swooped across a picture postcard setting. It took my breath away.

The desire to see what many consider the most beautiful bird in tropical America brings thousands of people every year to this biological reserve 113 miles (182 km) northwest of San José. But the Monteverde reserve is not just quetzals: There are more than 400 species of birds, 490 species of butterflies, 100 species of mammals, and 2,500 species of plants. It is the only known home of the golden toad, a two-inch brilliantly colored amphibian: males are orange, females yellow and black with patches of scarlet. But none has been seen since 1989. Only time will tell if another species has disappeared. The preserve also is home to the tapir. (But there is a greater chance of seeing tracks than this wary, once-common, now-endangered animal itself.) From March to August, you are likely to hear the booming call of the three-wattled bellbird. At any time of year, the fantastic variety of epiphytes covering the trees in this cloud forest is dazzling: there are more than 300 species of orchids (blooms are most profuse in March) and 200 of ferns. Gently press the moss covering a tree trunk to get an idea of how thick it is. There are checklists on birds and mammals and an informative nature trail guide. A map of the trails is also available at the visitor center. The preserve is open from 7:00 a.m. to 4:00 p.m. year-round. (It can be closed for special anniversary activities October 6 and 7.)

Monteverde Cloud Forest Preserve is not a national park, but it is within the Arenal Conservation Area. It is managed by Costa Rica's Tropical Science Center, a nonprofit scientific research and education organization based in San José. Founded in 1972, the reserve encompasses some 27,181 acres (11,000 ha) on the Continental Divide in the Tilarán Mountain Range, protecting both Atlantic and Pacific watersheds and containing eight ecological life zones.

The mean temperature at Monteverde is in the low 60s (16°-18°C). The annual rainfall is about 118 inches (3,000 mm). Bring your rain gear and rubber boots, or rent boots at the preserve; trails can be muddy. Though little rain falls from December through March, mist rolls in on strong trade winds from the Atlantic, and moisture forms on the abundant forest vegetation, dripping from the canopy to the ground. For the observant, this "indirect rain" is a striking demonstration of the importance of forest conservation. Without trees and forest plants to collect and disseminate this water, the mist would vaporize in the hot dry air to

White-faced monkeys (Photo by Ree Strange Sheck)

the west, and rivers that flow to the lowlands would carry less water. That is why the small group of dairy-farming Quakers from the United States who settled in this area in the 1950s set aside 1,369 acres (554 ha) to protect the watershed. That parcel is now part of the reserve, leased to the Tropical Science Center for management.

To both protect habitat and ensure visitors a worthwhile experience, only 25 people at a time are allowed on each of the five trails. Priority is given to those coming for the preserve's guided natural history walks, led by bilingual, naturalist guides. A slide show is part of the tour. Reservations for the walks can be made through hotels or directly with the preserve. In addition to public areas with marked trails and longer trails for backpackers, the preserve has areas where almost no use is allowed and others that are restricted to scientific investigation. The heaviest visitation is from December through May. Backpackers must make reservations for use of the shelters.

Overnight accommodations at the preserve's field station are limited to four rooms for about thirty-five people, with the space often filled by researchers and students. Baths, with hot water showers, are shared. However, hotels are available in the nearby towns of Monteverde and Santa Elena. Parking space is very limited at the preserve. The hotels can arrange transportation, or you can walk the 1.5 miles (2.5 km) from the cheese plant in Monteverde. Birds spotted along the roadside are your reward. The gift shop is worth a visit.

Transportation: By car, you can reach the Monteverde Cloud Forest Preserve either from the Inter-American Highway, turning north at Sardinal or Lagarto, or from Arenal, coming south through Tilarían, Quebrada Granda, and Santa Elena. On either route the last portion is unpaved and rough. Express buses run between San José and Monteverde, but it is a good idea to buy your ticket in advance if you do not want to stand for the four-hour trip. (See Practical Extras.) There are also public buses from Puntarenas and Tilarían to Santa Elena, with taxi service from Santa Elena. (See the description of the town of Monteverde in chapter 6 for other transportation possibilities.)

Rates: The entrance fee for day visits is $8 per person, $4 for students with an identification card. Children under twelve are admitted free. Guided walks led by bilingual guides are $23 per person, including admission and slide show. The use of shelters on backpacking trips costs $3.50 per night. A room and meals in the rustic field station is $20 per person.

Reservations: For overnight accommodations, telephone 645-5122, fax 645-5034. If you do not make a reservation, arrive before 4:00 p.m. Make reservations for guided natural history walks by calling the preserve or through your hotel.

Rancho Humo Ecotourism Center

The sun was still low in the eastern sky. From my vantage point atop a bluff, an iguana and I watched parrots move noisily from tree to tree below. Rays of light traveled over the green of Palo Verde National Park to shimmer on the waters of the Tempisque River. My feet were on the ground, but I had an aerial view, somewhat like looking at a living relief map.

The bluff is the site of the new Rancho Humo Hotel, across the Tempisque from Palo Verde. One does not have to go outside and sit with an iguana for this early morning treat—it can be savored from the attractive rooms. With binoculars, one can follow flocks of resident and migratory birds that live in this rich habitat.

The 24-room Rancho Humo Hotel, still under construction when I visited, is the upscale part of Rancho Humo Ecotourism Center, with swimming pools, restaurant, bar, gift shop, central air conditioning, and private baths with hot water.

Just down the hill, where I stayed, is a charming, rustic counterpart, Albergue Zapandí, built to resemble an Indian village. Eight rooms in four bamboo and thatch buildings around a central plaza have shared baths (with four showers, four toilets and no hot water), ceiling fans, and serve-yourself dining (good, ample food). The showers are open to the sky, so you can do a bit of bird-watching at the same time. In the community bath structure, guests can also wash out clothes *a la tica*, in a *pila*, a big cement sink-like contraption, and hang them up to dry. Don't be surprised if howler monkeys hang around to watch in trees by the clearing.

Puerto Lapas, connected by trails through the forest as well as by road to the hotel and albergue, is the operations center for water trips for the ecotourism center. It is a delightful place in itself, with indigenous architecture in a thatched snack bar/dining area and in structures for showers and toilets close to the pier on the Tempisque River. (Note the unusual shower heads: perforated gourds.) *Lapas* means scarlet macaws, and there are some here.

Rancho Humo has two 18-passenger, one 10-passenger, and one 4-passenger fiberglass motorboats for trips to nearby Isla de los Pájaros, to Chira Island in the Gulf of Nicoya via the Tempisque River from Puerto Chamorro, on the Bebedero River to where it flows into the Tempisque, and to Puerto Níspero where the Tempisque Ferry docks. All the boats are equipped with life jackets, cushions, first aid kit, and water pump, and they are covered as a protection from rain or the hot Guanacaste sun.

In addition to water excursions, guests can visit Barra Hondo and Palo Verde parks or hike or go by horseback in forests and through the floodplains on the ranch. You can also go along raised dikes to see some of the 279 species of birds identified in the area, including the roseate spoonbill, anhinga, jabiru, northern jacana, whistling-ducks, and various species of ibis, storks, and egrets. Sergio Montero, the operations manager, and I followed a busy armadillo for a bit. Other animals you are likely to see are porcupines, iguanas, deer, raccoons, coatis, and monkeys. The green-barked *palo verde*, the gumbo limbo (*indio desnudo*), *corteza amarilla* with its yellow flowers, and *tempisque* are among 148 species of trees identified so far. Sergio says guests are also invited to go along with the cowboys on their ranch chores.

The smiling, helpful staff is drawn mostly from surrounding communities.

Transportation: Driving, you can arrive either from Nicoya or the Tempisque ferry, taking dirt roads through Corralillo toward Puerto Humo. Boat transportation can be arranged from Puerto Chamorro, Bebedero, or Puerto Níspero at the Tempisque ferry. The two-and-a-half-hour trip costs $12 each for two people. There also is a bus from Nicoya to Puerto Humo, and light planes can land nearby.

Rates: At the Rancho Humo Hotel, singles are $46, doubles $80, with reduced rates for children under 12. The breakfast buffet is $6.50, lunch $10, and dinner $12; box breakfasts and lunches are available. A full American plan is $26. Food prices do not include tax. At Albergue Zapandí, a single is $25, a double $43. Breakfasts are $5, lunch and dinner $7, plus tax. Horseback riding is $5 per hour, and transportation from Nicoya to the albergue can be arranged for groups of four or more for $5 each. Credit cards are accepted.

Reservations: Telephone 255-2463, fax 255-3573.

Rincón de la Vieja Mountain Lodge

I almost did not get past the Colorado River at the entrance to Rincón de la Vieja Mountain Lodge. Cicadas were singing, a morpho floated above the river, shafts of sunlight sparkled on the rushing water, tall trees created a cathedral effect. Enchantment.

Enchantment might be the best word to describe what awaits one here on the slopes of Rincón de la Vieja Volcano, just outside the national park that protects it. One can visit bubbling mudpots and geysers, hike to hidden waterfalls, bathe in mountain streams or hot springs, ride horseback through pristine forest, and visit a mountain lake. Many of these activities are in the national park, but lodge guests also may explore trails in the primary forest on the surrounding farm, visit a neighbor's hot springs, and return to the Río Colorado to watch for birds and butterflies and soak up the energy and beauty of the place.

Owner Alvaro Wiessel is from a family with a history of more than 100 years in the area. The lodge was the family home. Today it contains a living area, dining room, kitchen, and rooms for guests. Alvaro has brought the number of rooms to 18 by adding guest cottages with private baths (but no hot water) and front porches with hammocks and chairs. Furnishings are simple but comfortable; some rooms have bunk beds. Beyond the lodge is a group of rooms built beside a small stream next to rich forest. The porch offers a comfortable place to sit and watch and wait for surprises from the natural world. A small swimming pool is in front of the lodge.

Among the showier birds spotted on the farm are violaceous, elegant, and orange-bellied trogons; the crested caracara; red-lored, mealy, yellow-naped, and white-fronted parrots; toucans; motmots; and the three-wattled bellbird. Mammals include howler and white-faced monkeys, deer, coatis, peccaries, and pacas. Tapirs live here, but it is unlikely you will see one.

In addition to the primary and secondary forest, Alvaro is reforesting some of his own land. Guests may also accompany farm workers on their rounds. The lodge has bicycles, tents, and horses for rent, and working cowboys can give riding instruction. These people, who have grown up here, are the local guides, though with advance notice, a bilingual tour guide can be arranged.

Transportation: Rincón de la Vieja Lodge is about 16 miles (26 km) northeast of Liberia; take the road through Curubandé off the Inter-American. The lodge provides transportation from Liberia for $30 for up to five people.

Rates: Rooms with shared baths are $18 per person; with private baths, they are $21 to $25. Breakfasts are $8, lunch and dinner $10 (served family-style). Box lunches are available. One-day tours to such destinations as Las Pailas, the volcano, and thermal springs range from $45 to $55. A two-day, one-night package that includes a tour to the volcano and Las Pailas is $140, while a two-night, three-day tour package is $350, including lodging, food, horses, and a local guide.

Reservations: Telephone 225-1073, fax 234-1676.

South

Bosque del Cabo

If you like nighttime by candlelight, scarlet macaws flying overhead, a private outdoor shower with water heated only by the sun on the pipes, and the sound of the sea as you drop off to sleep, then Bosque del Cabo is for you.

Perched above Matapalo Beach on the tip of the Osa Peninsula, this small wilderness lodge has perhaps just the right amount of comfort and adventure. The naturalist in me thrilled at the continu-

Bungalows above the sea at Bosque del Cabo (Photo by Ree Strange Sheck)

ous parade of tropical birds so easily seen. The explorer reveled in the horseback ride through a tropical storm, an encounter with a snake, and tracking howler monkeys on a forest trail. The romantic in me relished the private, thatched bungalows above the sea, mosquito netting draped gracefully over the beds, and a private outdoor shower with a forest for a backdrop. Four scarlet macaws flew over in perfect formation as I showered my first morning there.

I confess that I appreciated the modern bath with a flush toilet, the good food, and the comfortable beds. I enjoyed experiencing the bungalow at night with only candles or a kerosene lantern to warm the darkness. Doors fold back to open the front of each of the six bungalows to the sea and forest. The two deluxe bungalows have a king-size bed, wraparound deck, and big bathroom.

As I stood on my veranda, I counted a feeding flock of fifteen chestnut-mandibled toucans while the sounds of howler monkeys mixed with the sounds of the surf and a hummingbird whispering by my ear. The scarlet macaws are regular visitors.

Owners Philip Spier and Barbara Odio make visitors feel like welcome house guests. Attentive to their needs, they also give guests the space they want.

If you can tear yourself away from bird-watching and ocean-gazing (whales sometimes pass by), you can take an hour's hike to the gulf side of the peninsula to swim in gentler waters, walk the trail down to the small river, or go on a horseback ride to the ocean side of the peninsula to visit the tide pools along a deserted beach and walk up to the 30-foot (9-m) waterfall. There also are other horseback tours. Philip and Barbara will arrange for a biologist guide for tours and for surfing, sea kayaking, and deep sea fishing.

Restaurant hours are fairly flexible to meet the needs of both bird-watchers and late sleepers. Local fruits and vegetables are incorporated in the meals which include both typical Costa Rican and North American dishes. Soft drinks and beer are available in the bar during the day. Special dietary needs can be met with advance notice. A generator can provide electricity in the dining room in the evenings.

The young owners have been so busy creating Bosque del Cabo that they are just starting to compile bird and mammal lists. You can add to those lists while you are there if you wish. Philip and Barbara say they are beginners in natural history, but if so, they are avid students, and they like to share what they are discovering.

Transportation: You can take a direct bus from San José or fly on SANSA or Travelair to Puerto Jiménez. The taxi from Puerto Jiménez costs about $25 for the 10-mile (16-km) trip. If you choose the eight-hour drive from San José, you need four-wheel drive for the road south of Puerto Jiménez, which can be slippery and muddy and crosses several rivers without bridges.

Rates: For standard bungalows, single occupancy is $85 per day and double is $65 per person, meals included. Deluxe bungalows are $95 for a single and $75 each for a double. There is an extra charge for use of a credit card.

Reservations: There are no phones at Bosque del Cabo, so make your reservations by telephone or fax through the office in Puerto Jiménez: 735-5206.

Cabinas Chacón, Albergue de Montaña Savegre

At Cabinas Chacón, they do not talk about "if" you see a quetzal, they say "when." Roland Chacón, one of owner Efraín Chacon's eleven children, told me we would see one on our early morning tour, and we did. It was so easy. We drove up the mountain, and there it was, sitting in the tree he expected it to be in. The red, white, and green bird, so elusive in some places, seemed to appear as if on cue. Best months to see them are February through May.

The Chacóns' place in San Gerardo de Dota between Cartago and San Isidro de El General in the Talamanca Mountains is famous for quetzals and for hospitality. Efraín, who has lived here for thirty-seven years, started a dairy farm. People started coming to fish for trout in the Savegre River that flows through his property, and sometimes they stayed late. At first, Efraín and his wife took the visitors into their home to spend the night. Eventually, they built a cabin for them, and then in 1980, ecotourists began to arrive in the hope of spotting a quetzal.

Squirrel monkey, called *tití* in Spanish (Photo by Ree Strange Sheck)

Cabinas Chacón now has fourteen cabins, all with private bath and sitting room, and a spacious restaurant/bar to serve not only overnight but also day visitors and local folks. Be sure to bring your appetite; the food is good and plentiful, and fresh trout does make its way to the menu.

There is still a small dairy, and guests can visit the extensive apple orchards and packing plant on the property. All up and down the valley, apple, plum, and peach trees are replacing pastures on the steep slopes.

About half of the Chacón farm is in primary forest. There is a 5-mile (8-km) trail that takes two to three hours to hike (with fabulous views at times of the forest canopy) and a half-mile (1 km) one, too. For real hikers, a trail goes from the farm to Cerro de la Muerte. Roland suggests going there by car and walking back.

For those who just like gentle strolls, a walk along the country road in front affords a look at flowering trees, the rushing river that flows alongside, and a variety of birds. I watched a woodpecker gathering nuts. A good number of the more than 100 species of birds here can be seen from the cabin area. The quetzal is not the only flashy bird in the Dota Valley: trogons, emerald toucanets, and iridescent hummingbirds also lend color.

Animals that might be seen include porcupines, rabbits, white-faced monkeys, white-tailed deer, frogs, squirrels, and foxes. Local guides well versed in natural history can be hired for $10 per hour. Horseback riding is also $10 per hour.

Trout fishermen and ecotourists have been joined by scientists and students in this special place. The Quetzal Education Research Complex is Southern Nazarene University's tropical campus. A research laboratory is already in operation.

Cabinas Chacón is at 6,890 feet (2,100 m). The rainiest months are October and November, and there is generally little rain from December to June. You may need insect repellent for hiking on the higher trails. The cabins are simple and comfortable. Bring a jacket for the cool evenings.

Transportation: The turnoff for San Gerardo de Dota and Cabinas Chacón is at kilometer 80 on the Inter-American Highway south of San José. Buses going to San Isidro can let you off here, and the

Chacóns can pick you up. The $20 round-trip is on a 6-mile (10-km) attention-getting road with hairpin curves.

Rates: $50 per person including meals. Visa is accepted.

Reservations: Telephone 771-1732.

Genesis II

Walking through the cloud forest at Genesis II is like moving through a hanging garden in the mist. Bromeliads crowd every inch of space on the stately oaks. Mosses and mushrooms abound. I counted four orchids blooming on the same tree branch. Fallen blossoms from the canopy high above decorate the forest floor.

This cloud forest in the Talamanca Mountains, more than 7,740 feet (2,360 m) high, has an air of eternity about it. It seems to call for hushed tones, for quiet observation. Bird songs echo through the trees. It seemed appropriate that a collared redstart, known as the "friend of man," followed as we walked on the trail. Five mixed feeding flocks moved through the forest.

Birds bring many visitors to this 100-acre (247-ha) private reserve, located about 39 miles (62 km) south of San José. The current bird list has about 116 species, and owners Steve and Paula Friedman expect it to grow to 200. The resplendent quetzal is no stranger here. It is easily seen from March to June. The Friedmans reported seeing nine quetzals one day just from the balcony of their house.

The distinctive sounds of the three-wattled bellbird are heard here. There are collared trogons, black guans, emerald toucanets, silvery-fronted tapaculo, and hummingbirds—fiery-throated, magnificent, volcano, and purple-throated and gray-tailed mountain gems. Mammals are not as flashy but include sloths, armadillos, tayras, squirrels, and rabbits. The tracks of a tapir have been seen, probably visiting from the Río Macho Forest Reserve next door. One butterfly specialist told Steve that all the butterflies here are in the rare category. Twelve miles (20 km) of well-maintained trails and dirt roads let guests explore the area.

An optional side trip could include a visit to Dominical, or perhaps you can get in on a trip to the farm of Alexander Skutch, the well-known naturalist and ornithologist, near San Isidro.

Lodging at Genesis II allows a maximum of ten people in double rooms with shared baths. The facilities are humble, but the attention is first class. Paula turns out marvelous meals served family-style, using many garden-fresh fruits and vegetables grown on the property. She uses many of the recipes published in her *Quetzal Cookbook*, everything from typical Costa Rican dishes to lemon chicken and lasagna.

Steve directs young people in a volunteer program helping him to re-create forest on a piece of cleared land. Activities include research on species as well as tree planting and follow-up. The program attracts people from around the world who pay to spend their vacations on conservation work in this cloud forest. In their spare time, they teach English to adults and children in a school down the road.

And the name, Genesis II? Steve explained that he and Paula chose it to signify a "second beginning," where they would attempt to live on the land in a more proper, peaceful way.

Transportation: Buses from San José to San Isidro de El General can drop you off at the Cañon church near kilometer 58, where the Friedmans will pick you up. Genesis II is 2.5 miles (4 km) farther. Packages include transportation. If you are driving, watch for probably the most beautifully decorated roadside bus stop in Costa Rica. The Genesis II sign—colorful quetzals and bromeliads—is painted on it.

Rates: Weekly packages include lodging, meals, guides, transportation, laundry, and taxes. Singles are $700, doubles are $890. For three days, singles are $350, doubles $400. There also are non-package student rates.

Reservations: Telephone 288-0739.

Hacienda Barú

Four young coatis had dashed across the trail and scampered up a tree, quickly disappearing in a leafy world hidden from our eyes. We had watched a blue-black grassquit doing rapid little song-jumps, seeming to somersault in the air as it fluttered up and down from the same low branch. What sounded like a giant crashing through the forest turned out to be monkeys feeding noisily, knocking down fruit and throwing branches to the ground.

Jack Ewing's world—Hacienda Barú (Photo by Ree Strange Sheck)

This is Jack Ewing's world. He became interested in ecology about ten years ago, and today he operates Hacienda Barú just north of Dominical on the Pacific coast, a private nature reserve worth visiting. We had already gone by horseback to see pre-Columbian petroglyphs scattered in a field high above the Barú River Valley. Now we were working our way down by foot on trails that lead to lowland forest and eventually to mangrove swamps and sandy beach along the Pacific.

Jack wanted me to see a giant ceibo tree. I found out for myself that the jabillo tree has spines, and he explained that its wood is good for boats because the outside is resistant to salt water and the inside is usually hollow. Jack is an untiring student of the natural world, enthusiastic about sharing what he has learned and dedicated to its conservation.

He said some visitors arrive expecting boas to be hanging from the trees and jaguars to appear on the trails. Boas are on his reptile list, but you are not likely to see one. And no jaguars have been spotted here, though there are pumas, jaguarundis, and ocelots. More than 326 species of birds have been counted, 57 species of mammals (including bats), and reptiles and amphibians that run the gamut from caimans to red-eyed tree frogs and tiny, colorful, poison dart frogs. Humpback whales pass by offshore from December to April, and olive ridley and hawksbill sea turtles lay eggs on the beach from May through November. The hacienda helps with a nursery where about 2,500 baby turtles are hatched every year and released on the beach. Dolphins inhabit these warm waters.

About half of the 830-acre (336-ha) hacienda is forested, some in primary forest, some selectively logged a few years ago, and some regenerating on former pastureland.

Many visitors come to Hacienda Barú on day visits. There are a variety of hikes with native guides: a three-hour lowland walk through mangrove, riverbank, and seashore habitat; the popular six-hour rain forest hike; and an all-day trek that goes from the beach to the petroglyphs. There also are guided horseback tours to the lowlands, to the petroglyphs, and to the highlands above the river valley. Some can be combined with hikes.

A new opportunity to see the rain forest from a different per-spective is the canopy exploration adventure, for the physically fit only and generally limited to those between thirteen and sixty years of age. Instructors help you climb as high as 130 feet (140 m).

A night in the jungle is another option, camping in tents in the forest next to a shelter with flush toilets and shower. This may be your chance to see nocturnal animals, and bird-watching in the small clearing is excellent in the morning. Beach camping is also offered.

If your taste runs more to cabins, try Cabañas El Ceibo, six two- and three-bedroom units with kitchenette, bathroom with hot-water shower, and fans. A complimentary continental breakfast is served in an open-air dining room. The cabañas are near both forest and beach.

Before you start out on your tours, be sure to see Diane Ewing's orchid collection, 250 species and growing, in their backyard. She is responsible for the tasty meals and for riding herd on every-body's whereabouts. There are no phones here, so radio communi-cation is a way of life. Specialist John Hall is helping the Ewings create a living museum to help guests identify plants they will see in the forest.

Jack came to Costa Rica in 1970 to stay for four months, and the family followed shortly after. It looks as if they are going to stay. Stop by Hacienda Barú, and you will understand why.

Transportation: Bus and air service to Quepos and bus service to San Isidro de El General is a first step. Buses between Quepos and San Isidro pass by the entrance, just northwest of the Barú River. If you drive, stop by the El Ceibo gas station and information center on the road from Quepos. It is owned by the hacienda.

Rates: Per-person costs for activities include a lowland walk for $14, a rain forest experience for $28, an all-day trek for $33, a night in the jungle for $66 (with breakfast dinner, guides, and equipment), beach camping for $23 (including tent, bedding, breakfast, and dinner), and canopy exploration and three climbs for $110, with equipment, instruction, and lunch. These costs include a local guide; English-speaking naturalist guides are avail-able at $50 per day. Lodging in Cabañas El Ceibo is $46 per person for double occupancy.

Reservations: Telephone or fax 771-1903; if you get a recording, give the tour or accommodations you want, the approximate time of arrival, and the number in your party. It helps to give twenty-four-hour notice.

Lapa Ríos

The brochure for Lapa Ríos asks "Who says wilderness and luxury can't mix?" The owners of this 1,000-acre (405-ha) private reserve, John and Karen Lewis, thought it could be done, and set out to protect this piece of rain forest on the southeastern tip of the Osa Peninsula through a small, upscale ecotourism project that would have minimal impact on the environment while contributing to local development, education, and employment.

Located 10 miles (16 km) south of Puerto Jiménez where the Golfo Dulce meets the Pacific, Lapa Ríos is the result of their dream. The luxury wilderness resort has a spectacular main lodge that houses the reception area, restaurant, bar, and an outdoor terrace. Guests look up at the underside of the 50-foot (15-m) thatched palm roof. The intrepid can climb an open circular stair-way that makes four complete turns to an observation walkway three stories high. A 360-degree view encompassing the sea 300 feet (92 m) below and forest is the reward. The cliffside swimming pool next to the lodge has a dynamite view of the ocean.

Fourteen bungalows are built on three ridges below the main lodge. The first two are accessible to the lodge and pool by a wheel-chair ramp, but the rest require walking. My bungalow was 100 steps down. Each has a peaked thatched roof and gleaming floors of tropical hardwood. One wall is white stucco and cane; the other three are largely open, low wooden walls with screens above, bamboo rollups for privacy. Double louvered doors open onto a large private deck and small patio garden with an outdoor shower. The tiled bathroom has two sinks set in tropical hardwood and a large shower open to a view of the forest. Furnishings are primarily of bamboo. Each room contains two double beds with mosquito netting, desk, luggage racks, chairs with bright cush-ions,and ceiling fans. Battery chargers and razors can be used in the electrical outlets.

Pool and spectacular thatched dining room at Lapa Ríos (Photo by Ree Strange Sheck)

The Carbonara Beach down from the lodge is safe for swimming and has a number of tide pools. Surfers can find good waves nearby. Lapa Ríos uses local charter boat services for fishing, tours to Sirena Station at Corcovado and Caño Island, or a cruise on the Golfo Dulce.

A number of guided walks in the rain forest with a naturalist are available. A $15 beach walk that incorporates information about medicinal plants as well as wildlife takes about two hours, and a $25 three- to four-hour Rain-Forest Ridge Walk along a fairly level mountain ridge is a nice introduction to the biodiversity of tropical rain forests. Some 250 species live here, including the small green-and-black poison dart frogs, leaf beetles, army ants and the birds that follow their marches, howler monkeys, and boa constrictors. The $25, half-day Wet Waterfall Adventure will take you along the Carbonera River to a series of pristine waterfalls—this one is for the hardy.

A $20 night walk reveals some of the forest secrets not visible during the day. Bring your flashlight to see the eyeshine of nocturnal creatures. The road between Puerto Jiménéz and Lapa Ríos is good for birding. John told me one guest counted 45 species on this route. You can go with a guide if you like.

Horseback riding can be arranged, and guests can plant a tree on some of the 250 acres (100 ha) of regenerating forest on the property. The $25 fee goes into the Lapa Ríos reforestation program.

Meals are a treat; they look and taste great. Though food is included in the rate, there is no fixed menu: guests choose from several selections. Desserts are scrumptious. Restaurant staff members are well-trained and friendly—introducing themselves politely at the tables they serve. The restaurant is open to the public.

Transportation: Lapa Ríos provides transportation from Puerto Jiménez, which visitors can reach by either daily scheduled air service, charter flights, direct bus from San José, or charter boats or once-a-day launch service from Golfito.

Rates: Singles are $164, doubles $115 each, including meals and access to the private reserve. Off-season rates are lower. An extra charge is added for the use of credit cards.

Reservations: Telephone 735-5130, fax 735-5179.

Marenco Biological Reserve

There are no roads to Marenco Biological Reserve on the Osa Peninsula. You come in by either boat or plane.

Remote, set in a hillside clearing amidst lush premontane wet forest, the biological reserve is a center for natural history tourism. As you explore the miles of beach and forest trails on the reserve's 1,483 acres (600 ha), you can do some discovering of your own. In fact, you can sit on the balcony of your room and watch a veritable parade of exotic birds—parrots, toucans with their outrageous beaks, scarlet macaws, brightly colored tanagers. At certain times of the year, humpback whales pass by in the ocean below.

On forest trails you may encounter a slow-moving sloth or catch the scent of white-lipped peccaries. The resident naturalist guide will advise you to climb a nearby tree and wait until they pass if you meet a herd of the piglike peccaries. There is a subspecies of squirrel monkey, called tití in Spanish, that is endemic to southern Costa Rica and northern Panama. Watch for motion in the trees to spot them and the other three monkey species that live in Costa Rica: howler, white-faced capuchin, and spider.

You can rent one of the reserve's horses to go along the beach or forest trails, and you can walk to the cool waters of the Río Claro and take a dip beneath towering forest giants.

A nighttime visit to the tide pools reveals sea creatures you may never have seen before. Daytime snorkeling is good at coral gardens along Marenco's coastline, where you may see parrot fish, tangs, puffers, and angelfish. A boat tour to Caño Island, 11 miles (17 km) west of Marenco, opens up another underwater wonderland of octopuses, lobsters, moray eels, jacks, damselfish and triggerfish. Near the island you will probably see dolphins, and you may be startled by a manta ray. The forested island holds the secrets of both a vanished Indian culture and fabled pirate treasure troves.

A highlight for most travelers to Marenco is a day trip to nearby Corcovado National Park, entering at San Pedrillo and hiking along the beach and into the forest, up the Pargo River, where you have a chance to walk in an area of the large park that is little visited. Plant and bird life is outstanding, and a bilingual naturalist guide explains intricate biological relationships and points out what you often do not see in front of your very eyes. You know you are treading the turf of Corcovado's animal kingdom: the jaguar, giant anteater, tapir, agouti, ocelot, and kinkajou. After lunch, you hike along the San Pedrillo River to a pristine rain forest waterfall. A second option in Corcovado goes all the way to the magnificent waterfall at Llorona Beach. Not for the weak-kneed, the four-hour trek is up and down hills, through the tropical forest, across small streams, sometimes along the beach. There is time for lunch and a brief swim before the four-hour hike back. It is worth every aching muscle.

Marenco itself is a buffer zone that protects the park, employs local people, and offers the traveler a chance to taste the richness. Accommodations are pleasant. Bamboo and wood bungalows contain twenty-five double rooms, each with its own bath and a balcony open to a priceless view. Meals are served buffet style in high season in the large, open dining room.

The generator runs from 5:30 to 9:30 p.m.; bring a flashlight to complement the candle in your room after hours. The radio telephone is powered by solar energy. A small reference library with some preserved local flora and fauna is worth a visit. Crafts made by local people are also available in the Rain Forest Shop.

The busiest months are December through April at Marenco, which can house up to fifty guests. September and October are very rainy, but the off-season months can be pleasant, too.

Transportation: Package rates include round-trip transportation from San José. Non-package travelers should contact Marenco about land, sea, and air possibilities. Land/sea routes are usually through Uvita or Sierpe.

Rates: Package rates include transportation, meals, bilingual naturalist, and specified tours. A four-day, three-night package is $570 per person, double occupancy, including a tour to Corcovado and Río Claro. A five-day tour for $690 adds Caño Island, and there is a $390 three-day tour that goes only to Corcovado. Lodging and meals cost non-package travelers $85 for a single, $96 each for a double. Tour costs are $25 for the half-day Río Claro tour, $65 for Corcovado, and $75 for Caño. Credit cards are accepted.

Reservations: Telephone 221-1594. Fax (506) 255-1340. In San José, you may go by the office at El Pueblo Commercial Center. Any taxi driver knows where El Pueblo is.

Rainbow Adventures

Travelers take a forty-five minute boat ride north of Golfito along shores where steep forest meets the sea, past small, unpopulated beaches, to find a lodge with stained glass windows and turn-of-the-century antiques. Pleasant surprises are the order of the day at Rainbow Adventures.

I no sooner arrived than I spotted a green honeycreeper moving through tree branches next to my room, my first glimpse of that gorgeous bird. During my stay I witnessed a continuing, stubborn battle between a red-lored parrot and a yellow-naped woodpecker over a hole in a nearby tree trunk. The brilliance of the scarlet-rumped tanager flashed in the landscaped gardens around the lodge and two cabins. Five chestnut-mandibled toucans perched in a single tree just off the trail during the free introductory jungle walk. Fellow guests swore that the live-in scarlet macaw (who decided to stay after being brought here injured) actually poses for photographers, changing positions after hearing the click of the camera.

Rainbow Adventures is in a small clearing between mile-long Cativo Beach on the Golfo Dulce and primary and secondary forest behind. The 1,200-acre (486-ha) private reserve abuts the Esquinas addition to Corcovado National Park. If you can tear yourself away from the activity near the lodge and the warm waters of the gulf (85°F, 30°C), you can choose to fill your days with a wide variety of activities.

Hikes with a local guide include a two-hour trek to a 50-foot (15-m) waterfall, through the forest to the small hydro project that supplies electricity for Rainbow Adventures, or in-depth customized jungle hikes—perhaps to a big swimming hole above the waterfalls. The cost is $4 per hour for guided tours, boots provided. Animals more commonly seen include the agouti, banded anteater, coati, kinkajou, raccoon, tayra, iguana, Jesus Christ lizard, armadillo, and howler, spider, and white-faced monkeys. More than 100 species of birds are on the lodge list.

Rainbow Adventures hideaway on the Golfo Dulce (Photo by Ree Strange Sheck)

Boating activities include a birding trip on the Esquinas River through mangroves and primary and secondary forest, a dolphin tour, fishing, and snorkeling at a number of sites, where you may see parrotfish, angelfish, triggerfish, starfish, moray eels, octopus, sharks, sea turtles, or dolphins. Boat rental for these tours is $35 an hour, including guide, snorkeling gear, and safety equipment.

Another possibility is a $20 half-day boat trip to see the botanical gardens at Casa Orquídeas at San Josesito.

The lodge itself invites exploration. The first floor of the wooden structure has a lounge and dining room open to the gardens, the second has three double rooms that open onto a large veranda, and the third, called the penthouse, is open on three sides, with stained glass panels suspended between the waist-high wall and the roof. Antiques are scattered throughout, collected by owner Michael Medill of Oregon. All rooms have private baths with solar-heated water. The two secluded cabins have an open living area (with handwoven silk rugs) and two bedrooms and bath. The non-antique furnishings are handmade by resident crafstmen.

Delicious meals, including gourmet dishes, are generally served buffet-style, with most herbs and vegetables coming from the organic garden. Managers John and Catalina provide some very nice touches, such as having a guanabana fruit on hand to show guests when a drink made of guanabana is served. The garden provides produce such as pineapples, papayas, bananas, plantains, water apples, avocados, starfruit, anona, mamón chino, chestnuts, and edible hibiscus.

A seven-minute video about Rainbow Adventures can be rented.

Transportation: Rainbow Adventures arranges air transportation from San José to Golfito. A boat to Playa Cativo and the lodge is included in the package.

Rates: Cabins are $150 for a single, $180 for two people. In the lodge, second-floor rooms are $130 for a single and $160 for two people; the penthouse is $135 for a single and $165 for two. Prices include meals, soft drinks and snacks during the day, snorkeling gear, and a complimentary jungle walk.

Reservations: Telephone or fax 775-0220. In the U.S., telephone (503) 690-7750.

Robert and Catherine Wilson Botanical Garden

Even before you even arrive at the Robert and Catherine Wilson Botanical Garden, you will be glad you came. The trip south from San José on the Inter-American Highway takes you through high mountain páramo, lowland pineapple plantations, and then, off the Inter-American, back up along a ridge that was the Indian route from Paso Real to Panama.

The botanical garden lies in a rural agricultural setting 3.5 miles (5.6 km) south of San Vito, near Panama. It is some 206 miles (332 km) from San José. The lofty peaks of Amistad National Park reign to the northwest, sometimes appearing above the clouds.

Founded by the Wilsons in 1962, the garden is now owned by the Organization for Tropical Studies (OTS) and is used as a field station for its graduate-level courses in tropical biology and agroecology.

Fortunately for the natural history traveler, it is open for not only day visits, from 8:00 a.m. to 5:00 p.m., but also overnight stays. Space is at a premium in February and July because of courses, but it is worth a call even then to see if you can get in.

An internationally known collection of tropical plants awaits you on the 25 acres (10 ha) of planted grounds: 80 percent of the tropical and subtropical genera of palms are grown here—the second largest collection in the world—and many can be seen on the delightful Tree Fern Hill Trail. More trails await you: Heliconia Loop Trail; Bromeliad Walk; Orchid Walk (with more than two hundred native and exotic species); Fern Gully (Costa Rica has 800 species of ferns); Maranta Trail; Bamboo Walk. On the Natural History Loop, you will walk through Hummingbird Garden, with plants to attract this amazing creature. Costa Rica has 54 species of hummers; the garden has 24. A self-guided trail has sixteen information stations.

When you have had your fill of planted gardens, you can take off on trails that touch the adjacent 559-acre (226-ha) natural forest reserve area also belonging to OTS to see the orchids and palms and heliconias growing in their natural habitat. The River Trail offers excellent bird-watching.

Since 1983, the garden has been part of the Amistad Biosphere Reserve recognized by UNESCO. The garden and forest reserve contain about 2,000 native species of plants, 4,000 exotic species, 317 species of birds, 80 species of mammals, 71 species of reptiles and amphibians, and more than 3,000 kinds of moths and butterflies.

On Sundays especially, the garden is popular with area residents who come to spend the day. Admission to the park is 30 cents. Local outreach and education is a prime component of a program being implemented by Director Luis Diego Gómez and associate director Gail Hewson de Gómez.

Overnight facilities consist of beds for forty-eight people. Refurbished rooms, some with private baths with hot water, are quite comfortable—each with a desk and reading lamp. Four cabins have living room, refrigerator, balcony, and private bath. Meals are delicious, typical Costa Rican fare, served family-style, sometimes on an outdoor deck with impressive forest views. Day visitors can eat lunch at the garden with advance reservations. There is a washer and dryer for use by overnight guests. A small gift shop includes local handcrafts, some made by members of nearby Indian communities, books, T-shirts, pottery, and informative trail guides.

The Wilson Garden is located in a midelevation tropical rain forest. There is little or no rainfall from January through March, but the rest of the year there is heavy fog and, in general, afternoon rains. The annual rainfall is about 158 inches (4,000 mm). Year-round temperatures generally stay in the 70s (21° to 26°C) in the daytime and the 60s (16° to 21°C) at night.

Transportation: The road is paved from San José. By car, take the Inter-American Highway through San Isidro and Buenos Aires to 9.3 miles (15 km) past the El Brujo customs checkpoint. Turn left at the sign that says San Vito 45 km. Until a bridge is completed over the Terraba River, you cross by ferry. If you are in Golfito, you can reach the Wilson Garden via Ciudad Neily, turning north on Route 16 to Agua Buena. The taxi fare from Golfito is about $40. An express bus from San José to San Vito takes about five hours; buy your tickets in advance. Taxis in San Vito can get you to the garden.

Rates: Lodging and meals cost $79 per person for the cabins and $58 for the rooms. A day visit including lunch costs $12; without lunch, it is $6.

Reservations: Reservations are essential for overnight stays. Contact the Organization for Tropical Studies, telephone 240-6696, fax 240-6783. For lunch reservations for a day visit, telephone or fax 773-3278.

Tiskita Biological Reserve

My introduction to Tiskita Biological Reserve on the southern Pacific coast was two spectacular fiery-billed aracaris perched along the road and a group of six small squirrel monkeys cavorting through tree branches before we even reached the main lodge. Peter Aspinall, who owns Tiskita, can help you out with the name of the flashy bird if it is new to you as well as explain that you will see this subspecies of tití monkey only in southern Costa Rica.

If you enjoy birds or nature photography, you can have a field day without leaving the lodge. Planted nearby are hundreds of tropical fruit trees that draw birds like a magnet. We watched three chestnut-mandibled toucans casually eat a fruit breakfast. In the same tree were blue-crowned manakins, a lineated woodpecker, and blue-gray and scarlet-rumped tanagers. A bird book is left handy to help you identify what you spot, and there is a bird list so you will know if anyone has seen it before you. So far the list includes more than 275 species. Fifty-seven species of butterflies have been noted. Ask for the illustrated booklet on tide pools and the printed guide for the nature trail.

Since 1980, Peter has been growing exotic tropical fruits gathered from around the world on about 37 acres (15 ha) of his almost 400 acres (162 ha). His experimental station has the most extensive collection of tropical rare and exotic fruits in the country. Birds and guests alike can have their fill of more than 100 varieties, tasting such delicacies as star fruit (*carambola* in Spanish), passion fruit (*maracuyía*), guava, guanabana, custard apple (*anona*), jackfruit, *araza*, *abiu*, and dozens of others that are not yet household words. Peter's research on these fruits is intended to increase Costa Rica's nontraditional exports. Once, he reminds you, bananas and pineapples were considered rare and exotic fruits.

Animals also come out of the primary forest that covers more than half of his land to savor the fruits. You may cross paths with all four species of monkeys found in Costa Rica, with the coati, paca, white-lipped peccary, anteater, or cats such as the ocelot, jaguarundi, and margay. Trails take you through the fruit orchard, to a reforestation project of native and nonnative trees, to the beach at the bottom of the hill, and through the forest. There you find streams with clear pools where you can bathe in the company of kingfishers and hummingbirds, with giant trees spreading a canopy above. You can hike all the way to the hydroelectric system that, along with a backup diesel-powered generator, provides electricity to this remote place.

And remote it is. There is no telephone. Access is by air to a landing strip along the ocean or to Golfito and then by air again or overland to Tiskita. The 37-mile (60-km) drive from Golfito takes two-and-one-half hours. It is a fascinating trip through farm and ranch lands into a frontier region, crossing the Río Coto by ferry and fording other streams. A bridge now stretches across the Río Claro; I am sorry you will miss the adventure of driving through it, especially in the rainy season. That was something to write home about. When Peter first started coming to the area, he had to walk from where the boat left him. He first drove to the farm in 1980.

From the hilltop where the lodge and bungalows are located, you can look out at the Pacific and across to the Osa Peninsula. A visit to Corcovado National Park is an optional tour from Tiskita. A charter flight takes you to Sirena and back, allowing three to four hours to explore. It costs $90 per person, with a minimum of four.

Guests also can fish or surf. Nearby is the longest breaking left wave in the country, a 1,600-yard run at Punta Pavones. An Indian reserve borders Tiskita, which, by the way, is the Guaymi name for fish eagle. A visit to the Indian settlement can be arranged; dashing hats made by the Guaymis are for sale both at Tiskita and in San José at Costa Rica Sun Tours, which arranges visits to Tiskita and is operated by Peter's brother John. Horses can be rented for $25 per person.

Sleeping facilities at Tiskita include rooms separated from each other by a green area—a long, covered porch connects the rooms in front. Separate bungalows nestle against the forest, a short walk from the main lodge, with super baths that allow plenty of privacy yet are open enough to let you watch the birds while you shower.

The Aspinalls describe Tiskita as "five-star rustic." All the have private baths. The reserve's capacity is eighteen people.

Though fireflies sparkle in the evening, you will need your own flashlight for nighttime walks. In the rainy season, you will want rubber boots. Tiskita is closed in September and October because of the heavy rain.

Transportation: Round-trip costs from San José are included in package plans.

Rates: Daily rates are $92 for singles, $66 per person for doubles, including meals, trail map, and tax. If you are flying in, remember that domestic flights limit luggage to 26 pounds per passenger. Guided nature walks are $15. The basic package for three days and three nights (beginning Monday, Wednesday or Friday) is $495 per person for double occupancy, including air transportation, meals, hotel/airport transfers, and guided rain-forest and fruit-orchard walks; without the guided walks and hotel/airport transfers, the cost is $440. Ask about packages that combine stays at Tiskita with the Corcovado Tent Camp or Manuel Antonio. Four-day/four-night packages begin Thursdays and Saturdays. Ask for information about Fundación Tiskita, which has been set up to conserve and reforest land adjoining the lodge and to support local environmental education.

Reservations: Costa Rica Sun Tours, Apartado 1195-1250, Escazú. Telephone 695-5033, 255-2011; fax 255-3529. Sun Tours has an office at Avenida 7, Calles 3/5 in San José, where you can see photos and videos of Tiskita.

Caribbean

Aviarios del Caribe

At night, a flashlight revealed the yellow eyes of caimans along the bank of the Estrella River. At midmorning, from the same spot, I saw a river otter playing in the water, a purple gallinule strutting his stuff, and a little blue heron foraging at the river's edge. All of this from the upstairs veranda of the lodge at Aviarios del Caribe, 19 miles (30 km) south of Limón.

A private wildlife sanctuary that protects an island at the mouth of the Estrella River, freshwater canals and lagoons, and humid tropical forest, Aviarios del Caribe is a labor of love for owners Luis and Judy Arroyo. Gracious hosts, they warmly share with guests their lives and their vision of humanity as caretaker of habitat and creatures.

This particular habitat also includes sandy beaches and marshland along with the forest and waterways. Creatures there are monkeys, sloths, river turtles, sea turtles, frogs, lizards, butterflies, and aquatic, arboreal, migratory, and marine birds, plus birds of prey—264 species of birds so far. According to Luis, all six species of kingfishers found in Costa Rica are here, as well as the white-collared manakin, migrating orioles and warblers, collared aracaris, toucans, and even the black-crowned night-heron, which nests here but is uncommon in the Caribbean lowlands.

On a quiet canoe trip with Cali, a local guide who takes guests through the canals to the river's mouth and the Caribbean, we watched a boat-billed heron 15 feet (4.5 m) away as he watched us. I was almost within touching distance of a northern jacana, a pretty black and chestnut-colored bird with a striking yellow patch above its bill, before it took flight, revealing the yellow underside of its wing. When we got out of the canoe for a walk on the island, Cali deftly whacked off the top of a coconut with his machete—the liquid was marvelous in the morning heat.

On short trails through forest next to the lodge, you will probably see a sloth. You are sure to see one upstairs in the lodge—Buttercup has a private tree there, though she seems to prefer a corner of the soft couch. Judy nursed the injured baby three-toed sloth back to health after her mother was killed on the highway. Judy has an album she refers to as "Friends of Buttercup"—filled with photos taken by former guests who have sent back pictures.

The lodge has six bedrooms, all downstairs. The rooms are large with queen- or king-size beds, floor fans, and private baths with hot water. Fresh flowers say welcome, and there is a nice note from the maid, who, by the way guides a $10, two-hour night walk. Laundry service is available, and there is a small gym.

Upstairs is both an indoor and outdoor dining area and an inviting living area with a library, television/VCR, and tables for a variety of games such as chess, dominoes, Scrabble, and checkers. The outdoor terrace has lots of benches, an ideal spot for bird-watching—do not forget your binoculars. Next to the river is another covered deck and benches. The first time I met the Arroyos, Judy was cooking in a makeshift kitchen on that deck after the 1991 Limón earthquake. It hit just as they were finishing the lodge the first time, so they started over and have finished it again. The food is excellent.

The Arroyos will help arrange visits to other sites in the area. Cahuita National Park is only 6 miles (10 km) away.

Transportation: The entrance to Aviarios del Caribe is on the main highway from Limón to Cahuita. The San José-Sixaola bus passes three times a day, and the direct Puerto Viejo bus or buses from Limón will let you off right at the gate. A taxi from Limón is about $15.

Rates: Singles are $46 and doubles $68, including a full, delicious breakfast. Dinner is $12 per person from soup or salad to main dish to dessert. Lunch can be arranged as necessary. The canoe trip with a local guide is $25 per person and lasts up to three hours.

Reservations: Like many others along the Caribbean coast, the Arroyos are waiting for a telephone. In the meantime, fax 758-4459.

Cabinas Chimuri

For the traveler looking for adventure, a stay at Cabinas Chimuri outside Puerto Viejo de Limón may fit the bill. Mauricio Salazar, a Bribrí Indian, and his Austrian-born wife, Colocha, have a 49-acre (20-ha) natural reserve that offers an out-of-the-ordinary experience.

Traditional Bribrí structures house guests. Built on stilts, the buildings are of tropical wood and bamboo, the roofs thatched with cane. There are three doubles and one unit for four people, with shared baths (with shower-head hot water and flush toilets) a few steps away. You bring your own food and have use of a common kitchen, or, with advance notice, a cook can be arranged. Bedding is furnished. The complex is in a clearing surrounded by forest, and is reached via a five-minute foot trail from the road below. The Caribbean is 600 yards (500 m) from Chimuri.

Buttercup, the sloth that found a home at Aviarios del Caribe (Photo by Ree Strange Sheck)

The reserve offers good birding and a multitude of butterflies—a butterfly nursery is in the works. An afternoon in inviting pools in the river is great after a morning on the trails. Mauricio may accompany you at night to watch the animals in the forest. His eyes tell you he knows the jungle; his walk, that he is one with it.

Right on the reserve you are likely to see sloths, porcupines, agoutis, armadillos, tayras, coatis, anteaters, kinkajous, bats, poison dart frogs, boa constrictors, opossums, and iguanas. There are birds of prey, parrots, hummingbirds, trogons, motmots, jacamars, toucans, manakins, orioles, and tanagers. You can go on the trail by yourself or walk with Mauricio or trained local guides for about three hours at $10 per person. Bicycles and rubber boots may be rented. Bring repellent.

If you want to explore farther than the Chimuri reserve or the nearby Caribbean coast, there are optional tours. A one-day boat trip takes you on the Carbón River, which borders Cahuita National Park. A one-day walking tour takes you through abandoned cacao plantations to traditional Bribrí stomping grounds in the Kekoldi Indian reserve, where you will learn about plants used by the indigenous peoples for medicinal, construction, and other purposes. Along the trails you are likely to see a sloth, a raccoon, a toucan, iguanas, perhaps a snake.

The group, limited to five people, will stop by a friend's home to eat a picnic lunch and get a glimpse of life on the Indian reserve. The return is by a different trail. It is a hard trip, Mauricio says, intended for people in good physical condition.

If you are in really good condition, you can arrange for a three-day trip into the Talamanca Indian Reserve to experience a different type of vegetation, a wetter forest. Be prepared for rain, and bring insect repellent. The trip starts on a public bus to the beginning of the hiking trail. It is on foot to Suretka, Amubri, and farther up into the reserve, to an altitude of about 3,300 feet (1,000 m). On the return, you take a boat from Coroma to Suretka. A look at the map shows that the trek is in Costa Rica's frontier region with Panama. Trails are steep, and you will be carrying your own gear. Nights are spent in a Bribrí community house; bathing is Indian-style: in a creek. This trip is limited to six people, and Mauricio needs a week's notice to make arrangements.

Between the two of them, Mauricio and Colocha speak English, Spanish, German, and Bribrí. Hospitality is warm. If Mauricio's mother is visiting from the reserve, she may offer you a glass of *michilanga*, a delicious beverage of cooked plantain, coconut, and cinnamon. *Chimuri*, by the way, means ripe bananas in Bribrí, and a stalk is always hanging at the Salazars' house, where any hungry hand may reach out and take some.

Transportation: As you enter Puerto Viejo from Limón, watch on the right for the Cabinas Chimuri sign with a banana tree insignia on one side and a toucan on the other. From there, a short trail leads up to the cabins. Bus travelers should ask to be let off at the sign. (See Practical Extras for buses from San José or Limón.)

Rates: The double cabins cost $22 per day, the quadruple $33. The one-day tour is $25 per person. The three-day trip is $140 per person. Part of the tour fee is donated to the local Indian organization.

Reservations: Write to Mauricio Salazar, Cabinas Chimuri, Puerto Viejo de Limón, Talamanca, or call 758-3844 and leave a message. If you fax 758-0854, Mauricio or Colocha will call collect to confirm your reservation.

9
Nature Tour Companies: What They Offer

Nature travel tours in Costa Rica run the gamut from two people with a guide to a microbus of travelers, from hiking, bicycling, sailing, rafting, or kayaking to the standard overland tour by horseback, car, or bus. Just as Costa Rica is small and friendly, so are the nature tours I have tried out—no Greyhound-size buses trying to maneuver along narrow mountain roads, no herding people around like bodies that have to be moved. Chances are that by the time even a one-day tour is over, the guide will call you by name.

The companies included here specialize in nature travel. The listing begins with general nature travel, progressing to specializations: rafting/kayaking tours, cruises, and journeys to Tortuguero/Barra del Colorado. Finally, some of the companies outside Costa Rica that organize nature tours to the country are listed. Prices, of course, can change without notice. The listings of what each company offers are intended to give you an idea of the possibilities; they are not all-inclusive.

General Nature Travel

Two small companies that offer first-class nature travel are Geotur and Jungle Trails. Their bilingual guides are knowledgeable and personable.

Geotur is well known for its wildlife tour of Carara Biological Reserve. The one-day trip focuses on walks in the reserve but also includes a couple of hours at Jacó Beach for lunch, swimming, or a walk along the coast. At Carara, you not only see animals like monkeys, scarlet macaws, and crocodiles but may also get a close-up look through a telescope the guide carries, depending on the animal's cooperation, of course. Part of the $69-per-person fee is returned to Carara. Geotur is building and placing wooden nests for scarlet macaws in the reserve and on neighboring property under the watchful eyes of others who are also concerned about protection of this endangered species. According to Sergio Volio, the owner of Geotur, as many as 90 percent of the chicks in traditional nesting sites used by Carara's macaws are being poached to sell.

A day tour of Braulio Carrillo National Park is $69 with Geotur. Features include waterfalls, cloud forest, trails through lush vegetation, and encounters with wildlife. There is a stop at Costa Flores Farms, which has the world's largest collection of heliconias. A $69, one-day tour to San Gerardo de Dota is aimed at bird-watchers, with the big draw, of course, the chance to see the quetzal. Binoculars are essential. For hikers, there is a $45, half-day trek in the El Rodeo Forest Reserve above the University for Peace. Telephone 234-1867 or 224-1899, fax 253-6338.

Jungle Trails, *Los Caminos de la Selva* in Spanish, has an impressive array of tours and will customize expeditions throughout the country. An intriguing trip is the Let's Plant a Tropical Endangered Tree, in which people visit a native tree nursery in the Central Pacific area (where humid and dry forests meet) to learn what each tree is good for. Each person chooses one to plant at a watershed project in cooperation with Arbofilia (the Association for the Protection of Trees), a grass-roots ecological organization. After the tree-planting, a visit to Carara Biological Reserve shows what virgin forest is like. Part of the $75 cost buys the tree and contributes to Arbofilia. The fees for other tours also include donations to Arbofilia.

Other one-day tours with Jungle Trails, at $80 each, include walking through cloud forest on Barva Volcano, Braulio Carrillo, bird-watching or customized tours to any of the nearby parks or refuges, including an early departure for Poás to see the crater

Waterfall near Tango Mar on the Nicoya Peninsula (Photo by Ree Strange Sheck)

before clouds roll in. A $225, two-day trip combines either Barva and Poás or Braulio Carrillo, the Sarapiquí River area, and Poás, spending the night at Posada de Volcán Poás. (There is a minimum of four people.) A three-day trip explores Rincón de la Vieja on horseback. For $300, you can visit Cartago and nearby Lankester Gardens, go to Turrialba for a visit to CATIE, and then choose either a river trip or a visit to Turrialba Volcano or Guayabo National Monument—a three-day affair. Expeditions to Chirripó and Corcovado as well as to less-visited places such as Hitoy-Cerere, Caño Negro, and Barra Honda are available. Under a Trekking on Your Own program, Jungle Trails provides a hiking route with suggested campsites and information on necessary public transportation, and also will supply a guide if desired. On camping trips, all equipment except sleeping bags is furnished. The focus is on small groups. Telephone 255-3486, fax 255-2782. Jungle Trails' office is at Calle 38, Avenidas 5/7, near Centro Colón.

Costa Rica Expeditions, Horizontes Nature Adventures, and Costa Rica Sun Tours offer excellent nature-oriented tours of their own as well as booking a variety of tours offered by other companies.

Costa Rica Expeditions pioneered natural history travel in Costa Rica. A series of one-day trips under the heading of Tropical Forest Adventure offer travel with a professional naturalist for $69 to any of the following locations: Barva Volcano, El Tapir Private Reserve, Carara Biological Reserve, Cerro de la Muerte, Guayabo National Monument, Poás Volcano, Tapantí, or La Virgen del Socorro. Hiring a naturalist guide to accompany you on a private trip costs $154 a day; the guide plus transportation, covering 100 miles, is $314 a day. A day tour to Irazú Volcano and the Orosi Valley, including lunch, is $48. A half-day Poás tour is $28.

The company also has multiday packages that combine several destinations. For example, a nine-day trip for $1,425 per person (double occupancy, high season) includes in-country travel, lodging, guide, and some meals for either of the following: Costa Rica Odyssey, which combines the Monteverde Cloud Forest Preserve, Poás and Corcovado national parks, the Butterfly Farm, and whitewater rafting; or Costa Rica Explorer, which offers the Monteverde Cloud Forest Preserve, Arenal Volcano, EARTH (an agricultural school), Cahuita and Tortuguero national parks, and white-water rafting. You can write for a list of U.S. and Canadian companies that book trips for Costa Rica Expeditions, for the convenience of dealing with someone in your area. The company's white-water and Tortuguero tours are mentioned under specialty tours. Telephone 222-0333 or 257-0766, fax 257-1665. Costa Rica Expeditions owns the Monteverde Lodge, Tortuga Lodge, and Corcovado Lodge Tent Camp. Its office is at Avenida 3, Calles Central/2.

Horizontes specializes in nature adventures and in personalized service, for both groups and individuals. It works to provide just the right itinerary for what travelers want to see or do, taking into account physical abilities, budget, length of visit, and time of year. The staff wants to make sure clients do not take off on a trip that is too long or too tough.

Basically, Horizontes acts as a reservation center, booking arrangements with private reserves, hotels, naturalist guides, and nature companies that it feels will give people an excellent experience. The company handles both one-day and multiday tours. Its office is at Calle 28, Avenidas 1/3 (just north of the Pizza Hut on Paseo Colón). Telephone 222-2022, fax 255-4513.

Costa Rica Sun Tours operates two private nature reserves: Arenal Observatory Lodge and Tiskita Biological Reserve. The Arenal Volcano Night Tour is $70, including stops at Zarcero for the topiary and at the hot springs at El Tabacón. The tour operates every Tuesday, Thursday, and Saturday. A two-day, one-night tour is $195 with a bilingual naturalist, $165 with a driver and guide service only at Arenal. You can add a visit to Caño Negro Wildlife Refuge, La Pacífica, or Monteverde. Visits to Tiskita, a remote area south of Golfito, are $495 for three days and three nights. (See chapter 8 for details on tours to Tiskita Biological Reserve and Arenal Observatory Lodge.)

Sun Tours has a ten-day Pure Adventure tour that combines climbing on Mount Chirripó with exploring Corcovado and Caño Island—for those in good physical shape. The cost is $1,330 each, double occupancy. An eight-day Costa Rica Sampler takes in Braulio Carrillo, Carara, a cruise in the Gulf of Nicoya, and rafting, at $860 per person.

Boat trip to Caño Negro (Photo by Ree Strange Sheck)

The company will custom-design a multiday trip for you. Its office on Avenida 7, Calles 3/5 (one block north of the Aurola Holiday Inn) has an Eco-Center, which is a reservation and information center for a number of country lodges and private reserves. Drop by to see its videos and photographs of possible destinations. Telephone 255-2112 or 255-2011, fax 255-3529.

Tikal Tour Operators is a full-service travel agency that also specializes in nature travel. It has fixed departures for most one-day natural history trips, led by professional naturalists. For $69, there are tours to Guayabo park, horseback riding near Poás, or a Jungle Bus that goes to a coffee farm, Turrialba, Limón, a banana plantation, and Braulio Carrillo park. For $29, there is the Snakes of Costa Rica tour (to the Serpentarium and Clodomiro Picado Institute), or visits to Sarchí, Poás, Irazú, and Lankester Gardens.

Multiday trips cover the country. The Pacific Ecosafari goes to Manuel Antonio, Palo Verde, and Santa Rosa national parks, Tamarindo Wildlife Refuge, Carara Biological Reserve, the private reserve at Eco-Lodge, and Arenal Volcano. The cost is $749 each, double occupancy. The Caribbean Ecosafari includes Caño Negro National Wildlife Reserve, Tortuguero and Cahuita national parks, and the San Juan and Saripiquí rivers, for $823. Each of these tours takes eight days and seven nights. Other multiday trips feature mountain biking, rafting, wind surfing, diving, fishing, turtles, and a sports tour consisting of horseback riding, canoeing, biking, snorkeling, hiking, and river floating.

By the way, Tikal is helpful arranging an exit visa for visitors who overstay their legal limit. Telephone 223-2811, fax 223-1916. The office is at Avenida 2, Calles 7/9.

Guanacaste Tours is a regional company that includes a variety of historical/cultural and natural history destinations. Sample day tours, schedules, and prices are Tempisque River-Palo Verde, Tuesday and Friday, $75; rain forest and Arenal, Wednesday and Saturday, $90; turtle tour at Ostional, June through November, $50, Playa Grande, November to March, $40, and Santa Rosa and Los Inocentes, Thursday, $70. Bilingual biologist guides are available. Departures are usually from Guanacaste hotels, but are also from San José for Palo Verde and Arenal. Telephone 666-0306 or 234-8020, fax 666-0307 or 234-8022.

Rafting/Kayaking

Some companies that offer river tours are Costaricaraft, Costa Rica Expeditions, and Ríos Tropicales. All have trained, bilingual guides and good equipment. If you have never rafted or kayaked before, this is a new way to experience the natural world. There are trips for beginners, and each company offers instruction. All offer one-day trips year-round on the Reventazón near Turrialba (both rapids and calm stretches passing through spectacular landscape) and the Coribicí near Cañas (a float trip good for wildlife viewing, especially birds and monkeys), both at around $70. The one-day Pacuare trip is about $90.

Costaricaraft has a $220, two-day Pacuare River rafting trip, which is great for seeing wildlife. Rafters hike to a nearby waterfall. A four-day trip on the General River is $410. One-day Sarapiquí trips are also offered. Scheduled trips are from one to three days, but staff members also design custom packages. Kayaks may be rented. Telephone 225-3939 or 224-0505, fax 253-6934. The office is in San Pedro.

Costa Rica Expeditions offers a day-trip option on the Sarapiquí from May to November for $69 plus runs for experienced rafters on the Reventazón, in addition to the easy-to-moderate Reventazón run. Scheduled trips from June 15 to December 15 include up to two days on the Pacuare and up to four on the Chirripó. Telephone 222-0333 or 257-0766, fax 257-1665. The office is at Avenida 3, Calles Central/2.

Ríos Tropicales has both raft and kayak trips. A two-day Pacuare raft trip is $250, while the one-day Sarapiquí from July to January is $70. The company's four-day Río General trip runs from June to December only. There are also multiday trips to the Golfito area, to the Nicoya Peninsula near Curú Wildlife Refuge, and to Manuel Antonio. A ten-day rafting/kayaking adventure on the General, Reventazón, and Pacuare rivers is $1,470.

Trekking adventures are also offered for a minimum of six people by Dos Montañas, a division of Ríos Tropicales, either as part of a rafting or kayaking package or separately. Trips range from three to fifteen days and can focus on a destination such as Chirripó or involve treks in the rain forest, some of which allow for interchange with the Indian culture. There is also a one-day biking trip to Tapantí and an eight-day raft and ride tour. Telephone 233-6455, fax 255-4354. The office is at Avenida 2, Calle 32. The U.S. representative for multiday trips with Ríos Tropicales is Baja

Expeditions, at (800) 843-6967. It also has a branch in Manuel Antonio: Iguana Tours, which offers trips on the Savegre and Naranjo rivers and kayaking at Manuel Antonio and Isla de Damas.

Ríos Tropicales has a small outdoor store, Tienda de Aventura, with equipment for camping, hiking, climbing, and some water sports.

Cruises

Several companies offer day trips by yacht through the Gulf of Nicoya to Tortuga Island. Passengers are wined and dined during the daylong outing, with time for swimming, snorkeling, or just relaxing. The cost is about $70 from San José.

Calypso Tours, the originator of the island cruise to Tortuga Island, offers several packages that combine the island cruise with something else: a three-day, two-night visit to Monteverde for $347 per person; a two-day, one-night visit to Carara for $172; or a three-day tour to Tango Mar on the Nicoya Peninsula for $407. These prices are based on double occupancy. The company also has a ten-day charter trip to Coco Island on a yacht costing $850 per day. Telephone 233-3617, fax 233-0401.

Costa Sol Tropical Cruises offers a one-day trip to Tortuga on weekends, but will also make other bookings. Telephone 239-2000, fax 239-4839. Fantasia Island Cruise, telephone 221-8477 or 222-4752, fax 223-1013, also has gulf trips.

Cruceros de Sur has multiday sailing trips on the *Temptress*, a cruise ship with a capacity of 60 passengers, air conditioning, and private baths. The staff includes bilingual naturalists and diving and photography instructors. (The ship has its own photo lab.) The seven-day Pacific Voyage visits Curú National Wildlife Refuge, Corcovado and Drake Bay, Caño Island, Manuel Antonio park, and Carara. The high season cost is $1,495 per person, double occupancy. A three-day Curú Voyage includes the wildlife refuge and also Corcovado and Manuel Antonio for $745. The price and length are the same for the Caño Voyage, which includes Manuel Antonio, Caño Island, Corcovado, and Carara. Rates are lower from June to September. The *Temptress* travels at night, so you have the

Folk dances offered on island cruise tour (Photo by Ree Strange Sheck)

daytime to enjoy the destinations. The guides are knowledgeable, and both food and personal service are excellent. The company also offers 10-day diving trips to Coco Island for $2,495 per person. Telephone 220-1679, fax 220-2103.

Canal Trips—Tortuguero/Barra del Colorado

Four companies that offer package trips along the canals in the Caribbean lowlands are Adventure Tours, Costa Rica Expeditions, Cotur, and Ilan-Ilan. This is definitely a trip where the journey is as important as the destination. The April 1991 earthquake that struck hard on the Caribbean coast made access by canal from

Limón difficult. Larger boats sometimes depart now from Hamburgo, and some companies are using the Sarapiquí/San Juan rivers.

Adventure Tours is affiliated with Río Colorado Lodge in Barra del Colorado, where overnight guests stay. With more peaceful conditions along the northern border with Nicaragua, Adventure Tours has reopened the route Río Colorado Lodge pioneered, a two-day, one-night tour on the Río Sarapiquí to the San Juan River (on the frontier) and then on the Colorado River, which flows through Barra del Colorado National Wildlife Refuge. The trip includes lodging at Río Colorado Lodge and a visit to Tortuguero National Park. There is an optional nighttime turtle tour from mid-July through September for $25. The $196 river trip is aboard the twenty-four-passenger *Colorado Queen*, departing from Puerto Viejo de Sarapiquí and returning through Limón and Braulio Carrillo. Telephone 232-4063, fax 231-5987. The office in the Hotel Coribicí. In the U.S. and Canada, telephone (800) 243-9777, fax 813-933-3280.

Costa Rica Expeditions offers a two-day, two-night tour to Tortuguero, a bus through Braulio Carrillo National Park, the canal trip, guides, lodging and meals at Tortuga Lodge, and a return by air. The cost of $365 each for two people drops to $265 for four. A one-day, one-night tour starts at $199 each for four people, $299 for two. Telephone 257-0766, fax 257-1665. The office is at Avenida 3, Calles Central/2.

Cotur has a three-day, two-night tour to Tortuguero for $218, double occupancy, with accommodations at the Jungle Lodge and the canal trip on the *Miss America* going and coming. A two-day, one-night tour is $160. Air transportation is arranged for an additional charge. Departures are Tuesday, Friday, and Sunday. Telephone 233-0133, fax 233-0778. The office is at Paseo Colón/ Avenida 1, Calle 36.

Ilan-Ilan has a three-day, two-night visit to Tortuguero, cruising on the canals in the *Colorado Prince* or *Tortuguero Prince*. On the way, there is a stop at Braulio Carrillo and a banana operation. Lodging is at the Hotel Ilan-Ilan. The trip costs $215 per person, including three guided jungle walks. The two-day, one-night tour is

$162 per person. There is an optional turtle observation tour from July to September. Telephone 255-2031 or 255-2262, fax 255-1946. The office is on Paseo Colón just west of the Children's Hospital.

Some U.S. Companies with Nature Tours to Costa Rica

Many tour companies offer trips to Costa Rica. Here are a few of those that specialize in nature travel.

Costa Rica Connection has a nine-day, eight-night national parks tour that begins at $1,670 from Los Angeles or $1,445 from Miami, with visits to Tortuguero and Manuel Antonio parks. It can be extended to Santa Rosa and Corcovado parks. A donation to foundations that support national parks and private reserves is made for each parks tour sold. Specialty tours focus on birding, orchids, beaches, adventure, and language and culture. The eight-day, seven-night Costa Rica Odyssey tour combines the Monteverde Cloud Forest Preserve, beaches, a Pacific island cruise, and sightseeing in San José. Prices begin at $1,449 per person from Los Angeles. Send for their brochure. Telephone (805) 543-8823, fax (805) 543-3626. The address is 975 Osos Street, San Luis Obispo, CA 93401. In the U.S., telephone (800) 345-7422.

Geo Expeditions has a ten-day natural history tour, Costa Rica Explorer, that focuses on Poás and Tortuguero national parks, Monteverde Cloud Forest Preserve, Arenal Volcano, and Caño Negro, accompanied by first-class naturalist guides. The high-season cost is $1,516. The eight-day Best of Costa Rica Tour takes in Corcovado, Caño Island, Arenal Volcano, and Monteverde, for $1,195. Costs do not include international airfare. Telephone (800) 351-5041 or (209) 532-0152, fax (209) 532-1979. Or write to Box 3656, Sonora, CA 95370.

The biologists and ecologists of Geostar Travel design tours for visitors with natural history interests. Naturalists lead the ten-day Costa Rica Explorer to Monteverde Cloud Forest Preserve, Poás, Arenal Volcano, Caño Negro, and Tortuguero, plus a trip on the Reventazón River and a stay at EARTH, an agricultural school. The cost during the high season is $1,516. The ten-day Odyssey tour visits Monteverde, Poás, and Corcovado and also includes visits to a butterfly farm and white-water rafting. It costs $1,425 in the high season. Birding and botanical tours also are offered. Telephone (800) 624-6633 or (707) 579-2420, fax (707) 579-2704. The address is 1240 Century Court, Santa Rosa, CA 95403.

Wildland Adventures offers tours as well as an individual trip planner that lets you build your own program. The eleven-day Tropical Trails Odyssey travels to Poás, Monteverde, Palo Verde, Tarcoles (near Carara), and the Osa Peninsula. The Wildlands Hiking Safari, also eleven days, goes to Palo Verde, Arenal Volcano, Cahuita, and Manzanillo Wildlife Refuge, including a boat trip on the Bebedero and Tempisque rivers, a hike to natural hot springs, a stop at the Selva Verde forest and butterfly garden, and a hike in the Cocles Indian Reserve with a native guide. These tours are limited to fourteen people. For prices, telephone (800) 345-4453 or (206) 365-0686; fax (206) 363-6615. The address is 3516 NE 155th, Seattle, WA 98155.

Osprey Tours specializes in individual and group travel to Latin America. It offers natural history tours with a bent toward birding, along with general natural history, botany, archaeology, and geology. Escorted or guided tours include Palo Verde park, Caño Negro Wildlife Refuge, Lomas Barbudal and Carara biological reserves, and Monteverde. The company has tours for travelers who want to "go rustic" or stay in luxury hotels, travel by bus, rental car, or horseback, or charter a plane. There are two offices: Box 030211, Fort Lauderdale, FL 33303-0211, telephone (305) 767-4823, fax (305) 767-4824; and Box 832, West Tisbury, Martha's Vineyard, MA 02575-0832, telephone (508) 645-9049, fax (508) 645-3244.

Preferred Adventures does customized individual travel as well as tours for birders, horticulturists, and natural history travelers. Prices range from $1,355 for ten days to $2,795 for fourteen days, excluding airfare to Costa Rica. Telephone (612) 222-8131, fax (612) 222-4221. The address is One West Water Street, Suite 300, St. Paul, MN 55107.

Americas Tours and Travel offers individual itineraries emphasizing Costa Rica as a nature destination. It encourages travel to the private reserves and to less-visited parks and reserves as well as the more popular ones. Telephone (206) 623-8850 or (800) 553-2513, fax (206) 467-0454. The company is at 1402 Third Avenue No. 1019, Seattle, WA 98101-2110.

Laughing Heart Adventures offers nine-day sea kayaking tours to Costa Rica, traveling in the Gulf of Nicoya and along the Pacific Coast of the Nicoya Peninsula. The cost is $1,385, plus international air fare. The focus is on nature, with qualified guides. Both arrival and departure nights are spent in a hotel; the rest, camping out. Telephone (800) 541-1256 or (916) 629-3516. Or write to Box 669, Willow Creek, CA 95573.

Practical Extras

International Airline Information

In San José

Airline	Address	Reservations	Airport
Aero Costa Rica	La Uruca, in front of Shell station	296-1111	443-2707
American	Across from Hotel Corobicí, Calle 42	257-1266 441-0841	441-1168
Continental	Avenida 2, Calles 19/21	233-0266	442-1904
LACSA	Calle 1, Avenida 5	231-0033	441-6244
Mexicana	Calle 38, Avenida 5	222-1711	441-9377
SAHSA	Avenida 5, Calles 1/3	221-5561 221-5774	441-1064
TACA	Avenida 3, Calle 40	222-1790	441-5090
United	La Sabana	220-4844	441-8025

Reservation Numbers—United States and Canada

Aero Costa Rica	(800) 237-6274, (800) 320-8111, United States
American	(800) 433-7300, United States and Canada
Continental	(800) 525-0280, United States
LACSA	(800) 225-2272, United States and Canada
Mexicana	(800) 531-7921, United States (800) 531-7923, Canada
SAHSA	(800) 327-1225, United States
TACA	(800) 535-8780, United States
United	(800) 241-6552, United States

Costa Rican Tourism Institute

San José
Plaza de la Cultura
Calle 5, Avenidas Central/2
Telephone 222-1090
442-1820 (airport office)
(800) 327-7033, United States
Fax 223-5452

Private Information Service

INFOtur: Computerized Information Service
San José
Avenida 2, Calle 5
Telephone 223-4481 or 223-4482, fax 223-4476
Branch office in Liberia
Access via computer:
1. (506) 257-2000 or (506) 253-2000
2. For net users, the code is 0712211201000
3. Press H (capital) and enter
4. Press Ninfrac-211201000 and enter
5. Communicate via menus, using first two letters of option. In internal level, use number codes.

Embassies in San José

United States
Rohrmoser, road to Pavas
 in front of Centro Comercial
 (any taxi driver can take you)
Telephone 220-3939

Canada
Edificio Cronos, sixth floor
 Avenida Central, Calle 3
Telephone 255-3522 or 228-5154

France
Road to Curridabat, near Indoor Club
Telephone 225-0733 or 225-0933

Germany
Avenida 5, Calles 40/42
Telephone 232-5533 or 222-6671

Great Britain
Edificio Centro Colón, eleventh floor
Avenida Colón, Calle 38
Telephone 221-5566 or 221-5816

Holland
Los Yoses
Telephone 234-0949 or 234-0950

Italy
Los Yoses, Avenida 10, Calles 33/35
Telephone 224-6574 or 234-2326

Japan
Residencial Rohrmoser,
400 meters west,
100 north of La Nunciatura
Telephone 231-3140 or 232-1255

Spain
Calle 32, Paseo Colon/Avenida 2
Telephone 222-1933 or 222-0994

Switzerland
Centro Colon, fourth floor
Paseo Colón, Calle 38
Telephone 221-4829

Transportation Tidbits

Ferries

Puntarenas ferry (Puntarenas-Playa Naranjo on Nicoya Peninsula) Telephone 661-1069, car fee about $9, passengers a bit more than $1 each

Leaves Puntarenas 3:30 a.m., 7:00 a.m., 10:50 a.m., 2:50 p.m., 7:00 p.m.
Leaves Playa Naranjo 5:10 a.m., 8:50 a.m., 12:50 p.m., 5:00 p.m., 9:00 p.m.

Tempisque ferry (across mouth of Tempisque River) Telephone 685-5295, car and driver about $3, passengers less than 25 cents each

Leaves Puerto Níspero (mainland side) at 5 a.m. and Puerto Moreno (on the peninsula) at 5:30 a.m., continuous service until 7 p.m.

Paquera Launch (Puntarenas to Paquera on Nicoya Peninsula)
Telephone 661-2830 or 661-1444, extension 118, passengers only,
less than $2 each
  Leaves Puntarenas from behind market at 6:15 a.m., 11:00 a.m.
and 3:00 p.m.
  Leaves Paquera at 8:00 a.m., 12:30 p.m. and 5:00 p.m.

Domestic Airline Scheduled Service
SANSA
San José office at Calle 24, Paseó Colón/Avenida 1, Telephone 233-0397
  or 233-3258; fax 255-2176
Daily flights to Golfito, Nosara, Quepos, Sámara, Tamarindo
San José to and from Barra del Colorado, Palmar Sur, Tambor, and
  Tortuguero on Tuesday, Thursday, and Saturday
San José to and from Coto 47, daily except Sunday
Quepos to Palmar Sur to Puerto Jiménez to San José on Monday,
  Wednesday, and Friday

Travelair
San José office at Tobias Bolaños Airport in Pavas, Telephone 220-3054,
  fax 220-0413
Daily flights to Barra del Colorado, Carrillo, Golfito, Nosara, Palmar
  Sur, Puerto Jiménez, Quepos, Tamarindo, Tambor, Tortuguero

Taxis
If you have access to a phone directory, you can look in the yellow
pages for taxis, or your hotel can call one for you. Here are a few in
San José, since public phones do not have phone books.
Taxis Unidos—221-6865, 441-0333 (airport)
Coopetico—253-5838, 253-5691
Taxis San Jorge—222-0025, 221-3434, 221-3535

Intercity Buses

These are the addresses of bus stops in San José for the cities indicated, phone numbers, and length of trip. Sometimes there is a terminal; sometimes there is only a sign on the street indicating the bus stop. Check with the ICT Information Office or INFOtur for departure times, and to make sure the bus stop has not been moved.

Airport (Juan Santamaría): Avenida 2, Calles 12/14 (24-hour service, leaving every 10 minutes from 5:30 a.m. to 7:00 p.m., then less frequently), 222-5325, 20 minutes

Alajuela: Avenida 2, Calles 12/14 (same as above), 222-5325

Barva Volcano-Braulio Carrillo: From central market in Heredia bus to Paso Llano), three times daily, twice on Sunday, then walk to park

Braulio Carrillo National Park: Calle 12, Avenidas 7/9 (every half hour from 5:30 a.m. to 7:00 p.m.), 223-1276 (this is the Guapiles bus; get off at the ranger station)

Cahuita: Avenida 11, Calles Central/1, three times daily (this is the bus for Sixaola), 221-0524, 4 hours

Cañas: Calle 16, Avenidas 3/5 (buy ticket in advance), five times daily, 222-3006, 3 hours

Cartago: Avenida 18, Calle 5 (every ten minutes from 5:00 a.m. to 7:00 p.m., then less frequently), 232-5350, 45 minutes

Ciudad Quesada (San Carlos): Calle 16, Avenidas 1/3 (every hour from 5:00 a.m. to 7:30 p.m.), 255-4318, 3 hours

Ciudad Quesada-La Fortuna: Municipal bus station in Ciudad Quesada (take bus for El Tanque), 460-0326, 1 hour

Ciudad Quesada-Arenal-Tilarán: Municipal bus station in Ciudad Quesada (goes through Fortuna and around Lake Arenal and Volcano), 4 hours

Fortuna: Calle 16, Avenidas 1/3, 232-5660, 4½ hours

Golfito: express bus, (buy ticket in advance), 221-4214, 8 hours

Heredía: Calle 1, Avenidas 7/9, (every 10 minutes from 5:00 a.m. to 10:00 p.m.), 233-8392, 25 minutes; or microbuses from Avenida 2, Calles 10/12

Jacó Beach: Calle 16, Avenidas 1/3, 232-1829, 2½ hours

Junquillal: Calle 20, Avenida 3 (daily express), 221-7202, 5 hours

La Cruz or Peñas Blancas: Calle 16, Avenidas 3/5, 238-2725, 6 hours

Liberia: Calle 14, Avenidas 1/3 (several express buses daily, ticket in advance), 222-1650, 4 hours

Limón: Avenida 3, Calles 19/21 (hourly from 5:00 a.m. to 7:00 p.m., through Braulio Carrillo), 223-7811, 2½ hours

Limón-Cahuita-Puerto Viejo: Leaves from Radio Casino in Limón, four times daily

Manuel Antonio: see Quepos

Monteverde: Calle 14, Avenidas 9/11 (tickets in advance), 222-3854, 4 hours; or La Toruma Youth Hostel, Avenida Central, Calles 29/31, 224-4085, 645-5051 (in Monteverde)

Monteverde-Tilarán: from Santa Elena (3 km from Monteverde), 3 hours

Nicoya: Calle 14, Avenidas 3/5 (buy tickets in advance, 222-2750, 6 hours

Nosara (Garza and Guiones): Calle 14, Avenidas 3/5, 222-2750, 5 hours

Playa del Coco: Calle 14, Avenidas 1/3, 222-1650, 5 hours

Puerto Jiménez (for Corcovado): Calle 12, Avenida 7/9 (twice daily), 771-2550, 8 hours

Puerto Viejo de Limón: Avenida 11, Calles Central/1 (bus for Sixaola, get off at El Cruce), 221-0524, 4½ hours; or direct to Puerto Viejo, once daily

Puerto Viejo de Sarapiquí: Calle 12, Avenidas 7/9, 4 hours; or the Río Frío route through Guapiles, Avenida 11, Calles Central/1

Puntarenas: Calle 12, Avenidas 7/9 (every 40 minutes from 5:00 a.m. to 7:00 p.m), 222-0064, 2 hours

Puntarenas to Quepos: Main bus station in Puntarenas, twice daily, 777-0318, 3½ hours

Quepos and Manuel Antonio: Calle 16, Avenidas 1/3, express from lot beside Hotel Musoc (advance tickets in adjacent market), 223-5567, 3½ hours

Quepos-Dominical-San Isidro: Municipal market in Quepos (twice daily), 771-1384, 3½ hours

Sámara and Carrillo beaches: Calle 14, Avenidas 3/5 (daily express), 222-2750, 6 hours

San Isidro de El General: Calle 16, Avenidas 1/3 (every hour from 5:30 a.m. to 5:00 p.m., advance tickets), 222-2422, 3 hours; in San Isidro get bus for San Gerardo de Rivas (233-4160) for Chirripó

San Isidro-Puerto Jiménez: Next to church (twice daily), 773-3010, 5 hours

San Vito: Avenida 5, Calle 16 (advance tickets), 222-2750, 5 hours

Santa Cruz: Calle 20, Avenidas 1/3, 221-7202, 5 hours

Sarchí: Calle 16, Avenida 1/3, express, 1½ hours; or bus to Sarchí from Alajuela, from Avenida Calle 8, Avenida Central/1 in Alajuela; 441-3781

Tamarindo: Calle 14, Avenida 3/5, 222-2750, 223-8229, 5½ hours; or Calle 20, Avenidas 3/5, 221-7202, 6 hours

Tilarán: Calle 14, Avenidas 9/11, four times daily, 222-3854, 4 hours

Turrialba: Calle 13, Avenidas 6/8 (hourly express from 5:00 a.m. to 10:00 p.m.), 556-0073, 1½ hours

Zarcero: Calle 16, Avenidas 1/3 (hourly bus from 5:00 a.m. to 7:30 p.m.—Ciudad Quesada bus), 255-4318, 1½ hours

Metric Conversion Tables

To change	to	Multiply by
Hectares	Acres	2.4710
Meters	Feet	3.2808
Kilometers	Miles	.6214
Millimeters	Inches	.0394
Centimeters	Inches	.3937
Square kilometers	Square miles	.3861
Liters	Gallons (U.S.)	.2642
Kilograms	Pounds	2.2050

Temperature

Celsius to Fahrenheit: multiply by 9/5 and add 32.

Fahrenheit to Celsius: subtract 32 and multiply by 5/9.

Here are some reference points to save some of the math:

Celsius	Fahrenheit
0°	32°
10°	50°
20°	68°
30°	86°
35°	95°
40°	104°

Fauna: English and Spanish Names

English	Spanish
Agouti	Guatusa
Lesser anteater, tamandua	Oso hormiguero
Silky anteater	Serafín
Armadillo	Cusuco
Bat	Murciélago
Bird	Pájaro, ave
Butterfly	Mariposa
Caiman	Caimán
Coati	Pizote
Cougar, mountain lion	Puma, león
Crocodile	Cocodrilo
Brocket deer	Cabra de monte
White-tailed deer	Venado cola blanca
Frog	Rana
Gopher	Taltusa
Jaguar	Jaguar, tigre
Jaguarundi	León breñero
Kinkajou	Martilla
Scarlet macaw	Lapa
Margay	Caucel, tigrillo
Howler monkey	Mono congo
Spider monkey	Mono colorado, mono araña
Squirrel monkey	Mono tití, mono ardilla
White-faced capuchin monkey	Mono cara blanca
Ocelot	Manigordo
Opossum	Zorro
River otter	Nutria, perro de agua
Paca	Tepezcuintle
Parrot	Loro
Collared peccary	Saíno
White-lipped peccary	Cariblanco
Raccoon	Mapachín
Skunk	Zorro hediondo

English	Spanish
Sloth	Perezoso, perica
Snake	Serpiente, culebra
Squirrel	Ardilla, chisa
Tapir	Danta
Tayra	Tolomuco
Toad	Sapo
Turtle	Tortuga

Recommended Reading

A Naturalist in Costa Rica, Alexander F. Skutch. Gainesville: University of Florida Press, 1971.

The Costa Ricans, Richard Biesanz, Karen Zubris Biesanz, and Mavis Hiltunen Biesanz. Englewood Cliffs, N.J.: Prentice-Hall, 1982.

Costa Rican Natural History, edited by Daniel H. Janzen. Chicago: University of Chicago Press, 1983.

The Butterflies of Costa Rica and Their Natural History, Philip J. DeVries. Princeton: Princeton University Press, 1987.

Costa Rica National Parks, Mario A. Boza. Madrid: Incafo (for Fundación Neotrópica de Costa Rica), 1988.

The Rivers of Costa Rica: A Canoeing, Kayaking, and Rafting Guide, Michael W. Mayfield and Rafael E. Gallo. Birmingham, Ala.: Menasha Ridge Press, 1988.

Journey through a Tropical Jungle, Adrian Forsyth. Toronto: Greey de Pencier Books, 1988.

A Guide to the Birds of Costa Rica, F. Gary Stiles and Alexander F. Skutch. Ithaca: Cornell University Press, 1989.

The New Key to Costa Rica, Beatrice Blake. San José: Publications in English, 1991.

The Quetzal and the Macaw: The Story of Costa Rica's National Parks, David Rains Wallace. San Francisco: Sierra Book Club, 1992.

Index

Other Books from John Muir Publications

Travel Books by Rick Steves
Asia Through the Back Door, 4th ed., 400 pp. $16.95
Europe 101: History and Art for the Traveler, 4th ed., 372 pp. $15.95
Europe Through the Back Door, 12th ed., 434 pp. $17.95
Europe Through the Back Door Phrase Book: French, 112 pp. $4.95
Europe Through the Back Door Phrase Book: German, 112 pp. $4.95
Europe Through the Back Door Phrase Book: Italian, 112 pp. $4.95
Europe Through the Back Door Phrase Book: Spanish & Portuguese, 288 pp. $6.95
Mona Winks: Self-Guided Tours of Europe's Top Museums, 2nd ed., 456 pp. $16.95
See the 2 to 22 Days series to follow for other Rick Steves titles.

A Natural Destination Series
Belize: A Natural Destination, 2nd ed., 304 pp. $16.95
Costa Rica: A Natural Destination, 3rd ed., 320 pp. $16.95 (available 8/94)
Guatemala: A Natural Destination, 336 pp. $16.95

Undiscovered Islands Series
Undiscovered Islands of the Caribbean, 3rd ed., 264 pp. $14.95
Undiscovered Islands of the Mediterranean, 2nd ed., 256 pp. $13.95
Undiscovered Islands of the U.S. and Canadian West Coast, 288 pp. $12.95

For Birding Enthusiasts
The Birder's Guide to Bed and Breakfasts, U.S. and Canada, 288 pp. $15.95
The Visitor's Guide to the Birds of the Central National Parks: U.S. and Canada, 400 pp. $15.95 (available 8/94)
The Visitor's Guide to the Birds of the Eastern National Parks: U.S. and Canada, 400 pp. $15.95
The Visitor's Guide to the Birds of the Rocky Mountain National Parks, U.S. and Canada, 432 pp. $15.95

Unique Travel Series
Each is 112 pages and $10.95 paper.
Unique Arizona (available 9/94)
Unique California (available 9/94)
Unique Colorado
Unique Florida
Unique New England
Unique New Mexico
Unique Texas

2 to 22 Days Series
Each title offers 22 flexible daily itineraries useful for planning vacations of any length. Included are "must see" attractions as well as hidden "jewels."
2 to 22 Days in the American Southwest, 1994 ed., 192 pp. $10.95
2 to 22 Days in Asia, 1994 ed., 176 pp. $10.95
2 to 22 Days in Australia, 1994 ed., 192 pp. $10.95
2 to 22 Days in California, 1994 ed., 192 pp. $10.95
2 to 22 Days in Eastern Canada, 1994 ed., 192 pp. $12.95
2 to 22 Days in Europe, 1994 ed., 304 pp. $14.95
2 to 22 Days in Florida, 1994 ed., 192 pp. $10.95
2 to 22 Days in France, 1994 ed., 192 pp. $10.95
2 to 22 Days in Germany, Austria, and Switzerland, 1994 ed., 240 pp. $12.95
2 to 22 Days in Great Britain, 1994 ed., 208 pp. $10.95
2 to 22 Days Around the Great Lakes, 1994 ed., 192 pp. $10.95
2 to 22 Days in Hawaii, 1994 ed., 192 pp. $10.95
2 to 22 Days in Italy, 1994 ed., 208 pp. $10.95
2 to 22 Days in New England, 1994 ed., 192 pp. $10.95
2 to 22 Days in New Zealand, 1994 ed., 192 pp. $10.95
2 to 22 Days in Norway, Sweden, and Denmark, 1994 ed., 192 pp. $10.95
2 to 22 Days in the Pacific Northwest, 1994 ed., 192 pp. $10.95
2 to 22 Days in the Rockies, 1994 ed., 192 pp. $10.95
2 to 22 Days in Spain and Portugal, 1994 ed., 208 pp. $10.95
2 to 22 Days in Texas, 1994 ed., 192 pp. $10.95
2 to 22 Days in Thailand, 1994 ed., 192 pp. $10.95

22 Days (or More) Around the World, 1994 ed., 264 pp. $13.95

Other Terrific Travel Titles
The 100 Best Small Art Towns in America, 256 pp. $12.95 (available 8/94)

Elderhostels: The Students' Choice, 2nd ed., 304 pp. $15.95

Environmental Vacations: Volunteer Projects to Save the Planet, 2nd ed., 248 pp. $16.95

A Foreign Visitor's Guide to America, 224 pp. $12.95

Great Cities of Eastern Europe, 256 pp. $16.95

Indian America: A Traveler's Companion, 3rd ed., 432 pp. $18.95

Interior Furnishings Southwest, 256 pp. $19.95

Opera! The Guide to Western Europe's Great Houses, 296 pp. $18.95

Paintbrushes and Pistols: How the Taos Artists Sold the West, 288 pp. $17.95

The People's Guide to Mexico, 9th ed., 608 pp. $18.95

Ranch Vacations: The Complete Guide to Guest and Resort, Fly-Fishing, and Cross-Country Skiing Ranches, 3rd ed., 512 pp. $19.95

The Shopper's Guide to Art and Crafts in the Hawaiian Islands, 272 pp. $13.95

The Shopper's Guide to Mexico, 224 pp. $9.95

Understanding Europeans, 272 pp. $14.95

A Viewer's Guide to Art: A Glossary of Gods, People, and Creatures, 144 pp. $10.95

Watch It Made in the U.S.A.: A Visitor's Guide to the Companies that Make Your Favorite Products, 272 pp. $16.95 (available 7/94)

Parenting Titles
Being a Father: Family, Work, and Self, 176 pp. $12.95

Preconception: A Woman's Guide to Preparing for Pregnancy and Parenthood, 232 pp. $14.95

Schooling at Home: Parents, Kids, and Learning, 264 pp., $14.95

Teens: A Fresh Look, 240 pp. $14.95

Automotive Titles
The Greaseless Guide to Car Care Confidence, 224 pp. $14.95

How to Keep Your Datsun/Nissan Alive, 544 pp. $21.95

How to Keep Your Subaru Alive, 480 pp. $21.95

How to Keep Your Toyota Pickup Alive, 392 pp. $21.95

How to Keep Your VW Alive, 15th ed., 464 pp. $21.95

TITLES FOR YOUNG READERS AGES 8 AND UP

American Origins Series
Each is 48 pages and $12.95 hardcover.
Tracing Our Chinese Roots
Tracing Our German Roots
Tracing Our Irish Roots
Tracing Our Italian Roots
Tracing Our Japanese Roots
Tracing Our Jewish Roots
Tracing Our Polish Roots

Bizarre & Beautiful Series
Each is 48 pages and $14.95 hardcover.
Bizarre & Beautiful Ears
Bizarre & Beautiful Eyes
Bizarre & Beautiful Feelers
Bizarre & Beautiful Noses
Bizarre & Beautiful Tongues

Environmental Titles
Habitats: Where the Wild Things Live, 48 pp. $9.95

The Indian Way: Learning to Communicate with Mother Earth, 114 pp. $9.95

Rads, Ergs, and Cheeseburgers: The Kids' Guide to Energy and the Environment, 108 pp. $13.95

The Kids' Environment Book: What's Awry and Why, 192 pp. $13.95

Extremely Weird Series
Each is 48 pages and $9.95 paper. $12.95 hardcover editions available 8/94.
Extremely Weird Bats
Extremely Weird Birds
Extremely Weird Endangered Species
Extremely Weird Fishes
Extremely Weird Frogs
Extremely Weird Insects
Extremely Weird Mammals
Extremely Weird Micro Monsters
Extremely Weird Primates
Extremely Weird Reptiles
Extremely Weird Sea Creatures
Extremely Weird Snakes
Extremely Weird Spiders

Kidding Around Travel Series

All are 64 pages and $9.95 paper, except for *Kidding Around Spain* and *Kidding Around the National Parks of the Southwest*, which are 108 pages and $12.95 paper.

Kidding Around Atlanta
Kidding Around Boston, 2nd ed.
Kidding Around Chicago, 2nd ed.
Kidding Around the Hawaiian Islands
Kidding Around London
Kidding Around Los Angeles
Kidding Around the National Parks of the Southwest
Kidding Around New York City, 2nd ed.
Kidding Around Paris
Kidding Around Philadelphia
Kidding Around San Diego
Kidding Around San Francisco
Kidding Around Santa Fe
Kidding Around Seattle
Kidding Around Spain
Kidding Around Washington, D.C., 2nd ed.

Kids Explore Series

Written by kids for kids, all are $9.95 paper.

Kids Explore America's African American Heritage, 128 pp.
Kids Explore the Gifts of Children with Special Needs, 128 pp.
Kids Explore America's Hispanic Heritage, 112 pp.
Kids Explore America's Japanese American Heritage, 144 pp.

Masters of Motion Series

Each is 48 pages and $9.95 paper.

How to Drive an Indy Race Car
How to Fly a 747
How to Fly the Space Shuttle

Rainbow Warrior Artists Series

Each is 48 pages and $14.95 hardcover.

Native Artists of Africa
Native Artists of Europe (available 8/94)
Native Artists of North America

Rough and Ready Series

Each is 48 pages and $12.95 hardcover.

Rough and Ready Cowboys
Rough and Ready Homesteaders
Rough and Ready Loggers (available 7/94)
Rough and Ready Outlaws and Lawmen (available 6/94)
Rough and Ready Prospectors
Rough and Ready Railroaders

X-ray Vision Series

Each is 48 pages and $9.95 paper.

Looking Inside the Brain
Looking Inside Cartoon Animation
Looking Inside Caves and Caverns
Looking Inside Sports Aerodynamics
Looking Inside Sunken Treasures
Looking Inside Telescopes and the Night Sky

Ordering Information

Please check your local bookstore for our books, or call **1-800-888-7504** to order direct. All orders are shipped via UPS; see chart below to calculate your shipping charge for U.S. destinations. **No post office boxes please; we must have a street address to ensure delivery.** If the book you request is not available, we will hold your check until we can ship it. Foreign orders will be shipped surface rate unless otherwise requested; please enclose $3 for the first item and $1 for each additional item.

For U.S. Orders Totaling	Add
Up to $15.00	$4.25
$15.01 to $45.00	$5.25
$45.01 to $75.00	$6.25
$75.01 or more	$7.25

Methods of Payment

Check, money order, American Express, MasterCard, or Visa. We cannot be responsible for cash sent through the mail. For credit card orders, include your card number, expiration date, and your signature, or call **1-800-888-7504**. American Express card orders can only be shipped to billing address of cardholder. Sorry, no C.O.D.'s. Residents of sunny New Mexico, add 6.2% tax to total.

Address all orders and inquiries to:
    John Muir Publications
    P.O. Box 613
    Santa Fe, NM 87504
    (505) 982-4078
    (800) 888-7504